Oman

the Bradt Travel Guide

Diana Darke

www.bradtguides.com

Bradt Travel Guides Ltd, UK
The Globe Pequot Press Inc, USA

edition
3

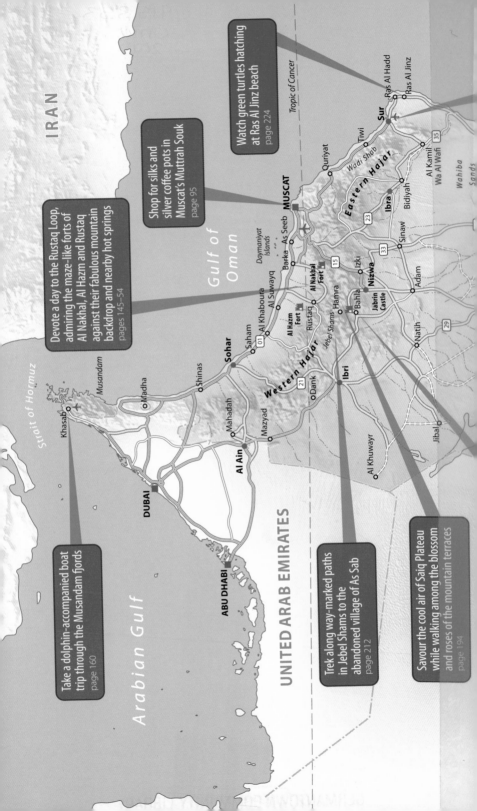

IRAN

Watch green turtles hatching at Ras Al Jinz beach
page 224

Shop for silks and silver coffee pots in Muscat's Muttrah Souk
page 95

Devote a day to the Rustaq Loop, admiring the maze-like forts of Al Nakhal, Al Hazm and Rustaq against their fabulous mountain backdrop and nearby hot springs
pages 145–54

Take a dolphin-accompanied boat trip through the Musandam fjords
page 160

Trek along way-marked paths in Jebel Shams to the abandoned village of As Sab
page 212

Savour the cool air of Saiq Plateau while walking among the blossom and roses of the mountain terraces
page 194

UNITED ARAB EMIRATES

Arabian Gulf

Gulf of Oman

Strait of Hormuz

Musandam

Khasab

Madha

Shinas

Mazyad

Mahadah

Al Ain

DUBAI

ABU DHABI

Sohar

Saham

Al Khaboura

Al Suwayq

Barka

As Seeb

MUSCAT

Quriyat

Tiwi

Wadi Shab

Sur

Ras Al Hadd

Ras Al Jinz

Tropic of Cancer

Daymaniyat Islands

Al Hazm Fort

Rustaq

Al Nakhal Fort

Hamra

Jebel Shams

Bahla

Jabrin Castle

Nizwa

Izki

Al Wafi

Al Kamil

35

Bidiyah

Ibra

Sinaw

Adam

Natih

Eastern Hajar

Western Hajar

Wahiba Sands

23

33

15

01

21

Dank

Ibri

Al Khuwayr

Jibal

29

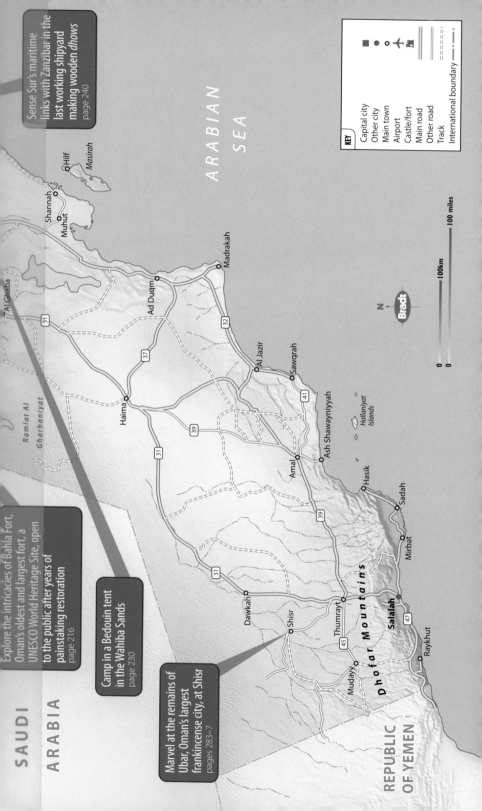

SAUDI

ARABIA

SAUDI ARABIA

Al Ghaba

31

Ramlat Al Gharbaniyat

37

Haima

31

39

Ad Duqm

32

Al Jazir

Sawqrah

41

Ash Shawayniyyah

Amal

39

Hallaniyat Islands

Hasik

Sadah

Mirbat

Dawkah

Shisr

Thumrayt

45

Mudayy

Salalah

Dhofar Mountains

47

Raykhut

REPUBLIC OF YEMEN

Masirah

Hilf

Shannah

Muhut

ARABIAN SEA

Explore the intricacies of Bahla fort, Oman's oldest and largest fort, a UNESCO World Heritage Site, open to the public after years of painstaking restoration page 216

Camp in a Bedouin tent in the Wahiba Sands page 230

Marvel at the remains of Ubar, Oman's largest frankincense city, at Shisr pages 283–7

Sense Sur's maritime links with Zanzibar in the last working shipyard making wooden *dhows* page 240

N

Bradt

0   100km
0   100 miles

KEY

■ Capital city
● Other city
○ Main town
✈ Airport
🏰 Castle/fort
Main road
Other road
Track
International boundary

Oman
Don't
miss...

Dhow shipbuilding in Sur
Traditional craftsmanship and skill that has died out elsewhere in the Gulf

(SS) pages 240 and 242

Coral reefs near Mirbat
Warm waters and colourful fish make Oman's south coast a diver's paradise

(SS) page 269

Oman's unique *falaj* irrigation channels
Water is carefully rationed and distributed according to age-old systems, agreed by consensus
(SS) page 171

Bilad Sayt
A rare gem hidden high in the Jebel Akhdar range
(BO/S) pages 148–9

Nizwa Fort
The colossal tower took 12 years to build and has three sets of internal defences
(OMOT) pages 203–5

Oman in colour

above Preparing hands and feet for henna painting — a custom enjoyed by Omani women on special occasions like weddings (OMOT)

left Traditional fishing methods are still used along Oman's 1700-km-long shoreline (OMOT)

below Camel racing remains Oman's most popular spectator sport, especially along the Batinah coast (OMOT)

pages 30–1

above   Omani men enjoy playing traditional games like dominoes (AS/S)

right   The date harvest continues throughout the summer months, forming a vital part of the Omani economy (CE/S) page 192

below right   Clay pots from the famous factory at Bahla (IP/S) page 217

below left   Locally produced fruit and vegetables on a market stall at Muttrah Souk (SS) pages 95–6 *above*   Muscat's spectacular Grand Mosque is the only one in Oman to allow non-Muslims inside (OMOT) page 120

left   The colourful Muscat harbour with Merani Fort in the background (OMOT) page 100

below   The huge model frankincense burner in Riyam Park overlooks the Muttrah corniche (OMOT) page 96

AUTHOR

Diana Darke, an Oxford Arabist, has written 16 books on the Near and Middle East, acquiring a rich appreciation of the region, its people, their culture and preoccupations during the 30 years she has lived and worked there. She communicates this in her guides, which are recognised as the leaders in their field, bringing countries to life through a host of colourful insights and through the inhabitants themselves. The book contains detailed itineraries and maps, with a wealth of practical information on transport, treks, hotels and restaurants.

AUTHOR'S STORY

My first exposure to Oman was in 1980 when I was offered a contract to work for the Oman Research Department as their Head of Media. I was already familiar with the Levant and Egypt, but not the Arabian Peninsula. A whole new world opened up to me, as Oman at that time was closed to tourism. Only a handful of expatriates were allowed in, after first obtaining a No Objection Certificate, something that was only issued to those in bona fide employment. On weekdays I was working in a bilingual environment with Omani colleagues and at weekends they would take me to the interior to visit their families and their villages. We shared food, climbed mountains, explored wadis and forts, enjoying nature and wildlife in the raw. Some of them kept gazelles as pets for their children. When the contract came to an end after a year, I wept as the plane took off, looking down over the mountains I had grown to love for what I feared might be the last time.

But luck was on my side. Twenty years later, while posted in neighbouring Dubai, the chance arose to write a guide to Oman. After many visits and long weekends, often accompanied by my young children, this Bradt guide was born. Yes, there are many more tarmac roads and highways, many more hotels and the Capital Area has changed almost beyond recognition, but in essence Oman and its people are the same – hospitable, charming, traditional and dignified. It has learnt from the mistakes of its neighbours, and has not rushed headlong into frantic development. Its political stability and its Arabian heritage are intact. Oman remains a real place.

PUBLISHER'S FOREWORD   *Hilary Bradt*

Oman came to my attention when we first published *Zanzibar*, many years ago. I learned about the historic links between the two countries – going back to the 1800s when, bizarrely, Zanzibar was the capital of Oman – and thought that any country in the Middle East that was once governed from East Africa would be a perfect addition to our list. Oman is now firmly established as a holiday destination, and – as the book itself moves into its third edition – Diana Darke continues to unearth the very best attractions and hotels to satisfy visitors who no longer have to rely on the trade winds to reach this exotic country.

Third edition published November 2013
First published 2006

Bradt Travel Guides Ltd, IDC House, The Vale, Chalfont St Peter, Bucks SL9 9RZ, England
www.bradtguides.com

Print edition published in the USA by The Globe Pequot Press Inc, PO Box 480, Guilford, Connecticut 06437-0480

Text copyright © 2013 Bradt Travel Guides Ltd
Maps copyright © 2013 Bradt Travel Guides Ltd
Photographs copyright © 2013 Individual photographers (see below)
Project Managers: Greg Dickinson & Claire Strange
Cover research: Pepi Bluck, Perfect Picture

ISBN: 978 1 84162 471 6 (print)
e-ISBN: 978 1 84162 775 5 (epub)
e-ISBN: 978 1 84162 677 2 (mobi)

British Library Cataloguing in Publication Data
A catalogue record for this book is available from the British Library

Photographs Alamy: Heimbach/Friedrichsmeier Archive (H/FA/A); awl-images.com: Michele Falzone (MF/AWL); Diana Darke (DD); Marco Muscarà, www.marcomuscara.com (MM); Omani Ministry of Tourism (OMOT); Shutterstock: BMJ (BMJ/S), Chameleons Eye (CE/S), Wim Claes (WC/S), Copit (C/S), Erni (E/S), Kokik (K/S), Philip Lange (PL/S), Lightpoet (L/S), Johannes Dag Mayer (JDM/S), Byelikova Oksana (BO/S), Ivan Pavlov (IP/S), Styve Reineck (SR/S), Andrea Seeman (AS/S); SuperStock (SS)

Front cover The medieval village of Misfat al Abriyeen is surrounded by a date plantation (MF/AWL)
Back cover Bedouin man near Nizwa (MM); Wadi Shab, one of Oman's most beautiful ravines (IP/S)
Title page Yiti Beach is south of Muscat (IP/S); Mosaic detail on Muscat's Grand Mosque (PL/S); Evening sun (OMOT)

Maps David McCutcheon FBCart.S; colour map base by Nick Rowland FRGS

Typeset from the author's disc by Wakewing, High Wycombe
Production managed by Jellyfish Print Solutions; printed in India
Digital conversion by the Firsty Group

Acknowledgements

Diana Darke would like to acknowledge the help of Omani friends and colleagues too numerous to mention, but especially the late Sheikh Saif Al Harithy; a special debt of gratitude is also owed to Mike and Barbara Baddeley for their excellent company chasing butterflies in many wadis, and to Paul Flaherty in Musandam and Andy Coulson for arranging access to Muscat's forts. Thanks also to Sandra Shields for her work on previous updates. More recently, thanks are due for their helpful feedback to Zeid Hashim, Michael Shaw, Gerard Sellek, John Cochrane, Jock Moilliet, Gordon Rattray, Robert Fitton, Kate Turnbull, Linda Scott, Gary and Leona Badham, Paul Schmidtberger, Giorgio Balzarro, Graeme Brooks, Linda Warminger, Alan Benson, Mike and Leslie Robbins, Glen Thompson, David Orkin, C E J Mallock, Michael Jones, Jane Bell, Michael Spiller, Maggie Jeans, Richard Woodhead, Stephan and Kathrin Schilling, and Marty Barreca.

DEDICATION

To Chloë and Max, with many happy memories of shared adventures.

UPDATES WEBSITE AND FEEDBACK REQUEST

At Bradt Travel Guides we're aware that guidebooks start to go out of date on the day they're published – and that you, our readers, are out there in the field doing research of your own. You'll find out before us when a fine new family-run hotel opens or a favourite restaurant changes hands and goes downhill. So why not write and tell us about your experiences? Contact us on ☏ 01753 893444 or e info@bradtguides.com. We will forward emails to the author who may post 'one-off updates' on the Bradt website at www.bradtguides.com/guidebook-updates. Alternatively you can add a review of the book to www.bradtguides.com or Amazon.

Contents

LIST OF MAPS

NOTE ABOUT MAPS

Several maps use grid lines to allow easy location of sites. Map grid references are listed in square brackets after listings in the text, with page number followed by grid number, eg: [94 A1].

Introduction

In a region notorious for religious extremism, turbulence and unrest, it is a relief to find a country characterised by calm and composure. Amid uneasy Middle Eastern neighbours, Oman and the Omani people sit peaceably – strong and silent.

Geographically, it is a place of awe-inspiring natural landscapes: mountains, ravines, cliffs, canyons, desert and coastline endure, unchanged, under an incessant Middle Eastern sun. Politically, Oman is stable and so offers a safe environment – as safe as any can be anywhere today. Financially it is strong with oil, agriculture and fisheries industries, and now its emerging tourism sector.

Considering that when Sultan Qaboos took over in 1970 there were only 5km of surfaced roads, three schools (all primary, and for boys only), one hospital (run by American missionaries), no police force, newspapers, radio or television stations, the scene today is incredible. The advances in all aspects of society are astounding.

Oman's modern mindset has facilitated its entrance on the global scene ensuring its future prosperity, while simultaneously improving the lives of its people. With today's juxtaposition of old and new in the country, Oman serves to endow us with an appreciation of the qualities of both ways of life. Although the modern way may be anathema to the late British writer and explorer Wilfred Thesiger, who valued the trials and rewards of life as the Bedu lived it in the Omani desert, it cannot be denied that the Omanis today at the very least have a fundamentally improved lot. Indeed the reason why the country has been slow to embrace tourism is because of concerns to preserve the old ways of life – the culture and the heritage. This is demonstrated today in the restoration projects of historic sites, aimed at keeping Oman's history intact and its story alive. Four areas are now UNESCO World Heritage Sites. The Omani people too are keen, proud and enthusiastic in showing and sharing their country's fruits (both literally and figuratively) with you.

With a varied wilderness terrain of desert, wadi, mountain and ocean, there is huge scope for adventure, eco- and cultural tourism. From the fjords and barrenness of Musandam to the sand deserts of the Wahiba and Empty Quarter, from the Hajar mountain range to the green monsoon area of Dhofar in the south, the draw of Oman lies in the outdoors – in its nature.

There are figures in history, myth and legend who have travelled, lived and explored Oman. The Queen of Sheba, Alexander the Great, Pliny the Elder, Vasco da Gama, Marco Polo, Freya Stark, Ibn Battutah, Lawrence of Arabia, H St J B Philby, Wilfred Thesiger and Ranulph Fiennes have all passed through, leaving invaluable writings behind. They provide a fascinating link to the past, illuminating the country for us today.

Construction projects are carefully planned and masterminded, and schemes like The Wave, which incorporates international-class hotels, a residential village, restaurants and retail and leisure facilities, including an 18-hole international-standard golf course, have been able to go ahead in spite of the economic climate, with 50% of residential property bought by Omani nationals and 50% by foreigners, mainly from Europe and the subcontinent.

Although it is considered an upscale destination for the discerning traveller, and Omani policy is to encourage small numbers of high-spending visitors, it is still possible to tour the country keeping an eye on the financial outlay, and this guide makes specific suggestions for budget travel. If this is not a concern, ultra-modern and busy Dubai makes a perfect contrasting partner for a twin-centre getaway, something which the Omani government is now keen to promote.

If you are from the West, and still in a fast-paced Western mode, the heat is soon likely to change that and slow you to a more leisurely mode. After any extended length of time here, you may even find yourself developing the *inshallah* mentality, meaning 'if God wills it, it will happen'; and bukra, 'sometime after tomorrow'.

The Oman of old is largely intact; and thanks to the enlightened policies of a liberal-minded, peace-loving, democratic sultan, we now have been invited in.

Part One

GENERAL INFORMATION

Location Southeastern edge of Arabian Peninsula at 21°N, 57°E
Neighbouring countries United Arab Emirates, Saudi Arabia, Yemen
Size 309,500km^2 approx
Population 3.1 million (CIA World Factbook 2012)
Life expectancy Male: 74; female: 77 (CIA World Factbook 2012)
Capital Muscat Capital Area; population 1,200,000 (CIA World Factbook 2012)
Other main towns Salalah, Nizwa, Sohar, Sur
Ports Mina Qaboos, Mina Raysut, Muttrah, Sohar
Climate Predominantly arid, with regional variations. Summer (April–September) finds coastal regions hot and humid with the interior hot and dry (average 40°C); winter (October–March) is warm and dry throughout, with high mountain areas becoming cold, sometimes with snow. Rainfall is rare and irregular.
Status Monarchy
Sultan and head of state Qaboos bin Said (from 1970)
Ethnic divisions Arab, Baluchi, south Asian (Indian, Pakistani, Sri Lankan, Bangladeshi) and Zanzibari
Languages Arabic (official), English (widely spoken), Baluchi, Urdu, Swahili, Hindi, Indian dialects. German and French spoken in larger hotels.
Religion Predominantly Muslim: Sunni (50%), Ibadhi (45%), Shi'a (2%); other 3% (mainly Hindu, Christian, and Buddhist)
Chief exports Oil, dates, copper, silverware, fish
GDP US$72.23 billion
Currency Omani rial (OMR/RO)
Exchange rate £1 = RO0.58, US$1 = RO0.39, €1 = RO0.50 (August 2013)
National airlines Oman Air, Gulf Air (of which the Omani sultanate owns one-third)
International telephone code +968
Internet domain .om
Time GMT+4
Electrical voltage 220–240v AC; British three-pin plugs widely used
Flag Three equal horizontal bands of white, red and green with a broad, vertical, red band on the hoist side; the national emblem (a *khanjar* dagger in its sheath superimposed on two crossed swords in scabbards) in white is centred at the top of the vertical band.
National emblem The khanjar (a silver-sheathed curved dagger)
National holidays Non-religious: New Year's Day (1 January), National Day (18 November), Sultan's Birthday (19 November); religious (dates alter each year according to the Islamic Lunar Calendar): Eid al Fitr (at the end of Ramadan), Eid al Adha (during the Hajj), Mawlid al Nabi (Prophet's Birthday), Muharram (Islamic New Year). See page 59 for dates.

1

Background Information

If your intentions are pure, how can you be harmed by the wind of a donkey?

GEOGRAPHY

Oman is located on the southeastern edge of the Arabian Peninsula and is bordered by Yemen (in the southwest), Saudi Arabia (in the west) and the United Arab Emirates (in the northwest). The second-largest country in the peninsula, after Saudi Arabia, it covers an area of around 309,500km², and is roughly the same size as the UK; it is bigger than Syria, Jordan and Lebanon put together.

Oman has a near-pristine coastline that extends to a total of some 1,700km, from the Musandam Peninsula to the Empty Quarter desert. The northern coastline sits on the Gulf of Oman and constitutes about a third of its total length. The remaining two-thirds sit on the Arabian Sea, which is the portion of the Indian Ocean between the Arabian Peninsula on the west and the Indian subcontinent on the east. The Gulf of Oman is one of the world's most important strategic waterways, providing a shipping lane for oil from the Gulf States. Tankers pass through the Strait of Hormuz – a narrow waterway linking the Persian Gulf (or Arabian Gulf) with the Gulf of Oman – that laps the northernmost part of Oman, Musandam.

The country's topography is varied, with mountains in the north and south, sand desert and gravel desert in the central plain, with areas of oases, and coastal plains. Roughly 82% of the land is made up of sand and gravel desert and valleys, about 15% is mountainous and the remaining 3% is coastal plain. The Hajar mountain range rises up out of the Strait of Hormuz at the northernmost tip of the country and continues southward, like a spine, for approximately 600km.

The name Oman is thought to mean 'the abode' or 'the land', though other local traditions hold that it was named after 'Uman Ibn Qahtan, Oman's legendary first inhabitant. Its formal name is the Sultanate of Oman or Saltanat 'Uman, but it is simply known as Oman in everyday speech.

Despite the potential for trade links beyond its shores Oman is insular in character, cut off from its neighbours by deserts, mountains or sea. Its own terrain is varied and striking, its geographic mix of mountain, desert and coast leading to different lifestyles and occasionally conflicting values. The scarcity of essential natural resources, such as water and fertile land, meant that it was only with a great deal of sustained effort that any people, city or district could rise above bare subsistence level.

CLIMATE

Oman is predominantly arid but, because of its size and topography, the climate tends to vary from one region to another. It is perhaps easiest to split the country

Traditional Arab geographers have divided the country like the human anatomy. The head is the Musandam Peninsula, called Ru'us Al Jibal (Head of the Mountains), the backbone or spine is the Hajar Mountains, while the back (Arabic: Al Dhahirah) is the stretch from the mountains to Buraimi. The interior (Al Dakhiliyah) encompasses the Jebel Akhdar range (green mountain) and the historic towns of Nizwa and Bahla; the stomach or underbelly (Al Batinah) is the fertile coastal plain down to Muscat. The bulge from Muscat south to Sur and its hinterland is the eastern province of As Sharqiya (Sharq, meaning 'east'). Jaa'lan (named after its inhabitants known as the 'People of the Water Beetle') is in the eastern coastal stretch of this region extending from Sur to Masirah Island. Al Wusta region is the empty midriff of the country covered by the vast dry gravel plain, stretching for 800km between the Hajar Mountains in the north and the Dhofar Mountains in the south. This plain (also known as the Nejd) is edged by the perilous Empty Quarter (Rub' al Khali) – a vast desert of sand that extends into Saudi Arabia. The huge gravel desert of the Jiddat Al Harasees is also in Al Wusta region, Harasees being the name for the local Bedu tribe. The southernmost region is Dhofar, the capital of which is Salalah.

into four when thinking of climatic variations: the coastal regions, the interior, the mountains and the Dhofar coast, and then consider the two Omani seasons of winter and summer.

The coastal regions are very hot and humid in the summer, while the interior is very hot and dry. In the winter months both the coastal areas and the interior are pleasantly warm and dry. There is little rainfall in the country and this is always irregular. However, when the occasional localised storms do occur (any time between October and March, with a tendency towards December and January, and largely in northern Oman), it is not unusual for them to be so heavy that *wadis* (watercourses) are in flood, causing havoc on the roads, especially the Muscat–Nizwa road, which is crossed by many wadis running off Jebel Akhdar, and the Muscat–Sur road, crossed by the wadis running off the eastern Hajar mountain range. Hailstorms are another winter phenomenon, sometimes falling so hard that people are injured and taken to hospital, livestock killed and crops damaged. Cyclones are rare, but in June 2007 Cyclone Gonu struck the coastline south of Muscat, causing much damage to the coast road and to the entrance of Wadi Shaab.

Temperatures in Muscat (northern coastal) can range from 32–48°C in the summer (April to September) and 25–36°C in the winter (October to March), making winter the best time to visit. January and February are the coolest months with average temperatures of 25°C. From March onwards temperatures begin to climb, reaching the 40s, together with high humidity. June and July are the hottest months and so the outdoors can become off-limits. Temperatures can also vary enormously: in July it can reach 48°C in the northern oil-producing desert areas round Fahud, but reach only 13°C on Jebel Shams. Hotels, restaurants, shopping malls and cars are well air conditioned and provide essential respite.

The high mountain areas enjoy a fairly moderate climate throughout the year, although in the winter the areas of high altitude can get cold. Night-time temperatures on Jebel Shams, Oman's highest mountain, at 3,048m (10,000ft) can reach below freezing point, and there is occasional snow.

In the south, the small band of land (roughly 240km long by 3–30km wide) between the Dhofar Mountains and the coast has its own microclimate. The temperature stays around a constant 26°C, with the phenomenon of the southwesterly monsoon rains – the *khareef* – running from around mid-June till mid-September. Dense fog and rains revive the parched flora, giving rise to a lush, green landscape, and so the Dhofar region is at its most beautiful in September and early October, making it the best time to visit. Visitors from other GCC (Gulf Co-operation Council) countries, as well as Omanis from the north, take advantage of this Dhofar spectacle, the temperature being moderate here by Middle Eastern standards. By November the greenery has vanished.

NATURAL HISTORY with Andrew Grieve

The diverse nature of Oman's climate and terrain provides the perfect habitat for thousands of species of plant, animal, bird and marine life and makes the country an ideal destination for lovers of nature and the outdoors.

Enthusiastically 'green' in its outlook, Oman has possibly the most enlightened policy on conservation in the Middle East, and is one of the world's top-ten environmentally committed countries. It is party to international agreements on biodiversity, climate change, desertification, endangered species, hazardous wastes, marine dumping, Law of the Sea, whaling and ozone layer protection. In 1984 it became the first Arab country to create a ministry dedicated to environmental issues, and environmental protection laws have been in place since 1974. In addition to preserving its historical monuments and forts, it is committed to preserving and protecting the natural habitat of its unique species of flora and fauna, and has established several designated nature reserves, protected sites and research centres. Responsibility for this comes under the Ministry of Regional Municipalities, Environment and Water Resources, through its Directorate of Nature Conservation. Oman is a member of CITES (the Convention on International Trade in Endangered Species of Wild Fauna and Flora), which forbids any commercial trading in specific live or dead animals and animal parts.

The most popular of the reserves is indisputably the Daymaniyat Islands (along the Batinah coast, see page 134), which is a designated bird sanctuary, but is excellent for both its marine and birdlife. Indeed it is Oman's only marine-protected area. Nineteen species of dolphin and whale have been recorded in Oman's waters and the Daymaniyat Islands are probably one of the best locations from which to spot them. Boat trips for dolphin-, whale- and birdwatching can be easily arranged (there is a no-landing policy throughout the bird-breeding season between May and October), and the area is also a highly ranked world dive site.

The protected turtle-breeding beaches at Ras Al Hadd and Ras Al Jinz are popular places to visit, the turtles being another strong tourist draw. There are seven species in the world, of which five occur in Oman and four breed. A visitor and research centre has been established at the turtle reserve at Ras Al Jinz, where an on-site ranger leads you to the sea's edge in the dark for your night-time turtle-watching adventure.

Other reserves have been established to protect the natural domain of mammals including the two species of gazelle, striped hyena, Arabian leopard, Arabian tahr, Arabian oryx, Blanford's fox, Nubian ibex and Gordon's wild cat. The Saleel Nature Reserve at Al Kamil and Al Wafi (in the Sharqiya region) is home to Arabian and sand gazelle and other animals, in addition to rare varieties of tree, namely *samr* (*Acacia tortilis*) and *ghaf* (*Prosopis cineraria*). A nursery has been established here to propagate and preserve Oman's endangered wild flora.

Although its central focus is on the endangered Arabian oryx, the Arabian Oryx Sanctuary in the Jiddat al Harasee-is (in central Oman) is also home to Arabian leopard, the two species of gazelle, Nubian ibex, red fox, Gordon's wild cat, sand cat, caracal, honey badger and others.

Jebel Samhan, in the Dhofar region, was declared a national nature reserve in 1997. The highest point in Dhofar at 1,800m, it is believed to be home to the Middle East's largest population of the endangered Arabian race of leopard, which is being continuously monitored. Research was also launched in 2006 to monitor the Arabian leopard in Musandam. Other species found in the Jebel Samhan reserve include the striped hyena, Gordon's wild cat and Blanford's fox.

The five Halaniyat Islands off the Dhofar coast are an important breeding ground for turtles and seabirds, although not yet designated a nature reserve. A turtle-counting and tagging programme has also been set up on Masirah Island, one of the most important turtle-nesting sites in the world, with approximately 30,000 loggerhead sea turtles laying their eggs annually. The importance of Oman for sea turtles is highly significant and the opportunity for turtle viewing unrivalled.

The area from Ras Al Hadd down to the southern borders of Oman and for 200 nautical miles out to sea from the coast has been declared, by the International Maritime Organization (IMO), a protected marine area, conserving the sea's resources by regulating tourist and ship activity.

The commissioning of books and studies covering the country's wild flowers, butterflies, birds and other forms of wildlife has made Oman one of the best-documented countries of the Middle East in this field. As visitors it is important that we are aware of Oman's conservation policies and respect the habitats and environs of the wildlife of the country. Note that collecting seashells, abalones or turtle eggs is strictly prohibited. So too is hunting or disturbing wild animals and birds. Driving over the sand is also illegal.

ECOSYSTEMS Oman can be broadly split into three ecosystems: the mountains of northern Oman, including Musandam; the desert plains or plateau of central Oman; and the escarpment woodlands and monsoon belt of Dhofar in the south. These very different environments support and sustain their own unique types of flora and fauna. Professor Reginald Victor of Sultan Qaboos University speaks of the importance of a National Biodiversity Strategy and Action Plan (NBSAP) for the country, which would aim (under the guidance of the World Zoo Organisation) to conserve these ecosystems or habitats.

FLORA The northern mountains (including the Musandam Peninsula) and the Dhofar region contain 80% of Oman's 1,204 species of flora, of which about a hundred are endemic to Oman or regionally in Arabia. Nurseries (including mangrove) have been established at the Saleel Nature Reserve (in the Sharqiya region), the Qairoon Hairiti (in Dhofar), Qurum Natural Park (in Muscat) and the Botanical Gardens at Sultan Qaboos University (also in Muscat). These provide some, albeit limited, facilities and potential for flora conservation, both *in situ* (in its natural habitat) and *ex situ* (removed from its natural habitat).

Oman's most famous plant is the *Boswellia sacra*, which produces the frankincense resin. Found only in Dhofar (in the south), and parts of east Africa, it is a gnarled and unattractive-looking tree which grows only to 3–4m. One tree can produce up to 20kg of frankincense in a season, and at the height of the trade 2,000 years ago over 3,000 tonnes of the spice were exported by camel caravan or by boat to the wealthy civilisations of Egypt, Greece, Rome and India. In recent times, however, the trade in frankincense has declined to an insignificant level. Research is currently ongoing into the cancer-curing properties of frankincense, as it is thought to contain an agent that stops the cancer spreading, by resetting the DNA code. The ancient Egyptians considered it to be the sweat of the gods.

A remarkable tree to look out for in the Dhofar region, particularly between Wadi Darbat and Wadi Hinna near Mirbat, is the grotesque-looking baobab *Adansonia digitata*, a species more familiar in the African savanna.

Mid 2004 saw a large coastal afforestation project take place with approximately 188,000 mangrove trees planted in the lagoons (*khors*) along Oman's coastline. A permanent mangrove nursery and research centre has also been established at Qurum Natural Park.

Rose water, extracted from the desert rose (*Adenium obesum*), is used extensively in Oman in the preparation of *halwa* (see box on page 152), as well as in perfumes, in incense (especially at Eid and weddings), in *kahwa* (see page 65) and in traditional medicines. The roses are cooked for three hours and the water then stored for 40 days before being bottled and sold.

FAUNA

Mammals Around 76 species of mammal have been recorded in Oman of which one, the endemic Dhofarian shrew, is critically endangered. In addition to some of those detailed below, another endangered mammal in Oman is the Arabian jird, while other larger species include Blanford's fox, Rüppell's sand fox, red fox, fennec fox, honey badger, caracal, Gordon's wild cat, sand cat, Cape hare, Indian-crested porcupine, small-spotted genet, white-tailed mongoose, Arabian wolf, striped hyena, Brandt's hedgehog, Ethiopian hedgehog and rock hyrax.

Arabian leopard The endangered Arabian race of leopard, Arabia's largest cat, survives only in the remote mountains of southern Oman and in Musandam. Usually solitary, it comes together with other leopards only for breeding. The Nubian ibex and rock hyrax form the bulk of its diet. An important sanctuary for the leopard is Jebel Samhan Nature Reserve. A survey into the animal is being carried out both here and, more recently, in Musandam. Modern techniques of camera-trapping and satellite collars have meant that the ecology of this shy and very secretive animal has been studied for the first time.

Arabian white oryx The globally endangered Arabian white oryx, which is a type of antelope, was extinct in Oman by the early 1970s due to excessive hunting. In 1975, Sultan Qaboos launched the Operation Oryx programme. This captive breeding programme was conducted at the sultan's Omani Mammal Breeding Centre, Bait al Barakah (at Seeb, near Muscat), with donated animals from London Zoo, the Hadhramaut (Yemen), Jordan, Kuwait, Saudi Arabia and Arizona, utilising the knowledge of the World Wildlife Fund, the Fauna Preservation Society and the International Union for Conservation of Nature and Natural Resources, who assisted with the project. The oryx were then reared at Jaaluni in the Jiddat al Harasees in central Oman, before being successfully reintroduced into the wild there in the early 1980s. UNESCO had proclaimed the Jiddat al Harasees a World Natural Heritage Site, but in 2007 withdrew this status as the numbers dwindled and the park size was reduced by 90% (see box on page 250). There is also the Arabian Oryx Sanctuary near Al Kamil on the edge of the Wahiba Sands.

Like camels, the timid oryx are supremely well adapted to a desert environment, conserving their water intake and requiring a drink only every few months. Their lifespan is around 19 years. It is thought that the mythical unicorn legend stemmed from the oryx, whose two horns, when viewed from the side, appear as one.

Arabian and reem gazelles The largest single population of Arabian gazelle (over 10,000 in 2003) can be found in the Arabian Oryx Sanctuary (see page 251). The male has thick horns while the female's horns are finer and straighter, and they feed on shrubs and grasses.

The reem gazelle (sand gazelle) is a less common species and can be found on the sandy terrain at the edges of the Empty Quarter. In contrast to the Arabian gazelle, the reem gazelle gives birth to twins. The reem gazelle, like the Oryx, can cover long distances searching for new pastures.

Arabian tahr This south Asian goat-antelope, with short curved horns, is one of the rarest animals in the world and is an endangered species. Its name means 'half-goat'. The ideal habitat for the tahr is at altitude, between 1,000m and 1,800m, and so the Wadi Sarin Tahr Reserve in the Hajar ash Shaqi (eastern Hajar) Mountains, and the mountains of northern Oman, including Musandam, are its natural home. The Arabian Tahr Project began in 1976 and continues to work for the animal's conservation.

Nubian ibex The Nubian ibex, another globally endangered species, is a wild mountain goat that lives in small groups. During the annual mating season, groups of up to 30 animals come together, with the large adult males fighting for the right to breed. The Nubian ibex can be found in the Arabian Oryx Sanctuary and in the Jebel Samhan Nature Reserve. It does not occur in northern Oman.

Reptiles There are around 64 species of reptiles in Oman, of which at least 21 are endemic to Arabia and seven are globally threatened. Only three species of amphibian are known from Oman, with the Dhofar toad an Arabian endemic. Geckos, agamas, lizards, skinks and snakes are well suited to survive in abundance in mountain and desert areas. Apart from the rarely seen horned viper, carpet viper, puff adder and the Arabian race of cobra, the remaining nine snake species are harmless. The mountains of northern Oman contain three nationally endemic species of geckos and five regionally endemic geckos and lizards. A common and widespread species worth looking out for in the Dhofar region is the Arabian race of chameleon.

Birds (*Andrew Grieve*) According to the Oman Bird Records Committee (OBRC), which publishes an official bird list, a total of 514 bird species had been recorded in Oman by 2013. Familiar widespread wintering species in Oman include cormorant, cattle egret, spoonbill, greater flamingo, shoveller, little stint, ruff, black-tailed godwit, kingfisher and stonechat. Other more sought-after wintering species in different parts of Oman include Indian pond heron, pallid harrier, steppe eagle, imperial eagle, lesser sand plover, pintail snipe, great black-headed gull, Egyptian nightjar, citrine wagtail, red-tailed wheatear, eastern pied wheatear, plain leaf warbler, Isabelline shrike and rose-coloured starling.

Many geographical influences can be detected in Oman's breeding birds, with the influence of India provided by yellow bittern and pheasant-tailed jacana nesting in Dhofar, and grey francolin, Indian roller, purple sunbird and Indian silverbill along the Batinah coast. The mangroves along this coast also support interesting species including red-wattled plover and the white-collared kingfisher, an endemic subspecies. Typical African species that are resident in the

Oman sits at the crossroads of three continents: Europe, Africa and Asia, and is therefore well placed along bird migratory routes, which makes it an excellent location for seeing transitory species as well as interesting resident and wintering birds. The best times to see the migrating species are from late August to November and from February to May, with December through to February being the best for winter birds and also the coolest time of the year. Most of the indigenous species can be seen in the winter though some breeding species do not arrive until May, particularly in Dhofar.

There are good birding sites in every region of the country (see regional chapters for further details). The coastal *khors* (lagoons) offer perfect spots for wintering and migrating waterbirds including ducks, waders and terns. The Daymaniyat Islands hold substantial numbers of breeding bridled and white-cheeked terns, with small numbers of common noddy, ospreys and western reef herons. The Sawadi Islands and Fahal Island (about 4km off Ras al Hamra, in the Capital Area) hold breeding sooty falcons, with the latter site also having nesting red-billed tropic-birds; boat trips around Fahal Island can easily be arranged from Muscat (see page 104). Al Ansab Lagoons (about 30km west of Muscat) and Qurum Natural Park in Muscat itself are good places to see typical Omani breeding species such as grey francolin, red-wattled plover, laughing dove, little green bee-eater, yellow-vented bulbul, Arabian babbler, purple sunbird and Indian silverbill.

Barr al Hikman and Masirah Island (the latter is accessible by ferry only) hold perhaps a million wintering waterbirds, mainly herons, egrets, waders and gulls. Mouth-watering species such as crab plover and great knot are present in winter, the latter found south of the Shannah ferry terminal for Masirah Island when the tide is rising. A good area to watch at high tide is Film, 19km south of the town of Al Hij, where great white egrets, greater flamingos, crab plover, terek sandpiper, broad-billed sandpiper and slender-billed gulls can be seen.

Other locations offering good birdwatching opportunities include Musandam, where breeding Lichtenstein's sandgrouse, chukar and Hume's wheatear, and wintering eastern pied wheatear, red-tailed wheatear, Eversman's redstart and plain leaf warbler can be seen. The Sohar Sun Farms (Batinah coast) offer first-class year-round birding with many passage and wintering species of note including a small number of the globally threatened sociable plover. The desert oasis and resthouse of Qitbit (see page 283) on the desert road between Muscat and Salalah is an excellent place to stay over to see desert species such as crowned and spotted sandgrouse and hoopoe lark. A series of *khors* along the Dhofar coast each side of Salalah are also excellent sites for a range of waterbirds throughout the year, particularly Khor Taqa and Khor Rawri (sometimes spelt Rouri). For the Arabian endemics and Dhofar specialities, the wooden ravines inland of the coast are the places to visit in the spring, particularly Ayn Hamran just 22km from Salalah.

Birdwatching excursions can easily be arranged through many of the tour operators in Muscat (see pages 76–8). They cost around RO30 per person for a half-day tour. Several books have been published by the authors Hanne and Jens Eriksen, who operate birding tours in Muscat. Readers might like to get hold of a copy of their *Birdwatching Guide to Oman* (see page 299) or any other of their publications.

Dhofar region include the huge lappet-faced vulture, Verreaux's eagle, spotted thick-knee, namaqua dove, green pigeon, African scops owl, African paradise flycatcher, shining sunbird, black-crowned tchagra, Rüppell's weaver, African silverbill and African rock bunting. Some of the summer visitors to Dhofar are also typically African in distribution, with the striking didric cuckoo, brightly coloured grey-headed kingfisher, Forbes-Watson swift and singing bush lark all breeding during the monsoon period.

The remaining breeding species are mainly Arabian endemics, seabirds, desert species or typical European and Mediterranean birds. The Arabian endemics include Arabian partridge, Arabian wheatear and the rather plain-looking Yemen serin, which all breed in Dhofar. Yellow-vented bulbul (north and south Oman) and Tristram's grackle (Dhofar only) are mainly restricted to the Middle East. The elegant and graceful sooty falcon, osprey and crab plover all breed on island groups such as Masirah, Daymaniyat and Halaniyat. Breeding seabirds and herons on these islands feature striated heron, western reef heron, red-billed tropic bird (also breeds on mainland sea cliffs), masked booby, socotra cormorant (Arabian endemic), sooty gull, swift tern, white-cheeked tern, bridled tern, common noddy and Saunder's tern. Jouanin's petrel probably breeds and is another endemic to the region.

Desert and mountain species are typified by golden eagle, striated scops owl, sand partridge, cream-coloured courser, four species of sandgrouse, black-crowned finch-lark, Dunn's lark, desert lark, hoopoe lark, long-billed pipit, Hume's wheatear, scrub warbler, trumpeter finch and house bunting. Palearctic species that breed around the Mediterranean and also in Oman include little bittern, Egyptian vulture, black-winged stilt, collared pratincole, turtle dove, blue-cheeked bee-eater and southern grey shrike.

The shy Houbara bustard is a desert bird that by 1996 was near to extinction in other parts of Arabia, where it was largely hunted out by Arab falconers. Now protected by CITES, it is also the subject of a conservation survey in Oman, whose anti-falconry laws add further protection. Jaaluni in the Jiddat al Harasees in central Oman is a good place to look for this species.

For further information visit www.birdsoman.com.

Butterflies (*Andrew Grieve*) There are around 80 classified species of butterfly in Oman, none endemic to either Oman or Arabia, and many can be seen in either Musandam or Dhofar mainly between October and May. Familiar colourful species such as swallowtail can be seen in northern Oman while the similar African lime butterfly can be seen in the Dhofar region. A large bright species likely to be seen in all parts is the plain tiger, a large orange butterfly with black wing tips. As with the birds, many species are typical of neighbouring continents, particularly Africa. Jebel Akhdar (in the interior) is another good area for a range of species.

Marine life The waters of the Arabian Sea and the Gulf of Oman provide diverse marine habitats, which give rise to and accommodate an abundance of sealife. At least 900 species of fish and around 85 varieties of hard and soft coral exist in Oman's waters, which firmly places the sultanate on any diver's itinerary. Rays, honeycomb moray eels, barracuda and frogfish are just some of the species of fish that inhabit these waters. Coral varieties such as table, black, whip, teddy bear and cabbage coral can all be found here, Fahal Island offering the widest variety in one location. For information on diving, see the regional chapters; for books on the subject, see page 299.

Whales, dolphins and sharks Omani waters are home to 19 species of whale and dolphin, which include blue whale, sperm whale, humpback whale, Cuvier's beaked whale, pygmy killer whale, orca or killer whale, Bryde's whale, false killer whale, dwarf sperm whale, melon-headed whale, common bottlenose dolphin, spinner dolphin, Indo-Pacific humpback dolphin, long-beaked common dolphin, pan-tropical spotted dolphin, striped dolphin, rough-toothed dolphin and Risso's dolphin. Fahal Island is reportedly a good place to spot dolphins aplenty though the best whale-watching areas lie off southern Oman. Ras Janjari near Mirbat is a particularly good land-based viewing point. Oman is a member of the International Whaling Commission and follows the CITES regulations, which prevent all these species from being traded. The Whale and Dolphin Research Group is a voluntary organisation which works within the Environment Society of Oman (ESO) and shares the same excellent website (*www.environment.org.om*). The various sharks spotted in Omani waters include leopard sharks, whale sharks and black-tip reef sharks. They are said not to have a taste for human flesh, so do not be too alarmed if you spot a few telltale fins.

Sea turtles The other creature to merit its own sanctuary is the sea turtle, particularly the green turtle, on designated beaches at Ras Al Hadd and Ras Al Jinz on Oman's southeastern tip. These two sites are the main natural breeding areas for up to 13,000 green turtles each year. Permits, which used to involve a lot of rigmarole, can now easily be obtained at the entrance or arranged at your hotel in the region, and tourism is monitored to safeguard the turtles' environment. For further details see Turtle Beach Resort (see pages 244–5) and Ras Al Jinz Centre (see page 245).

There are five species of turtle (out of the world's seven) that populate the coasts of Oman, four solely for the purpose of laying their eggs: the olive ridley, the loggerhead, the endangered green and the critically endangered hawksbill turtle, which nests in some number on the Daymaniyat Islands. The fifth species, leatherback turtle, occurs as a visitor offshore. Over 30,000 female loggerhead turtles nest on just 14km of beach on Masirah Island. The green turtle is a protected species in Oman. These marine turtles can live for up to 200 years and most only start to breed once they are between the ages of 30 and 50. Each female can lay up to 100 eggs in a clutch and several clutches in a breeding season. She spends hours covering them up in the holes she has dug for their protection. She then returns to the water (keeping close by) for a fortnight before she returns to lay another clutch, in a cycle that is repeated up to eight times in the season. It will be another two to four years (depending upon the species) before a female will lay more eggs. The eggs take around two months to hatch, and the sight of tiny baby turtles emerging from the sand is extraordinary. They struggle through the sand, making their way to the sea, but only a small proportion will make it, as many are eaten *en route* by seagulls and other predators.

CONSERVATION

Wildlife conservation is actively carried out at the country's nature reserves. However, for endangered species, the two principal centres are the Arabian Oryx Sanctuary at Jaaluni, in the Jiddat al Harasees (Al Wusta region), and the Oman Mammal Breeding Centre at Bait al Barakah, in Seeb (Muscat region). Mammals being bred in captivity in these locations include the Arabian oryx, the Arabian tahr, Arabian gazelle, Arabian wolf, the white-tailed mongoose, the striped hyena and Gordon's wild cat.

UNESCO WORLD HERITAGE SITES Oman has four sites on the UNESCO World Heritage Site list. These include: Bahla Fort (1987) in the Dakhiliyah region; the

Aflaj irrigation systems of Oman (2006); the Land of Frankincense (2000) in the Dhofar region, which includes the archaeological sites at Shisr and Sumharam/ Khor Rori; and the archaeological sites at Bat, along with neighbouring Al Khutm and Al Ayn (1988) in Al Dhahirah region.

HISTORICAL OVERVIEW

Archaeological evidence and historical writings enable us to track Oman's history over a 5,000-year period. Sohar is believed to be the ancient 'Majan' referred to in Mesopotamian texts of the 3rd millennium BC. Majan means 'copper mountain' and it is the copper industry that is known to have sustained Oman for over 4,000 years.

Oman's people have historically been astro-navigators, sailors and merchant traders, occupying, as they did, a prime geographical position on the sea trading route between eastern and western continents. The indigenous natural resources of copper and frankincense (both extremely important commodities in the past) transformed the country's prosperity in ancient times through trade with ancient Egypt, Greece, Rome and China, to where these goods were shipped. Evidence of Oman's prosperous seafaring history can be found in ancient texts.

Islam did not arrive in the region until AD630. There was a short rule by the Portuguese in the 16th century, who were expelled in 1650 by Sultan bin Saif al Yarubi. The Ya'arubi dynasty continued to rule until the Persians invaded in 1741. They were expelled in 1749 by the founder of the present-day dynasty, Imam Ahmed bin Said. The presence of numerous castles and forts in virtually every village is testament to Oman's uneasy warring past – serving as protection from both outside invaders and neighbouring tribes.

Historic figures have passed through. The legend of Sindbad the Sailor, of *Arabian Nights* fame, is believed to have originated here around the 10th century AD. T E Lawrence (or Lawrence of Arabia) was a British soldier and author famed for *Seven Pillars of Wisdom*, an account of his desert campaigns with the Arabs. The Land of Frankincense (a UNESCO World Heritage Site) links the Queen of Sheba to the region. Wilfred Thesiger, an explorer and writer, lived and travelled with the Bedu of southern Arabia in the 1940s. His writings illuminate the traditional way of life in Oman, which he deeply cherished. Oman is home to the famed 'Atlantis of the Sands' (the lost city of Ubar), alluded to in the Koran, the Bible and *Arabian Nights*.

Since 1975, immense changes to the country's prosperity and outlook under the leadership of the well-respected Sultan Qaboos have been achieved, made possible by the country's oil reserves. Oman has been carefully modernised and now sits as a newly opened destination for the discerning traveller, offering top-class international hotels. For the near future, new top-end leisure resorts will continue to augment Oman's prosperity through tourism, offering international-standard golf courses, spas, shops and restaurants, as well as property for sale on the international market.

CHRONOLOGY There is no specific history section in this guide, since historical background is woven into the text as and when relevant. For an overview therefore, the following detailed chronology is provided as a handy reference and summary.

c3000BC	Earliest-known references to Oman, as Majan found at Ur in Sumeria, confirming it as a thriving and wealthy seafaring state, the source of Mesopotamian (the Tigris and Euphrates region of Iraq) copper. Settlement and graves at Bat established.

2500–2000BC	Umm Al Nar period of rich trade between Oman and Mesopotamia, mainly in copper. Camels domesticated for transportation. Wadi Jizzi sites founded.
2000BC	Rise of Dilmun (Bahrain) eclipses Oman's trading power.
2000–1300BC	Wadi Suq period where Oman's main trading partner is Dilmun. Sites at Samad and Ras Al Jinz established.
1300–300BC	Iron Age. Frankincense trade using caravan routes through Arabia to the north. Sites of Ubar, Khor Rori, Lizq and Bowshar established.
c1000BC	*Falaj* system of irrigation introduced to Oman, probably by Persians.
24BC	Roman army attempts to reach frankincense lands of southern Arabia but is defeated by climate and disease.
AD130	Yemeni Adnani (Ghafiri) tribes settle in Oman after years of wandering in the Nejd of Saudi Arabia.
AD200	Yemeni Azdite (Hinawi) tribes migrate to Oman after the bursting of the Maarib Dam.
AD200–400	Sassanians in power, having moved from Iran down the Gulf. Sassanian governors in Sohar and Rustaq.
AD400	Persians ransack Sumharam.
AD400–500	Christianity arrives in Oman with suggestions of an early Nestorian church in Sohar and an Omani bishop.
AD630	Amr Ibn Al As, Muhammad's general, arrives in Oman to convert the country to Islam. Oman is one of the first lands to embrace Islam fully and abandon Arabian paganism. Hinawis, after Muhammad's death, follow Ibadhi puritanical Islam, while Ghafiris follow Sunni orthodox Islam.
AD633	Battle of Dibba. Arab tribes of Oman defeat the Sassanians.
AD750	Julanda bin Masud elected first imam (spiritual leader) of Oman. Oman remains under imam rule until 1154.
8th–10th century	Oman is a rich country and Baghdad (capital of Abbasid Caliphate) sends expeditions to obtain large tribute from it. Nizwa becomes the Omani capital.
9th–10th century	Extensive trade with the Far East and India, *en route* to the wealthy Abbasid court of Baghdad. Sohar enjoys great wealth and takes over from Nizwa as the capital. Interior of Oman deteriorates, attacks by Qarmathians, but Sohar is unaffected on the coast as trade routes flourish.
1151	Dynasty established by Banu Nabhan.
13th century	Hormuz, island settlement in the strait of the same name, becomes the region's most important trade centre, despite no water supply on the barren rocky island. It becomes independent of the mainland and remains unchallenged until the arrival of the Portuguese in the 16th century. Qalhat becomes the Omani capital.
1330	Ibn Battuta, north African traveller and geographer, visits and describes Nizwa.
1428	Dynastic rule challenged by the imams.
1507	The first Europeans, the Portuguese under Albuquerque, reach Oman. They burn Oman's fishing fleets and pillage the towns of Qalhat, Quriyat and Muscat, followed by Sohar. Their commercial success is based on supply of spices (pepper, cinnamon, camphor, nutmeg and cloves) to European markets. The coastal area and city and port of Muscat under Portuguese control.

1527	Forts of Jalali and Merani built by the Portuguese in Muscat harbour.
1624	First imam of the Ya'arubi dynasty begins with Sultan ibn Saif.
1649–68	The navy is built up and expeditions undertaken to liberate Omani settlements.
1650	The Portuguese evicted from Oman after 150 years of coastal domination by Sultan ibn Saif, the powerful Ya'arubi leader. Oman is independent from this point on.
17th–18th century	Oman under Ya'arubi rulers dominates the Gulf and trade routes to east Africa. By the end of the 18th century the Omanis controlled an extensive empire, ruling Mombasa and Zanzibar.
1698	The east African coast from Mogadishu to Cape Delgado controlled by Oman, beginning a period of great Omani wealth.
1724–39	Hinawi ('northern' faction and descendants of the Qahtan) against Ghafiri ('southern' faction and descendants of the Nizar) civil war results in virtual anarchy.
1741	End of Ya'arubi dynasty.
1743	Persian invasion of Batinah coast. Persians retained control until 1749.
1749	Founding of the Al Bu Said dynasty by Ahmed bin Said from his capital in Rustaq. (Today's Sultan Qaboos is the current representative of the Al Bu Saids.)
1786	Oman's capital formally moves to Muscat from the interior.

PORTUGUESE NAVAL DOMINATION

The golden age of the Persian Gulf under the Hormuz princes ended with the arrival of the Portuguese in the Indian Ocean. The beginning of the end was when Vasco da Gama reached India in 1498, guided by an Omani navigator. In the following 30 or so years the Portuguese carried out a series of devastating attacks on key strategic points and secured maritime domination of the Arabian seas. The Portuguese were able to achieve this through great organisational skills, benefiting from strong political and economic direction from their homeland, and inspired by religious crusading zeal. On a more down-to-earth level they also had new and faster ships and superior arms.

Their aim was to monopolise trade, in particular the long-distance luxury trade of the Indian seas. They took Hormuz in 1507, but though they built some forts and bases in the region, their practice was to leave power in the hands of local governments as much as possible and to rule indirectly. This avoided the manpower demands, expense and trouble of a direct European administration. The Portuguese were repulsed from the Gulf in the mid 17th century by the combined forces of the Iranian Safavids and the English, leaving Oman and its chief port city Muscat to dominate the Gulf until the British again established European supremacy in the 19th century. Portugal's rule was too loose rather than too harsh, and it was remarkable that such a small country was able to retain control of an area as vast as the Indian Ocean for as long as it did. In the period from the end of the Portuguese domination in the mid 17th century until the 19th century, the English, Dutch and French all sailed the Gulf, but their interests were commercial rather than political. Gradually over the course of the 19th century, the British increasingly allied themselves with the Omanis against the Arab 'pirate' sheikhdoms.

1750–1800	Oman is wooed by Britain and France, both seeking political alliance and favour. French influence dwindles, weakened by the Napoleonic Wars. Napoleon lands in Egypt *en route* to India. Muscat would have been on his route, but he never got that far, having been forced to retreat from Egypt. Conservative tribes in the interior elect their own imam, feeling that the sultan in Muscat has grown too liberal.
1798	Treaty of friendship with Great Britain signed.
1800	Muscat is threatened by Wahhabi invasions from Saudi Arabia, so now it seeks alliance and support from Britain.
1804	Sultan Al Bu Said is killed by pirates, and Said bin Sultan comes to power at 18, after killing his cousin to make way. His 50-year reign brings Oman the greatest prosperity it has known since Ya'arubi days, principally from Zanzibar and Arab east Africa in the form of slaves.
1820	General treaty of peace signed between Britain and the main sheikhs of the region. The British East India Company, whose concerns in the Gulf had begun for purely commercial considerations, became gradually more political as first the company, then the British government, took upon itself the business of 'preserving peace at sea'. Throughout the first half of the 19th century, Muscat and Oman was the most powerful state in Arabia, ruling Zanzibar until 1861, and coastal parts of Persia, Kenya and Pakistan.
1822, 1839, 1845, 1873	Anti-slavery treaties established with Britain.
1839, 1846, 1891	Treaties signed with Britain for friendship, commerce and navigation.
1840	Sultan Said moves to Zanzibar and visits Oman less and less frequently. The elected imams in the interior become more and more powerful and remain very separate from Muscat and the coast.
1856	Said dies, leaving one son to rule in Muscat, another in Zanzibar.
1861	Split between Muscat and Zanzibar formalised when Zanzibar agrees to pay an annual amount to Muscat, not by way of tribute, but by way of compensation for Muscat renouncing all claims on Zanzibar, and as an adjustment to the inequality of the two sons' inheritances from their father Said.
1890	Zanzibar is parcelled out to Britain as a protectorate.
1860–95	Oman is weakened by Wahhabi incursions from the north and west, and by dissension within the ruling family. Its economy is weakened by Britain's pressure to suppress slaving activities.
1890–1910	Rivalries between Britain and France for influence in Muscat. Sultan Faisal bin Turki dies and the tribes of the interior refuse to recognise his son Taimur as imam.
1920	Treaty of Seeb to bring peace between the people of Muscat and the tribes of the interior, confirming that each will respect the other, with the sultan recognising the imam as a spiritual leader and allowing him limited jurisdiction over the interior. The treaty is mediated by the British to avert the possibility of civil war. Omani naval power declines with the advent of steam vessels.
1924	Exploration for oil begins.
1932	Oman's total budget is £50,000, made up of a few fish and date exports, customs' receipts, the Zanzibar subsidy and the oil concession rental.

1932	Taimur resigns as sultan and retires to Bombay where he dies in 1965.
1938	Said bin Taimur, his 22-year-old son, takes over, having been educated at a British school in India. Oman has been on the verge of bankruptcy since the Zanzibar split of 1857. Said bin Taimur balances the books, never going into debt, believing this is the best course of action for the country. He wrote: 'From 1933 to this present day there has been no financial deficit in the government's budget.'
1950s	Said bin Taimur attempts to regain total control of the interior, backed by the British because they want to prospect for oil and therefore require the sultan's authority to be absolute, and, in addition, for Oman's borders with Saudi Arabia and Abu Dhabi to be clearly defined. Saudi Arabia ousted from Buraimi oasis by Said, the imam and the British in a rare show of unity. Said occupies the imamate dual capitals of Nizwa and Rustaq and annexes the interior.
1951	The Sultanate of Muscat and Oman achieves full independence from Britain.
1954	A serious search for oil commences.
1957–59	Rebel war between interior tribes who elect a puppet imam (Ghalib) supported by Saudi and Egyptian aid, and the sultan in Muscat with his army and British support. After the war Said retreats to Salalah and rarely leaves the city.

THE TRUCIAL COAST

In the early 19th century Britain's main concern in the Gulf was to secure its imperial communications to India. When some of its ships got caught up in the Gulf in the war that had been ongoing for some years between the Omanis and the Arab sheikhs of the Gulf coast, they viewed it as simple piracy. They had no understanding of the cause of such attacks, no realisation that they were casualties of a local naval and trade war. Instead, they accused the Wahhabis (a highly conservative Islamic group) of initiating attacks on British shipping and talked of the 'predatory habits' of the maritime Arabs. With Omani support the British attacked 'the pirates' three times between 1805 and 1820, and then imposed a maritime peace, which had the effect of forbidding the Arab states of the Gulf to fight one another at sea without British permission.

Over the next few decades a series of other treaties followed, some formal, some informal, for establishing a set of special privileges for those who co-operated with the Western powers and restricted their participation in the slave trade. In this way insidiously and over a long period, Britain's policy of 'non-interference' in the Gulf States' internal affairs in practice radically altered the tribal status quo, and removed the method by which Gulf principalities and city-states used to dominate each other and vie for position in the Gulf. Britain saw itself as a benevolent policeman in the Gulf, preventing piracy, slave trading and maritime war. It also saw itself as gradually introducing, true to the imperial philosophy of the time, progress and civilisation to the Arab Gulf states. As a result of these truces, the Arab side of the Gulf became known as the 'Trucial coast'.

Said bin Taimur had a horror of debt and strove never to become dependent on creditors. In his only public statement, made in January 1958, he wrote: 'Doubtless it would have been easy to obtain money in various ways, but this could only have been by a loan with interest at a set percentage rate. This amounts to usury, with which I completely disagree, and the religious prohibition of which is not unknown.' Having seen the mistakes of his predecessors he also decided it was dangerous to delegate – better to do everything oneself to be sure it was done as you wanted. The sultan followed these principles utterly consistently, controlling every issue in his country in minute detail, leading, alas, to a rigid form of centralised administration which became increasingly inappropriate in the 1960s, though it may have been suitable in the 1940s and 1950s. When PDO (Petrol Development Oman) announced in 1964 that it had found oil in commercial quantities and would start exporting in 1967, the sultan could have easily obtained credit, but he never took a penny because of his debt principle. He continued to sit, apart from it all, mistrusting all, unapproachable except by those who had obtained special permission to visit Salalah and who had arranged a prior appointment. Those who were fortunate enough to meet him were generally won over by his charm and powers of persuasion.

1959	Development department is set up to administer the subsidy provided by Britain after the Jebel War. It has three divisions: health, agriculture and public works. Health comprises a few underfunded clinics. Agriculture is two experimental farms in Nizwa and Sohar completely unsupported by the sultan, and public works is road building and repair, a division which took six years to complete the 150-mile graded track from Azaiba to Sohar. No piece of machinery can be purchased without the sultan's authorisation.
1964	Shell discovers oil in commercial quantities at Fahud, which later provides the finance for the transformation of the undeveloped kingdom to a modern state. Smaller oilfields are established at Natih and Yibal.
1967	First oil exports from the fields of Fahud, Natih and Yibal, yielding revenues small by Middle Eastern standards, but of enormous importance to Oman. Oman now has an oil-based economy for the first time. Said refuses to spend any money on development projects, opposes any change and seeks to keep Oman isolated from the modern world. Britain withdraws from Aden. Russian and Chinese imperialists fill the vacuum left. The Marxist-led Dhofar War begins with the aim of overthrowing the sultan and taking control of Oman and the Strait of Hormuz.
1970	Qaboos (aged 30) stages a non-violent coup against his father Said with British support. Said bin Taimur goes to London in exile. Sultan Qaboos takes over power. Country's name changed to 'Sultanate of Oman' as opposed to 'Muscat and Oman' and a modernisation programme is launched, financed by income from oil.
1970–75	Qaboos begins the task of building up Omani infrastructure, Mina Qaboos Port in Muttrah, health care and schooling in a series of five-

	year development plans. The Omani rial is established to replace the Indian rupee and the Maria Teresa dollar. End of the Dhofar War, with British military assistance, including elite SAS units.
1976	Qaboos marries but later divorces. He has no children.
1981	Oman plays a key role in establishment of six-member Gulf Co-operation Council, whose other members are Saudi Arabia, Kuwait, the UAE, Bahrain and Qatar.
1982	Memorandum of understanding with UK signed, providing for regular consultation on international issues.
1986	Oman's first university, called Sultan Qaboos, opens.
1990	Majlis Ash Shura created, comprising 82 elected members from the *wilayats*.
1994	Women given the vote in the nomination process for the Majlis Ash Shura.
1998	Port of Raysut opens with world-class container terminal facilities.
1999	Oman's oil reserves are estimated at five billion barrels; gas reserves are estimated at 900,000 barrels a day. Tourism is estimated to contribute a mere 1% to gross national product. Oman and the neighbouring United Arab Emirates (UAE) settle their border disputes.
2001	The Sultan Qaboos Grand Mosque opens at Bowshar.
2002	The new world-class Sohar Industrial Port project gets under way, managed by the Sohar Industrial Port Company (SIPC), which is a joint venture between Oman and the Netherlands. It will be a major hub in the upper Gulf and Indian Ocean region.
2003	All Omani citizens over the age of 21 are given the power to vote.

THE MILITARY

The SAF (Sultan's Armed Forces) was formed in 1958 from various loosely organised groups with military assistance and a subsidy from the British government. It initially had a British colonel as its commander, but by the mid 1970s it had grown to include over 13,000 personnel, an expansion forced on it by the bitterly fought Dhofar War against Marxist-led guerrillas from south Yemen. It used to be top-heavy with British officers on secondment and many of these stayed as contract officers on leaving the British army. In recent years though, strenuous efforts have been made towards Omanisation, with Omanis increasingly taking the place of senior British officers. The subsidy Britain paid to SAF stopped in 1967 when the sultan was thought to have enough money from oil revenues to pay for it himself. In the Gulf wars, the 2001 US invasion of Afghanistan and the 2003 invasion of Iraq, Oman (Masirah Island) acted as a base and staging post for both Britain and the US. In 2001, Oman hosted the British army in exercise Saif Sareea II (which translates as 'Swift Sword'), in which 12,500 members of the SAF also participated. It was an exercise to practice rapid deployment and test equipment in severe conditions, but it so transpired that the Afghan invasion intervened. Today the SAF consists of the Royal Guard, land forces, the Royal Navy of Oman (RNO) and Royal Air Force of Oman (RAFO). The RNO is thought to be one of the most modern in the region and RAFO is highly respected. It acts more as a para-police force than a military machine, entirely appropriate for a country like Oman.

2004	The Ministry of Tourism established, tourism being a major component of the government's economic diversification plan to move away from its reliance on oil. The first female government minister is appointed.
2006	Productive activities in the port of Sohar commence. Royal decree announces a new property law, which enables foreign freehold ownership of real estate on designated major tourist developments such as The Wave. Oman and the US sign a free trade deal.
2007	Cyclone Gonu, the most powerful cyclone in the region for decades, hits the Gulf, disrupting oil production, destroying areas of coastline south of Muscat, killing over 50 people and causing over US$4 billion of damage. Oman's Oryx Sanctuary is removed from UNESCO's World Heritage site list after the herd dwindles and the government reduces the park size by 90%.
2009	Somali pirates hijack a cargo vessel off the coast of Oman, the first such attack in the area. First residents move into The Wave.
2010	Scottish firm Aggreko wins £50 million power supply contract. Muscat holds the Asian Beach Games.
2011	First ever outbreak of discontent in wake of Arab Spring protests across the region. Young Omanis demand more jobs, higher salaries, media freedom and an end to corruption. No calls for regime change. Two protestors die in Sohar at the hands of security forces. Qaboos responds by creating 50,000 new jobs in the public sector, increasing benefits and raising salaries.
2012	Activists are put on trial for criticising the government online. Six are given jail sentences of 12–18 months and fined US$2,500 each. Amnesty International issues a statement of support for the detainees. Most are subsequently released. Qaboos reshuffles his cabinet in response to protests, removing three ministers.
2013	Peaceful protests are permitted but freedom of expression and assembly remain limited. Cabinet outlines plans to limit the expatriate workforce to 33% of the population. Qaboos promises youth participation in nation-building through entrepreneurship and investment opportunities.

GOVERNMENT AND POLITICS

Prior to 1970, Al Said leaders assumed the political title of 'Sultan of Muscat and Oman', which implied the existence of two separate and irreconcilable political sectors. Indeed, coastal Muscat was more cosmopolitan and secular, largely because of its international trading history, whereas the interior was more insular, tribal and religious, ruled by an imam with traditional Ibadist ideologies. Under Sultan Qaboos's leadership (since 1970) the country was reconciled under the title the 'Sultanate of Oman', and has carefully and cautiously recognised its position within the global scheme, and embraced an international, diplomatic mindset.

Administratively, Oman today is divided into eight regions (or five regions and three governorates) and these regions are in turn divided into administrative areas, or *wilayats*, each overseen by its own chief governor, or *wali*. Under Sultan Qaboos, as head of state, the government remains essentially autocratic: there is no prime minister and the sultan can accept or reject any legislation. Political parties are still banned, the death penalty is still in force, the internet is monitored and the media

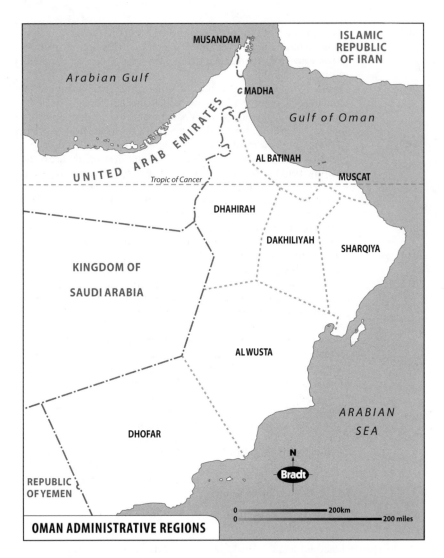

OMAN ADMINISTRATIVE REGIONS

exercises self-censorship. However, he has recognised that such a situation will not go on indefinitely: 'The time will come when this will have to stop and the voters' decision will be final.'

In 1970, when Qaboos came to power, the sultanate had diplomatic relations with just three countries. Now it has relations with over 140, as well as belonging to a network of over 105 regional and international organisations including the United Nations and the Gulf Co-operation Council (GCC). There are currently two female Omani ambassadors. Unusually for the Gulf, Oman maintains good relations with Iran.

The Council of Oman (Majlis Oman) is a bicameral system, comprising the Consultative Council (Majlis al Shura) and the State Council (Majlis al Dawla). The Consultative Council was inaugurated in 1991 and was originally made up of 59 publicly elected members, representing each of the 59 *wilayats* (districts/areas)

THE *WALI* SYSTEM

Outside of Muscat, Oman is administered by *walis* (local governors). The sultan appoints them himself, and they then report back to him via the Ministry of the Interior. The *wali* is responsible for all civil matters in his district (*wilayat*) and there are 59 *wilayats* in the country. This has been the system for many centuries, throughout the sultanate, and before that the imamate, except that at times, especially in the 19th century, they evolved into near-independent city-states, defying any attempts at centralisation. Before oil the *wali* might, if he was lucky, have an old Land Rover and even an old wireless link to Muscat. Some places, like Izki, had neither. The *wali* in Sur had a wireless but no Land Rover and was once on tour on his donkey when the wireless operator received an urgent message that he should report to Muscat. The *wali* was fetched and given the message, whereupon he caught a *dhow* and was in Muscat 12 hours later. There, he was made to wait three days for an audience with the minister of the interior on a matter that was trivial. The *wali* of Buraimi was once likewise summoned and kept waiting for four months until he was allowed to return. Such treatment was not regarded as unusual.

of the country. As a result of increases in the population, this has now expanded to 83, to include further representation for the *wilayats* with a population in excess of 30,000. The number of women on the Consultative Council has been increased from one to 15. This council acts as a consultative body only, proposing legislation and expressing views on laws once they are passed. It covers legal matters, the economy, health, education and the environment, but has no say in Oman's foreign defence or security policies. The committees, of which it is composed, have free rein to interrogate ministers. Elections are held every three years.

The State Council has 53 members who are appointed by the sultan on a three-year renewable term. Members are selected for their high status in society, their experience, reputation and expertise. The State Council acts as the upper chamber,

THE *QADI* SYSTEM OF LAW

Islamic or shari'a law applies to all members of the community and a *qadi* (Arabic judge) serves alongside the *wali* in every *wilayat* to administer justice according to this law. There is then a chief Qadi's court in Muscat. In all Arab countries where shari'a law applies it is interpreted more or less strictly in accordance with the outlook prevalent in that country. For Oman this is an Ibadhi interpretation of Islamic law, which aligns it closely to the teaching of the Koran and the Hadith (traditions) of the Prophet, right up to the 1970s when Sultan Qaboos's father, Said bin Taimur, saw no reason to alter matters. Since Qaboos's accession in 1970 however, there has been a modernising shift towards adapting shari'a law to cope with situations of the 20th and 21st centuries while still adhering to shari'a principles. Most Arab countries have had to face this issue of how to modernise Islamic law, and most have adopted a compromise where the legal system is based either on English law, or on the French Napoleonic code, depending on their historic associations. Owing to its long-standing links with Britain, and Sultan Qaboos's own ties to the British way of life, Oman favours the British legal system.

playing a central role in the country's development. It holds four 'ordinary' sessions each year, with the option to hold further 'extraordinary' sessions. This council has the power to review and revise draft laws and submit proposals to the sultan and the Council of Ministers. Each of the councils includes female members, albeit in a marked minority. Sultan Qaboos is the longest-serving ruler in the Middle East, since the demise of Colonel Qadhafi of Libya.

ECONOMY

Prior to 1970, the economy was based on the export of dates, limes, fish and skins, and otherwise the country had a subsistence economy based on agriculture and fisheries. Today, the agriculture and fishing industries still constitute the largest employers of the population, followed by government, then service industries, manufacturing and construction. Ironically oil and gas employ the lowest percentage of the population despite generating the largest income for the economy.

The Omani economy is still largely dependent on oil revenues, despite the fact that this dependency has been substantially reduced. In 1982, oil and gas provided 62% of GDP; this was reduced to 38% by 1998, and the decline continues, currently at 35% of GDP; the aim is to reduce it to 19% by 2020 and to expand the non-oil sectors, thereby diversifying the economy. Oil and gas account for 85% of government revenue at present, but by 2020 the aim is to reduce that to less than 70%.

Today, defence and security account for a large portion of government spending. The LNG (Liquefied Natural Gas) plant near Sur, the Raysut Port in Salalah and now the Sohar Port will be critical to its economic future.

ECONOMIC DIVERSIFICATION AND VISION 2020 Oman is a relatively small oil-producing state and the remaining years of oil production are said to be limited. This fact, coupled with a drop in oil prices in the second half of 1997, revealed a vulnerability within the Omani economy and alerted the government to the need to diversify its economic base away from its reliance on oil. The country's focus has now shifted to other areas, such as trade and tourism, manufacturing and building, construction and real estate, the directives of which have been outlined in its Vision 2020 economic programme.

Tourism Tourism in Oman is still underdeveloped and is one of the most important areas identified for expansion. Until the 1980s no-one was allowed into Oman without a No Objection Certificate (NOC) which could only be obtained through an Omani sponsor. If you simply wanted to visit the country out of curiosity, you were not allowed in. Journalists in particular were almost never

---

BRITAIN AND OMAN – THE SPECIAL RELATIONSHIP

Every year around 2,000 Omanis come to Britain to study at schools, universities and training institutes, a higher number than from any other country in the Arab world, and around 7,000 British citizens live and work in Oman, the largest western expatriate group in the country.

Britain also has a strong defence relationship with Oman, thanks to Sultan Qaboos being a graduate of Sandhurst. Nearly a hundred British military personnel are on loan to the Oman Armed Forces at any one time, the second largest such group in the world.

BUYING PROPERTY AS A FOREIGNER

The Omani government in the mid-2000s introduced new laws permitting foreigners to buy property, but only within integrated tourism complexes like The Wave close to Seeb, Muscat Hills Golf & Country Club, Blue City near Sawadi on the Batinah coast, Jebel Sifah, Barr Al-Jissah and Yiti Resort south of Muscat, and the Salalah Beach Resort. The rules have been a touch confusing in the past but now the government has clarified that property owners will qualify for a full two-year residence visa, extendable to immediate family members, once the title deed has passed to the buyer's name. There have been some delays in the completion of these projects, thanks to the global financial crisis, but all are going ahead. While the property is under construction, registered buyers are entitled to multiple three-week visiting visas. By opening up the country to foreign investors and simultaneously expanding the country's tourism infrastructure, the thinking is that projects such as these will play a big role in offsetting the country's future reliance on oil revenues. Property ownership in these complexes is 75% foreign, mainly Indian nationals. Prices are reasonable and very stable, with a one-bed flat costing around £90,000 and a three-bed villa with pool £300,000. Foreign owners are also permitted to have 'buy to let' arrangements. The property can be sold any time after its construction is complete, and residency then passes to the new owner. If you die owning Omani property the laws of your native country apply to inheritance, so make sure you have a valid will. If no heirs present themselves within a year the Ministry of Tourism will manage the property for up to 15 years, then take ownership itself.

Useful websites: www.expatarrivals.com and www.engelvoelkers.com.

allowed in and were regarded with great suspicion. This rigorous entry system was devised by the sultan's father, Said bin Taimur, and in his day his own personal permission had to be obtained for entry. The first organised group of tourists – 14 of them – visited the country in 1983, led by the wife of a former ambassador. Today, Oman is far more accessible and accommodating, and ecotourism and adventure tourism are being actively promoted. Oman offers a more peaceful travelling option than neighbouring tourist-dense Dubai and is the most successful example in the Middle East of how a country can be gradually modernised without giving up its cultural identity. In 2012 Oman was the only Arab country to feature in the National Geographic's 20 Top Tourist Destinations, showing how its politically stable image has made it a direct beneficiary of the tourist fallout from Arab Spring countries like Egypt and Syria. Tourist numbers touched 2 million that year.

Restoration and development plans for the tourism industry

The Ministry of Tourism has instigated restoration projects to develop old stone buildings, restoring original mountain tracks, introducing *barasti* (palm frond) shades and toilets and providing proper signage. There are plans to develop mountain villages as exclusive retreats to showcase Oman's distinct heritage, culture and natural attractions. Even the children can undergo a one-year programme to equip them with the tools to interact with tourists, which includes an English-language course.

The aim of the Omani government is to double tourist revenue and increase it to 5% of GDP by 2020. As over 50% of the population is estimated to be under 18, it is hoped the tourism sector will absorb many young Omanis entering the job market. Unlike neighbouring Dubai, which encourages visitors from all backgrounds, Oman has repeatedly stressed its desire to encourage upmarket tourism, focusing on cultural and heritage attractions. Backpackers will remain something of a rarity for the foreseeable future. Travel restrictions have now been eased and visitors from over 75 countries can get a visa, valid for either ten days (RO5) or one month (RO20), on arrival at Oman's entry points (see pages 43–4). There is a joint visa facility with Dubai, from which Oman obviously hopes to attract some of Dubai's 5 million visitors. Seeb/Muscat International Airport and Salalah International Airport are both being upgraded to handle more incoming flights, and Oman Air has acquired new planes and expanded its European destinations, now flying direct to Paris, Frankfurt, Munich, Milan, Zurich and London. Salalah has seen a particularly marked increase in air passenger arrivals, up 25% in 2012, with Oman Air, FlyDubai, Qatar Airways and Air Arabia all increasing their year-round flights.

Employment and Omanisation Half a million jobs are currently filled by cheap hard-working imported labour that sends remittances abroad. Under the government's Vision 2020 directive, the country plans to get Omanis doing this work. Omanis are more willing than most GCC nationals, but there is still a long way to go in attitudes and training. This is the country's biggest concern. Over 50% of the population is under 18, which puts a huge pressure on youth employment. The government's solution, apart from encouraging Omanis to take on more lowly jobs (eg: petrol-pump attendants, waiters, cleaners, tailors and shop assistants) currently occupied by expatriate subcontinentals, is to try to broaden the economic base, so that secondary and tertiary businesses will be created and thus begin to absorb the growing workforce. The target for Omanisation was for 95% of all jobs to be held by Omanis by 2020, but the process is proving slower than the government had hoped, with institutions such as banks and oil companies finding it very difficult to place suitable Omanis in middle-management jobs held by Indian and Pakistani managers who have ten to 15 years of experience behind them.

Infrastructure and development Huge improvements to the infrastructure have been made over the past few years, especially in the network of tarmac roads and highways, notably the Muscat Expressway. Streets that were nameless have now been identified and are clearly signed. Shell petrol stations abound, and so do Al Maha and Oman Oil.

New flyovers have been constructed, which seem to have eased the traffic flow considerably where once it amassed at roundabouts, and consideration has been given to pedestrians, who now have walkways that pass up and bridge over the main motorway. New highways have been completed from Muscat to Sur along the coast, and from Muscat to Salalah, transforming the timings of journeys.

PEOPLE

The Omanis are a conservative people, and a respect for their privacy and their religion are courteous gestures from any visitor to their country. They are friendly and giving, and keen to communicate and demonstrate their culture and heritage to those who are interested. They are known for their hospitality and are deeply committed to a sense of family. Omanis are generally keen to assist and welcome outsiders. Broadly, they have a relaxed, laid-back *bukra* mentality. '*Bukra*' means 'tomorrow', which implies they will do something 'tomorrow', but in reality means 'at some point in the infinite future'. You are likely to hear '*inshallah*' often, which means 'if God wills it, it will happen'.

The true indigenous Omanis did not originally live on the coast but in the interior. Some 45% of the population belongs to the highly conservative Ibadhi sect (see box on page 28), one of Islam's earliest sects. The merchant classes on the other hand lived on the coast along the Batinah, and the leading ones among them were the Baharina, originally of Persian ancestry, and the Shi'ites, together with the Khojas or Hyderabadis, who are Shi'ites of Indian origin. Their families often had strong trading links up and down the Gulf, with cousins and brothers running businesses in Bahrain, Kuwait, Dubai and Qatar. The other class of non-indigenous Omanis are the Beluch who also tend to live in specific quarters of the coastal towns. The Sunnis, who now form about 50% of the population, are concentrated in Sur and the Sharqiya, and in Dhofar.

POPULATION STATISTICS The total population of Oman is around 3.1 million, of which some 80% are Omanis and 20% are expatriates, mainly Indian and Pakistani, with a few thousand from other Arab countries, Europe and the US. Muscat is commonly thought to be the most densely populated city but the Batinah coast in fact has a greater population; half of Oman's total population lives in Muscat and

THE STATUS OF WOMEN IN OMANI SOCIETY

Since Sultan Qaboos came to power in 1970 women's status in the Sultanate has been transformed. They now enjoy fair treatment and, broadly, equal opportunities in education and in the workplace. They increasingly take up careers in teaching, medicine and banking and can become members of the Majlis al Dawla, and occupy other senior government positions, unlike elsewhere in the Arabian Peninsula. Sultan Qaboos's philosophy is made clear from the following speech: 'Many years ago I said that if the energy, capability and enthusiasm of women were excluded from a country's active life, then that country would be depriving itself of 50% of its genius. I have taken very good care that this should not happen to Oman, and I look forward to the further progress of women in my country with the greatest pleasure and confidence.' The sultan has forbidden the full face veil for women in public office.

That said, there is still a strong traditional element in Omani society, especially among the Ibadhi shaikhs, who resist such change. In 2011 a new decree declared that women could share in the financing of the home, but it was abolished a year later after tribal pressure. In 2012 women tried to establish a cycling club near Nizwa, but the tribal shaikhs mobilised against it. In the brief Omani uprising of January to May 2011 women were vocal in calling for greater emancipation. 'We have suffered from four sultans,' one woman said, 'our political sultan before Qaboos, our tribal sheikh, our religious imam and our own father.'

Shari'a law also remains a problem, under which women cannot marry without the consent of their male guardian, sons inherit twice as much as daughters and the testimony of a woman is worth half that of a man. The words of the Ibadhi *mufti* (religious leader) sum up the problem: 'Women are naturally seductive,' he said, 'so segregation should be applied in school and in the workforce.' Undeterred, the Sultan continues to champion women's rights and has established a new body with the aim of reforming education in Oman.

Each main tribe has its paramount or senior sheikh who is consolidated in this position by the sultan, though not appointed by him. The sheikh acquires his position through the consensus of the tribe, not by hereditary succession. He is responsible if the tribe commits an offence, and he receives from the sultan the traditional tribal tribute. The interesting question is the relationship between the sheikh and the nearest *wali* (local governor), and the answer depends on the sheikh's power in relation to the *wali's* influence. The sheikh, like the *wali*, generally approaches the sultan via the Minister of the Interior. Oman is one of the few remaining places in the Arab world where the tribal system continues to matter and remain strong, though of course its force is inevitably waning. Even so, rivalries between tribes still occasionally flare up, though today they are more likely to be over allegiances to different football teams.

the Batinah. Approximately 78% of the population is classed as urban. The least-populated region is Al Wusta, closely followed by Musandam.

Many families, especially the men, believe that to have fewer than six children suggests unmanliness and conveys a lack of status. Such views are gradually being modified, however, and the average size of an Omani household has reduced to around six members. Birth control is gradually becoming more common. The average age for men to get married is 35, for women between 28 and 30.

LANGUAGE

Despite the ethnic mix, Arabic remains overwhelmingly the spoken and official language of Oman. The larger indigenous population means that the dominance of Arabic is unchallenged, unlike in the United Arab Emirates next door, and the numbers of immigrant Indian and Pakistani workers are not enough to have a significant impact on Omani culture. The Arabic spoken here is also one of the purest dialects. As a foreigner you may find yourself questioning this, since the bulk of the staff in hotels, restaurants, shops and businesses still tend to be English-speaking Indians, whose labour is cheaper and who are in any case more prepared than Omanis to do such jobs. A serious effort is being made by the government to change these attitudes through the Omanisation programme (see page 24).

Spoken Arabic here is close to the classical, written Arabic, equating to the erstwhile BBC English, but you will have to be quite determined to use it in the Capital Area. In the interior, however, it is often the only language spoken. Arabic is everywhere on street signs and in advertisements so there is plenty of opportunity to practise your Arabic alphabet (but don't panic, the English translation invariably accompanies it).

Arabic is, by the very nature of its structure, an extremely rich language, capable of expressing fine shades of meaning, and this is reflected in the wealth of Arabic literature, especially poetry. The average English tabloid reader is said to have a working vocabulary of 3,000 words, whereas the Arab equivalent is said to have about 10,000 (see pages 291–2).

There are also many interesting features of the language which hint at the nature and attitudes of the Arab mind, notably the existence of only two tenses, perfect and imperfect: there is no future tense. In the Arabic concept of time there is only one distinction that matters: has something been finished or is it still going on?

Another curiosity is that the plural of inanimate objects is treated grammatically as feminine singular, a characteristic which invites speculation.

The written Arabic language together with Islam is one of the few unifying factors in the Arab world. It means that newspapers published in Egypt can be distributed and read from Morocco to Iraq and even down to Yemen. In the spoken language however, the 22 countries of the Arab League also express their individuality, to the extent that a Moroccan and an Iraqi speaking their local dialect will understand each other only with difficulty. In order to communicate therefore they have to compromise and speak a form of modern classical Arabic which is understood by educated Arabs everywhere, and it is this middle Arabic which you generally speak as a foreigner. The Arabic spoken in the Gulf is the closest to classical Arabic as you might expect, since the Arabian Peninsula has been least influenced by external factors and has never been colonised by a foreign power. By contrast, the forms of spoken Arabic furthest away from the pure written classical Arabic are Lebanese and Egyptian, since these countries have been most exposed to foreign influences.

RELIGION

The official religion of Oman is Islam, and has been since the 7th century, originally of the Ibadhi sect which is very conservative and traditional in approach. Sunni Muslims, the mainstream of orthodox Islam throughout the region, are now estimated to account for half the population. The Indian and Pakistani expatriates are a mixture of Muslims, Hindus and Christians. Oman is tolerant of other religions and the presence of churches and temples demonstrates this.

The Islamic religion follows the five pillars of faith. These are the professing of faith (Shahadah), the making of prayers (Salat), fasting (Sawm), the giving of charity (Zakat) and the pilgrimage to Mecca (Hajj). Salat occurs five times a day at dawn, noon, mid-afternoon, 1½ hours before sunset and at sunset. Muslims are alerted to this by the *muezzin*, who chants a call to prayer from the mosque.

The Islamic calendar is calculated from the Hejira, which is the day of departure of the Prophet from Mecca to Medina. For the year 2000, the Hejira year was 1421.

RAMADAN Ramadan is the holy month, when Muslims abstain from eating, drinking and smoking between sunrise and sunset for 30 days. Non-Muslims are affected because it is considered disrespectful to be seen eating, drinking (in any

MOSQUE ETIQUETTE

This is something that varies from country to country across the Arab world, but in the Arabian Peninsula non-Muslims are not generally allowed to enter mosques, as the assumption is that they will be unsuitably dressed and only be interested in taking pictures of everything. The same applies in Oman, but there is an exception – the massive modern Sultan Qaboos Grand Mosque in Al Ghubrah near Muscat, which opens to non-Muslim visitors from 08.30–11.00 every day except Friday. Children under 10 are not allowed. Women are given full-length gowns with hoods to comply with Muslim dress custom. Photography is permitted. This is a good opportunity to see mosque architecture and design, with a separate prayer hall for women and a public library (early mosques were always places of learning often combined with schools/colleges).

form) or smoking in public places during daylight hours in Ramadan. As a result most restaurants are closed (though large hotels keep a screened-off area for non-Muslims), bars are closed and hotels are not permitted to serve alcohol publicly. Even after sunset, throughout Ramadan alcohol is not sold in restaurants or bars, and therefore many are shut down. Consumption of alcohol is permitted only in the privacy of your home or hotel room. Working hours are shorter, with later starts and earlier finishes. Ramadan is looked forward to and enjoyed by Omanis, as it is a time for self-restraint, religious reflection, and visiting friends and family after dark, when social activity tends to go on into the small hours. During Ramadan, government offices and banks are open from 08.00 till noon, Saturday to Thursday. As it follows the lunar calendar, Ramadan moves forwards each year (falls earlier) by about 11 days.

IBADHISM

The Ibadhis, named after Abdullah Ibn Ibadhi (c AD683, the second half of the first Muslim century), were the most tolerant subdivision of the puritanical Kharijites, who bitterly opposed Ali, the fourth caliph, and the right of the Quraysh tribe, the most powerful Meccan tribe, to choose the caliph. They wanted the Islamic state to return to how it had been before the power struggle of Ali and Mu'awiya, and believed the best person for the caliph should be chosen irrespective of his relationship to the Prophet's family. This disagreement played itself out in Basra (Iraq) and ended in persecution and exile for the Ibadhis. Some took refuge in Oman and some in Libya, Tunisia and Algeria, where they still survive.

The main doctrinal point on which they differ from Sunnis and Shi'a (the two main Islamic subdivisions), is that they do not feel it is essential that a visible leader must exist at all times. If there is no-one suitable, then they feel it is best to wait until someone suitable appears. From the 8th century onwards imams were appointed in Oman as spiritual, political and military leaders, best described as tolerant puritans. The Ibadhis were sometimes known as 'quietists' who believed in achieving things through quiet dignity and reasonableness, not through fanatical confrontations. The mosques reflect this style and tend to be simple and devoid of decoration except round the mihrab niche and the windows. Minarets were not used except on the coast, and in the interior the call to prayer was traditionally made from the roof, reached by an outside flight of steps.

Ibadhism has always been tolerant of Christians and Jews, allowing them to practise their own religions in Oman. Even so, in the coffee-pouring etiquette where guests were always served in order of importance, Christians often came last, after the poorest Muslim in Ibadhi areas, while in Sunni areas Christians sometimes even came higher than the wali in the coffee hierarchy. Singing is suppressed by Ibadhi Muslims as a frivolity, but most Arabs have a natural sense of rhythm and love of music, which tends to escape when they are happy and contented. Superstition runs deep too, and Islam has never completely wiped out old Semitic beliefs in blood sacrifice, fetishism and animism of ancient idolatry. The Ibadhi areas are predominantly in the interior around Nizwa, becoming increasingly diluted as you go northwards to Buraimi, and also in the Jebel Akhdar, which provided the refuge for Ibadhism and the imamate during periods of outside interference and dominance.

EDUCATION

In 1970, prior to the current sultan coming to power, there were only three schools in the whole of Oman: one in Muscat, one in Muttrah and one in Salalah; they were for boys only. Now the situation has turned around and there are over 1,000 government-run schools and over 100 private schools providing equal schooling opportunities for boys and girls. In 1986 the Sultan Qaboos University, the first university in Oman, was established, and now there are over 20 universities and higher education institutions in the country. Adult literacy centres are plentiful throughout the country, and Oman can now boast one of the highest literacy rates in the Arab world, at 86% for men and 74% for women.

CULTURE
OMANI TRADITIONAL DRESS
Men The *dishdasha* is the ankle-length robe worn by Omani men. Usually white in colour for daytime wear or in the workplace, official and formal, this also comes in a variety of colours for evening and special occasions. The tassel at the neck is called the *furakha* or *farusha* and it is customary to perfume this.

The *kumah* (or *kummar*) is the small embroidered cap worn by Omani men. The embroidery comes in a variety of colours and floral or geometric designs to match the *dishdasha*. On formal occasions a *musr* (or *mussar*) (turban) is often worn. The *khanjar* (a curved sheathed dagger) is worn, attached to a belt (made from either leather or cotton fabric), also worn on special occasions (see *The Khanjar* box on page 30). The *assa* (stick) is another part of the Omani traditional costume, which was used for practical purposes in the past to control camels, but these days is more of a decorative appendage. On the feet, leather sandals are worn. On formal occasions, a *bisht* (cloak) may be worn that in part covers the *dishdasha*. The edges are embroidered in gold or silver threads.

Women Underneath the *abaya* (a black cover-all gown worn in public), Omani women can be found wearing brightly coloured traditional ankle-length dresses and headscarves made from a range of fabrics in a variety of styles, according to region and/or personal taste. The name of each part of the costume varies from region to region. Broadly, the woman's *jallabia* (dress) is usually worn over *sirwall* (trousers) and with a *lihaf* (head shawl). In some regions a *burka* (face mask) is worn. Some women wear Western clothes, but cover up with the *abaya* outside the home. Fabrics are embroidered with lace, sequins, jewels, beads, coins and other materials. Tailors are plentiful throughout the country and so costumes can be speedily made to order according to any personal design. It is traditional for women to have their hands and feet painted with henna at times of celebration. Traditionally, kohl was drawn on the eyes and indigo on the face on special occasions, festivals and weddings. Henna is still used today, pasted on the hands and feet in various patterns and designs which, when dried, leave an orangey-brown decorative stain.

TRADITIONAL SPORTING EVENTS
Bullfighting This takes place on Friday afternoons in the winter months at several places along the Batinah coast. Unlike Spanish bullfighting, the sport in Oman is bloodless. Two Brahmin bulls (who are pampered as pets) fight until the first is knocked down or runs away. The event begins at 16.00 and lasts just a few minutes. The bulls lock horns in a test of strength, trying to push each other over into the sand or make them run away. There is no prize money, only honour and prestige for

THE KHANJAR

The *khanjar* is a curved, sheathed dagger, which encapsulates and symbolises the Omani identity. In the past the *khanjar* had a utilitarian purpose, and served as an essential piece of weaponry used to protect against wild animals or the enemy. Today it is valued and respected, and proudly worn as part of a male Omani's traditional dress on special occasions and for official ceremonies. Its image is used on the Omani flag.

The article itself can be broken down into three pieces: the knife, the sheath and the attaching belt, and different skills are required to fashion each piece. The price of such a souvenir is largely determined by the material used in its handle. This can be ivory, rhino horn or sandalwood, sandalwood being the cheapest. Although it is no longer permitted to obtain further stocks of ivory or rhino horn, the remaining stocks are reportedly still used until their eventual depletion. It is illegal to export such material though, so you will need to opt for the sandalwood variety if taking one out of the country as a souvenir.

the winner, something that would render it unworkable as an activity in Dubai. In Oman, however, traditions are still valued for their own sake, thereby making this bullfighting a natural spectacle refreshingly devoid of commercialism. No hurt comes to the bulls, as they are matched in age, strength and weight by a panel of judges, and a rope is tied to each bull so that they can be separated if need be. The bulls are often given heroic names from Islamic literature, such as Antar, or even names of American wrestlers. It is noticeably an all-male event. The fun is in watching the crowd scramble when the bulls get too close and watching the owner try to retrieve his fleeing bull at the end. See page 130, for further details.

Camel breeding and racing Intricately linked with Omani tradition and culture, the camel is an integral part of the country's culture and history, stemming back to references in the Koran. Known as 'the ship of the desert' or 'the beast of burden', they were also traditionally sources of milk and meat. In Dhofar today, where there are about 60,000, this is still very much the case: meat and milk are taken from them and they are considered part of the household. Indeed, a female can produce up to 20 litres of milk per day, depending on her reproduction programme, which is low fat and reportedly good for the human stomach. Elsewhere select camels have bypassed their traditional use and instead have been bred since birth for racing. Much like thoroughbred horses they are fed a healthy diet, groomed and trained, and can become great financial assets to their owners, differing considerably in appearance from their conventional cousins. A good racing camel can still fetch a price of RO30,000 or more.

Camel racing has become a popular and commercial sport in the Arabian Peninsula. In Oman camel-racing events are held at tracks in many areas throughout the country on occasions of celebration, such as National Day and other public holidays. It is most popular in the Batinah region, which is the camel-rearing hub of the country, as well as Seeb (in the Muscat region) and Al Mudaybi and Al Kamil (in the Sharqiya region). Al Abiadh camel racetrack is located about 30km from Sinaw, off the Sinaw–Mahawt road and attracts some top-quality camels. Admission is free.

Barka has several racetracks and camel pens. Racing camels are strictly bred and trained specifically for the sport, and represent big business, competing at both national and international events, warranting their own Directorate-General of Camel Affairs. Omani thoroughbreds are well known in the region and in demand. The training season runs from June to October and the racing season from September to March. Races are generally run 06.00–09.00 at weekends, and are announced in the local papers; a list of camel-race locations and dates is given on www.omantourism.gov.om.

Equestrian events Oman is famous for its pure-bred Arabian horses and has a centuries-old horse-breeding history. In 1983 the Oman Equestrian Federation was formed, promoting equestrian events. Each winter the federation organises a national show-jumping competition, attracting entries from the Royal Stables at Seeb, the Royal Oman Police, the Royal Guard of Oman and various private stables. It takes place at the Enam Equestrian showground in Seeb – one of the best riding arenas in the world; the Duke of Edinburgh, Prince Philip, participated in one such event in 1991. A Royal Equestrian Show is held every five years at the Royal Stables,and a Royal Meeting held annually where the Royal Stables compete with other horses bred in Oman. Oman is a member of the World Arabian Horse Organisation (WAHO; *www.waho.org/Reports/Oman*).

ARTS AND CRAFTS

Traditional crafts The craft industry was once an important part of Oman's economy, with artisanal skills handed down from generation to generation. It is artefacts such as pots from Bahla, decorative chests, silver bracelets, *khanjars* and coffee pots that most embody the spirit and identity of Oman; they are tangible samples of its ancient tradition and heritage – symbolic of place and the spirit of a people.

OMANI PROVERBS

In a country where illiteracy was the norm till the 1970s the literary tradition was oral, with storytelling and poetry featuring as the main evening entertainments, though Oman's chief claim to fame was always in its proverbs. Proverbs in the Arab world have a very long and important tradition, and the Arabs were the first to gather their own collections as early as the 9th century AD, though they were not translated into English till the 16th and 17th centuries. The origins of some go back long before Islamic times, and provide fascinating insights into the folk wisdom of different cultures. Some are common across the Middle East but others are specific to a country. For example, the following proverbs on corruption all show a slightly different take, revealing slight differences in national attitudes:

'May God protect the vineyard from its guardian' (Lebanese)

'To destroy the cobweb, destroy the spider' (Maltese)

'It is from the head that the fish first stinks' (Turkish)

'When cat and rat join forces the country is destroyed' (Omani)

The proverbs quoted at the start of each chapter in this book are all specifically Omani.

Jewellery Women's necklaces and bracelets, whether in silver or gold, play an important part in marriage ceremonies in Oman – a bride's dowry is expected to contain a certain amount of jewellery. The wealth and status of a family may be judged by the jewellery worn by the women. There is a belief that its wearer will be protected from the evil eye (see box on page 67). Silver is said to be representative of the moon and gold representative of the sun.

Pottery Bahla, in the Dakhiliyah region, is famous for its potters and potteries. Today there are two working factories there, which you can visit to watch the potters at work. Traditionally these pots were used as water containers and dispensers.

Incense burners These *majmars*, made from clay, are ubiquitous and make the perfect gift or keepsake of Oman. Salalah's frankincense souk (in Dhofar) or Muttrah Souk (in the capital) are two prime locations for these items. Some are painted in bold colours.

Mandoos These are Omani chests which have been traditionally used to store valuables. It is said that this stemmed from a Portuguese tradition which Oman inherited when it was invaded in the 16th century. Today, *mandoos* can be bought in a variety of sizes (down to jewellery-box size) and are usually made from either walnut or rosewood. On the surface they are inlaid with brass, gold or silver, in Islamic and geometric designs, and sometimes decorated with precious stones. You will spot them all over Oman, in hotels, official buildings, offices and private homes as decorative furnishing. They are sometimes referred to as bridal chests.

Omani doors Intricately carved doors have been a tradition, and today you will find that their usage has been extended: the carved door – or rather a modern imitation of the traditional Omani door – is now used as a coffee-table top. These

SILVER

Oman has a long silver-smithing heritage. The material has been used for centuries, and expertly handcrafted into articles of jewellery and ornaments, perhaps the most famous of which is the *khanjar*, a curved dagger, worn by men (see box on page 30). In the past, Omani men as well as Omani women wore decorative silver. They carried keys on fine chains, had silver money holders, tweezers in silver cases, silver toothpicks and ear cleaners on silver chains.

Most of the old silver was unfortunately melted down before traders realised the value of antique silver pieces, so there is remarkably little genuine old silver left. Experienced Omani silver dealers can tell whether a piece is from the Batinah, the Sharqiya or Dhofar.

Headpieces can be very heavy, weighing 2kg or more, and are worn on special occasions, usually when seated. Dhofari bracelets are adorned with coral beads and spiky silver washers threaded on to elastic. Women's silver necklaces often display Koranic inscriptions, and amulets, anklets and bangles are all intricately engraved. Other articles fashioned from silver include rose-water distillers, incense burners, trays, small engraved silver boxes (used for storing kohl or jewellery) and coffee pots (also made from copper).

INDIGO

The colour of the outer garment (*abaya*) and face mask (*burka*) worn by women throughout Arabia was always thought to be black, but in fact it was indigo – from the only natural plant that was suitable for dyeing clothes. It once grew wild over large areas, but farmers began to cultivate it and extract the natural dye, and sell it in tablet form to the professional dyers of the towns. The wild plant used (*nil*) was pulled out and soaked in water for two days; the dye in the leaves would sink to the bottom and the surface water would be drained off. The pasty residue was hung out on a thick cloth to dry for two or three days, and then cut into small tablet-like segments. Before the advent of the pharmacy, the drying and healing properties of indigo were utilised to cure skin diseases and heal wounds such as the umbilical cord on a newborn baby or on a boy's penis after circumcision.

Over the past 20 years or so the industry has all but disappeared, and the dye is instead imported from India.

can be found for sale in many of the artisan and souvenir shops in Qurum, or in the souk at Muttrah, as well as in other artisan workshops scattered throughout the country.

2

Practical Information

Eat onions wherever you find them and eat as much garlic as you can get.

WHEN TO VISIT

The **winter season** (October to March) is the peak time to visit Oman as the temperature is broadly on a par with summer in the Mediterranean. The **summer season** (April to September) is the cheaper option, as it is generally deemed too hot for most visitors – temperatures can reach around 48°C, though by sightseeing in the early morning or late evening, a carefully planned visit is still possible. Hotel prices differ depending on the season.

During the winter season the **Muscat Festival** is an annual 22-day event running from late January until late February (see box on page 114), when traditional Omani villages are erected at a few specific locations in the city and artisans demonstrate Oman's array of traditional crafts. Funfairs, rides and fireworks all add to the festivities of this time, when Oman promotes its culture and heritage. It is an interesting time to visit as you get a taste of Oman condensed into one area, although, inevitably, early-evening traffic gets extremely busy and congested, especially going towards Qurum Natural Park and Azaiba Beach. The hotels too can become full, and some prices may even be increased a little.

During the weeks of **Ramadan** (see pages 27–8 and 59), no alcohol is served in restaurants, bars or private clubs, and minibars in hotel rooms tend to be emptied. You are permitted to order alcohol to your room through room service, but this must be consumed within the privacy of your room. No independent restaurants are open in the day at all, and hotel restaurants that are open have their windows draped over and obscured for discretion and in order not to offend local sensibilities. Ramadan, then, may or may not affect your choice of time to visit the country.

HIGHLIGHTS

BAHLA FORT Oman's oldest and largest fort, a UNESCO World Heritage Site, newly opened after years of restoration work (see pages 214–16).

SUR Sense the country's maritime links with Zanzibar while strolling in the last working shipbuilding yard for wooden *dhows* (see pages 240–2).

MUTTRAH SOUK AND CORNICHE Meander through the narrow alleyways of an old Arabian/Indian souk just behind the attractive corniche, still very much in use by local people (see pages 95–6).

UBAR/SHISR Marvel at the haunting remains of Oman's largest frankincense city, linked with the legendary 'Atlantis of the Sands' (see pages 284–7).

THE RUSTAQ LOOP Take in three of Oman's greatest forts, Al Hazm, Al Nakhal and Rustaq, against their fabulous mountain backdrop and nearby hot springs (see pages 145–54).

JEBEL SHAMS Trek along waymarked paths to the abandoned mountain village of As Sab (see pages 212–13).

SAIQ PLATEAU Drink in the clear cool air while walking among the blossoms and fragrant roses of the mountain terraces and villages (see pages 194–8).

MUSANDAM Enjoy a boat trip through the mountainous fjords accompanied by leaping dolphins, then picnic on Telegraph Island (see pages 161–9).

RAS AL JINZ Spend the sunrise with baby turtles as they hatch out in their protected reserve and scurry across the sand towards the sea (see page 245).

DESERT EXPERIENCE Camp out in the remote Wahiba Sands in a Bedouin tent among the silent dunes with camels for companions (see pages 230–3).

SUGGESTED ITINERARIES

One week is fine for a holiday here, but if you want to get a fuller taste of what Oman has to offer you will need to travel out of the Capital Area. The average stay is ten days. Three weeks is a great amount of time, which will allow for a full round trip where you will see pretty much everything. Below are itineraries that may be helpful in giving you some idea of how much time to allot to each location. Juggle these around to suit your preferences.

DAY TRIPS FROM MUSCAT
- The Rustaq Loop (see pages 145–54) makes a great day out. Take along a picnic and find a spot at the Nakhal Springs. A 4x4 is not necessary.
- Nizwa (see pages 199–206) can be visited as a full-day trip from Muscat. Steeped in history, it provides a real sense of the Oman of old. A 4x4 is not necessary.
- Take a wadi trip (either independently or with a tour operator) to Wadi Bani Auf (see pages 148–9); it will give you an idea of the amazing mountain scenery of the country. You reach an incredible mountain village oasis (Bilad Sayt) at the top, along with the dramatic Snake Canyon. A 4x4 is necessary here.

OVERNIGHT TRIPS
- Visit Ras Al Hadd or Ras Al Jinz to see the turtles. Stay overnight there, or in one of the Sur hotels.
- Take a boat trip to the Daymaniyat Islands, stay in Sohar, visiting the Sohar Fort and museum.
- Visit the highest mountain, Jebel Shams, and the forts of Bahla, Jabrin and Tanuf, staying at a hotel in Nizwa.

SHORT VISIT If your time in the country is limited, here are some recommendations for sites relatively close to Muscat.

If you have time for only one old town, make it Nizwa. Located in the interior, it is truly evocative of the Oman of old. If you have time for only one wadi trip, make it Wadi Bani Auf, where you can climb in your 4x4 up the mountainside, taking in spectacular gorges and ravines, and finally witness the amazing thriving village of Bilad Sayt that clings to the side of the mountain. If you can do one short trek along a ravine, go to Wadi Shab (on the coastal road to Sur), and let the boys guide you along and show you the cavernous mountain pool at the end – the peace and the colours of nature here are outstanding. If you can fit in a souk, make it the historical souk at Muttrah, where you can take in the ambience of Muttrah harbour. If you can, visit Al Bustan Palace Hotel, one of the best hotels in the world, with its awe-inspiring atrium. For a unique culinary experience, try Mumtaz Mahal Restaurant by Qurum National Park for excellent Indian food and service, topped with views over the capital. Finish your meal with a snake coffee (a liqueur coffee where alcohol is lit and the flame poured down the long, peeled skin of an orange) and watch it being made at your table.

ONE WEEK

Day 1 Muscat Old Town – Al Alam Palace; Jalali and Merani forts; Bait Al Zubair; Muttrah corniche and souk; The Grand Mosque, Al Bustan Palace Hotel visit; overnight Muscat.

Day 2 Birkat Al Mawz Fort; Nizwa Fort and souk; Bin Ateeq for traditional Omani food; Tanuf ruins; overnight Nizwa.

Day 3 Hamra Old Town; Misfah mountain village; Wadi Ghul, Jebel Shams; Bahla Town, fort and souk; Jabrin Castle; Wadi Dank scenery; overnight Nizwa/Bahla.

Day 4 Return towards Muscat visiting Fanja old citadel; Al Nakhal Fort; Ain Ath-Thowrah Hot Springs; overnight Sawadi.

Day 5 Rustaq Town and fort; Al Hazm Fort; Barka Fort; overnight Muscat.

Day 6 Take a cruise around the bays of Muscat (this can be arranged through any tour operator). Shopping excursion to Qurum plazas or City Centre (after Seeb/Muscat Airport, but before Seeb village). Visit to Qurum Natural Park.

Day 7 Rest and relax in Muscat.

TWO WEEKS With an additional week you can add on a flight to Khasab in Musandam, where you can take a half-day *dhow* cruise to Telegraph Island and do a half-day mountain safari tour in a 4x4 with driver/guide. You can reach Musandam by air, ferry or road (see pages 158–9).

Day 8 Drive the inland route to Sur, visiting *en route* Bidbid Fort; Samad ash Shan; Ibra ruined quarter; overnight in Ibra.

Day 9 Collected by tour company to take a desert safari through Wahiba Sands. The dunes require a 4x4 vehicle and a skilled, experienced driver with knowledge of the terrain, and it is best to pre-arrange a trip with a tour operator in Muscat, or with one of the tour operators listed in this chapter (see pages 39 and 76–8), so you will have an accompanying driver/guide. If you choose to visit the Wahiba independently, it is strongly recommended that you follow at least one other vehicle and have at least one experienced person in the group, in the interests of your safety. Watch the sunset in the desert and stay at a desert camp.

Day 10 On towards Al Ashkhara. Visit Bani Bu Hassan Fort; Ras Al Hadd, Ras Al Jinz. Arrange evening visit to turtle beach with Ras Al Hadd Beach Hotel (tours start at 21.00) or at the Ras Al Jinz Turtle Beach Camp. Stay overnight.

Day 11 On to Sur; tour *dhow* shipbuilding yards; Qalhat; using the new coast road you can return from Sur along the coast to Muscat via Wadi Dayqah and Tiwi.

Day 12 Fly to Khasab; take mountain safari tour with driver/guide (can be arranged on arrival, but you might like to pre-book); stay overnight.

Day 13 Morning *dhow* cruise; fly to Muscat in the afternoon; overnight Muscat.

Day 14 Flight home.

THREE WEEKS With a third week you can fly to Salalah – the land of frankincense – and spend three days visiting the main sights (three days is really all you need). Then return to Muscat and drive up to Sohar for a couple of nights, exploring Sohar itself and its hinterland, with copper mines, the Arja ziggurat and medieval stronghold of Hawra Burghah. Return to Muscat and relax until your flight home, buying your souvenirs in Muttrah Souk or in the shopping complexes in Qurum.

TOURIST INFORMATION

In 2004, the Ministry of Tourism (*Directorate General of Tourism, PO Box 550, Muscat, PC113;* ℡ *24 588700;* e *info@omantourism.gov.om*) was founded – evidence of the sultanate's commitment to promoting its tourism sector. It is located at Azaiba (before the Azaiba roundabout) on the left-hand (coastal) side of the highway. The official online tourist service for Oman is www.omantourism.gov.om. There are no tourist information offices in the country, so you have to approach private tour operators for information on tours. See opposite.

TOURIST BOARDS AND PR COMPANIES Oman now has representation in the following countries: the UK and Ireland, France, Benelux, Germany, Spain, Switzerland, Australia and New Zealand, the United States and Hong Kong.

⚏ UK and Ireland Representation Plus
11 Blades Ct, 121 Deodar Rd, London SW15 2NU; ℡020 8877 4508; e oman@representationplus. co.uk
⚏ Australia and New Zealand Air Marketing
Level 11, 99 York St, Sydney, NSW 2000, Australia; ℡+61 9244 1841; e bill@airmaketing.com.au
⚏ Benelux BrouwerBetist Hoge Gouwe 93, Post Bus 277, NL 2800, AG Gouda; ℡+31 182 670244; ; e rbrouwer@brouwerbetist.nl; www. brouwerbetist.nl

⚏ French-speaking countries Oman Tourism Office France, Embassy of Sultanate of Oman, 50 Av d'Iena, 75116 Paris; ℡+33 1 47 20 56 06; e omantourism@wanadoo.fr
⚏ German-speaking countries Sultanate of Oman Representative – Germany, Interface International, GMBH Petersburger Strabe 94, 10247 Berlin; ℡+49 30 4225 6027; e kzwiersinterface@t-online.de

TOUR OPERATORS

UK Package holidays from London Heathrow start at around £1,250 per person for a week, including scheduled flights, airport transfers and bed and breakfast accommodation. For the up-to-date listing of UK-based tour operators who specialise in Oman, consult www.travel-lists.co.uk/lk1oman. A handful that have been recommended are:

Corinthian ☎01372 469300; e info@ corinthiantravel.co.uk; www.corinthiantravel. co.uk. Specialists in the top-end luxury tailor-made holiday market.

Gane & Marshall International ☎01822 600600; e holidays@ganeandmarshall.com; www. ganeandmarshall.com An Africa specialist which now offers excellent trekking holidays in Oman, ranging from 1–9 days, fully organised with donkey support, local guide & transport. Treks are run in the western & eastern Hajar mountains, the Musandam Peninsula & the Capital Area around Muscat.

Oman Holiday Architects ☎01242 253073; e mail@omanholidayarchitects.net; www. omanholidayarchitects.net. Purely specialising in Oman, this Cheltenham-based company offers tailor-made quirky holidays with a great deal of insider knowledge.

Omantravel Hanwell, Oxon OX17 1HR; ☎01295 730950; www.oman-travel.co.uk. Oman specialist offering tailor-made holidays for all budgets.

Rainbow Tours ☎020 7666 1250; www. rainbowtours.co.uk. Rainbow Tours offers a comprehensive, specialist Oman programme, which takes in the beaches, the interior & the culture.

Safari Drive ☎01488 71140; e info@ safaridrive. com; www.safaridrive.com. Specialises in private, tailor-made safaris & offers trips to the Wahiba Sands with a Bedouin guide.

The Shaw Travel Company ☎01635 47055; e esonia@shawtravel.co.uk; www.shawtravel. com. Shaw Travel specialises in luxury holidays to Oman using Gulf Air & tailors your itinerary to suit.

Steppes Travel 51 Castle St, Cirencester, Glos GL71 1QD; ☎0845 0756117; e enquiry@ steppestravel.co.uk; www.steppestravel.co.uk. Specialises in private holidays based on personal specifications, ranging from a couple of days to a couple of months. See advert on page 34.

Wild Frontiers ☎020 7736 3968; e info@ wildfrontiers.travel.com; www.wildfrontiers.travel. com. Offers stylish & original small group tours, using local ground handlers so all costs go to the local economy. Christmas in Arabia, an 11-day tour including Dubai. See advert on page 70.

World Odyssey ☎01905 731373; e pbirley@ world-odyssey.com; www.world-odyssey.com. Exclusive luxury-end tour operator offering tailor-made holidays, such as the 10-day Essence of Arabia tour & the 14-day full tour including Salalah, with a good mix of culture & wildlife.

US

Travcoa ☎866 591 0070; e requests@travcoa. com; www.travcoa.com. Luxury tailored holidays in small groups to Oman, with local guides & lecturers.

US Dive Travel 15050 Cedar Ave, St Paul, MN, USA 55124 7047; ☎952 953 4124; www. usdivetravel.com. Diving specialists operating out of Muscat's Radisson Hotel.

OMAN Major tour operators based in Oman usually have head offices in Muscat and tours need to be booked at least three or four days in advance. It is normal to make a 50% deposit by credit card when you book, then pay the rest when you are collected at the start of the tour, be it at the airport or from your hotel. See pages 75–8 for listings.

RED TAPE

VISAS All visitors require visas and these can be easily purchased on arrival at Seeb/ Muscat International Airport or at any of the border posts (after filling in a form), for visitors from 63 countries; a new short-term business/tourist visa is available costing RO5 for up to 10 days, which can be extended for a further 10 days for a further RO5. A 30-day business/tourist visa costs RO20 and is extendable for a further 30 days for another RO20. Cruise ship visitors are entitled to a free visa if their visit is for less than 48 hours. Make sure you pay in Omani cash, because if you pay by credit card or non-Omani currency the rate is higher, around US$20, when it should be closer to US$15. For all nationalities, under 18s are free. Your passport should be valid for at least six months from the date of entry. Multiple entry visas can be applied for in advance from your local Omani embassy, allowing visits of up to three weeks and are valid for three months from date of entry, at a cost of RO50. They are usually only granted to businessmen and your passport must be valid for at least a year from date of entry. Free visas are issued on the border into the UAE and are valid for 60 days (see pages 43–4). Unusually for the Arab world, having an Israeli stamp in it is not a problem. Visas to Yemen are obtainable on the border at Sarfait for all EU nationalities and for nationals of the USA, Australia and New Zealand. They cost US$30 and are valid for one month from entry, three months from issue. In this case your passport must not contain an Israeli stamp. The position can change, so it's best to check beforehand either with the Royal Oman Police (e *ropnet@omantel.net.om; www.rop.gov.om*), the Foreign and Commonwealth Office (www.gov.uk/government/world/oman) under Oman travel advice, or try the very informative Destination Oman website (*www. destinationoman.com*).

CUSTOMS REGULATIONS Firearms, narcotics and pornographic material are banned. Magazines, videos and books are sometimes confiscated and examined for subversive or overtly sexual material. Alcohol may be purchased and brought into the country by non-Muslims on entry at the Arrivals duty-free shop at Muscat International Airport, situated just before baggage reclaim. The limit is two litres per person, 100ml of perfume and 400 cigarettes. There are spirits and also some wine at UK supermarket prices. Alcohol is not sold in supermarkets or shops and is only available to residents on a liquor licence, but it is available at licensed hotels, bars and restaurants. Alcohol is forbidden in private vehicles at land border crossings and vehicles are searched quite thoroughly to find it among parties of expatriates travelling over from Dubai for weekends or holidays. If found it is confiscated and you are fined. There are no restrictions for camera equipment, computers or music players.

As for taking goods out of the country, be aware that some handles of the more expensive *khanjars* (curved tribal sheathed daggers) are made from rhino horn or ivory. It is illegal to take these out of the country and indeed import them to your own. Although these materials are no longer allowed to be used in the making of *khanjars*, the authorities still permit the old stocks to be used up. Cheaper varieties of *khanjar* are widely available as souvenirs (see box on page 30).

DEPARTURE TAX On leaving Oman, there is no departure tax.

EMBASSIES AND CONSULATES

OVERSEAS

❸ Austria Waehringer Strasse 2-4/24/25, 1090 Vienna 9th Quarter; ☏+43 1 310 8643–4/8644/8684

❸ Bahrain Bldg 37, Rd 1901, Diplomatic Area, Manama 319, PO Box 26414; ☏+973 293 663

❸ Cyprus (consulate) 113 Prodromou Str 2064 Strovolos, PO Box 4670; ☏+357 2 663 300

❸ Denmark (consulate) Strandvaenget SB, Dk 8240 Risskov; ☏+45 8617 5072

❸ Egypt 52 Al Higaz Str Al Muhandesin, Cairo; ☏+20 2 303 6011, 303 5942/5673

❸ France 50 Av D'Iena – 75116 Paris; ☏+33 1 47 23 01 63

❸ Germany Clayallee 82, Berlin; ☏+49 30 810050

❸ Ireland (consulate) 10A Lower Camden St, Dublin 2; ☏+353 1 478 2504

❸ Italy Via Della Camilluccia 625, 135, Rome; ☏+39 06 3630 0517/0545

❸ Jordan Jebel Amman, between 4th & 5th Circle, PO Box 20192, Amman 11110; ☏+962 6 568 615–7

❸ Kuwait Al Odeilia Plot 3, 3rd St, Villa 25; ☏+965 2561 956–7

❸ Lebanon Al Remla, Al Bida Venezuele Str, Al Tyser Bldg, PO Box 135900 Beirut Shouran; ☏+961 1 856 555

❸ Netherlands Konginnegracht 27-2514 AB, The Hague; ☏+31 70 361 5800, 363 3969

❸ Qatar Ibn Aiqassim St No 41, Villa No 7, Alhilal Area, Doha; ☏+974 670 744–6

❸ Russia 109180 Moscow, Staromonetny per, 14 Bldg 1; ☏+7 095 230 1255/1587/2052

❸ Saudi Arabia Al Raed Quarter, opposite King Saud University, PO Box 94381 Al Riyadh 11693;

☏+966 1 4823 120/067. Hajj & Endowment Affairs Attaché, Al Ribat Hse, Makkah Al Mokarama; ☏+966 1 5432 314

❸ South Africa (consulate) 3rd Fl, Export Hse, cnr of Maude & West St, Sandown, Sandton, PO Box 2142, Fourways, 2055; ☏+27 11 884 0999

❸ Syria Mezzeh Westvillas, Al Ghazzaui Str PO Box 9635; ☏+963 11 6110 408, 6622 506, 6130 003, 6622 194

❸ Tanzania (consulate) Hse No 2277, Vuga, Zanzibar PO 2100; ☏+255 54 30 700/066

❸ Turkey Mahatma Gandhi Cad 63, Gazi Osman Basha, Ankara; ☏+90 312 4470 630–1; e oman@marketweb.net.tr

❸ UAE Al Mushraf Area, next to Emigration Dept, Saeed bin Tahnon Str, Abu Dhabi; ☏+971 2 463 333

❸ UK 167 Queens Gate, London SW7 5HE; ☏+4420 7225 0001/1622 (consular section); e omanembassy@btconnect.com

❸ US 2535 Belmont Rd NW, Washington, DC 20008; ☏+1 202 387 1980; e emboman@erols.com

❸ Yemen Al Hoboob Corp St, Sub Baghdad St, PO Box 105, Sana'a R Y; ☏+967 1 208 874–5

IN MUSCAT Many countries have embassies in Oman, and these are largely concentrated in the Shatti al Qurum diplomatic area of Muscat (close to the As Saruj area). Opening hours generally are 08.00–14.00, with some slight variations. They are closed on Fridays and Saturdays.

❸ Austria PO Box 2070, PC 112, Ruwi; ☏24 793135, 793145; e maskat-ob@bmaa.gv.at; www.austriantrade.org; location: Moosa Abdul Rahman Hassan Complex, Bldg No 477

❸ Bahrain PO Box 66, PC 115, Madinat Al Sultan Qaboos; ☏24 605074–5, 605133; location: Shatti Al Qurum, Way No 3017, Villa No 1345

❸ Belgium (consulate) Al Wattayah, Al Rawahy Bldg; ☏24 562033, 563011

❸ Canada (consulate) Flat 310, Bldg 477, Way 2907, Moosa Abdul Rahman Hassan Bldg, A'Noor St, Ruwi; e canada_consulate_oman@hotmail.com

❸ Cyprus (consulate) PO Box 603, PC 113; ☏24 590200, 590285; location: Al Azaiba, J&P Camp Azaiba

❸ Denmark (consulate) PO Box 1040, PC 112, Ruwi; ☏24 708304; location: W J Bldg, MBD

❸ Egypt PO Box 2252, PC 112, Ruwi; ☏24 600411, 600982; location: Diplomatic Area, Jami'at al Dowal al Arabiya St

❸ Finland (consulate) PO Box 84, PC 113; ☏24 702133; location: Getco Tower, MBD Area, Bldg No 1704, Way No 2726

❸ France PO Box 208, PC 115, Madinat al Sultan Qaboos; ☏24 681800; www.ambafrance-om.org; location: Al Khuwair, Diplomatic Area, Jami'at al Dowal al Arabiya St

❸ Germany PO Box 128, PC 112, Ruwi; ☏24 832164, 832482; f 24 835690; e diplofrg@omantel.net.om

❸ Iran PO Box 3155, PC 112, Ruwi; ☏24 696944, 696947, 696919; location: Diplomatic Area, Jami'at al Dowal al Arabiya

❸ Ireland (consulate) PO Box 424, PC 113, Ruwi; ☏24 701282, 797083; location: OC Centre, 8th Fl, Suite 807

❸ Italy PO Box 3727, PC 112, Ruwi; ☏24 560968, 564832, 564838, 695223; e ambamasc@omantel.net.om; location: Al Qurum, Hse No 842, Way No 2411

❸ Jordan PO Box 70, PC 130, Al Azaiba; ✆24 692760–1; location: Diplomatic Area, Jami'at al Dowal al Arabiya St
❸ Kuwait PO Box 1798, PC 112, Ruwi; ✆24 699626–7, 696095; location: Diplomatic Area, Jami'at al Dowal al Arabiya St
❸ Lebanon PO Box 67, PC 118; ✆24 695844, 693208; location: Shaati al Qurum, Villa No 1613, Way No 3019
❸ Netherlands PO Box 3302, PC 112, Ruwi; ✆24 603706, 603719; location: Shaati al Qurum, Villa No 1366, Way No 3017
❸ New Zealand (consulate) PO Box 520, PC 113, Muttrah; ✆24 794932, 795726, 786039; location: Muttrah St, Bldg No 387, Way No 3007
❸ Norway (consulate) PO Box 89, PC 112, Ruwi; ✆24 708304, 703289; location: WJ Towell Bldg
❸ Portugal (consulate) PO Box 1812, PC 112, Ruwi; ✆24 561400; location: Al Watteyah, Al Asfoor Furnishing
❸ Qatar PO Box 802, Muscat; ✆24 691152–4; location: Diplomatic Area, Jami'at al Dowal al Arabiya St
❸ Russia PO Box 80, PC 112, Ruwi; ✆24 602894; location: Shaati al Qurum, Way No 3032, Surfait Housing
❸ Saudi Arabia PO Box 1411, PC 112, Ruwi; ✆24 601743–4, 601791; location: Diplomatic Area, Jami'at al Dowal al Arabiya St
❸ Spain (consulate) PO Box 3376, PC 112, Ruwi; ✆24 698381; e spanishconsulatemct@hotmail.com or spaconsl@omantel.net.om; location: Shatti al Qurum, Villa No 1386, Way No 2818
❸ Sweden (consulate) PO Box 1, PC 112, Ruwi; ✆24 708693; location: 8th Fl, Bahwan Business Centre Bldg
❸ Switzerland (consulate) PO Box 385, PC 118, Al Harthy Complex; ✆24 568202; location: Al Asfoor Plaza, Qurum, 1st Fl, Flat No 104
❸ Syria PO Box 85, PC 115, Madinat al Sultan Qaboos; ✆24 697904, 695917; location: Madinat al Sultan Qaboos, Al Inshirah St, Villa No 201
❸ Turkey PO Box 47, PC 115, Madinat al Sultan Qaboos; ✆24 697050–1; location: Shaati al Qurum, Villa No 3270, Way No 3042
❸ United Arab Emirates PO Box 55, PC 111; ✆24 600302, 600988; e uaeoman@omantel.net.om
❸ UK PO Box 300, PC 113; ✆24 693077, 609000; www.britishembassy.gov.uk/oman; location: Diplomatic Area, Jami'at al Dowal al Arabiya St
❸ US PO Box 202, PC 115, Madinat al Sultan Qaboos; ✆24 698989, 699049; oman.usembassy. gov; location: Diplomatic Area, Jami'at al Dowal al Arabiya St
❸ Yemen PO Box 105, PC 115, Madinat al Sultan Qaboos; ✆24 600815, 604172; location: Shaattti al Qurum, Bldg No 2981, Way No 1840

GETTING THERE AND AWAY

BY AIR Muscat International Airport (formerly Seeb Airport), located 40km west of the old town of Muscat (about a 40-minute drive), is the country's main international airport, receiving flights from most of the world's airlines, as well as operating domestic flights. Salalah Airport, in the south of the country, is the only other international airport, receiving flights from other GCC countries only, as well as domestic flights from Muscat (*for flight information* ✆24 519456/223).

Flight prices are always subject to change, and it is worth doing a thorough search online using sites such as www.ebookers.com. A standard direct return flight with Oman Air costs around £600 but rates drop once you start to explore indirect flights. Qatar Airways runs a flight that makes a brief stop in Doha and costs around £425 return, and Gulf Air has something similar, while British Airways and Emirates return fares cost around £480. Flights from London Gatwick are often a little cheaper than from Heathrow. If you are looking to cut costs more, find the cheapest flight to Dubai, then catch a bus to Muscat. This also saves you the Oman visa fee, thanks to a special deal. See pages 39–40. From the US there are no direct flights to Oman.

National carriers
✈ Gulf Air ✆+44870 777 1700; Muscat ✆24 482777; www.gulfair.com. Oman is one of 3 owner states of Gulf Air, which has the most frequent flights into Muscat of any of the international airlines, servicing not only Europe

but also the US, Asia, Africa & Australia. It operates direct daily flights from London Heathrow.

✈ **Oman Air** Sales office, Ruwi ☎24 531111; www.omanair.aero; Holidays ☎24 765129. The national carrier has flights from Muscat to destinations that include Abu Dhabi, Al Ain, Bahrain, Beirut, Cairo, Chennai (Madras), Cochin, Dammam, Dar es Salaam, Delhi, Doha, Dubai, Hyderabad, Jeddah, Kochi, Kuwait, London, Mumbai (Bombay), New Delhi & Trivandrum, as well as domestic flights to Salalah (in Dhofar) & Khasab (in Musandam).

Other airlines

✈ **Aeroflot** ☎24 704455; www.aeroflot.com
✈ **Air Arabia** ☎24 700828; www.airarabia.com
✈ **Air France** ☎24 562153; www.airfrance.com
✈ **Air India** ☎24 799801; www.airindia.com
✈ **Air New Zealand** ☎24 700732; www.airnewzealand.co.uk
✈ **British Airways** ☎24 568777/565123; www.ba.com
✈ **Cathay Pacific** ☎24 789818; www.cathaypacific.com
✈ **EgyptAir** ☎24 794113; www.egyptair.com
✈ **Emirates Air** ☎24 404400; www.emirates.com
✈ **Etihad Airways** (Abu Dhabi) ☎24 823555; www.etihad.com
✈ **Japan Airlines** ☎24 704455; www.jal.com
✈ **KLM Royal Dutch Airlines** ☎24 566737; www.klm.com
✈ **Lot Polish Airlines** ☎24 796387; www.lot.com
✈ **Lufthansa German Airlines** ☎24 796692; www.lufthansa.co.uk
✈ **Qantas** ☎24 559941; www.qantas.co.uk
✈ **Qatar Airways** ☎24 771900; www.qatarairways.com
✈ **Saudi Arabian Airlines** ☎24 789485; www.saudiairlines.com
✈ **Sri Lankan Airlines** ☎24 784545; www.srilankan.aero
✈ **Swiss International Airlines** ☎24 796692; www.swiss.com

BY ROAD Oman borders three countries, but almost all entries by road are through the United Arab Emirates. It is not advisable to access Oman from Saudi Arabia as the border crossing simply heads into the Empty Quarter with no towns or settlements. Crossing into Yemen from Salalah is possible by local bus, but not for women travelling solo, who will be refused entry. See pages 39–40 for visa requirements.

Border crossings with the UAE From the United Arab Emirates there are six entry points: Hatta border (at Wadi Hatta and Al Wajajah); two Buraimi borders – one at Wadi Jizzi (coming from Sohar to Buraimi) and one at Jebel Hafeet (leading to Ibri/Nizwa); and Khatmat Milahah border (from Fujairah). The final two entry points are into Musandam in the north (from Ras al Khaimah emirate into Bukha, and from Fujairah emirate into Dibba). The journey from Dubai to Muscat International Airport takes approximately five hours and is a straight, uneventful drive through desert plain.

Tourists coming from the UAE by road will have their UAE visa cancelled on exit at the border posts, and Omani visas issued on entering the sultanate. All European and US nationals are eligible to get visas upon arrival at the borders, after filling in a form and paying the visa fee. For all other nationalities, and any other border post concerns, check with the Royal Oman Police via its website (*www.rop.gov.om*). It is then necessary to pass through immigration and customs formalities.

Visits to Musandam and Buraimi in Oman are a little more complex, as they each require a crossover into UAE territory. Although Buraimi is in Oman, it is frustratingly necessary to cancel your Oman tourist visa, as it is tightly juxtaposed with Al Ain (UAE) and the border posts lie quite a way out of Buraimi/Al Ain Town. Fortunately, the UAE offers a free-of-charge visit visa (see *www.uaeinteract. com/travel/visas.asp*), but it is nevertheless frustrating to endure the rigmarole of the paperwork and having to pay for the issuing of another Omani visa (which will last for one month from the new date) in order to continue your journey in Oman. There are no restrictions for women travelling alone, although lone female travellers are seemingly questioned more thoroughly at the border.

If you have rented a car in Oman and are taking it into the UAE (even simply in transit to Musandam or to Buraimi) then it is necessary to gain permission from your car-hire company and to confirm that the car is fully insured in both countries.

BY SEA No passenger ships terminate at Muscat, only cargo vessels, and these use Muttrah and Salalah ports. An increasing number of cruise ships do call into Muscat as part of their itinerary or do day-long stops at Khasab (Musandam), Muttrah and Salalah (Dhofar).

HEALTH *with Dr Felicity Nicholson*

PREPARATIONS From a health perspective, Oman is a relatively safe country to visit. Vaccinations are usually required only for longer-term visitors or those staying in rural areas. There are pharmacies, clinics and good private medical-care facilities throughout the country. The heat of the country does mean that it is important to drink plenty of water.

Vaccinations The only compulsory vaccine for visitors is the yellow fever vaccine if you are arriving from a yellow fever endemic area, such as sub-Saharan Africa or South America within six days. A valid certificate is then required, which is active ten days after vaccination and lasts for ten years. If the vaccine is contraindicated then ask your doctor or travel clinic (see page 45) for an exemption certificate and wherever possible obtain a letter from the Oman Embassy in your starting country to accept this.

Generally, however, it would be wise to be up to date with tetanus, diphtheria and polio and hepatitis A vaccine. Long-term visitors and expatriate residents are usually advised to have typhoid vaccine and hepatitis B injections. A course of pre-exposure rabies vaccine (see page 45) is also advised for long-term visitors who will be in rural areas. It is best to check with your local clinic several weeks before departure. Yellow fever is required only for those travelling from infected areas.

Malaria There is a sporadic risk of both benign and malignant malaria due to importation of cases from other countries. In 2010 local outbreaks were reported in North Sharqiya region. Anti-malarial tablets are not recommended for the majority of travellers.

Extra protection Although malaria tablets for prophylaxis are not recommended it is important to protect yourself from mosquito bites, so keep your repellent to hand at all times. There are a variety of diseases that can be transmitted by mosquitoes including Dengue fever, a viral illness transmitted by day-biting Aedes mosquitoes. You should use a product that contains 50-55% DEET and apply as often as is necessary. Remember to reapply after being in water.

You also need either a permethrin-impregnated bednet or a permethrin spray so that you can 'treat' bednets in hotels. Permethrin treatment makes even very tatty nets protective and prevents mosquitoes biting through the impregnated net when you roll against it; it also deters other biters. Putting on long clothes at dusk means you can reduce the amount of repellent you need to put on your skin, but be aware that malaria mosquitoes hunt at ankle level and will bite through socks, so apply repellent under socks too. Travel clinics usually sell a good range of nets, treatment kits and repellents.

Rabies Rabies is carried by all mammals (beware the village dogs) and is passed on to humans through a bite, scratch or a lick of an open wound. You must always assume any animal is rabid and seek medical help as soon as possible. In the interim, scrub the wound with soap and bottled/boiled water for ten minutes, then pour on a strong iodine or alcohol solution. This helps stop the rabies virus entering the body and will guard against wound infections, including tetanus.

If you intend to have contact with animals and/or are likely to be more than 24 hours away from medical help, then pre-exposure vaccination is advised. Ideally three doses should be taken over a minimum of three weeks. Contrary to popular belief these vaccinations are relatively painless.

If you are exposed as described, treatment should be given as soon as possible, but it is never too late to seek help as the incubation period for rabies can be very long. Those who have not been immunised will need a full course of injections together with rabies immunoglobulin (RIG), but this product is expensive (around US$800) and may be hard to come by: another reason why pre-exposure vaccination should be encouraged in travellers who are planning to visit more remote areas.

Tell the doctor if you have had pre-exposure vaccine, as this will change the treatment you receive. And remember that, if you do contract rabies, mortality is 100% and death from rabies is probably one of the worst ways to go.

Travel clinics and health information A full list of current travel clinic websites worldwide is available at www.istm.org. For other journey preparation information, consult www.nathnac.org and look under the Country Information tab. Information about various medications may be found on www.netdoctor.co.uk/travel.

Personal first-aid kit Pharmacies are so plentiful throughout Oman that it is not the end of the world if you don't take your own personal first-aid kit. However, if you prefer to go prepared, then the following may be helpful.

- A few small plasters or dressings
- Suncream
- Painkillers
- Antiseptic cream
- Insect repellent (only needed if camping, and then only in some remote areas)

IN OMAN
Medical facilities In the late 1960s there were only three hospitals in the country and eight out of ten babies died within ten months of conception. Old and young alike were riddled with trachoma (a contagious disease of the eye). Tuberculosis was common, as were malaria and chronic anaemia. Leprosy was endemic with no enforced segregation. Flies were everywhere, transferring disease from the faeces of villagers to their food with regularity and crawling over the faces of oblivious children.

Today, the situation in Oman is remarkably different. There is an extensive public health service, which is free to Omanis. Foreigners, however, are often expected to pay cash to use these services, and costs can be high. Private medical services are excellent, with many well-equipped clinics and hospitals. Cosmetic surgery is widely available, as is laser eye surgery (tried and tested to full satisfaction by the author in Al Shatti Hospital in Muscat). Travel insurance is advised as medical treatment can be costly for foreigners. Those with specific medical conditions should wear medical alert tags and carry a list of medications related to their condition. Health expenditure now accounts for 3% of GDP.

Hospitals All main hospitals with emergency rooms are in the Capital Area. The main government hospitals are Al-Nahda (↖ *24 831255*), Ibn Sina (↖ *24 876322*), Khoula (↖ *24 563625*) and The Royal Hospital (↖ *24 599000*); and the main private hospitals are Al Shatti (↖ *24 604263*) and Muscat Private Hospital (↖ *24 583600*).

Pharmacies Muscat Pharmacy has branches throughout the country at Ruwi, Al Saruj, Al Khuwair, Al Ghubra north, Al Mawaleh, Sohar, Al Hail, Hamriya and Salalah. A few are open 24 hours in the capital, the details of which appear in any of the English-language newspapers.

LONG-HAUL FLIGHTS, CLOTS AND DVT

Any prolonged immobility, including travel by land or air, can result in deep vein thrombosis (DVT) with the risk of embolus to the lungs. Certain factors can increase the risk and these include:

- Previous clot or close relative with a history
- People over 40 but greater risk over 80 years
- Recent major operation or varicose veins surgery
- Cancer
- Stroke
- Heart disease
- Obesity
- Pregnancy
- Hormone therapy
- Heavy smokers
- Severe varicose veins
- People who are very tall (over 6ft/1.8m) or short (under 5ft/1.5m)

A deep vein thrombosis (DVT) causes painful swelling and redness of the calf or sometimes the thigh. It is only dangerous if a clot travels to the lungs (pulmonary embolus). Symptoms of a pulmonary embolus (PE) include chest pain, shortness of breath, and sometimes coughing up small amounts of blood, and commonly start three to ten days after a long flight. Anyone who thinks that they might have a DVT needs to see a doctor immediately.

PREVENTION OF DVT
- Keep mobile before and during the flight; move around every couple of hours
- Drink plenty of fluids during the flight
- Avoid taking sleeping pills and excessive tea, coffee and alcohol
- Consider wearing flight socks or support stockings

If you think you are at increased risk of a clot, ask your doctor if it is safe to travel.

If someone was seriously ill with much pain, the old Arab practice was to apply the *wussum* burn. A girl who had been bitten by a poisonous snake on one leg, thus had a series of deep burns inflicted on her other leg that was then brushed with fresh camel dung. The effect was to outweigh the original pain, and sometimes to cause gangrene and death. The old customs ran deep and even in the late 1960s a trained Omani doctor commented: 'Our people will burn and bleed a patient through trying to cure him before they would even think of taking him to the American hospital in Muttrah. That is done only as a final resort when all else has failed.'

Freya Stark in her travels in southern Arabia commented on the same tendency. As a consequence of having two windows in every wall there were often strong draughts in Arab houses. Many caught measles, shivering, then bronchitis and pneumonia, as she herself did. But as she noticed: 'Few came to the chemist. They preferred to run hot irons down their backs.' She also noted that the people of the Hadramaut had a horror of soap or scent, convinced it weakened or even killed you if you were already poorly. After measles no-one would use it for 41 days.

Emergency An ambulance service has been introduced in certain urban locations, using US equipment and US-trained staff. Otherwise, the availability of roadside or ambulance assistance is poor. The Royal Oman Police will assist in an emergency.

Emergency services ☏9999

Drinking water Outside of the Capital Area, water should be regarded as being potentially contaminated. Bottled water, or water that has been boiled, is advised for drinking, brushing teeth and making ice. Several brands of bottled water are from Oman's own mountain sources.

Protection from the sun The summer months (April–September) can be extremely hot. Be careful to keep your skin covered and wear loose-fitting clothes for comfort. Sunglasses and hats will provide welcome relief and are recommended. Do use a sunscreen or at least a high-factor protection cream, ideally 25SPF or above, and reapply after swimming. Try to keep out of the sun between 11.00 and 15.00 when the sun is strongest. Drink plenty of liquids to keep yourself well hydrated.

SAFETY

The crime rate in Oman is low and the streets of the capital are safe even for lone travellers after dark.

WOMEN TRAVELLERS Oman is one of the easiest Arab countries for foreign women to travel in without hassle, if their dress and demeanour are appropriate. There is no risk for women in using taxis, buses or hiring a car. In the city, despite the fact that the hotel bars and private clubs are a male domain (in Omani culture), you will find that, broadly, Omanis are chatty, relaxed and helpful. Their temperaments generally are very easy going and good humoured. For a lone female traveller, Omani men (and for that matter Omani women, who are increasingly to be found independently in public places) make excellent, respectful and supportive company. The important thing is to wear unprovocative loose-fitting clothing and to conduct yourself with politeness and friendliness, but making sure a respectful distance is maintained.

GAY AND LESBIAN TRAVELLERS As in many Muslim countries, homosexuality is illegal in Oman. Partners travelling together should be discreet and especially careful to make no overt physical contact with each other. If caught engaged in homosexual practices, especially with a local Omani, the penalties for Westerners range from deportation to imprisonment. It is not a topic for discussion in any social situation with Omanis.

TRAVELLING WITH CHILDREN Like all Arabs, Omanis love children and, as a result, hotels and restaurants welcome them warmly, though high chairs are a rarity. Children love the desert, the mountains and the beaches, and their greatest danger will be sunburn, so take care to protect them properly. There is a growing number of fast-food outlets, and many restaurants offer child menus or child discounts. Supermarkets and chemists sell nappies, as well as baby food in jars and packets.

WHAT TO TAKE

CLOTHES For comfort, loose cotton clothing is best and a pullover will often be required in the evenings in the winter months (October–March). In the top-class hotels dressing for dinner is normal, while in the smaller hotels, especially inland, the style is much more informal. For more details, see page 65.

Footwear A lot of the exploration involves walking on rocky and uneven surfaces so ensure your footwear can cope.

Other useful items There are pharmacies and food stores throughout the country and so medicines, plasters, batteries, etc will all be readily available. In Muscat there are several large supermarkets and one hypermarket that have excellent stocks of virtually everything you can get at home. For female travellers, it may be an idea to take a tampon supply – only a few of the supermarkets stock Tampax, and most places sell only the non-applicator variety. You will find that some pharmacies keep these under the counter too. Sanitary towels are widely available.

CHANGING SOCIAL PATTERNS

As Omani society becomes more urbanised and western, traditional patterns of society are changing. In the cities Omani women now get married later, often not till aged 28–30, while most men wait till the age of 35. There are fewer arranged marriages and Omani men as a rule take only one wife, unlike many of their counterparts elsewhere in the Gulf. The average number of children per family has now dropped from six or seven to four, a direct result of the rise in women's education. Some Omani women will even now marry foreigners, if their families agree.

Electricity/plugs Unusually for a Middle Eastern country, Oman has British-style square three-pin plugs, thanks to its close historic ties with Britain.

Camping equipment Camping equipment can be hired from tour operators (see page 123). In addition there are local shops in every village selling pots, pans, and odd bits and pieces that are cheap enough and will equip you for your trip.

MONEY AND BUDGETING

CURRENCY The currency is the Omani rial (RO). One rial is made up of 1,000 baizas (bzs). The Omani rial is pegged to the US dollar at RO1 = US$2.60 and the exchange rate has therefore been very stable for a number of years.

The rates of exchange in August 2013 were as follows: £1 = RO0.58, US$1 = RO0.39, €1 = RO0.50.

CASH It is best to change money in Oman as the rates are better than can be obtained overseas. ATMs are plentiful throughout the country (there are several HSBC points in Muscat and Salalah and in other large towns) and offer the best exchange rates; avoid airport money changers as they offer poor rates. Up to RO300 in cash can be withdrawn per day. Be aware that banks do not like to change foreign cash.

TRAVELLERS' CHEQUES If you prefer to use travellers' cheques, these, as well as major currencies, can be exchanged for Omani rials at banks, bureaux de change, the airport and at larger hotels. Travellers are advised to purchase travellers' cheques in US dollars to avoid additional exchange rate charges. The exchange rate at hotels is usually worse than at a bank or money changer (sometimes up to 17% lower), but has the advantage of convenience, and where the amounts concerned are small the effort entailed in finding a bank and queuing during its opening hours scarcely warrants the saving. Banks outside Muscat will change only American Express travellers' cheques.

CREDIT CARDS Credit cards are widely accepted in hotels, restaurants, shopping complexes, petrol stations and businesses throughout Oman. It is recommended that you advise your credit card provider that you intend to use the card in Oman, and in that way you can be assured that you will encounter no hiccups and gain full approval. In smaller hotels, shops, souks and restaurants it is likely that you will need cash, especially in the interior. In the traditional souks, cash is mainly used, as it also allows for easy bargaining, which is expected in this setting as a matter of course.

TIPPING In hotels and restaurants a 15% service charge is added to the bill, so tipping over and above this is a matter of personal choice. It will, however, be appreciated. Any other tipping, for example for hotel porterage, airport assistance, room service or taxi service, is appreciated, but not expected. Around 10% is the norm.

GETTING AROUND

BY AIR Within Oman there are domestic flights to Khasab in Musandam (four days a week; cRO40; 1½hrs) and Salalah in Dhofar (twice a day; cRO72 return; 1½hrs), operated exclusively by Oman Air (see page 43).

Gordon Rattray (www.able-travel.com)

Having wheelchair access is not yet obligatory for Oman's tourist facilities, and the further you venture from Muscat, the more challenging life becomes for travellers with mobility problems. However, the tourist industry is growing rapidly and this is having a positive influence on what is available for the disabled traveller. On top of this, Omani culture is one of exceptional hospitality and friendliness, and therefore local people will always offer support and help.

ACCOMMODATION Since most hotels have been built post-1980, access is fairly good. The government has been putting pressure on hotels to provide special facilities and many have responded well (especially in Muscat and in Salalah). This does not mean these hotels will all have roll-in showers and grab handles, but some have a small number of dedicated bedrooms, and lifts and access ramps make movement within the public areas of the hotel easier. Generally, access to the pool areas in these larger hotels is quite good, but many still only have ladder entry. Exceptions (albeit expensive) are The Chedi (see pages 79–80), and the Al-Bustan Palace (see page 79), where pools have gradual steps. Access to beaches is never easy, but, as always, staff are willing to help. Hotels with specially adapted rooms include Al Bustan, The Chedi, Grand Hyatt, Muscat InterContinental, Golden Tulip Resort (Khasab), Radisson Blu, Shangri-La's Barr Al Jissah Resort and the Crowne Plazas.

GETTING AROUND

In general As with tourist accommodation, most public buildings have been built in the past 30 years, meaning they are fairly accessible. In the cities, the situation is constantly improving and several modern shopping malls and pedestrian areas even have disabled toilets and access ramps. The main mosques and museums don't cater especially for wheelchairs, but most are fairly flat with wide doors and level access. If you are intending to visit forts and castles, you can expect to find them as inaccessible as they were designed to be. There is ramped wheelchair access to Bait Zubair Museum, Muttrah Souk and the Sultan Qaboos Grand Mosque.

By road There are some taxis with wheelchair access in Oman, but not many, so you may need help when transferring in and out of the vehicle. This will be even more likely if you are planning to venture off the beaten track as 4x4s are higher than normal cars. Drivers/guides are normally happy to assist, but are not trained in this skill, so you must thoroughly explain your needs and always stay in control of the situation.

Distances can be great but thankfully the condition of the roads throughout the country is excellent. However, if you plan to go off-road in any way, for example a wadi trip, or a desert or mountain safari, then it will be bumpy. Anyone prone to skin damage should take extra care. Place your own pressure-relieving cushion on top of (or instead of) the original car seat and if necessary, pad around knees and elbows.

Anyone planning to use Oman's coach network should be aware that it does not cater for disabled travellers. Therefore, depending on your ability, you may need assistance to get on and off buses.

By air Aisle chairs are used for international arrivals in Muscat, making entering and exiting the aircraft easier for non-ambulant people, and Muscat International Airport has disabled toilets. The local carrier – Oman Air – is also reported to be of a high standard, though that is not to say that an aisle chair and full facilities are to be expected at every domestic terminal.

ACTIVITIES Local operators have assured me that the dolphin-watching and desert and wadi visits should all be possible. More challenging activities like trekking or *via ferrata* (mountain routes traversable by fixed cables, ladders and bridges) would obviously require more planning, but, again, depending on your ability and motivation, they are not out of the question.

HEALTH General healthcare in Oman is excellent. However, as with anywhere, you must understand and be able to explain your own particular medical requirements. Comprehensive insurance is essential, and be sure the insurance company is aware of any existing medical conditions.

Pharmacies are well stocked, but it is always advisable to take all necessary medication and equipment with you, and to pack this in your hand luggage during flights in case your main luggage gets lost.

Oman is hot all year round, but every hotel is equipped with air-conditioning units for your comfort. Aerosol water sprays are widely available at chemists, and provide welcome relief as an instant cooling aid, although a cheaper and more environmentally friendly device is a plant-spray bottle filled with water.

SECURITY Oman is a relatively safe travel destination and the crime rate is low. However, it is worthwhile remembering that, as a disabled person, you are more vulnerable. Stay aware of who is around you and where your bags are, especially during car transfers and similar. These activities often draw a crowd, and the confusion creates easy pickings for an opportunist thief.

SPECIALIST OPERATORS There are, as yet, no operators which specialise in disability travel to Oman. Having said that, most travel companies will listen to your needs and try to create an itinerary suitable for you. For the independent traveller, it is possible to limit potential surprises by contacting local operators and establishments by email in advance.

FURTHER INFORMATION The most accurate and up-to-date information is available from tour operators. I found the following people most helpful:

Peter and Margaret at Omantravel +44 (0)1235 200444; e margaret@omantravel.uk.com; www.omantravel.co.uk
Sasha at Muscat Diving & Adventure Centre +968 24 485 663; e sasha@holiday-in-oman.com; www.holiday-in-oman.com
Oman Association for the Disabled +968 24 605 566. Mainly for nationals but does give some information for visitors.

BY SEA A ferry service runs north from Muscat to Musandam, consisting of two catamarans, the *Shinas* and the *Hormuz*, completing the journey in less than five hours. It runs north twice a week on Sundays and Thursdays, returning Tuesdays and Saturdays, and costs around RO25. The ferry begins from Sultan Qaboos Port and stops and Dibba and Lima before reading Khasab. There is also a ferry to Khasab that departs from Shinas on Sundays and Thursdays, returning on Tuesdays and Saturdays. The passage takes three hours, cutting the car journey time by two hours. The round trip costs RO22 per adult and RO15 per car. Both routes are operated by National Ferries Company (*800 72000;* e *reservation@nfc.om; www.nfc.om*); tickets can be bought through tour operators in all the larger hotels or reserved by email. There is also a car ferry run by NFC linking Khasab and Lima, a small town in the Musandam not readily accessible by road, that runs five times a week. On Sundays it also connects with Shinas as a round trip.

There is currently a daily ferry from Shannah to Masirah Island, leaving at high tide and taking about 1½ hours. This is the only way to reach the island.

BY ROAD The road network in Oman is excellent, so a saloon car is largely all you need to get about. The six-lane Muscat Expressway is good (although the roads around the capital can be confusing; see pages 73–4 for further details), and so too are the dual carriageways in the capital, along the Batinah coast, and south along the coast to Sur. There are good single carriageways inland to Nizwa, Sur, Ibri and down to Salalah, and traffic is generally light. Roads are also excellent to Dubai. Directions are clearly signposted in phonetic English, so getting around is easy.

There are, however, a few off-road trips where a 4x4 is necessary, and these can easily be hired, though you should always check the small print to make sure

---

OMAN ON A BUDGET – SOME IDEAS

Oman is not a cheap destination for the visitor, but it is possible to tour the country on a budget if you are prepared to forgo some comforts and luxuries. These pointers may help.

1 Fly to Dubai (cheaper than Muscat) and get a bus to Muscat (5hrs, RO9 return). This way the Omani visa fee is waived at the border (see pages 41 and 56).
2 You can eat very cheaply at the unlicensed Indian and Omani restaurants and coffee shops. A meal for two with drinks is likely to be under RO5.
3 Buy fresh breads of all varieties, hot chicken, delicatessen foods, pre-prepared salads, fruits and cold drinks from any of the supermarkets for great beach or mountain picnics. A litre bottle of water costs around 250bzs, and canned drinks cost around the same. A whole chicken straight off the rotisserie costs only RO1.
4 Camping will reduce your costs considerably, but do not attempt it in the hot months from April to October. November to March are the best months, with November and March the best of all. This is obviously only possible outside towns. In rural areas camp well away from villages. Beach camping is possible south of Muscat (see page 123).
5 Car-hire companies operate within residential areas, and these are a little cheaper than those in the airport. If a 4x4 is not necessary, go for a saloon, which is significantly cheaper. Petrol is very cheap (under RO10 to fill a 4x4 tank), and taxi fares can mount very quickly within the Capital Area, making it cheaper to hire a car, especially if the cost is shared between several people.

you are covered when driving off-tarmac. Alternatively, if you arrange these trips through a tour operator, rather than going independently, the vehicle and driver/guide will be provided and included in the price with no insurance worries. The Wahiba Sands, the Empty Quarter and the wadi trips each require a 4x4. As such it may be an idea to hire a saloon, then pay a tour operator for a trip into the Wahiba or your first wadi-bashing experience. They can either drive you from the capital to your destination, or collect you from your hotel in the region.

Driving is on the right-hand side of the road, so all vehicles are left-hand drive. Muscat rush hour is from 07.00–09.00 and from 16.00–18.00, and roads are also very busy on Thursday afternoons when everyone leaves their offices for the weekend. Be sure to carry your driving licence and hire-car agreement and insurance with you in case you are asked to produce them at any time. In the event of an accident, however slight, the police must be called and the vehicles involved not moved till they have arrived. Driving under the influence of alcohol renders your insurance void in the event of an accident and carries heavy fines or even a ban. Wearing a seatbelt is mandatory and the fine for non-compliance is RO10. You can also be fined up to RO50 for driving a car that is too dirty! It is against the law to drive while using a mobile phone. A two-wheel drive is not covered for damage incurred while being driven off-road, so think carefully before you drive off the tarmac.

Be aware that there may be camels, goats or donkeys crossing the road at any time. Oncoming cars may flash their headlights at you to warn you to slow down for a possible hazard up ahead.

The speed limit on the highways is 120km/h (75mph) and all hire cars are fitted with an insistent beeper which is triggered automatically if you exceed this speed

6 A cheaper option for getting around is to use the shared taxis or microbuses operating in the capital (see page 74) and the Oman National Transport Company coaches for inter-city travel (see page 57).

7 Cheapest of all is to hitchhike, though bear in mind that Westerners are not expected to do this unless they are destitute students, and solo women should definitely not consider it. Omanis have been told foreigners coming to their country will bring wealth, so the 'something for nothing' mentality does not go down well. Always offer your lift some money for the petrol. The correct gesture to indicate you want a lift is to hold out your right arm straight and waggle your hand downwards. The Western custom of sticking out a thumb is a gesture with obscene overtones.

8 If you're lucky enough to have Omani friends or acquaintances, or know expats with Omani residence, then it is likely at some point that you will be invited along to one of the many private clubs in the cities. Here you will save a fortune on food and drink, which are expensive in hotels.

It is possible to stay in Oman for RO40 (around £25) per day, staying in a budget hotel, renting a saloon car and eating in the local coffee shops and budget restaurants. This figure can be reduced further if you forgo the hire car, or intend to camp in the country (although if you're camping, you will need the car for all the necessary equipment). In this case, you can get by here on a rock-bottom budget of RO25 (around £15) per day.

limit. The speed limit in urban areas is 80km/h. The tolerance on speed cameras, of which there are many in the Capital Area, is +9km/h.

In the Muscat area, especially around Muttrah and Qurum, an increasing number of parking spaces require pay and display tickets. Make sure you always have some coins on you for the meters: half an hour costs 50bzs. Parking is free on Fridays.

Shell, Al Maha and Oman Oil fuel stations abound throughout the country. The BP stations have now been replaced with Oman Oil garages. Fuel is cheap – approximately RO9 (£15, US$23, €18) to fill a 4x4 tank. Most fuel stations have toilets (albeit in various states of cleanliness), and some have shops selling foodstuffs and drinks, very cheaply.

Vehicle assistance The AAA (Arabian Automobile Alliance) (✆ *24 697800*), provides 24-hour roadside assistance.

Car hire There is no difficulty in getting a hire car in Oman. Plenty of car-hire firms have desks immediately in Muscat International Airport arrivals area and the upper-range hotels have car-hire desks/offices within, if you prefer to wait until you are rested before arranging things. The budget and mid-range hotels will also arrange a car for you on request. So, don't worry if you haven't pre-booked; you are bound to find something. Most companies will drop a car off at your hotel. Some car-rental companies reuse paper, resulting in an ID theft risk. The Omani car registration documents can, for example, be photocopied on to the back of a photocopy of other people's passports or driving licences. This practice is also commonplace in Dubai, even with big companies, so always double check and get them to change it if necessary.

As in most places you will be asked for a copy of your passport, your driving licence (either from your country of origin or an International Driving Permit) and a credit card or cash for a returnable deposit. Drivers have to be 21 or over. Rates for small cars range from RO17 per day or RO80–100 for a week, including insurance. A 4x4 jumps up to approximately RO40 per day. The costs usually include 200km mileage, collision damage waiver, theft waiver, third-party insurance and local taxes. Personal accident insurance is optional, and costs around RO1 per day, and mileage above 200km is charged at approximately RO0.08 per kilometre. Check on child-seat availability in advance as you may have to bring your own. In the glove box you will often find a clear plastic tube: this is the standard piece of kit required for siphoning petrol from one tank to another, and if you come across an Omani who has run out of petrol in the interior, he will know how to go about it. Petrol is cheap – RO5 buys 42 litres. Petrol stations are open 24 hours and an attendant fills the tank for you.

If you intend to cross any of the border posts into the UAE (even if simply in transit to Musandam or Buraimi) it is necessary to obtain permission from your car-hire company and to confirm that the vehicle is insured in both countries. This usually costs a little extra. It is not possible to rent a car in one country and leave it in another. In your own car it is possible to cross any of the borders as long as your insurance covers you to do so. For more details about crossing borders, see page 43.

Note that, if returning your hire car to the airport, you need to go back to the arrivals desk (even though you are departing) as there are no car-rental desks in departures. So remember to park the vehicle closer to this end of the airport entrance.

Always keep documentation with you in case of an accident or a police stop. The majority of the car-rental companies listed here are in Muscat. Where they have branches in Salalah, this has been indicated.

🚗 **Advantage Car Rentals** CCC, Qurum:
\24 561910; e touroman@shanfari.com;
www.shanfari.com
🚗 **Al Hadaf Car Rent** \24 497684, 99
357953. This is a local car-hire company with
an office in Ghubra. It might save a few pounds,
although the organisation may take a little bit
more effort.
🚗 **Al Ibtisama Rent-a-Car** Rex Rd, Muscat:
\24 751177
🚗 **Al Maskry Car Rentals** Ghubra, Muscat:
\24 505923, 595241; e almaskrey@ omantel.net.
om; www.almaskryrentacar.com
🚗 **Al Miyasa Rent-a-Car** Salalah (Al Salam St,
next to Redan Hotel): \23 296521
🚗 **Arabian Tours Company** Salalah & Muscat:
\23 290088
🚗 **Avis Rent-a-Car** Ruwi: \24 692940; Avis
Muscat Airport: \24 519176, 510342; Avis
Intercontinental: \24 607235, 601224; Avis Al
Bustan Palace Hotel: \24 703242; Avis Sheraton
Oman: \24 799899; Avis Grand Hyatt:
\24 696596; Avis Crowne Plaza: \24 566526; Avis
Salalah (Al Nahda St): \23 2022582, 235 582;
e avisoman@omantel.net.om; www.avis.com
🚗 **Budget Rent-a-Car** Muscat Airport:
\24 510816–7; Salalah Crowne Plaza: \23 235160;
Salalah Airport: \23 290097; Al Falaj Hotel:
\24 794721, 702311; Sur Plaza Hotel: \25 443777;
Ruwi Hotel: \24 561910; e budgetom@omantel.
net.om.
🚗 **Europcar** \24 700190–1; Muscat Holiday
Inn: \24 684093; Muscat Airport: \24 521369,
519014; Salalah Airport: \99 341814; Salalah
Hilton: \23 212460; Sohar: \26 840753; Sur
Beach Hotel: \25 540735; e euro@omantel.net.
om; www.europcar.com

🚗 **Global Car Rental** Shatti al Qurum:
\24 697140; Sur: \25 541007; e glowbal@
omantel.net.om
🚗 **HertzNational Travel and Tourism**
Wattayah: \24 566208; Muscat Airport:
\24 521187; e nttoman@omantel.net.om;
www.nttomanhertz.com.
🚗 **Mark Rent-a-Car** Hatat Hse, Muscat:
\24 562444, 565567, 560975; Muscat Airport:
\24 510033; www.marktoursoman.com
🚗 **Payless Car Rental** Muttrah, Muscat:
\24 567261, 561482
🚗 **Qurum Beach Hotel Car Hire** Qurum Beach
Hotel, Muscat: \24 564070; Shuram Shatti al
Qurum, Muscat: \24 696299
🚗 **Sixt** Muscat Airport: \24 520224, 510224;
Al Khuwair: \24 600793, 600835, 600896; Crowne
Plaza Hotel: \24 561427; Sheraton Oman:
\24 704455, 704458; Salalah: \23 290908,
294665; www.sixt-oman.com
🚗 **Thrifty Car Rental** Al Khuwair:
\24 489248, 489648; Muscat Airport:
\24 521189; Salalah Airport: \23 290082, 99
323619; Salalah City Centre: \23 211493; Qurum:
\24 567785; Muttrah Business District:
\24 784275; e haditha@omantel.net.om;
www.thriftyoman.com. The Thrifty desk at Muscat
Airport is very helpful.
🚗 **Toyota Rent-a-Car** Crowne Plaza Hotel,
Muscat: \24 561427, 561437; Muscat Airport:
\24 510224, 510933; Salalah Airport:
\23 290908, 294665; e tracbest@omantel.net.om
🚗 **Value Plus Rent a Car** \24 597265;
Muscat Airport: \24 510292; Sohar: \26 842557;
Salalah: \23 210125; e vic@otegroup.com; www.
valueoman.com

By taxi Taxis are frequent and reliable and are the easiest means of transport
in urban areas of Oman. With their orange-and-white colouring they are
particularly conspicuous. It is a good idea to agree the fare beforehand, as taxis
are unmetered, and there have been many stories of foreigners paying two or
three times the going rate. The usual rate from Muscat Airport to Qurum is RO8,
and this price is now fixed by the central airport taxi kiosk (see page 74). All taxi
drivers are Omani nationals as this has been designated a protected profession.
They can be hailed on any street, and, on quieter roads, if the driver sees you
walking he may sound his horn to see if you need a taxi. The system is that you
can share one of these taxis with other people if your destinations happen to tally,
which is obviously cheaper, but in practice with foreigners the taxi drivers just
tend to charge more and keep the taxi private to you. Tipping is not necessary,
unless you particularly want to.

Practical Information   GETTING AROUND

2

The maximum safe depth is to the tops of the tyres. Cross where the water is at its widest, as this tends to be where it is shallowest and with the weakest current. Keep your speed down if the water is fairly shallow so you do not splash your electrics. With deeper water, enter slowly in 4x4 low gear (first or second), then keep the revs high once the front grille is in the water to create a slight bow wave with a trough under the engine.

If your engine does get drowned do not attempt to start it as water may have entered the tops of the pistons via the exhaust or air filter, which could result in a bent crankshaft or, in the worst case, a piston breaking through the side of the engine. Tow the vehicle out of the water, remove and dry the spark plugs, dry the ignition system, then turn on the ignition, which will pump the water out of the combustion chamber. Once the water is out, you can reassemble the spark plugs and leads (taking care to get them in the right order!), then try the ignition or push start if your battery is low.

By pre-booked taxi There are now several taxi firms that offer a 24-hour pre-booking service, and these are based in Muscat. They are fitted with meters so the price is fixed. The vehicles are clean and safe and are recommended for solo women travellers especially at night. If the timing is very important, such as to catch a plane for example, ring again about an hour beforehand to double check, if you have booked more than a day ahead.

🚗 **Allo Taxi** 📞 24 697997
🚗 **City Taxi** 📞 24 603363
🚗 **Hello Taxi** 📞 24 607011

If you require something special, a chauffeur-driven limousine service is available and can be arranged through most of the larger hotels or at the information desk in Muscat Airport.

BY BUS For longer journeys you might like to consider taking a bus. The long-distance ones have air conditioning and a toilet, and stop at regular intervals for refreshments. Bollywood and kung fu movies are the staple fare of on-board entertainment, which will either help you to sleep or keep you awake, depending on your inclination. From Muscat it is possible to get a bus from Ruwi Bus Station (just off Al Jaame Street along from the Sheraton Hotel) to Salalah (in the south), Nizwa (in the Dakhiliyah), Sohar (on the Batinah coast), Buraimi (in the Dhahirah), Ibra and Sur (in the Sharqiya), and Dubai and Abu Dhabi (in the United Arab Emirates). Buses make several stops along the way at allocated pick-up/drop-off points, the first being at Muscat International Airport. It is recommended that you make your booking a few days in advance, though it is possible to join any of the coach services on the spot if space allows, and simply pay your fare to the driver. The air-conditioned buses take around 40–45 people. No food is provided on the coaches so you might like to take some snacks and drinks along with you. Children under 12 travel for half price. Journeys that take you into Dubai, Abu Dhabi and Buraimi cross border posts where the coaches stop for the necessary visa procedures. Visas to the UAE are issued free at the border (see page 43).

Oman National Transport Company (*Muscat office* ☏ *24 492948; Salalah office* ☏ *23 292773;* **e** *ontc01@omantel.net.om; www.ontcoman.com*) This is state owned and the only company to offer the full range of destinations: Salalah, Dubai, Buraimi, Abu Dhabi, Sur and Sohar. There is a detailed timetable on its website, some details of which are shown below.

Ruwi to Salalah The Salalah Express, taking 12 hours from Ruwi Bus Station to Salalah Central Market, with children under 12 half fare. You can pick up the bus at any designated ONTC stop, including the one at Muscat International Airport. Rest stops are made at Ghaba Resthouse and Al Ghaftain Resthouse. It is best to check on the website for the up-to-date timings. Some people find the overnight bus to Salalah is preferable to relieve the boredom of the largely featureless landscape *en route*. If you are on a tight budget it also saves one night's accommodation.

Other routes are **Muscat to Salalah (route 100)**, **Muscat to Buraimi (route 41)**, **Muscat to Ibri (route 54)**, **Muscat to Sur (route 55)** (stopping at Ibra and Al Mintrib), **Muscat to Abu Dhabi (route 202)**, **Muscat to Dubai (route 201)** and **Salalah to Dubai (route 102).**

Gulf Transport Company (☏ *24 790823, Salalah office* ☏ *23 293303)* This company operates daily coach services from Muscat to Salalah and from Salalah to Dubai.

Salalah Line Transport (*Muscat office* ☏ *24 709709; Salalah Office* ☏ *23 293323;* **e** *sltsalalah@yahoo.com*) This company offers coach services to and from Salalah only. It runs three daily services from Ruwi Bus Station in Muscat and three from Salalah.

BY MINIBUS Minibuses (sometimes called baiza buses) can also take the form of 14-seater small van-type vehicles, which can be flagged down at the many stops along the highway. They are certainly the cheapest way of getting around and are used largely by the Asian workforce. A trip from Ruwi to Muscat costs around 200bzs.

MAPS Detailed maps of Oman are available through regional publisher Explorer, which produces a good road map and also a mini map of Muscat. Apex Press and Publishing also produces a good map of Muscat. These can be bought online (*www.amazon.co.uk*) before departure, more cheaply than in the country itself. The Ministry of Tourism also produces a decent free road map of the whole country, marking all the new highways, with the bonus of good city maps of Muscat, Muttrah, Sohar, Sur, Nizwa and Salalah on its reverse.

ACCOMMODATION

Muscat is home to some excellent four- and five-star hotels such as Al Bustan Palace, the Grand Hyatt, the Radisson Blu, The Chedi, and the Shangri-La Barr al Jissah Resort (which comprises two five-star hotels and one six-star). There are many mid- and budget-range hotels too, which offer good, clean accommodation, so it is a misconception that the country can be visited only by the more affluent traveller. Hotel apartments are a cheaper way of staying for longer periods in one place, and a growing number of these can be found in the Muscat/Ruwi area. As tourism increases, the facilities and services available are likely to improve and become more competitive. In the off-season summer months many hotels advertise attractive discounts, while in the high seasons of autumn and spring, especially at festival times, there is a lot of pressure on availability of rooms. Government resthouses offer good value for money and can be found along the main highways throughout the country. A few youth hostels have also recently opened. Free-range camping is permitted anywhere well away from habitation or on undeveloped beaches. A range of listings is given in each chapter.

EATING AND DRINKING

Travelling around the country you will find plenty of local coffee shop-type restaurants. Although these are very basic, they offer a good, cheap way to eat when you are on the road. Chicken, mutton and fish are frequently on the menu. Vegetarians are also well catered for, with a big range of vegetarian *mezze* or starters based around tomatoes, onions and aubergines on offer in all Arabic restaurants. Large numbers of Indians are also vegetarian by religion so many Indian restaurants offer a range of vegetarian dishes.

Each of the resthouses scattered about on the main highways has a restaurant, and although these are basic and unlicensed, the curries tend to be very good. Snacks can be bought at the food stores found beside most petrol stations, and within the shops of the petrol stations themselves. Supermarkets sell a good range of food and soft drinks suitable for picnics, and the Omanis themselves have a strong picnicking tradition, with the favourite weekend pastime involving the whole extended family bundling into the car, taking large quantities of food out into the countryside and sitting on carpets with the children running round while the men wrestle with the

Typical Omani cuisine is quite simple, with rice eaten as the main accompaniment to beef, mutton, chicken or fish. Spices are used to flavour the meat and fish, not hot and spicy ones but rather more subtle and aromatic ones like cardamom, cinnamon, cumin, ginger, turmeric and saffron. Salads are simple lettuce, cucumber and tomato with a slice of lime for dressing. A few local dishes to look out for are *maqbous*, a saffron-coloured rice dish cooked over spicy meat; *harees*, a wheat-based dish with chicken, tomato, onion and seasoning; *rabees*, boiled baby shark fried with liver (a Dhofari speciality); *shuwa*, marinated meat (goat, mutton, calf or camel) cooked for 12 hours in an earth oven with date juices and spices, wrapped in banana leaves and served on a giant communal tray called a *fadhl*; and *mashuai*, a whole spit-roasted kingfish with lemon rice. The main meal is eaten at midday, with a lighter evening meal. Food is always eaten with the right hand only.

Favourite local drinks are *laban*, heavy salty buttermilk and yoghurt flavoured with cardamom and ground pistachios. Fresh fruit juices are also made from local fruits like mango, banana, pineapple and pomegranate, and are very cheap by Western standards. The sweet sticky *halwa* is a popular dessert, made by men, with the recipe handed down from generation to generation. After the meal bitter cardamom coffee is traditionally served from brass long-spouted coffee pots into tiny china cup-like bowls.

barbecue and the women prepare the other food. Higher-end restaurants can be found in any hotel in any town and these generally are licensed. The star rating of the hotel is indicative of the price range of the restaurant. The Bin Ateeq small chain is good for Omani cuisine, served in the traditional way at floor level (unlicensed); you will find these at Muscat, Nizwa and Salalah. The capital has many excellent mid- to high-end restaurants both inside and out of hotels.

PUBLIC HOLIDAYS

RELIGIOUS Each year, the religious holidays move forward by approximately 11 days in accordance with the lunar calendar. For festivals, see relevant chapters.

Prophet's Birthday (*Mawlid al Nabi*)	13 January 2014, 3 January 2015, 24 December 2016
Ramadan	28 June–28 July 2014, 18 June–17 July 2015, 8 June–8 July 2016
Eid al Fitr (end of Ramadan)	28 July 2014, 17 July 2015, 8 July 2016
Eid al Adha (conclusion of the pilgrimage)	4 October 2014, 23 September 2015, 12 September 2016
Islamic New Year (*Muharram*)	15 November 2013, 4 November 2014, 25 October 2015

NON-RELIGIOUS
New Year's Day	1 January
Renaissance Day	23 July
National Day	18 November
Sultan's Birthday	19 November

SHOPPING

The main shopping complexes are in the Qurum area of Muscat. These are in the form of modern, air-conditioned malls and plazas, selling perfumes, gold, souvenirs, furniture made in India (to Omani style), household goods, stereos, computers, mobile phones, sports equipment, clothing and photographic equipment. Shopping is not cheap (for better deals you might like to take a trip to Dubai), but it is good to have a wander, simply to spot all the things in Arabia that are familiar to us in the West. Largely, it is home from home: Gap, Bhs, Next and the Body Shop all have a presence here, and so do the ubiquitous McDonald's, KFC, Pizza Hut and Burger King. Marks & Spencer (at Al Mawaleh) is now also here, so there is no need to panic if you have forgotten to pack your underwear.

A traditional shopping trip is a must, and the souk (or traditional market) at Muttrah is the place to go for this Arabian experience, selling souvenirs, crafts, jewellery, perfumes and oils, wooden chests, fabrics, *dishdashas*, etc, not forgetting frankincense (see box on pages 276–7). Souks have been part of Omani culture for centuries, and every town and village in the country has one. It is a traditional marketplace, which doubles up as a meeting place. Those selling fruits and vegetables are well worth a visit, displaying a fantastic array of bright colours.

SOUVENIRS Omani silver *khanjars* (daggers), traditional Omani silver jewellery, coffee pots and small silver boxes all make excellent souvenirs. A real antique *khanjar* will cost anything up to RO600 but souvenir imitations are available from RO40. Old Bedouin silver jewellery is also becoming increasingly scarce and pricey. Silver Maria Theresa dollars, which used to be the country's unit of currency, can still be bought fairly cheaply at around RO5. Omani rose water, perfumes, frankincense and myrrh are cheaper, smaller, yet still distinctive souvenirs. Frankincense, or *bakhoor* (a mixture of fragrances; see *Frankincense* box on pages 276–7 for further details), and a frankincense burner make the perfect gift – Oman being famed for its frankincense production and trade throughout history. Slightly more intriguing, and certainly a topic of conversation when you get back home, would be the *hookah* pipe, also known as the *sheesha* or *nargileh* or just as the water-pipe. Larger items are the Omani and Indian chests, and the Omani coffee tables (which use the concept of the traditional Omani door as the table top), which can be shipped or air freighted to you in your home country. The *mandoos* (Omani chests) come in all sizes, so the smallest (which is jewellery-box size) may be a more practical purchase, in terms of transporting it home. See pages 89–90, for artisan/furniture shops. The *dishdasha* makes a souvenir gift to be worn, and is great to wear about the house after a shower or as a dressing gown. For the consumable small gift for friends and family, Omani dates are good and you can always combine this with a packet of Omani coffee (mixed with cardamom), which will undoubtedly evoke memories of your Oman experience. Visit the souk at Muttrah for your souvenirs.

WORKING HOURS

Government sector/ministries 07.30–14.30 Sun–Thu, closed Fri–Sat
Private sector 08.00–13.00 & 16.00–19.00 Sun–Thu, 08.00–noon Fri
Banks 08.00–13.00 Sun–Thu, 08.00–noon Fri, closed Sat

Shopping malls 09.00–13.00 & 16.00–22.00 Sat–Thu, 16.30–22.00 Fri
Souks 08.00–13.00 & 16.00–21.00 Sat–Thu, 16.30–21.00 Fri

ACTIVITIES

The terrain of Oman, along with its climate, makes it perfect for the adventure tourist with a love of the outdoors. Since mountain and desert dominate the country's geography, mountain trekking, rock climbing, caving and wadi driving (see box on page 131) are all widely available (see page 123). The treks, climbs and caves are graded in terms of difficulty. There are now over 200 bolted climbing routes in the mountains,

OMAN'S CHANGE OF WEEKEND

Back in the 1980s and for years before that, Oman had just one day off a week – Friday. Then it extended in stages, first to include Thursday afternoons, then to the full two days of Thursday and Friday. Since 1 May 2013, Omanis and resident expats have had to adjust to another big change. Oman has, by official decree of the Sultan, changed its weekend from Thursday/Friday to Friday/Saturday to bring it line with its neighbour the UAE, and, as of July 2013, Saudi Arabia has followed suit too. Qatar, Bahrain and Kuwait were already on the Friday/Saturday weekend.

As well as aligning Oman's banks and businesses with its fellow Gulf countries, the change also means that Omani offices now have at least four days of overlap with western offices on the standard Saturday/Sunday weekend, a huge improvement from the previous two and a half days of overlap which obviously used to lead to big delays in communication. Local businesses can see the logic but are finding that business is slower on Thursdays and Saturdays while people adjust their shopping habits. The National Ferries Company has changed its timetable to reflect the likely change in passengers' preferred travel times, and other businesses such as supermarkets across the country are making similar adjustments, changing the day of their weekly imports from Thursdays to Fridays. The Sultan also included in the decree an announcement ordering private companies to give their employees the same number of religious holidays as civil servants currently enjoy, in order to make private sector jobs more appealing. Traffic patterns have also changed, with Thursday afternoons and Saturday afternoons now becoming much busier on the roads.

and for the real enthusiasts there are even *via ferrata* wire-lines in places such as the upper reaches of Snake Gorge. The Ministry of Tourism (*www.omantourism. gov.om*) has developed a set of walking tours and a booklet describing these routes. There are spectacular gorges and old mountain villages to see, and camping is very popular. The beaches are also public so you can walk a full 20km along the sand from Qurum to Seeb, for example. If you prefer water-based activities, then scuba diving, sailing, snorkelling, canoeing, dolphin and whale watching, *dhow* cruising and game fishing are all available. See pages 125–6 for details of specialist local tour operators offering these activities. Nature and wildlife lovers can birdwatch, turtle watch, camp or picnic in the mountains or quiet coastal bays. If local history or architecture is of interest, there are museums, mosques, forts and castles to explore (and these proliferate throughout the country). Culture lovers now also have the Royal Opera House Muscat (*www.rohmuscat.org.om*) to satisfy their need for high-level opera, ballet or theatrical performances, often from internationally renowned touring companies (see page 88). For those keen on physical fitness, there is a good selection of gyms and health clubs within the hotels, with swimming pools and tennis and squash courts attached. The beaches or beach roads are perfect for jogging. Visiting the souks (marketplaces) provides a fascinating glimpse into traditional Oman, while air-conditioned, modern shopping complexes give it its familiar Westernised feel. If you want to do nothing, there are some excellent, luxury hotels, some with private beaches, where you can simply relax.

For details of excursions beyond Muscat, including more details of the options available, see pages 123–6.

ENTRY FEES AND PERMITS Oman's focus on the promotion of its tourism industry means that its forts and other historical buildings of significance are on rolling schedules to undergo restoration programmes. As a result, one or other of the forts is always likely to be closed for restoration, because their mud-brick constructions require regular maintenance, especially after heavy rains.

It costs between 500bzs and RO1 to visit most forts (payable at the door); others have no-one at the door and you can wander around freely with no charge; and some appear to be locked up at odd times during the day. So do interpret the opening times shown in this guide generously.

It is no longer necessary to obtain permits from the Ministry of Culture and National Heritage (opposite the Zawawi Mosque in the ministries area of Muscat) to visit forts and archaeological sites. For turtle-watching sites you can easily get a permit from the Ras Al Hadd Hotel, or your tour operator, or at the entrance

A LAND GIFT FROM THE SULTAN

Every Wednesday announcements are made in the local paper giving the names of people who are being given their automatic 600m² of land by the state. Men have been entitled to this gift from the Sultan since 1970, but in 2010 the law was amended to allow women to benefit as well. Unmarried women are prioritised, as are divorced women. Everyone is entitled to this land in the province where they were born, hence the massive land housing boom around Muscat in areas like Bawshar. The plot size is generous, enough to build a spacious detached villa with a large garden. The usual pattern is to start by building a high wall round the perimeter for privacy, then to continue as and when funds permit.

of the Ras Al Jinz site itself. To dive the Daymaniyat Islands, the permit is easily obtained for you by any dive centre arranging the dive trip, at a rough cost of RO30 for two dives. The bureaucracy has been relaxed as part of the country's initiative to facilitate tourism.

The **Historical Association of Oman** (\ 24 563074; e *patricia@cfbtoman.com; www.hao.org.om*) organises regular talks (usually at the PDO oil exhibition club in Qurum) and field trips in appreciation of Oman's past.

PHOTOGRAPHY

The scenery of the country is superb for photography. The only places where it is not permitted are government and military buildings. Photographing Omani women can be offensive to them – it is safest to ask permission (and permission should generally be asked of men as well). '*Mumkin sura, minfadluk?*' is Arabic for 'May I take your picture, please?' If it's a woman, it is likely that you will be refused. By contrast, Omani men are usually happy to be photographed.

MEDIA AND COMMUNICATIONS

NEWSPAPERS The English-language newspapers in Oman are the new-entry *Muscat Daily,* which now boasts the largest circulation in the Sultanate, with 33,000 copies sold daily, Sat–Wed; *Times of Oman* (e *times@omantel.net.om; www. timesofoman.com*); the *Oman Observer* (*www.omanobserver.com*); the *Oman Tribune;* and *The Week. Muscat Daily* is owned by Apex Publishing and caused a stir by covering the 2011 Sohar protests extensively. Foreign newspapers can be bought in the larger hotels, supermarkets and in some bookshops, but they are not cheap.

MAGAZINES *Oman 2day* is an excellent publication in handy small size, with lots of up-to-date information and good photo-led articles on adventure days out around the capital. It also has reviews of cars and restaurants. Foreign magazines are readily available, but are expensive.

TELEVISION AND RADIO There is one terrestrial television broadcaster in Oman which is the state-owned Oman TV, run by the Ministry of Information. It broadcasts two channels, one in Arabic with the other in English.

The Sultanate of Oman FM service is the local English-language radio station, broadcasting daily. Radio Oman is the official state broadcaster, operated by the Ministry of Information, running two channels, in Arabic and English. The BBC World Service is also available.

TELEPHONE The country code for Oman if dialling from abroad is 968 followed by the local number. International calls made from Oman are cheapest from 21.00 until 07.00. Local calls are around 25bzs for three minutes.

Public telephones accept phonecards, which can be bought at petrol stations, supermarkets and some small shops.

Landline numbers are six digits and are prefixed with a two-digit area code (eg: 24 for Muscat, 23 for Dhofar, 26 for Musandam and the Batinah, and 25 for the interior and Sharqiya).

Mobile phones Your first option is to check with your mobile phone provider in your country of residence as to whether there is network coverage in Oman and establish with them the cost of calls. If there isn't coverage, and if you intend to visit Oman regularly, an option worth considering is to purchase a pay-as-you-go mobile phone in Muscat. To top up your balance scratch cards are used, and these are readily available at petrol stations, supermarkets and in some small shops, in amounts of RO1.50, RO3 and RO5. They last an age. **Hayak** top-up cards are used for Oman Mobile phones (*www.omanmobile.om*) and **Nawras** are used for Oman Telecommunications (*www.omantel.net.om*). Mobile numbers are usually prefixed with 99 or 95.

Useful telephone numbers

AAA (car breakdown services) ☎24 605555
Directory enquiries ☎198 (from abroad
☎+968 24 600100)
International directory ☎143
International operator ☎195
Emergency services ☎9999
Royal Oman Police Muscat☎24 560099;
Salalah☎23 290099

Recorded news in English ☎1105 (including chemists on duty)
Flight information ☎1101, 24 519223
Foreign exchange rates ☎1106
Talking pages ☎24 600100

INTERNET Oman's internet service provider is Omantel. Internet cafés (or cyber cafés) can generally be found within the shopping complexes at Qurum and Al Khuwair, and some exist within the rows of shops down side streets in any residential area throughout the country. They charge far less than the hotels and are well worth a visit. There is something quite intriguing, after retrieving communication from London, in passing groups of laid-back Omanis in *dishdashas* and sandals gathering to smoke *shisha* al fresco next door. The old and the new sit side by side like respectful neighbours. So aside from the financial saving made by visiting an internet café on the street, there is also the experience to be had; instead of being obscured from local culture inside the hotels, you are amid it. The internet in Oman is monitored and any site considered offensive to the religious, moral, cultural

---

ARABIC LANGUAGE SCHOOLS

Oman is capitalising on the flight of foreigners wanting to learn Arabic from the previous favourites of Egypt, Syria and Tunisia. The turbulence of the Arab Spring barely touched Oman and it continues to be seen as a rare model of stability in the Arab world. The biggest Arabic language school is the Muscat-based Center for International Learning in Oman (☎ *968-24-551041; www.omancenter.org*) run by the National Council on US-Arab Relations in Washington DC). They run intensive Arabic language programmes at three levels – Beginner, Intermediate and Advanced – in both Omani dialect and media Arabic. All classes are taught by native Omani instructors trained in TAFL. They offer six-week summer immersion programmes, three-, six- and 12-month programmes, as well as evening classes. Accommodation can be with an Omani family for complete immersion, or in shared one-/two-bedroom flats in bustling neighbourhoods. Offering even more immersion is the Noor Majan Training Institute in the more remote town of Ibri, two hours' drive inland from Muscat (*www.noormajan-institute.com*). Accommodation is with host families, with small classes of up to six students and four-week courses of four hours' teaching per day at Beginner, Intermediate, Advanced I and Advanced II levels.

or political mores will be blocked. Publications are also censored with the same criterion in mind. Many hotels now offer free internet.

POST OFFICES Post offices are open 07.30–14.00 Sunday–Thusday. They close at 11.00 on Fridays and are closed all day Saturday. The post offices aren't always easy to find, but there is one in every district in Muscat, usually with the Omani flag flying above the building. This is the cheapest way of sending postcards or parcels home, a postcard to any country outside the GCC region costing only 200bzs. More expensive, but more convenient is to ask your hotel to do it for you. Some bookshops and newsagents also sell stamps.

CULTURAL ETIQUETTE

On greeting, Omani men will shake hands. For friends and family the handshake is accompanied by kissing, which is a gentle touch to both cheeks, and is sometimes repeated for close friends. Kissing between men in this way is common. Some will lightly touch noses. It is not customary to shake an Omani woman's hand unless she offers it first. It is quite common for Omani men to shake hands with foreign women as Omanis are highly aware of this cultural difference. Omanis themselves never shake hands with the opposite sex, especially if they have never met before.

If you are invited to an Omani's home, it is customary to remove your shoes at the door before entering the house. *Kahwa* (a strong, bitter coffee, flavoured with cardamom) and dates are offered, and it is considered impolite to refuse, even if you are not hungry or thirsty. Once the first cup of coffee (served in a tiny bowl-like container) is consumed, it is then fine to refuse further top-ups. To indicate that you have finished, the cup is gently shaken (or tilted) from side to side. The right hand is used for traditional Omani eating from a communal plate, and the same is used for drinking. This is usually performed at floor level. It is quite normal for gatherings to be single-sex groups. At Omani mealtimes there is not much talk. This is normal as the focus is on eating, so do not feel you have to make small talk to fill the silences. The custom is to leave almost immediately after eating. Often the food is served late, so the talking and socialising take place beforehand.

DRESS CODE Considering Oman is a Muslim country, the dress code is relatively relaxed. As a gesture of respect it is advisable for both men and women to wear loose clothes that cover the shoulders and knees and are therefore not too revealing. Shorts, T-shirts and sleeveless tops are fine for the beach, but to be avoided in the shopping complexes and souks, or for touring the villages and sites of the interior (where the dress code is more conservative). Men, too, should avoid shorts except in the city or on the beach. Lightweight and loose-fitting cotton blouses, trousers and skirts are perfect all year round, and for your comfort in the winter, lightweight jackets, jumpers or shawls may be needed. Swimwear, preferably one-piece, not bikinis, is fine for private hotel beaches and pools. Omani women will swim fully clothed, even including their black *abaya*. During the holy month of Ramadan it is respectful to observe the dress code strictly.

BUSINESS ETIQUETTE

In business, it is advisable to wait for the Omani party to initiate the greeting. As in social etiquette, men will shake hands with other men, and some (probably most) will shake hands with foreign women. It is better for a businesswoman to wait for an Omani man to offer his hand. A customary greeting is *salaam alaykum*, meaning 'peace be with you'. This is followed by *kaif halek*, meaning 'how are you?' When offered coffee, it is considered impolite to refuse. It is acceptable, however, to refuse refills. The left hand is considered unclean. Always eat with the right hand. Showing the bottom of your shoe or foot is offensive, and so too is the 'thumbs up' gesture. Gifts are not necessary. If you do offer one, it will be opened in private. When offered a gift, it is impolite to refuse. On visiting an Omani's home take a gift of chocolates, nuts or dates, not flowers. Do not come empty-handed. Non-Muslims are not allowed to enter mosques, the exception being the Sultan Qaboos Mosque in Muscat. Do not discuss the subject of women, even if to enquire about an Omani man's wife or family. Avoid admiring an item to excess, as your host may feel obliged to give it to you.

Expect communication to be slow. Do not feel obliged to speak in periods of silence. Meetings can often be interrupted by phone calls and visits from friends and family. Bear in mind that the Omani doing all the talking is often not the decision-maker. The decision-maker will often be the silent observer.

BUSINESS DRESS CODE For foreign businessmen, a jacket and tie are usually required for business meetings. Long trousers and preferably a long-sleeved shirt (fully buttoned to the collar) should be worn. Men should avoid wearing visible jewellery.

For foreign businesswomen, high necklines are a must and sleeves at least to the elbows are expected. Skirts should cover the knees well and preferably be ankle-length. As with the general social dress code, clothes should not be figure-hugging; aim for a baggy, loose-fitting look.

TRAVELLING POSITIVELY

When travelling through Oman there are many small things you can do to give something back to the place you have the privilege of exploring. Every action, no matter how small, counts.

Respect the locals and their right to privacy. Bear in mind that it is their home territory, so when driving in a 4x4 in remote areas, do not drive straight through

ARABIC NAMES

The structure of Arabic names is quite different from what we are used to in the West. Everyone has a name given at birth, often taken from the Koran, such as Muhammad, Ali or Fatima. This is then followed by *bin* meaning 'son of' in the case of a boy, or *bint* meaning 'daughter of' for a girl, followed by the name of their father, such as Muhammad bin Ahmad or Fatima bint Ahmad where a brother and sister's father is called Ahmad. The final part of the name is the family or tribal name, which is very important and helps distinguish between the thousands of Muhammads and Fatimas. So a full name might be Muhammad bin Ahmad Al-Harithy, showing that this Muhammad bin Ahmad is from the Harithy tribe. Again, unlike in the West, when a woman marries she does not change her name to her husband's, but simply stays the same, as her tribe has not changed – the total opposite of what we might expect. Arabs find it very odd, given the supposed equality of women in our society, that Western women generally take their husband's name on marriage.

The concept of the Evil Eye is common throughout Turkey and the Arab world and extends into Oman even though its origin is Roman, not Islamic. Early Roman mosaics such as those found in Antakya (ancient Antioch) in modern Turkey have graphic depictions of a huge human eye being attacked by a range of weapons and surrounded by devils, illustrating the concept behind it, namely that to openly admire something that belongs to someone else will cast an evil spell on it and bring harm. To protect from this, there are set prayers from the Koran that people can say and expressions such as 'Mashallah' (literally 'what God wills'). The commonest form of protection however is the glassy blue eye which can be bought everywhere and is to be seen widely hanging in people's cars, homes and elsewhere, often on key rings, bracelets and pendants. Newborn babies are always given such pendants by their families and close friends to protect them from the envious glances of admirers.

the middle of a village, but explore on foot. It is also essential to show respect by being dressed conservatively, with women especially being well covered up with loose clothing at least to the knee and at least three-quarter-length sleeves, no cleavage, tight-fitting tops or bare shoulders. The less flesh on display the better. Naked swimming in wadi pools is a no-no. Ask permission before taking any photographs, and be aware that Omani women and girls will often refuse. Omani men and boys will often enthusiastically oblige. If you have a digital camera, showing Omani children their picture on the screen invariably delights them.

Look after your immediate environment. Limit your water usage. Do not leave water running. Take a shower, if you can, rather than use the bath. Turn lights off in hotel rooms when they are not absolutely necessary. Reuse towels (hang them back on the rail, so they will not be considered laundry). Limit your use of air conditioning, if possible. Always dispose of your own rubbish after camping or picnicking.

Purchase any locally made artefacts. Buy a pot from the Aladawi pottery factory in Bahla, or buy a rug from the locals selling their weavings in Jebel Shams and Jebel Akhdar. Don't forget the essential purchase of frankincense and a burner – you will have become part of an ancient trading history in this commodity. Every small amount you give helps to sustain the heritage and keep alive long-standing Omani traditions.

Eat at local restaurants and coffee shops – your valued rials will help in keeping these small businesses running. Buy some fruit at a souk or roadside stall. Stay at any of the static camps in the country, for example those in the Wahiba Sands; these make trips out to Bedouin camps where you will share lunch in a traditional home. Simply by demonstrating their way of life to you, the Bedu are able to benefit financially, so by using the camps, you are making a contribution to their living.

Respect the rules when visiting nature reserves and sanctuaries. Take care not to disturb the wildlife in any way. This is their habitat. Adhere to the list of dos and don'ts when it comes to viewing the nesting turtles (see box on page 243). Don't touch the coral when scuba diving or snorkelling – it causes damage.

An opportunity to assist with the Arabian leopard survey in Musandam is offered through www.responsibletravel.com, which is collaborating with conservation authorities in Oman. The aim is to expand the knowledge of the leopard in this vicinity. You might like to play a part.

Practical Information TRAVELLING POSITIVELY

2

www.stuffyourrucksack.com is a website set up by TV's Kate Humble which enables travellers to give direct help to small charities, schools or other organisations in the country they are visiting. Maybe a local school needs books, a map or pencils, or an orphanage needs children's clothes or toys – all things that can easily be 'stuffed in a rucksack' before departure. The charities get exactly what they need and travellers have the chance to meet local people and see how and where their gifts will be used.

The website describes organisations that need your help and lists the items they most need. Check what's needed in Oman, contact the organisation to say you're coming and bring not only the much-needed goods but an extra dimension to your travels and the knowledge that in a small way you have made a difference.

Make that little bit of extra effort to find out more about the local charities shown at the end of this chapter. You might be able to help. Perhaps you can volunteer your time, knowledge or assistance in bringing awareness to their cause in some way when back in your country of residence. There may be a new project under way at the time of your visit. Do give them a call.

Let's be responsible and conscious tourists in the sultanate.

CHARITIES AND ORGANISATIONS

A'Noor Association for the Blind PO Box 910, Al Khuwair, Code 133; e anoorab@omantel.net.om; e (email address of the vice-president, who speaks good English) bshahbal@hotmail.com

Association for Early Intervention for Children with Special Needs 24 496960; e earlyint@omantel.net.om; www.aei.org.om. Looks after children from birth to 6 years of age. Hassan Moosa (99 324882) is responsible for marketing & fundraising.

Association for the Disabled www.oad-oman. org. Looks after those above 16 years of age.

Association for the Welfare of Handicapped Children PO Box 1056, Muscat; 24 596502; www.awhc.info. Looks after children from 6–15 years of age.

Cancer Awareness Group 99 383070. Fat'hiya al Hinai & Yuthar al Ruwahy are the two most senior ladies.

Dar Al Atta e daralatta@yahoo.com. A newly formed charity that gives assistance to underprivileged families.

Geological Society of Oman www.gso.org.om. Established in 2001, this organisation promotes geotourism in Oman (considered one of the world's best 'geo parks') & facilitates knowledge-sharing

in the geologic community of the country, advancing the science & increasing awareness in the lay community of the importance & relevance of its work.

Historical Association of Oman 24 563074; e patricia@cfbtoman.com; www.hao.org.om. Organises regular talks (usually at the PDO oil exhibition club in Qurum) & field trips in an appreciation of Oman's past. The membership secretary is Rosemary Hector.

Omani Charitable Organisation Al Khuwair St 33, bldg no 173, Muscat; PO Box 1998, Ruwi PC 112; 25 687998; www.oco.org.om. Established in 1996, to assist needy families, orphans, senior citizens & the disabled.

Royal Geographical Society www.rgs.org. Promotes geographical research & advances geography, nationally & internationally. The Queen is patron. In Oman it runs the Wahiba Sands Project.

United Nations Children's Fund (UNICEF) – Oman www.unicef.org/infobycountry/oman.html. International aid agency assisting & advising Oman on all aspects of child development, malnutrition reduction, education & protection.

Part Two

THE GUIDE

3

Muscat مسقط

Telephone code 24

> *We who have seen Muscat and its custom houses are not amazed at the sight of a donkey dragging its own girth.*

Your first encounter with Oman is likely to be with its capital city Muscat – the hub of all international flights. On arrival at Muscat International Airport it is possible to take an immediate short domestic flight south to Salalah in the province of Dhofar, or north to Khasab in the Musandam peninsula; you may even choose to drive directly up the Batinah coast or into the interior. But generally, after your flight, it is likely that you'll want to rest where you land, and so Muscat will provide your first impression of the country.

Muscat proper is a small old port and harbour town, situated about a 30–40-minute drive away from the airport, and home to the Sultan's Palace, Al Alam. But since the discovery of oil in commercial quantities in 1964, and the subsequent coming to power of Sultan Qaboos bin Said in July 1970, surrounding residential areas, which were once small villages, have expanded under the modernisation programme, spilling over and outwards. Muscat, as a governorate, in fact stretches from Seeb (the town to the west of Muscat International Airport) out to Muscat Old Town (approximately 35km away, on the eastern tip) and southwards down to Quriyat. So today, when people speak of Muscat, they tend to be speaking of Muscat in this broader sense, which encompasses the whole governorate or Capital Area.

Muscat is that rare thing in the Middle East, a modern, clean yet overwhelmingly traditional city. Beautified since 1970 under the careful instruction of Sultan Qaboos, it appears almost like a developer's model town made large. Date-palm trees and neat, manicured, grassed areas flank the faultless motorway that threads this narrow, elongated piece of land between the mountains and ocean and speeds you along with ease to your hotel. Once away from the initial hubbub and slight congestion of the exit road of the airport, you will find yourself funneled into an elaborate and elegant network of ring-roads, roundabouts and flyovers, which can be a little bewildering at first, especially at night. But by day you can only be impressed by the clean and cared-for appearance of Muscat. Under the capital's unrelenting blue sky, camel-coloured mountains trail you to your right and blue ocean trails you to your distant left; deep-green grassed verges and white low-level buildings complete the picture. The boldness of nature's colours and the power of nature's heat are conspicuous. Muscat appears confident and prosperous and, like its people, self-respecting and proud.

HISTORY

With a population of around 1.2 million, Muscat is Oman's capital and its largest city, home to over a third of the country's inhabitants. Its port has always been

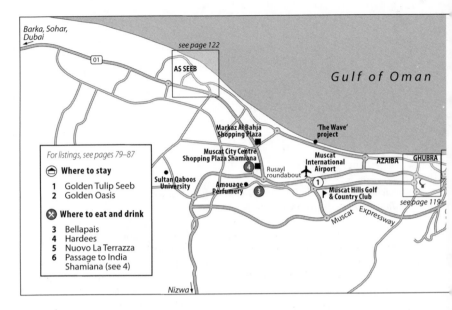

Barka, Sohar, Dubai

see page 122

see page 119

Gulf of Oman

AS SEEB

'The Wave' project

Markaz Al Bahja Shopping Plaza

Muscat City Centre Shopping Plaza Shamiana

Muscat International Airport

AZAIBA   GHUBRA

Rusayl roundabout

Sultan Qaboos University

Amouage Perfumery

Muscat Hills Golf & Country Club

Muscat Expressway

Nizwa

For listings, see pages 79–87

🛏 **Where to stay**
1 Golden Tulip Seeb
2 Golden Oasis

❌ **Where to eat and drink**
3 Bellapais
4 Hardees
5 Nuovo La Terrazza
6 Passage to India
   Shamiana (see 4)

its *raison d'être* and in Ptolemy's 1st century AD *Map of Arabia* it is identified as *Cryptus Portus* (the Hidden Port), reference to its position tucked out of sight and ringed with mountains. Over the centuries it has been an important trading centre and pottery found in the area confirms it had very early contact with the Indus Valley. The port was usually in the control of local indigenous tribes, but in the 3rd century it was conquered for a time by the Persian Sassanids. With the Arabian conquests and the conversion to Islam in the 7th century the port flourished and grew. The Abbasid Caliphate of Baghdad was able to capture it for a time in the 11th century, but then it reverted to local control till the Portuguese conquest in 1507. The Portuguese slaughtered all the men, women and children of the town after they resisted, then went on to pillage and occupy it, holding it for over a century. Their commander Afonso de Albuquerque wrote after the conquest:

> Muscat is a very large and populous town, flanked on both sides with high mountains and the front is close to the water's edge; behind, towards the interior, there is a plain as large as the square of Lisbon all covered with salt pans. There are orchards, gardens and palm groves with wells for watering them by means of swipes and other engines. The harbour is small, shaped like a horseshoe, and sheltered from every wind.

The Ottoman Turks captured Muscat from the Portuguese for two short periods in the 16th century, but in 1650 the local imam sent an army of fighters who eventually forced the Portuguese to leave. The Persians made a few attempts to take the port in the 18th century, destabilising the region, but the Al Bu Said dynasty, which has ruled Oman ever since, saved the situation and restored Muscat to local control.

GETTING THERE

BY AIR All international airlines serving Oman fly into Muscat International Airport on the western edge of the Capital Area, close to the coast and a 30–40-minute drive from the centre. See also page 420.

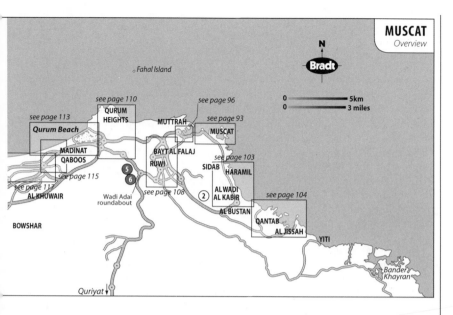

There is a currency exchange desk immediately in front of you as you enter the airport building from the plane, and you need to pay for your tourist visa here. There are no longer any forms to fill in on arrival. Visas cost RO20 for a month or RO5 for ten days and may be paid for in foreign currency or by credit card. If you pay in foreign currency, you will be given your change in rials.

Once through passport control/immigration, there is a small duty-free shop on the left, which also sells alcohol. You are permitted to take two litres into the country (and if you are staying at one of the upper-range hotels, you might like to consider doing so, if you want to save a small fortune on the cost of the same in the minibar in your room). A little further on past this shop are the luggage carousels. Once you have taken your luggage through the security check, you reach the arrivals area where there are some cafés, a cashpoint (that accepts a multitude of cards) and plenty of car-rental desks. In the departures area there are two business-class lounges on the ground floor. If you don't have access to these, take the escalators up to the first floor, where there is a licensed bar, some cafés, a bookshop, music shop, souvenir shop and a small duty-free shopping area.

Airport transfers If you walk across the footbridge opposite the airport, you can catch a minibus (600bzs/per person) or a taxi (RO8) into the city centre.

OVERLAND See page 43.

GETTING AROUND

ORIENTATION As the Capital Area is replete with flyovers and roundabouts, if you are intending to hire a car, some familiarisation with the names of the suburbs prior to your drive will be time well spent. The city is not at all large, but it is stretched out and constantly expanding. While the modern six-lane highways and ring-roads that thread through it are wonderful for residents, for the newcomer it can become confusing when they suddenly split, cross over themselves and continue in distorted figure-of-eight shapes to circumnavigate the mountains, which have a constant looming presence throughout the capital. This can create havoc with your sense of direction and once you have taken a wrong turn it can be very tricky to correct yourself. If you think of the airport roundabout as the starting point, the first roundabout/flyover you meet (going towards the old town of Muscat) is Azaiba (or Ghala), then Ghubra (or Bowshar), Al Khuwair, Qurum, Wuttayah, Wadi Adai, Hamriya, Ruwi, Al Burj, then Bait Al Falaj. Once you have mastered the position of these, and the various ring-roads, then finding your way to specific locations becomes a lot easier. The Muscat Expressway (also known as Madinat Sultan Qaboos Street), a three-lane motorway completed in 2012, runs for 55km just 2km inland from Highway 1 (known as Sultan Qaboos Street), the original main highway. Beginning at the main inland route to Nizwa near the airport it ends at Al-Nahdah Street in Qurum, where it joins into the original highway. It has 12 intersections, but can be tricky for newcomers unfamiliar with which exit to take. It also gets severely congested in rush-hour, so it is advisable to stick to the older Sultan Qaboos highway instead.

Be prepared for several different spellings of the same place names on road signs, in books and on maps. This is because of varying interpretations of the transliteration of the Arabic. Many of the roundabouts in the capital are adorned with giant model sculptures, and these have significance for that particular area. Coffee pots, incense burners, fish, boats and books all appear. When obtaining directions, the roundabouts are frequently referred to, in simple terms, by the model that sits on them. For example, the roundabout that is close to the Sultan Qaboos University displays a large model book, and so is often called 'the book' roundabout; and the one at the top end of the Muttrah corniche (coastal road), close to the group of budget hotels and fish souk, is referred to as 'the fish' roundabout.

BY TAXI Taxis are certainly the easiest option for getting around in the capital, especially if you are unfamiliar with the lie of the land. They are a distinctive orange and white, and because they are not metered you will have to bargain. All taxi drivers are Omani in line with the Omanisation principle. Omani men enjoy working in 'transport'. Their English is generally good in the Capital Area, less so in the interior. They function either as shared taxis where others get in too and you share the fare, or else you hire the whole taxi privately so no one else can get in, in which case the fare is obviously more.

Taxi fares (the private as opposed to shared variety) between suburbs should cost about RO4, though roguish taxi drivers may try to charge you RO7–10 if they think they can. Thankfully, from the airport the system is different, as there is now a central taxi control office just outside the exit of the arrivals area. You tell the man in the office your destination, the fare is fixed, you pay and receive a chit in exchange. You are then met by a driver with a copy of the same chit and escorted to the car and driven away. For all other journeys fares should be agreed before getting in. The official taxi fare from Muscat Airport to Muttrah/Muscat Old Town is roughly RO12 and it takes about 40 minutes to cover the 40km. A transfer to any of the central hotels, such as the Radisson Blu, Grand Hyatt or Intercontinental (about 20km away), will take roughly 15–20 minutes and will cost around RO9. See also page 56 for pre-booked taxis.

BY HIRE CAR There is no difficulty in renting a car at Muscat International Airport, though you may decide to rent from your hotel rather than have the stress of negotiating the unfamiliar road network after a long flight, especially if you arrive at night. Plenty of well-known car-hire firms operate both here and from local hotels. There are also some cheaper local firms throughout the city. Don't worry if you haven't pre-booked; you will certainly find something (for details and car-hire firms, see pages 54–5).

BY MICROBUS Local white microbuses seating about 12–14 people pass the airport regularly between 07.00 and 22.00, and run all the way along the coast to Ruwi, Muttrah and Muscat, costing 500bzs. There is a bus stop outside the airport and you can flag one down if it has room. For travelling around within the Capital Area these microbuses are the cheapest option, and journeys from one suburb to another cost about 200–300bzs. The maximum fare on a microbus within the Capital Area (Greater Muscat) will be 500bzs. In Ruwi the microbuses cluster around Al-Jaame Street opposite the main bus station, and in Muttrah they gather round the Muttrah Bus Station.

BY MINIBUS By far the cheapest way to get around is by minibus – medium-sized vehicles known as baiza buses (because it costs only a few baizas for the journey), which operate in the city area. They can be hailed at any of the bus stops on the main highway, and run to all of the Muscat suburbs. Fares are charged according to your destination, and you pay on entry. This mode of transport is regularly used by Oman's large Asian labour force, but rarely by Western visitors. At busier times, be prepared to become closely acquainted with other passengers; the 'packed-in-like-dates' situation may be off-putting for some.

BY BUS Another good option in Oman is to travel by bus and there are a handful of operators in the capital. From Muscat it is possible to get a bus trip to Sur (in the Sharqiya) and Salalah (in the Dhofar region), making stops at strategic points in the interior (Dakhiliyah region) – Nizwa, for example. Buses also travel to Dubai and Abu Dhabi in the United Arab Emirates, making stops at Sohar (in the Batinah region) and Buraimi (in the Dhahirah) along their respective routes. For all bus information see pages 56–7.

ON FOOT It is not easy to walk around Muscat as the city is so stretched out, and in the summer months it is just too hot. Nevertheless, the introduction of the occasional pedestrian walkway over the main highway makes things a lot safer; pedestrians dashing across the busy road used to be a common, if heart-stopping sight. One exception is the way-marked trail from Riyam Park into the mountains and round to Muttrah harbour (see box on pages 94–6). Otherwise I would suggest saving your walks for the endless stretches of beach, all of which are public.

TOURIST INFORMATION

See page 39.

TOURS AND OPERATORS

ORGANISED TOURS Many tour companies operate within the capital (listed on pages 76–8), each offering the usual array of tours. They are regulated by the Ministry of Tourism. If you don't want to make the arrangements yourself, explain your requirements to your hotel and they will arrange things for you; they usually work closely with one or two tour operators. Guests can be picked up from any of the city hotels (or from a private address) and this is included in the price.

Tour options The stock tours offered in Muscat include **sunset *dhow* cruises** (a *dhow* being a traditional wooden boat, part of Oman's seafaring history) along the coastal bays of Muscat, half-day **city tours** (which include the Sultan Qaboos Grand Mosque at Azaiba, Al Alam Palace in Muscat Old Town, the Portuguese forts of Mirani and Jalali, Muttrah Souk, Bait Al Zubair Museum and Al Bustan Palace Hotel), **dolphin-watching tours**, **snorkelling and diving tours** and **fishing safaris**.

Off-road **4x4 safari tours** are largely to destinations beyond the Capital Area, and include trips up into the mountains, into the wadis and into the desert. A 4x4 is essential, and it is advisable to go through a tour operator who will provide the vehicle and an invaluable driver/guide.

For safety and comfort, these 4x4 trips offered by tour operators are based on four passengers in one vehicle with a driver/guide, and cost upwards of RO150. Some tour companies allow you to join a tour in a convoy, if you have your own rented 4x4, and this will work out cheaper, but of course you miss the information provided by the guide *en route*, and you also take responsibility for the driving, which requires skill and experience. It is better to leave the driving to the guides, and more or less essential to do so for trips into the Wahiba Sands (Sharqiya) and the Empty Quarter (Dhofar). Wadis may be more manageable for the inexperienced, but only if dry. Some of the roads up into the *jebels* (mountains) can be narrow and precipitous. In this case, it is still recommended that at least two vehicles go in convoy. If in doubt, arrange your trip through a tour operator rather than drive independently.

The 4x4 tours can work out expensive if you are a lone traveller for a 4x4 and driver/guide for the day, as the price is the same irrespective of if you are one or four passengers. In such a situation, and if you would like to bring the cost down substantially, enquiries at any of the tour operators will establish whether it is possible for you to join another car for your chosen trip. However, you may prefer the privacy of your own car and driver/guide, regardless of cost.

TOUR OPERATORS Below is a list of the majority of tour operators in existence in Oman. These are all based in Muscat but arrange tours throughout the whole of the country. Some have desks within the upper- to mid-range hotels and this is generally the most convenient way to arrange a trip.

Arabesque Travel PO Box 1244, Muscat 131; www.arabesque.travel. Offers a full range of tours including trips starting from Dubai. Self-drive 4x4 & private tours from 1 to 4 days, as well as tailor-made private tours.

Al Azri Tours PO Box 877, PC 611, Nizwa; ✆ 25 412368. This small company specialises in tours of Nizwa Old Town, walking & trekking in the Jebel Akhdar, as well as camping & camel safaris in the Nizwa area.

Bahwan Travel Agencies PO Box 282, PC 113; ✆ 24 704455, 706798; e topclass@ omantel. net.om or lakshmy@bahwantravels.com; www. bahwantravels.com. Has several offices in the capital & is one of the biggest tour operators.

Locations in the Central Business District, MQ Shopping Centre; ✆ 24 601192, Ruwi; ✆ 24 706134, Sabco Centre; ✆ 24 564678, Golden Tulip Hotel; ✆ 24 510720, Al Khuwair, ✆ 24 603898; Salalah, ✆ 23 294665, 290908. Established 25 years, offering a full range of tours & safaris. Helpful & knowledgeable staff.

Desert Adventures ✆ 95 201107. For group tours & expeditions; also offers cruises on a 30ft boat (15 passengers). Camping & expedition equipment meets international quality & safety standards. Wahiba Sands & Coastal Adventure (2 days, 1 night); Sea Adventure (full-day cruise) snorkelling, fishing, dolphin watching, beach BBQ; Wilderness Challenge – specialising in adventure education for the young, the Wilderness programmes focus on team building, personal development & leadership for those aged 14–18 (3 days, 2 nights) .

Desert Discovery Tours PO Box 99, Madinat Al Sultan Qaboos, PC 115; 24 493232, 99 328858, 99 418664; www.desertdiscovery.com. This company's facilities include Al Areesh Desert Camp in Wahiba Sands, Al Naseem Turtle Beach Camp at Ras al Junaiz (close to the turtle reserve), Al Qabil Resthouse (approx halfway between Muscat & Sur, & a good stop-off point), as well as mobile camping units. It offers professionally guided tours from one person to a large group, including cultural, historical & adventure tours.

Eihab Travels PO Box 889, PC 113; 24 796387, 796282; e inbound@omantel.net. om. Located in Muttrah high street. Offers city tours, day trips, car hire & domestic flights.

Elite Travel & Tourism PO Box 36, 116 Mina Al Fahal; 24 499797; e info@eliteoman.com; www. eliteoman.com. Specialises in luxury travel, culture & nature tours, soft adventure & golf.

Global Tours 24 484156, 695959, 695994; e globtour@omantel.net.om, globaltoursoman. com. Located at Al Khuwair. For wadi & dune bashing, camping & caving, & all the usual tours.

Golden Oryx Tours 24 489853, 99 810889; e info@golden oryx.com; www.goldenoryx. com. This company offers the Muscat city tour, the Nizwa & the Grand Canyon tour, dolphin-watching tour, Wadi Shab trail, Rustaq, desert adventure & oasis trail, & the giant green turtles of Ras al Hadd tour.

Gulf Ventures PO Box 1938, PC 130, Al Azaiba; 24 490733; www.gulfventures.com. Long-established company with the full range of tours, day trips & safaris. Specialises in trekking.

Hud Hud Travels PO Box 479, PC 115, Medinat Qaboos; 92 920670; contact@hudhudtravels. com; www.hudhudtravels.com. Provider of professionally run luxury private expeditions & one-off innovative events in remote locations in the Wahhiba Sands & the Hajar Mountains.

Mark Tours PO Box 3310, PC 112, Ruwi; 24 562444, 565567, 560975, 561466; e marktour@omantel.net.om or admin@ marktoursoman.com; www.marktoursoman.com. Main office is in Hatat Hse at Wadi Adai roundabout [map page 73], plus a desk at Muscat Airport & in the Radisson Blu Hotel [117 C4], also a franchise in Salalah. Will send you a list of tours on request.

Mezoon Travels PO Box 629, PC 100; 24 796680; e info@mezoontravel.co.om; www.mezoontravel. com. Located in Al Burj St, Ruwi. Established more than 25 years with branches in Salalah (23 297846) & Mina Al Fahal (24 568220), although all tours are arranged through the Muscat office. Offers an impressive, well-structured range of tours, trips & safaris through mountain, wadi & desert, including rock climbing & trekking, & can organise overnight camping tours, which are priced on any tailor-made route intended. Will send you a detailed list on request.

Midland Tourism PO Box 426, PC 113; 24 566524. Located in Qurum, & offering the full range of tours, including diving & hang gliding.

Multaqa Al Ebda'a Tourism PO Box 746, PC 112, Ruwi; 99 274755, 349399; e khaled_ wahaibi@ hotmail.com. Offers dolphin-watching trips, snorkelling trips, game-fishing trips, Muscat trip & bay trips, sunset cruises on a 28ft boat.

Muscat Diving & Adventure Centre   24 485663; e info@holiday-in-oman.com; www.holiday-in-oman.com. This company offers excellent adventure tours, from trekking to caving, with knowledgeable, qualified guides & equipment. Rock climbing, trekking, surfing, kayaking, game fishing, diving.

National Travel & Tourism PO Box 962, PC 113; 24 566046; e nttoman@ omantel.net.om. Also located at Wattayah, Qurum (24 564783), Salalah (23 295016), Buraimi (25 650716). Long-established large company with 45 4x4 vehicles & 2 buses, offering city tours, day trips, *dhow* cruises, camel & 4x4 safaris, & scuba diving.

Al Nimer Tourism m 089 550535; www. alnimertourism.com (at time of writing, the website was under construction). Located in the Ramada Hotel at Qurum Beach offering all the stock tours as well as parasailing, sea tours, water rides for families & children on the Matrix, Viper or Jumbo Dog (inflatables, towed by a speedboat), & camping trips.

Oman Discovery PO Box 3932, PC 112, Ruwi; 24 706424; e omandisc@omantel.net.om. A division of Khasab Travel & Tours offering a similar range of tours, trips & safaris but in the Omani heartland instead of Musandam.

Oman Geo Tours PO Box 122, PC 116, Mina Al Fahal; 24 536629, 600914. Located in Qurum. Specialises in geological & scientific tours, but offers other tours as well.

Oman Orient Tours PO Box 409, PC 113; ☏24 685066, 790700, 790567; e mctoffice@ orienttours.ae. Established over 15 years with branches throughout the Gulf, offering city tours, day trips, *dhow* cruises, camel & 4x4 safaris. Also in Salalah (☏*23 236038*).

OmanHoliday.co.uk ☏+968 95 116638; www. omanholiday.co.uk. Based in Hamriya in Muscat, has been operating for more than 20 years & will arrange bespoke trips for everyone from single visitors to large groups & business visitors.

Omani Travel & Tourism Bureau (OTTB) PO Box 532, PC 117; ☏24 789845–7; e otboman@omantel.net.om or niche@omantel. net.om. Also in Seeb (☏*24 421469*) & Buraimi (☏*25 655890*). Full range of tours from 2hr city tours to 20-day safaris, also fishing tours. Car hire, travel insurance, hotel reservations, domestic flights, & meet & greet.

Shanfari Travel & Tours PO Box 783, PC 100; ☏24 602710; e group@shanfari.com; www. shanfari.com. City tours, *dhow* cruises, adventure trips, camel & 4x4 safaris, turtle-watching.

Al Tamayim Tourism PO Box 244, PC 119; ☏24 571461, 601061. Located in Al Harthy Complex. A medium-sized company offering city & day trips by bus, *dhow* cruises, 4x4 safaris, airport transfers, meet & greet.

Tour Oman PO Box 1694, PC 114, Muttrah; ☏24 799966. Established 12 years, offering the full range of tours & trips including scuba diving.

Tours by Heide Beal PO Box 2031, PC 112, Ruwi; ☏24 795206. Based at Hotel Mercure Al Falaj, Heide Beal was the first person to run adventure safaris in Oman back in 1987. She offers tailor-made holidays from 1-day to 2-week study tours, including mountain trekking.

United Tours PO Box 599, PC 114, Muttrah; ☏24 787448; e utours@omantel.net.om; utours@unitedoman.com. Located in the CBD. Also in Salalah (☏*23 297948*). Large established firm with 40 4x4 vehicles & a fleet of buses offering the full range of tours, including comprehensive 8–12-day tours of Oman, camping, safari & culture.

Zahara Tours PO Box 833, PC 112, Ruwi; ☏24 400844; e arvind@zaharatours.com or harsh@zaharatours.com; www.zaharatours.com. Located in the CBD. Also at the Intercontinental Hotel (☏*24 699862*), Grand Hyatt Hotel (☏*24 696596*), Salalah (☏*23 202581, 202582*). Large established firm, IATA travel agents carrying stocks of over 21 international airlines, with Avis car hire, travel & diving insurance, & the full range of day trips, city tours, camel & 4x4 safaris, scuba diving & adventure trips.

OMAN IN THE ARAB SPRING

Oman's brief version of its own Arab Spring lasted just four months from January till May 2011, with most of the demonstrations taking place in Sohar among the student population. Young Omanis mainly saw it as an opportunity to make demands for better salaries and working conditions, demands which were met in full by an obliging government keen to quell the unrest. Thousands of new jobs were created in the police and public sector. The working week was reduced from six to five days, or from 48 to 40 hours, to banish the spectre of strikes in the hotel sector. As a result Omanis are now paid more than expatriates, but expatriates will not protest or go on strike.

The Arab Spring has also changed the dynamic of tourism in Oman to some extent. Before 2011, 80% of foreign visitors were from Europe – mainly the UK, Germany, Italy, France, Benelux, Austria and Switzerland. Post 2011 Arabs from Gulf countries were no longer able to spend their summers in Syria, Lebanon and Jordan, the northernmost Arab countries, so came to Oman instead. Now the balance is more like 50% European, 50% other Gulf countries. Summer occupancy in hotels used to be only 20%, when it was considered too hot for Europeans, but now occupancy in summer is closer to 45%, thanks to the increase in GCC visitors well accustomed to the heat.

The lion's share of Oman's hotels are in Muscat and the Capital Area, with greater choice here than anywhere else in the country. However, the range of what is on offer, as you might expect from Oman's stated policy of encouraging top-end tourism, is reflected in a preponderance of top-end hotels, with five- and four-star establishments that start from over RO100 per double room. To find reasonably priced mid-range and budget accommodation is harder, but the listings on pages 79–85 attempt to give a fair selection of places to consider. For atmosphere, the cheap hotels along the Muttrah corniche are the best, but if you want access to a beach at budget prices, head for somewhere like the Qurum Beach Hotel.

From the airport it is never too far to your hotel, irrespective of where you are staying in the city. The closest is the Golden Tulip, which is virtually opposite the airport; the farthest are Al Bustan Palace and the Shangri-La's Barr al Jissah both about a 40-minute drive away on good roads. A more central choice from which to explore the city would be The Chedi (about 15mins away from the airport), the Grand Hyatt, or the Intercontinental Hotel (both roughly 20mins away from the airport). The Radisson Blu is also a good central base (again about 15–20mins from the airport). Although it doesn't occupy a beach location, it does have a beach club located next to the Grand Hyatt.

Some hotels in the city provide a complimentary transit from the airport; this is certainly the case if you have booked a package holiday. For the independent traveller it may be a good idea to confirm with your chosen hotel whether this service is included.

If you prefer a self-catering arrangement, for a stay of a longer duration perhaps, hotel apartments are widely available around Muscat. Again these vary in quality, but all are basically clean and comfortable. You will often get a discount for a longer period of stay.

Note that all room rates are subject to a 17% government tax; some of the rates quoted here already include this (and this has been specified). In the same way, some of the rates quoted here include breakfast (also specified), whereas some don't.

LUXURY & UPMARKET

🏠 **Al Bustan Palace Hotel** [103 D4] (250 rooms) PO Box 1998, PC 114, Muttrah; ☎24 799666; e albustan@ritzcarlton.com; www. ritzcarlton.com/en/properties/albustan. About a 35–40min drive from the airport. Set on its own private beach within 200 acres of lush parkland, complete with helicopter landing pad & stark mountainous backdrop, the famous Al Bustan has recently had a facelift, while retaining its magnificent foyer & upmarket souvenir shops. Its bay location means that the sea is clear & calm. The hotel is regularly voted top in the Arabian Peninsula competition & is known as one of the finest in the world. Over half of its rooms overlook the sea. Sports & leisure facilities are extensive. Offers gourmet dining, inc a traditional Omani dinner for RO20 on Wed, a beach bar & restaurant & an award-winning buffet restaurant. A new spa building has been added to the facilities. The hotel's location is a little less exclusive since the Omani government decided to build a massive parliament complex just inland, housing the Majlis Oman, Majlis A'Shura & Majlis A'Dawla, along with VIP areas, an information centre, library & other offices. The new site of Oman's National Museum is also nearby in the Al Bustan bay. **$$$$$**

🏠 **The Chedi** [119 D2] (161 rooms) PO Box 964, PC 133, Al Khuwair, Muscat; ☎24 524400, 524401; www.ghmhotels.com. Located in north Ghubra (also known as Bowshar beachfront), this is one of the most stylish of Muscat's luxury collection of 5-star hotels & only about a 15min drive from the airport (7km). It is well signposted. It is a single- & 2-storey hotel & spa, with 1 deluxe room & private villas, 2 swimming pools, tennis courts, treatment rooms & a boutique (which is also an art gallery). There are sports facilities, 3 bars & 2 poolside *cabanas*. One of the bars is sunken & has a beautiful outlook past the glass-like stillness of the infinity pool & directly on to the postcard-like blue ocean. The intention is an uncluttered Zen experience of peace & tranquillity, with beauty & bathing rituals on offer, & body elixirs, in the form of massages, scrubs & wraps, for which there is a menu in your room. The award-winning restaurant (called 'The Restaurant') is regarded as one of the best in the city (✆ *24 524343; e restaurant@ chedimuscat.com*). There is a choice of Arabic, Asian, Indian & Mediterranean cuisine cooked in the 4 open-display kitchens, in addition to an extensive cellar, which houses over 300 imported wines on full display in the floor-to-ceiling glass library in the bar (called 'The Bar'). Alternatively, there is The Chedi Pool Side Cabana for evening dining, which serves a Mediterranean menu, & has a resident pianist entertaining you (Sat & Sun). There are 3 semi-private dining rooms, all with sea views, named The Datai, The Setai & The Legian. Suites are impressive, with high ceilings & minimalist designs. Outside, a maze of paved pathways leads to the pools & private beach. The understated décor here attracts a more European than Gulf Arab clientele, in contrast with the opulence of Al Bustan Palace & the Shangri-La.

$$$$$

⌂ **Grand Hyatt Muscat** [113 A4 & 115 A2] (280 rooms) PO Box 951, Shatti Al Qurum, PC 133, Muscat;✆ 24 641234; e hyattmct@omantel.net. om; www.muscat.grand.hyatt.com. About 20km from Muscat International Airport, this 5-star hotel is set in 10 acres of gardens, in a good central location on Qurum Beach. It has a stylish design in traditional Arabian architecture, said to have been conceived by a Yemeni prince, including a huge stained-glass window (14m high) through which you have views out towards the swimming pool & gardens. There are 4 restaurants & 2 bars. For those who would prefer to self-cater there are Crowne Suites with 2 or 3 beds adjacent to the hotel, with private kitchens & living rooms. The Sirj tea lounge, with its bold décor & sumptuous sofas, is opulent, &, coupled with the soft music from the grand piano, creates an atmosphere of sheer tranquillity. Perhaps take high tea here, with cakes & pastries, or have your business meeting. There is a superb Italian restaurant (The Tuscany), decorated as a Tuscan villa, complete with iron gate & courtyard; the Mokha Café is down the stairs, & serves buffet

b/fasts & Middle Eastern lunches & dinners; there is also a poolside Asian restaurant & bar (The Marjan). The John Barry Bar, with its sea theme, was named after the wreck of the SS *John Barry* which sank off the coast of Oman in 1944. It has a peaceful ambience & good entertainment later on by the resident pianist. The Copacabana is the hotel's nightclub, which is underneath the hotel & at the front. Club Safari is a 2min walk down the sloped entrance to the hotel. It is a great African-themed bar on 3 levels, with a snooker/pool area & a cigar lounge on the ground floor (Habana Café), a good, fun bar on the middle floor (Safari Pub) & a grill restaurant on the roof terrace (Grill House). Many excellent house bands play nightly in the Safari Pub & it can get full & lively after 22.00. There are all the usual 5-star facilities & services in the hotel, & watersports are available at the Hyatt Boat House (✆ *24 485663*) situated on the beach.

$$$$$

⌂ **Shangri-La's Barr al Jissah Resort & Spa** [104 D3] (680 rooms) PO Box 644, PC 113, Muscat;✆ 24 776666; e slmu@shangri-la.com; www.shangri-la.com/muscat. This is one of the newest additions to Oman's growing 5-star hotel assortment with the added tag of 'deluxe'. It is a resort of 3 top international-class hotels, set in 124 acres of landscaped gardens with a remarkable mountainous backdrop. Although this is the farthest hotel in the city from the airport it is still only a 40min drive on roads of excellent condition. This resort is sheer relaxation & escape, just as that offered by Al Bustan a few bays earlier. The 3 hotels are geared towards different target markets: Al Husn ('The Castle') is a 6-star luxury hotel, while Al Bandar ('The Town') is aimed at the business guest. Al Waha ('The Oasis') is aimed at families, providing a kids' club named 'Little Turtles', two kiddie pools & an internet café. The Chi Spa, adjacent to the gym, has treatment rooms in 12 private villas, & offers traditional Himalayan & Chinese treatments. There is a protected 'turtle cove' area where turtles come to nest, & a ranger informs & educates guests on how to respect the species & their natural environment. Guests of Al Bandar & Al Waha can use each other's facilities, & a lazy river can be swum or followed, adjoining the two. There is a central bar amid the pools & surrounding flower gardens. There are over 15 food & drink outlets in total. There is a dive school & watersports facilities, with a lifeguard present. Al

Husn remains exclusive, & with a huge chandelier from the Czech Republic, wall light shades from Morocco & carpets from Iran, the décor is opulent. When combined with 3 crystal-ceiling ballrooms with retracting walls (which allow it to convert into one impressive 700-seater), this place is seriously luxurious. Transfers from Muscat International Airport can be arranged for a hefty RO35. **$$$$$**

🏨 **Crowne Plaza Hotel Muscat** [113 G1] (207 rooms) PO Box 1455, PC 112, Ruwi; 📞24 660660; e mcthc@interconti.com; www. cpmuscat.com. The Crowne Plaza has a superb location perched on a cliff in Qurum Heights, overlooking Qurum Beach. This is one of Muscat's oldest established hotels & used to be the Gulf Forum Hotel. There is a Lebanese restaurant (Shiraz), an international buffet restaurant (Tropicana), Arabic food (Palm Café), casual dining (The Edge) & an English pub (Duke's Bar). It is recommended that you reserve a table in advance for any of these restaurants. There are good sports & recreational facilities & dive trips are arranged through Oman Dive Centre. **$$$$**

🏨 **Golden Tulip Seeb** [map pages 72–3] (177 rooms) PO Box 69, Muscat International Airport, PC 111; 📞24 510300; e admin@ goldentulipseeb.com; www.goldentulipseeb.com. This is the closest hotel to Muscat International Airport, & is situated next to the Oman International Exhibition Centre. Guests can use the facilities of the Oman Aviation Beach Club & the Oman Automobile Club (which has go-karting & an 18-hole brown (sand) golf course, located a few minutes from the hotel) & offers free transfer to these on request. There is an international restaurant (Le Jardin), with themed buffet nights, & nightclub. Seafood night is well worth seeking out, with an awesome buffet & endless wine included in the set price of RO15, open to non-residents as well. PADI dive course packages are also available. **$$$$**

🏨 **InterContinental** [113 D3] (261 rooms) PO Box 398, PC 114, Muttrah; 📞24 680000, 600500; e muscat@icmuscathotel.com or muscat@interconti.com; www.intercontinental. com. On Qurum Beach about a 20min drive from the airport (21km), close to Qurum Natural Park & the museums. Set within 35 acres of private well-maintained gardens, its brown-brick structure doesn't make it the most attractive building. It is a

little dated, but there is an efficient, friendly staff, & has good leisure & sports facilities. There is an American-style steakhouse (OK Corral), a Mexican restaurant (Señor Pico's), international snacks round the pool (Pool Deck) & Far Eastern food (Coconut Grove). The bar (Al Ghazal Pub) serves food & is popular with expats. It has a live band playing most evenings, & offers quiz nights, sport on the large-screen TV & a pool/snooker area. There is a good cocktail bar & restaurant (Trader Vic's [113 D3] 📞24 698028), situated just outside the front of the hotel & on the left (as you face it), serving Caribbean & Pacific food. **$$$$**

🏨 **Radisson Blu Hotel** [117 C4] (156 rooms) PO Box 939, PC 133, Al Khuleiah St, Muscat; 📞24 487777; www.radissonblu.com/hotel-muscat. Located in Al Khuwair, in a good elevated & central setting in the capital (on the mountain side rather than the sea side of the highway), this hotel is about a 10–15min drive from the airport (signposted from the highway, & situated just off Al Khuleiah St, at the one-way section). It has an excellent standard of modern décor & there is a great steak restaurant here (Al Tajin Grill), set opposite a romantic, dimly lit piano bar (The Coral), for pre- or post-dinner drinks. There is a nightclub (The Cellar – accessed around the back of the hotel & down the stairs), an all-day indoor & outdoor dining restaurant (Olivio's Coffee Shop), which is also a Wi-Fi zone, serving buffet & à la carte meals, & the Fontana Heath Club. The garden has a bar by the pool open late afternoon & evenings. The business centre provides free internet & computer services to all guests. The beach club for the Radisson is located next to the Grand Hyatt & transport is provided. The staff give an excellent smiling welcome, & a swift, efficient check-in & delivery of bags to your room. Reception offers a full explanation of what the cost of an overnight stay includes without being prompted. A courtesy bus will take you to the airport & also does trips to Muttrah Souk at 16.00 with pick-up at 19.00 on request. **$$$$**

🏨 **Sheraton Oman Hotel** [108 D4] (217 rooms, 24 deluxe suites) PO Box 3260, PC 112, Ruwi; 📞24 772772; e sheraton@omantel. net.om; www.sheraton.com. Roughly a half-hour drive from Seeb (40km), set in the Central Business District at Ruwi, this is a high-rise hotel, rated 5-star by the Ministry of Tourism. To get here keep straight on the main highway until you reach the Ruwi roundabout. Turn right here & follow the road all the way up to the T-junction, to the traffic lights at the very end. The hotel lies opposite these lights. In addition to its full sports facilities it has a 6-lane bowling alley. A beach resort has recently been added with a shuttle-bus service to Qurum (see next entry). There is an international restaurant (Green Mountain Restaurant) with various theme nights, including BBQ night, fish night & Thai night, an Italian restaurant (La Mamma), a French restaurant (La Brasserie), Le Croissant Coffee Shop, the Piazza Bar & Saba Disco. All outlets are licensed. There is no complimentary airport transfer service. **$$$$**

⌂ **Sheraton Qurum Beach Resort** [113 D3] (7 rooms) PO Box 3260, PC 112, Ruwi; ☎24 605945; e sheraton@omantel.net.om; www.sheraton.com. Located at Shatti al Qurum, this is the beach resort of the Sheraton Oman Hotel in Ruwi & guests from Ruwi can use the facilities here for free. There is a complimentary shuttle service from Sheraton Ruwi, leaving at 10.00/11.00/12.00 & returning in the afternoon at 15.00/16.00/17.00. All rooms have sea views, a gym & a swimming pool. The small resort is good for beach-sports lovers. There is an Arabic/Moroccan nightclub (Cleopatra Night Club) & Feeney's Irish Bar. Accepts credit cards. **$$$$**

MID-RANGE

⌂ **Al Madina Holiday Inn** [119 A5] (107 rooms) PO Box 692, PC 130, Al Azaiba, Muscat; ☎24 596400; e amhi33@omantel.net.om; www.holidayinn.com. This Holiday Inn, located in Ghala, has a coffee shop & licensed bars with live entertainment, as well as a Health Club with exercise machines. **$$$$**

⌂ **Al Falaj Hotel** [108 A3] (143 rooms) PO Box 2031, PC 112, Ruwi; ☎24 702311; e sales@omanhotels.com or reservationruwi@omanhotels.com; www.omanhotels.com/alfalaj. One of Muscat's oldest hotels, this is set in the Central Business District of Ruwi, off Al Burj St, & rated 4-star. Private beach facilities are available on request. On the 8th floor there is a Japanese restaurant (Tokyo Taro) & a pub (Le Pub) with live band & bar-food menu, & each has scenic views over the city. Al Falaj also has a Lebanese restaurant, an Indian restaurant & a coffee shop. The sports facilities include glass-sided squash courts. **$$$**

⌂ **Beach Hotel Muscat** [113 D3] (20 rooms, 20 suites) PO Box 86, PC 134, Mina al Fahal, Muscat; ☎24 696601; e reservations@beachhotelmuscat.com; www.beachhotelmuscat.com. This lovely small hotel is set close to the beach & the InterContinental Hotel. It is under friendly new Omani management & has a quaint design with rooms surrounding a small swimming pool. Its international restaurant is unlicensed. **$$$**

⌂ **Bowshar International Hotel** [117 A4] (38 rooms) PO Box 1842, PC 112, Ruwi; ☎24 491105; e bwshrhtl@omantel.net.com; www.bowsharhotel.com. To get here, come off the highway at the Ghubra roundabout. It is on the sea side of the highway, rather than the mountain side, 15mins from the airport, & is signposted. The hotel is rated 3-star by the Ministry of Tourism. Al Mas Brasserie is the hotel's licensed restaurant. Accepts credit cards. **$$$**

⌂ **Dream Resort** [map page 121] (30 rooms) PO Box 609, PC 121, Al Seeb; www.rameehotels.com/dream-resort.html. This is a modern hotel (about 4 years old) of international standard & is certainly the best if you are planning on staying in Seeb Town. It is within easy walking distance of the beach. Rooms surround the 2 pools & lead straight out to them if you request one on the ground floor. The hotel is rather in the middle of nowhere, so unless you're coming for a complete rest, & like to beach-walk, there is not a lot to see & do. There is the Café Lounge, an international restaurant & the Black Out nightclub. It also has a large screen for sporting events. **$$$**

⌂ **Haffa House Hotel** [108 B5] (120 rooms) PO Box 1498, PC 114, Jibroo; ☎24 707207; e reservations@haffahouse.com; www.haffahouse.com. This hotel is situated on Ruwi Street in the CBD & is affiliated to the Shanfari group of hotels (they have Haffa House & Samharam tourist village both in Salalah). It has a swimming pool & an unlicensed restaurant (Four Seasons). **$$$**

⌂ **Holiday Inn Muscat** [117 B3] (129 rooms) PO Box 1185, PC 111, Seeb; ☎24 487123; e mcthinn@omantel.net.om; www.holidayinn.com. There are 2 Holiday Inn hotels in Muscat, but the one in Al Khuwair has the more central & pleasant location. Live music features in the restaurants & bars, & on the 1st floor there is a pub (Churchill's), which provides a pub-food menu. There is also an African restaurant (Hakuna Matata). **$$$**

⌂ **Majan Continental Hotel** [119 C6] (159 rooms) PO Box 311, PC 115, Madinat Qaboos; ☏24 592900; e info@majanhotel.com or sales@ majanhotel.com; www.majanhotel.com. The hotel has a 24hr licensed coffee shop (Khaboura Café) & 5 bars with live bands performing daily. It can arrange diving packages to the Daymaniyat Islands, car hire & tours. Accepts credit cards. **$$$**

⌂ **Muscat Holiday Hotel** [off map 117, A4] (123 rooms) Al Khuwair; ☏24 487123; www. muscat-holiday.com. Clean & comfortable accommodation halfway between the airport & central business district. Good outdoor pool, floodlit tennis court & fitness centre. All-day dining & licensed bar. **$$$**

⌂ **Oman Dive Centre Beach Huts** [104 C3] (35 barasti huts) ☏24 824240–1, 99 379031; www.omandivecenter.com. Located in Bander Jissah, in its own tranquil bay, this offers an alternative-type stay in Muscat. When nearing Al Bustan you descend a hill. Partway down you take the right-hand exit directing you to Qantab & the Shangri-La Resort. This road winds up & over the mountains & when you come to a roundabout take a left. This will take you down into the private bay of the dive centre. You can no longer camp on the beach here, but equipped, traditional Omani *barasti* (made with palm fronds) huts with AC are available for rent. There is a licensed restaurant (The Odyssey ⊕ 07.00–16.30 & 18.00–22.00). This is a peaceful location where you can get on with the business of taking or completing your PADI course or doing a dive without distractions. **$$$**

⌂ **Ramada Qurum Beach** [113 C4] (92 rooms) PO Box 2994, PC 112, Ruwi; ☏24 603555; e ramadaom@omantel.net. om; www.ramadamuscat.com. This hotel has a good location very close to the beach & the InterContinental Hotel, about 10–15mins from the airport. Rated 4-star deluxe by the Ministry of Tourism, it is an Arabic-style construction & the room décor is of a good standard. Inside the hotel is Nauras Al Shatti Restaurant & the Petit Café. **$$$**

⌂ **Ruwi Hotel** [108 B5] (116 rooms) PO Box 2195, PC 112, Ruwi; ☏24 704244; e reservationruwi@omanhotels.com or sales@ omanhotels.com; www.omanhotels.com/ruwi.

This is one of a chain of 4 hotels, the others being Al Falaj (see page 82), Sur Plaza (Sur) & Al Wadi (Sohar). Set in the Central Business District at the 7th roundabout from the airport (Ruwi roundabout), this hotel has a 3-star Ministry of Tourism rating & has been operational for over 20 years. It has 2 licensed restaurants: the Coffee Shop offers all-day dining & Al Fakhr Restaurant has live entertainment from an Arabic band. There is also the Club Bar & the Mehfil Bar, each with live entertainment. There are 2 glass-backed squash courts. Accepts credit cards. **$$$**

⌂ **The Treasure Box** (also known as **Johnny International**) [119 C5] (36 rooms) Way 3709, Bldg 631, South Al Ghubra, Bawshar; ☏24 502570; e reservation@treasureboxhotels. com; www.thetreasurebox-muscat.hotel-rez.com. Unusual Omani boutique hotel in a modern, yet traditional, style of architecture that combines Omani hospitality with European standards & management. Located in a quiet residential area of Al Ghubra, within walking distance of the Grand Mosque, the hotel sits midway between the airport & Qurum Beach, a 10min taxi ride from either. Airport transfer RO10. **$$$**

BUDGET

⌂ **Al Bahjah Hotel** [map page 121] (52 rooms) PO Box 979, PC 121, Seeb; ☏24 424400; www.rameehotels.com. This hotel is located in Seeb on the one-way system in the town, about 15km from the airport. Its rooms have full facilities, including swimming pool. On-site restaurants & bars include Al Saadah Café, Keranadu Restaurant, Al Massarrat Sports Bar, Al Rafahia Arabic Restaurant & Al Marrah Indian Restaurant. If you are not staying here, it still makes a good stop for a cup of tea (400bzs) or something to eat, while visiting Seeb Town. Accepts credit cards. **$$**

⌂ **Corniche Hotel** [96 A3] (53 rooms) PO Box 1800, PC 114, Jibroo; ☏24 714707, 714636; e corniche_hotel@mjsoman.com. This hotel is in an excellent spot on the Muttrah corniche with superb views, an adequate restaurant & friendly staff. The sgl rooms have a shower only. Although the hotel is worn & tired-looking it offers a welcome bed for the night in a beautiful historic location. It is unlicensed & parking can be limited at times, There are a few chained parking spaces directly in front of the hotel, which can be reserved & unchained on request, or you can park directly opposite in front of the fish souk. Accepts credit cards. **$$**

🏠 **Hotel Golden Oasis** [map pages 72–3] (62 rooms) PO Box 353, PC 117, Al Wadi Al Kabir; 📞24 811655, 814062; e hotgoldn@omantel.net. om; www.hotelgoasis.com. This hotel is rated 2-star & is located on the road to Al Bustan. To get here, exit the highway at Al Wadi Al Kabir roundabout (about 25mins from the airport) & follow Al Wadi Al Kabir Street, which is the road running parallel to Al Bustan Street. It is on your left-hand side. The hotel has a licensed bar & 3 licensed restaurants with live entertainment: Mer-Maid Bar, Captain's Café, Ubar Restaurant & Cleopatra Restaurant. This makes a good base for divers using the Oman Dive Centre, a 5min drive away. The hotel provides a shuttle service & can organise courses & dive trips. Accepts credit cards. **$$**

🏠 **Ibis Muscat** [117 B4] (171 rooms) Dohat Al Adab Rd, Al Khuwair; 📞24 489890; www.ibis.com. Functional & neutral but comfortable & clean hotel with all-day restaurant & 24hr bar with snacks. **$$**

🏠 **Marina Hotel** [96 A2] (20 rooms) PO Box 500, PC 114, Muttrah; 📞24 713100, 714343, 711711; no direct website, but can be reserved through www.booking.com. The 3-star Marina is arguably the best of the hotels along Muttrah corniche & has a good restaurant, Dolphins Bar & Shark Night Club, all licensed. Even if you don't stay here, do take a trip up to the terrace floor 'P', where the restaurant & bar are located, for a fantastic view over the port, the corniche & the minarets of the mosques. Accepts credit cards. **$$**

🏠 **Qurum Beach Hotel** [113 G1] (64 rooms) PO Box 2148, PC 112, Ruwi; 📞24 564070; e qurumbeachhotel@hotmail.com. Located at Qurum Heights, this hotel provides good cheap accommodation & is in a great location with plentiful parking. Up the road to the entrance it is almost African in feel, on account of all the greenery around. It also has 2- or 3-bedroom apts, an international restaurant (Maymoon) & two licensed nightclubs either side, which can be a bit noisy into the early hours. Still, there's a real sense of the holiday feel about the place. The hotel will store your excess baggage if you are taking short trips up or down the country. Members of staff are friendly, professional & accommodating. You are a short walk away from the fantastic stretch of beach that runs from the Crowne Plaza Hotel all the way up past the Grand

Hyatt & InterContinental hotels. Fantastic value for money. Accepts credit cards. **$$**

🏠 **Ramee Guestline Hotel** [113 G1] (102 rooms) PO Box 191, PC 113, Muscat; 📞24 564443; www.rameehotels.com. This hotel has traditional Omani-style architecture & is in a good location close to Qurum Beach. It has an international licensed restaurant (Yamamah). Sea View Grill restaurant at rooftop. Accepts credit cards. **$$**

🏠 **Sun City Hotel** [108 B5] (35 rooms) Al-Jaame St, Ruwi; 📞24 789801. A bright modern hotel with big windows & spacious rooms right next to the Ruwi main bus station, making it convenient if you have a bus to catch. Friendly staff. **$$**

🏠 **Al Fanar Hotel** [96 A2] (48 rooms) PO Box 3738, PC 112, Ruwi; 📞24 712385, 713142; e alfanar@omantel.net.om. This grubby 1-star hotel is located in the group that sits at the end of the Muttrah corniche. It has an unlicensed restaurant. **$**

🏠 **Al Mina Hotel** [96 A3] (28 rooms) PO Box 504, PC 112, Ruwi; 📞24 711828; e minahotl@ omantel.net.om. Set on Muttrah corniche & offering scenic views, this hotel is rated 1-star by the Ministry of Tourism. Al Bahar & Al Safina are its licensed restaurants, serving Indian & continental cuisine. Accepts credit cards. **$**

🏠 **Al Nahdha Hotel** [96 B2] (48 rooms) PO Box 1561, PC 114, Jibroo; 📞24 714196; e alnahdhaa@ muscatcityhotels.com. Set on the Muttrah corniche with sea views & about 30km from Muscat Airport. There is a restaurant serving oriental & Arabic food, & a snack bar. Rendezvous is the rooftop garden, which has splendid views of the harbour (for private parties). **$**

🏠 **Naseem Hotel** [96 B3] (29 rooms) PO Box 360, PC 114, Jibroo; 📞24 712418. Located on the Muttrah corniche, close to the souk, all the very clean rooms have baths. There is no restaurant but it does provide room service with food from nearby eateries. Ask for a sea-facing room. **$**

HOTEL APARTMENTS

🏠 **ASAS Oman Hotel Apartments** [113 G1] (35 apts) PO Box 191, PC 113; 📞24 568515; e asasoman@omantel.net.om. Located at Qurum, near Qurum Natural Park, this complex comprises fully furnished en-suite apts, all with AC, equipped kitchens, washing machines, satellite TV, 24hr reception, daily housekeeping service, phone, business centre, temperature-controlled swimming pool & car park. There is disabled access & pets are allowed. There is also an unlicensed restaurant. Accepts credit cards. **$$$**

🏠 **Al Khuwair Hotel Apartments** [117 D4] (9 apts) PO Box 121, PC 115, Madinat Qaboos; ☎ 24 478171. This is one of 4 properties owned by the Safeer Hotels & Tourism Company (the others

are Safeer Plaza Hotel, Nuzha Hotel Apartments & Ghaba Resthouse). Large but run-down rooms. **$$**

🏠 **Safeer Plaza Hotel Appts** [117 C4] (44 suites) Al Kuliya St, Al Khuwair; ☎ 24 471000; www.safeerplazahotel-muscat.com. Big rooms, good value & service. 15mins from the airport. International restaurant. Car rental, packed lunches & tour desk in reception. **$$**

✕ WHERE TO EAT

Dispersed around the city are plenty of restaurants offering cuisines from around the globe. In addition to the ubiquitous Arabic and Indian cuisine, American, African, Chinese, French, Greek, Italian, Japanese, Mexican, Middle Eastern, Mongolian and Thai can all be found.

Most of the upmarket restaurants are situated within the five-star hotels, but other excellent places, like D'Arcy's Kitchen in the Jawaharat A'Shaati shopping complex, the Pavo Real (Mexican), the Mumtaz Mahal (Indian) or the Golden Oryx (Chinese/ Thai), for example, are independent. While hotel restaurants are usually licensed to serve alcohol, not all of the independents are, so you might like to check this before making your choice. See pages 79–85 for brief information on hotel restaurants – the star rating of the hotel generally reflects the price range of the restaurant.

The restaurants below are the ones outside of hotels and are in price-range order.

INDEPENDENT RESTAURANTS
Mid-range

✕ **Bellapais Restaurant** [map pages 72–3] ☎ 24 521100; ⏰ 12.00–15.00 & 18.00–23.00 Sat–Thu, 18.00–23.00 Fri. Located in the Rusail commercial complex, this pleasant licensed restaurant serves Greek cuisine, & offers take-aways & home delivery. Your steak is cooked at your table for you. **$$$**

✕ **Blue Marlin** [103 C2] ☎ 24 737288, 737291; e marina@omantel.net.om; www.marinaoman. net; ⏰ 09.30–23.00 Sun–Thu, 08.30–23.00 Fri, 08.00–23.00 Sat. Set within the marina complex at Marina Bander Al Rowdha, this international seafood restaurant is licensed, & you don't have to be a member to access it. Very popular al fresco breakfast buffets by the pool. **$$$**

✕ **The Golden Oryx** [108 B3] ☎ 24 702266, 706128; e goryx@omantel.net.om; ⏰ 12.00–15.00 & 19.30–midnight Sat–Thu, closed Fri. Located on Al Burj St, Ruwi, this licensed restaurant has an extensive menu including Cantonese, Schezwan, Beijing, Mongolian & Thai. It is also good for vegetarians. Dimly lit, it has a peaceful, pleasant atmosphere with instrumental versions of familiar songs playing softly in the background. The food is good, & the waiters are consistently

efficient & friendly. The Thai Pavilion at the back provides a nice, private spot for dining. Highly recommended. **$$$**

✕ **Mumtaz Mahal** [113 G3] ☎ 24 605907, 607103; ⏰ 12.00–14.30 & 19.00–23.30 Sat–Thu, 13.00–15.00 & 19.00–midnight Fri. Partly because of its hilltop location, which provides an elevated view over Qurum Natural Park & the city, & partly because of its good food, its ambience, its faultless waiter service, its dim lighting, & its very reasonable prices, this award-winning Indian restaurant is one of the best in Muscat. There is a good wine list, but if you are keeping an eye on costs, the carafe of house wine is cheap & easy to drink. From around 21.00, Indian musicians play softly on the low-level stage which fronts a calming waterfall feature. **$$$**

✕ **Murchi Curry House** [113 G1] Set within the Ramee Guestline Hotel. Offers excellent curry, is licensed, has good service & a pleasant atmosphere with live Indian music. **$$$**

✕ **O Sole Mio** [113 D3] ☎ 24 601343; ⏰ 12.00–16.45 & 19.00–23.00 Sat–Thu, 18.45–23.00 Fri. This is an excellent Italian restaurant with an extensive wine list & a live Filipino 2-piece band. On Shatti Al Qurum. **$$$**

✘ **Passage to India** [map pages 72–3]
✎24 568480, 563452; ⊕ 12.00–15.00 & 19.00–
23.30 Sat–Thu, evenings only Fri. This licensed
restaurant is located behind the Hatat House
compound, near Wadi Adai roundabout [map
pages 72–3]. Both the food & service are excellent
here, & there is an open kitchen where you can
watch your fresh bread & superb tender meats
being cooked. $$$
✘ **Pavo Real** [115 inset] ✎24 602603;
⊕ 12.00–15.00 & 18.00–midnight Sat–Thu,
evenings only Fri. A fun, licensed Mexican
restaurant at Madinat Qaboos with live music,
where friendly, attentive & smartly dressed waiters
serve you great food. Do go here for a good fun
night out. Try the cocktails! $$$
✘ **The Candle Bar** [113 A4] On the beachfront
just east of the Hyatt, this place has a terrace right
by the sea & offers simple food like mixed grill &
sandwiches. It is unlicensed but has very good
juices. The atmosphere is relaxing, a perfect place
to smoke *sheesha* or watch big football matches
with local people. In summer they rig up fans to
keep you cool. $$
✘ **D'Arcy's Kitchen** [113 D3] ⊕ 08.30–23.00.
This cheerful place, with its comfortable bamboo
chairs set out on the pavement, is open all day
long seven days a week, serving everything from
breakfast & light snacks to full meals. Housed
in the Jawaharat A'Shaati Complex near the
InterContinental Hotel. $$
✘ **Golden Dragon** [115 inset] ✎24 697374;
⊕ 12.00–15.00 & 19.00–23.30 Sat–Thu,
13.00–15.00 & 19.00–23.30 Fri. A licensed Chinese
& Thai restaurant in Madinat as Sultan Qaboos
(MQ) behind the shopping complex, offering a nice
ambience & décor. Also does take-aways. $$
✘ **Nuovo La Terrazza** [map pages 72–3]
✎24 571126; ⊕ 19.30–midnight daily. A good
Italian located behind Hatat House, close to the
Passage to India (see above). $$
✘ **Odyssey** [104 C3] ✎99 379031; ⊕ 07.00–
16.30 & 18.00–22.00 daily. Located at the
Oman Dive Centre, Bander Al Jissah, serving an
international menu. $$

Budget

✘ **Copper Chimney** [108 C4] ✎24 706420,
780207; ⊕ 12.00–15.00 & 19.00–midnight Sat–
Thu, 13.00–15.00 & 19.00–midnight Fri. Located
inside Fair Trade House in the Central Business

District (opposite British Bank), serving good
Indian food, licensed. $$
✘ **Grill House Co** [117 G2] Souk El Mal;
⊕ 09.00–21.00. Serves excellent buffets during
Ramadan. Very clean. Highly recommended. $$
✘ **Kamat** [map page 98, 108 B3, 117 E3]
✎24 479243, 793355, 783300; ⊕ 10.00–13.00
& 17.30–23.00 daily. Located in Khuwair/RexRd/
Ruwi. An award-winning Indian restaurant. $$
✘ **Kargeen Caffe** [115 inset] ✎24 692269;
e kargeen@hotmail.com or info@kargeencaffe.com;
www.kargeencaffe.com; ⊕ 09.30–15.00 & 17.00–
01.00. There are 3 of these vegetarian restaurants in
town, but the unique gem is located in the Madinat
Qaboos Shopping Centre area, within one of the
courtyards. This unlicensed café is segregated into
separate outdoor eating areas, some al fresco, some
tented, screened (to enable AC units to function),
benched & cushioned, some for traditional eating
at floor level, some for families, & some for smoking
shisha. Overall it imparts a real sense of being in
traditional Arabia. An attractive labyrinth & a true
oasis, where the bread & food on the international
menu is cooked outdoors in full view. The two other
Kargeen outlets are in City Plaza (at Al Khuwair) & Al
Harthy complex (in Qurum), but these are indoor &
not half as interesting. $$
✘ **Khana Khazana** [108 C4] ✎24 813466;
⊕ 12.15–15.15 & 19.00–23.30. Indian, Chinese
& Tandoori restaurant behind Pizza Hut in Ruwi
Souk St. $$
✘ **Khyber** [108 C4] ✎24 781901; ⊕ 12.00–
15.00 & 19.00–midnight. Indian cuisine in the
CBD, next to National Bank of Oman, licensed. $$
✘ **Morning Rose** [108 C4] ✎24 785960. Behind
Air India in the CBD in Ruwi, serving Indian, Arabic
& Chinese cuisine. $$
✘ **Al Deyar Restaurant & Cafe** [113 B3]
✎24 696247; ⊕ Sat–Thu. This local budget
restaurant occupies a good location close to the sea
(opposite Al Shatti Plaza). $
✘ **Automatic Restaurant** [117 C4] Qurum
(✎24 561500), Al Khuwair, behind the Radisson
Blu (✎24 487200) & Seeb (✎24 424343);
⊕ 12.00–midnight Sat–Thu, 13.00–midnight
Fri. Award-winning Lebanese food chain
restaurant serving Arabian, Mediterranean &
Lebanese food. Good servings & prices, but an
uninspiring name. $
✘ **Bin Ateeq** [117 B3] ✎24 603225. Open all
day, 7 days a week. Traditional Omani food. Next to

Shell petrol station on the Khuwair slip road. The Bin Ateeq restaurants (one in Muscat, one in Nizwa & one in Salalah) are highly recommended. They are very reasonable in price, & offer good tasty food served in the traditional Omani way at floor level. Some say the novelty of eating on the floor can soon wear off, but it is worth a try if your limbs permit. $

✕ **China Town** [110 A5] ☎24 567974; ⊕ 11.00–15.00 & 18.00–midnight Sat–Thu, 13.00–15.00 & 18.00–midnight Fri. Located at the Capital Commercial Centre (CCC) in Qurum, serving good Chinese food. $

✕ **Golden Spoon** [117 C3] ☎24 482263, 478215; ⊕ 11.30–15.30 & 18.00–midnight Sat–Thu, 13.00–15.30 & 18.00–midnight Fri. Located on the Khuwair slip road, between the ice skating rink & the Shell petrol station, near McDonald's, serving good Chinese & Indian food. Also at Seeb souk (☎24 424204). $

✕ **Intaqiah** [96 C4] ⊕ All day daily. On Muttrah Street within 100m of the back entrance to Muttrah Souq this low budget place is best after dark when its garden is attractively illuminated. It serves set meals freshly made every day, free of the constraints of a menu, accompanied by a selection of salads & *mezze*. $

✕ **Jean's Grill** [110 B6] ☎24 567666; ⊕ 07.00–23.30 daily. Located inside the Sultan Centre & upstairs at Qurum, this restaurant/café serves good buffet b/fasts. $

✕ **Woodlands Restaurant** [108 C5] ☎24 700192; ⊕ 12.00–15.00 & 18.30–23.30. Located in the CBD in the Europcar Building, serving Indian cuisine, licensed. $

Fast food

✕ **Happy Days** [117 C4] Near the Radisson Blu, serving burgers & *shisha*. $

✕ **Hardees** [map pages 72–3] At Qurum, Al Khuwair slip road, near airport roundabout, Ruwi, Seeb & Muscat City Centre food court. Chicken fillet served in a variety of ways. $

✕ **KFC** [108 C5] At Qurum, Al Khuwair slip road, Muscat City Centre food court, Ruwi High St, Seeb, near airport roundabout, Azaiba roundabout, Lulu Centre in Ghubra & Madina Plaza. $

✕ **McDonald's** [113 C4 & 117 B3] Behind the CCC at Qurum, Al Khuwair, Muscat City Centre food court, Ghala, Seeb & Saruj Complex. Selling the usual array of burgers, with the addition of the McArabia grilled kofta. $

✕ **Magic Wok Good** [map pages 72–3] Chinese fast food at Muscat City Centre food court. $

✕ **Papa John's Pizza** [115 C4] Serving pizza, in Ruwi CBD & Al-Madina Plaza, Madinat Qaboos. $

✕ **Pizza Hut** [108 C4 & 113 inset] 14 branches in Oman. Eat-in, take-away or home delivery. $

✕ **Pizza Muscat** [110 B6] At Al Khuwair & Al Harthy Complex in Qurum, serving pizza made with halal meat, salads & lasagne. $

✕ **Santino's Bistro Italiano** [113 D3] In Jawaharat A'Shatti & in Muscat City Centre food court. Serving antipasti, pizza, pasta, *calzone*, *risotti* & *insalata zuppa*. $

✕ **Shamiana** [map pages 72–3] At Muscat City Centre food court. Serving fast Indian food. $

✕ **Taza** [map pages 72–3] At Al Khuwair. Serving a burger with a difference in toasted *ciabatta*. $

PUB FOOD There are many pub-like bars inside the hotels and generally these all serve bar food. Again, the star rating of the hotel usually reflects the price bracket. **Churchill's** in the Muscat Holiday Inn (see page 83), **Duke's Bar** in the Crowne Plaza (see page 81), **Al Ghazal** in the InterContinental (see page 81), **Club Safari** in the Grand Hyatt (see page 80) and **Feeney's** in the Sheraton Qurum Beach Resort (see page 82) are some of the bars popular with expats and locals alike. The **Up Town** restaurant is like an English pub and located on Rex Road, Ruwi (☎ 24 706020).

COFFEE SHOPS Both **Costa Coffee** [113 B3] and **Starbucks** [113 F2] have a large presence in Muscat now, with outlets at Madinat Qaboos (MQ), Jawharat A'Shatti, Shatti al Qurum (beach road to the Crowne Plaza Hotel), Muscat City Centre food court, Muscat Airport, Lulu in Ghubra, **Oasis by the Sea** [113 D3] (Shatti al Qurum) and Al Asfoor Plaza in Qurum. Starbucks and **Marina Café** [113 F2] are the two coffee shops with an excellent location on the beach road running from Shatti al Qurum up to the Crowne Plaza Hotel.

ENTERTAINMENT AND NIGHTLIFE

BARS AND PRIVATE CLUBS There are no independent bars as such. Instead you will find 'pubs' and bars inside hotels and private clubs.

You can access a private club only as a guest of a member. If you are lucky enough to have Omani or expat acquaintants, then you can get food and drink in these clubs for a fraction of the amount you pay in the hotels. A couple of these are **Muscat Rugby Club** [117 G4] (*Al Khuwair;* ☎ *24 604890*) and **Civil Aviation Recreational Club (CARC)** [off map page 119 A1] (*Azaiba Beach;* ☎ *24 519424*).

CINEMAS Films are shown in the capital in English, Arabic, Hindi, Tamil and Malayalam. The cinemas listed below all show films in English.

🎬 **Al Shatti Plaza** [113 B3/4] Shatti al Qurum; ☎ 24 607360, 692656; ⊕ 13.30–midnight
🎬 **Ruwi Cinema** [108 C5] Ruwi; ☎ 24 780380; ⊕ 09.00–13.00 & 17.00–23.00

🎬 **Star Cinema** [108 C3] Central Business District, Ruwi; ☎ 24 791641; ⊕ 14.30–00.30
🎬 **Markaz al Bahja Cinema** Al Khoud; ☎ 24 540855; ⊕ 13.30–02.00

NIGHTCLUBS

☆ **Al Hamra** [103 D4] Al Bustan Palace Hotel; ☎ 24 799666
☆ **Saba Nightclub** [108 D4] Sheraton Oman Hotel; ☎ 24 799899

☆ **Sur Nightclub** [113 D3] InterContinental Hotel; ☎ 24 600500
☆ **Copacabana** [113 A4] Grand Hyatt Hotel; ☎ 24 641234

SHOPPING

Evening shopping is a popular pastime with Omani families. There are several modern, air-conditioned **shopping complexes** mainly in the Qurum area, where the highway splits [map page 110]. Each of these complexes, malls or plazas has its own selection of cafés, food courts and play areas and amusements for children, as well as fashion shops, upmarket brand-name products (such as watches and sunglasses), computer shops, sportswear outlets, CDs and DVDs, photographic retailers, electronics, perfumes, florists, opticians, interior design shops, artisanal handmade furniture and gifts, internet cafés, cards and bookshops, footwear, beauty products (for further details see pages 109 and 112). Among the biggest and most modern malls are Qurum Commercial Centre [110 A5] near the

Qurum interchange and Muscat City Centre [map pages 72–3], out past Muscat International Airport, with a gigantic car park and the French supermarket Carrefour as its anchor. There are small, modern souks in this mall and in the Sabco Centre [110 A5] and Capital Commercial Centre [110 A5], if you haven't the time to visit the real thing in Muttrah. The best English language bookshops are Family Bookshop and Magrudy's.

SUPERMARKETS The supermarkets (dotted about everywhere) have a fantastic selection of fresh fruit and vegetables, fresh breads and hot ready-to-go foods.

Al Fair is an excellent chain of supermarkets worth a browse around, especially if you fancy taking a picnic to the beach or into the mountains. Grab a hot rotisserie chicken, Arabic bread and hummus, *taboule* salad, fruits and cold drinks, and head to any close destination (there is plenty of spare beach available). Simply driving the short distance from Al Fair at A'Saruj to Al Shatti Street (the beach road leading up to the Crowne Plaza), parking the car and eating on the beach is great fun. Al Fairs are dotted about throughout the city, another one being at Madinat Qaboos shopping area.

The **Lulu** [108 B1 & 117 A4] chain has some excellent hypermarkets here, one near the Bait Al Falaj flyover/roundabout, another by the Ghubra flyover/roundabout (on the mountain side of the highway) and one at Darsait.

BAKERIES Branches of both the **Muscat Bakery** and **Switz** chains are dotted around the capital and the country and are worth a peek. Try those on the Khuwair slip road, in Ghubra, or Ruwi. You're never far away from a Muscat Bakery.

TAILORS Tailors' outlets too are ubiquitous. Virtually every parade of back-street shops in the city has its collection. Try Ruwi, Khuwair or Ghubra. You can take in an article of clothing and they will copy it for you very cheaply in a material of your choice, in no time at all; or, alternatively, select a design from their range of catalogues.

ART AND ARTEFACT GALLERIES AND SHOPS

Abu Qais Decoration and Trading Co [117 G2] Qurum, near Madinat Qaboos; ✆ 24 699956. Art exhibitions by local artists, Omani handicrafts.

Al Madina Art Gallery [115 C4] Rd 2, Villa 1691, Madinat Qaboos; ✆ 24 691380. Selling prints, watercolours & oils.

Bait al Muzna Gallery [map page 98] Old Muscat; ✆ 24 739204; e baitmgal@omantel.net. om; www.baitmuznagallery.com; ☉ 09.30–13.30 & 16.30–20.00 Sun–Thu, closed Fri & Sat. Opposite Bait al Zubair Museum in a traditional Omani villa, this gallery showcases both contemporary & traditional art by local & international artists.

Bait Al Turath [117 C2] Al Omani; ✆ 24 593719; ☉ 07.30–14.30 Sun–Thu, closed Fri & Sat. In a shopping plaza by the Porsche showroom in lower Al Khuwair by the ministries. Sponsored by the Omani Ministry of Heritage & Culture, this place offers traditional weaving, pottery & other crafts.

The Gallery [110 B6] Al Harthy Complex, Qurum; ✆ 24 562269. Selling fine art, originals & prints.

Jibreen Art Gallery [110 A5] Al Araimi Complex; ✆ 24 796925. Selling fine art, originals & prints.

Lamsat Al Khuwair; ✆ 24 698338. Selling paintings by local artist Saleem bin Sakhi.

Majid Trading Enterprises [110 A5 & B6] ✆ 24 563098, 562370. Located in Al Araimi Complex, Al Harthy Complex & inside the Grand Hyatt.

Majlis Gallery [off map 119 A1] St 44, Villa 57, Azaiba; ✆ 24 501057. Selling Arabian & colonial antiques, Omani chests, silver jewellery, coffee tables, frankincense candles.

Marina [110 A5] Al Araimi Complex, Qurum; ✆ 24 562221; www.marinagulf.com. Also in Muscat City Centre (✆ 24 537055) & in Jawharat a'Shatti (✆ 24 698884). Stocks rustic wooden furniture & other unique furnishings. Arranges international shipping.

Murtada AK Trading [96 B4] Al Noor market, Muttrah Souk; ☎24 711632, 793248. Selling original paintings by Omani artists, gifts, handicrafts & jewellery.

National Trading Co [115 B4] Al Inshirah St, MQ; ☎24 601066. Near the British Council, selling restored Arabian & Asian furniture, chests, doors, tables, Omani silver jewellery & weaponry.

Omani Heritage Gallery [113 D3] Jawaharat A'Shati Commerical Complex, Shati al Qu'rum; ☎24 696974. Selling Omani handicrafts made by Omani Artisans, a non-profit organisation. Very good for gifts & souvenirs, from jewellery to T-shirts with turtle motifs.

Raj Relics [119 D2] Ghubra; ☎24 593131; m 99 329842. Behind Bahar soap factory (near The Chedi Hotel), selling antique & reproduction furniture, Indian & Omani chests, antique doors, dining & coffee tables & artefacts.

Riqwa Oman [113 D3] InterContinental Hotel; ☎24 600500. Selling fine art & limited-edition prints.

SA Halela [96 B4] Behind Muttrah Souk; ☎24 712627. Selling original paintings by Indian artists.

Sabco Souk [110 A5] Sabco Commercial Centre, Qurum; ☎24 563943. Selling handicrafts & artefacts. Haggling expected.

Tamimah Gallery [map page 98] Muscat Old Town; ☎24 737683. Selling Omani antiques, chests, weaponry & silver jewellery. Phone for an appointment.

Yitti Art Gallery [110 A5] Al Khamis Plaza & CBD; ☎24 796073, 785696. Selling fine art, limited-edition prints & maps of Arabia.

OTHER PRACTICALITIES

USEFUL TELEPHONE NUMBERS
Hospitals
✚ **Khoula Hospital** ☎24 563625, 560455
✚ **Muscat Hospital** ☎24 738036
✚ **Al Nahdha Hospital** ☎24 707800, 837800
✚ **Quriyat Hospital** ☎24 645003

✚ **Royal Hospital** [119 B5] ☎24 592888, 599000, 590491
✚ **Al Shatti Hospital** ☎24 604263
✚ **Sultan Qaboos Hospital** ☎24 211151

MISSIONS
UNICEF PO Box 3787, PC 112, Ruwi; ☎24 602624, 601398; location: 1st Fl, Al Khuwair National Automobiles Bldg (BMW)

WHO PO Box 1889, PC 112, Ruwi; ☎24 600989, 602177, 605860; location: Ministry of Health Bldg

MEDIA AND COMMUNICATIONS
Post and courier services Post offices can be found in all residential districts and this is by far the cheapest way of sending letters, postcards or gifts home, costing just baizas rather than rials. Post offices are open generally from 08.00–14.00. As is common throughout the Middle East, post is delivered to PO box numbers, not direct to people's houses, and the onus is on them to come and collect their post from their local post office.

DHL [108 C4] Rumaila Bldg, 106 Sultan Qaboos St, Wattayah, PO Box 818, Al Hamriya 131, Muscat 112; ⊕ 07.00–21.00 Sat–Thu, 09.00–18.00 Fri.

FedEx [110 B5] Sinaw Hse, opposite Al Nahda Hospital; ☎24 793311. FedEx is represented in Oman by a service contractor. For further information call Oman Postal Express (☎24 833311).

Internet Internet cafés can generally be found within the shopping complexes at Qurum [110 A5] and Al Khuwair [117 D4], as well as within some residential areas in the rows of smaller shops on the street. These all charge far less than the business centres of the hotels.

WHAT TO SEE AND DO

There is a variety of things to see and do in the Capital Area, including scuba diving, dolphin-, whale- and birdwatching, *dhow* cruising, fishing, watersports, sailing, beach walking and jogging (for further information see pages 123–6). There are museums, mosques and forts to visit, or you can shop in the souks and modern shopping complexes. You can opt for a tour with one of the many tour operators (see pages 76–8) or hire a car and travel independently (see page 54). For the less active, there are endless beaches and bays within the capital that are crying out for you to relax, perhaps with a picnic. Or if you don't want to move, there is the beach or pool of your hotel. Public beaches tend not to have any facilities, just long stretches of flat sand, so be sure to take your own sun protection as there will be no shade. If you want to use the beaches of the big hotels, which are equipped with beach shades and showers, you can do so but at a price, usually around RO10 for a sunlounger for the day.

Birdwatching Birdwatching sites in the capital include Qurum Natural Park [113 F2], Al Ansab Lagoons, the gardens of the InterContinental (see page 81) and Grand Hyatt (see page 80) hotels, and any of the beaches.

In Qurum Natural Park species such as the purple sunbird, Indian silverbill, laughing dove, Indian roller, little green bee-eater, yellow-vented bulbul, graceful prinia, grey francolin, the common mynah and the house crow are likely to be spotted. On the beaches species such as western reef heron, swift tern and sooty gull will undoubtedly be seen. For further detailed information, the publications by Hanne and Jens Eriksen are highly recommended (for details see *Appendix 3*, page 299). Speak to any tour operator in the capital if you would like to join a set birding excursion.

DIVING

Dive sites Al Munassir wreck was offered by the Royal Navy of Oman for an artificial reef project and was sunk on 22 April 2003. It is a short boat trip from Marina Bander al Rowdha. Fahal Island, 4km offshore, is also a short ride away.

Diving here involves finning through an L-shaped tunnel through the island. There are many corals to be seen and the area attracts numerous sharks. Other popular dive sites include Cemetery Bay, Cat Island, just off the coast of the Marine Science and Fisheries Centre at Sidab, and the Kalbou area (east of Muttrah harbour). East of Al Bustan Palace Hotel (see page 79) there are the three bay areas of Bander Jissah, Bander Khayran and As Sheik. Any dive centre will provide you with further information.

Dive centres

⛵ **Muscat Diving & Adventure Centre** [113 A4] The Boat House, Grand Hyatt, Muscat, Shatti al Qurum; ☎ 24 602101; e diveco@omantel.net; www.holiday-in-oman.com. Operating from the beach of the Grand Hyatt & offering all of the stock dive tours around Muscat.

⛵ **Oman Dive Centre/Extra Divers Muscat** [104 C3] Barr Al Jissah; ☎ 24 824240–1, 99 379031; e muscat@extra-divers.li or info@omandivecenter.com; www.omandivecenter.com. Located in its own

peaceful bay, the Oman Dive Centre is a PADI Gold Palm 5-star resort & is managed by Extra Divers Worldwide. They have 4 custom-made boats & offer 1 dive RO15; 2 tank dives RO25; night dive RO15 (min 4 people); snorkelling RO12/6 am/pm. Courses include Discover Scuba (full day) RO36; Open Water diver (3–4 days) RO150; Advanced Open Water (5 dives) RO120. Dolphin watching RO17; coastal cruise RO17. For dives, proof of dive certification & logbook are required. It has 35 AC, equipped, traditional Omani *barasti* beach huts in which you can stay (RO35/40/45 low/mid/high season, includes b/fast & dinner, under 12s half price). There is a licensed restaurant called The Odyssey (⊕ *07.00–16.30 & 18.00–22.00*). To get there follow the road towards Al Bustan Palace.

As you descend the hill take the right-hand exit directing you to Qantab. This road winds up & over the mountains, towards the Shangri-La resort. When you come to the first roundabout take a left. This leads down to the dive centre. Camping is no longer permitted here.

HEALTH CLUBS Health and fitness clubs and gyms can be found in most of the hotels in Oman and, as expected, the standards vary according to the star rating of the venue. If you are resident in the country you can arrange annual membership at most of the clubs. If you are a guest, then usage is included in your room rate. Non-guests can use the gym and pool facilities of most hotels for the day, for a charge of approximately RO8 per person plus taxes – check with the specific venue.

BOWLING There is City Bowling [117 B3] (✆ *24 541277*) opposite the Holiday Inn Hotel in Al Khuwair, and one in Al Hail in the Markaz al Bahja. The Sheraton Hotel (see page 81) at Ruwi has a bowling alley (✆ *24 772772*) and a further bowling centre has been constructed opposite the Saruj Centre in Shatti al Qurum.

GOLF 'Brown' (sand) golf courses exist in Muscat. The first 18-hole green golf course on offer to the tourist in the Capital Area is the Muscat Hills Golf and Country Club [map pages 72–3] (*www.muscathillsgolf.com*). This is an internationally recognised PGA championship-standard golf course, with facilities for world-class tournaments, and is also the first full green golf course in Oman (there is a 9-hole green golf course at the Crowne Plaza, Salalah). There is a clubhouse, a restaurant, swimming pools, tennis and squash courts, as well as a driving range and a 9-hole practice course.

HORSERIDING [map page 121] The Royal Stables at Seeb (✆ *24 420444*) are considered one of the top riding arenas for watching equestrian events, although the best breeders and trainers are located in the Al Kamil and Al Wafi regions in the Sharqiya. The Royal Stables offers horseriding lessons and trails. Riding groups are kept small, in the interests of safety, and are accompanied by an experienced guide.

Other riding schools are based within easy reach of Muscat, at Qurum Natural Park and by the sea:

Qurum Equestrian School [113 F2] Qurum Natural Park; ✆ 99 832199. Signposted once inside the park. For an hour's ride it is RO10, but if there is a group of you, this reduces to RO8 pp, with a maximum of 6 people in the group.
Al Sawahil Horse Riding [113 F1] ✆ 95 177557; e ahmad-565@hotmail.com; ⊕ 16.00–19.00. Located at the seaside, behind the park, at Al Bahja, Al Hail. RO8 per hour for lessons; beach RO14 per hour for a ride along the beach. Beginners welcome.

Shah Mohammed al Khalili [113 F2] Qurum Natural Park; ✆ 99 386978. Shah Mohammed will meet you & your group at the main gate of the park. Beginners are welcome & can take a ride through the park & along the beach for RO10. For the more experienced, the ride can be tailored. An experienced guide accompanies all rides. Lessons are also available at RO12, but if you have a group of 4 people (which is the max for a group ride), this reduces to RO8.
Seeb Horse Riding Centre [113 F2] ✆ 24 603501, 694303. Horseriding trails.

ICE SKATING
Al Khuwair Centre Ice Rink [117 C3] ✆ 24 489492. Regular sessions 09.00–20.00 Sat–Thu, 11.30–20.00 Fri. Sessions cost RO2.50 including skates.

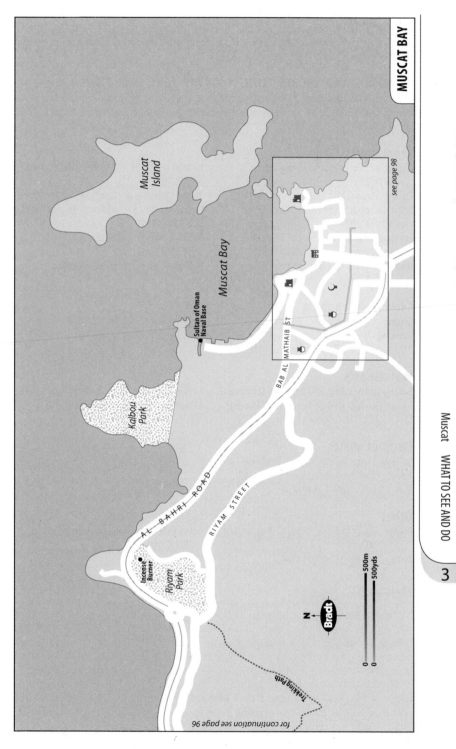

Muscat Island

Muscat Bay

Sultan of Oman
Naval Base

Kalbou
Park

AL BAHRI ROAD

RIYAM STREET

BAB AL MATHAIB ST

see page 98

Incense
Burner

Riyam
Park

Trekking Path

for continuation see page 96

N

Bradt

0   500m
0   500yds

MOTORSPORTS Oman Automobile Association in Seeb, (⚲ *24 510239, 510630, 522177; www.omanauto.org*) offers a range of go-karts, motorbikes, motorcross/dirt bikes, rallies.

ACTIVITIES AND SPORTS CLUBS FOR THE LONG-STAY VISITOR For those planning a longer stay in Oman, or, more specifically, in Muscat, there are excellent health clubs attached to the larger hotels, which you can join. There are also several sports clubs:

Team sports

Basketball Oman Basketball Association ⚲24 793802

Cricket Oman Cricket Association ⚲24 703142; British Cricket Club ⚲24 673910; Oman Cricket Club ⚲24 791270

Football Muscat United Football Club ⚲24 542920

Hockey RAH Hockey Club Muscateers ⚲24 675355

Netball PDO ⚲24 675334; Red Devils Costains ⚲24 595011

Rugby Muscat Rugby Club ⚲24 604890; Women's Rugby Team ⚲24 544806; Dhofar Nomads Rugby Club ⚲99 291548

Softball Muscat Softball League ⚲24 680453; m 99 336015, 99 235291

Volleyball Oman Volleyball Association ⚲24 705567

Cycling and running

Cycling Muscat Cycling Club m 99 324594

Running Muscat Hash House Harriers ⚲24 316127; Jebel Hash House Harriers ⚲24 494226;

Oman Athletic Association ⚲24 797233; Muscat Road Runners ⚲24 692903

Watersports

Sailing and boating [103 B2] Beach Catamaran Owners Club ⚲24 604307; Capital Area Yacht Club CAYC ⚲24 737712; Castaways Sailing Club ⚲24

494751; Civil Aviation Yacht & Beach Club ⚲24 519424; Marina Bandar Al Rowdha ⚲24 737288

Racquet games

Squash Muscat Squash League ⚲24 677414

Tennis Oman Tennis Association ⚲24 751402; Muscat Tennis League ⚲24 675210

Other

Bridge Muscat Ladies ⚲24 590167; Muscat Open ⚲24 797597

Darts Oman Darts Club ⚲24 618426

Game fishing Muscat Game Fishing Club m 99 322779

MUTTRAH مطرح

Muttrah is superficially similar to its close neighbour (Muscat Old Town, see page 97) with its bowl-shaped harbour and seafront crescent of impressive merchant houses. Its solitary fort is smaller than the Merani or Jalali forts in Muscat's bay, perched up on a rocky crag guarding the harbour. It has historically been out of bounds to visitors, in use by the military police, but it is now open to the public.

Muttrah has less political significance than Muscat, yet it has always been the larger of the two, with a bigger souk and at least three times the population. The port here was the traditional starting point for commercial caravans to the interior. The city gate was ceremonially shut and guarded at night until the 1970s.

The modern As Sultan Qaboos Port (completed in 1974) has replaced the ancient trading port and now fills most of the bay. The traditional industries of the area include perfumery, the crafting of silver and gold, weaving, textiles and fishing. Muscat gold is 21 and 22 carat. It is not as cheap as in the UAE, but cheaper than in Europe.

Close to the fish roundabout (As Samakah roundabout), at the beginning of the corniche, there is a group of budget hotels grouped together at the very end, and Al Mina Hotel is a little further along the corniche towards the souk (see pages 83–4). It is good to stay in one of these, if only for one night, to get a real sense of being in the Oman of old. Request a room at the front of the hotel for the views up the corniche.

If you need to pick up your emails, there is an internet café just past the Muttrah Souk entrance (400bzs/hr). If you don't want to walk the corniche, taxis are plentiful or you can flag down local microbuses which cruise the corniche or congregate around Muttrah bus station.

WHAT TO SEE
Muttrah Souk [96 B4] (⊕ *08.00–13.00 & 17.00–21.00 Sat–Thu, 17.00–21.00 Fri*) Muttrah Souk (or Souk al Dhalam – Market of Shades) is the oldest souk in Oman and the most popular with visitors. This is probably due, in part, to its accessibility and proximity to the airport (it can easily be visited by short-stay visitors), as well as the fact that it occupies such a scenic location on Muttrah harbour. Since completion of the modernisation project for the corniche for the 35th National Day (in 2005), the souk has been adorned with a domed entrance and is opposite pedestrian traffic lights. So, if you had problems finding the entrance before, you won't now. Once inside, be sure to avoid the Shi'ite Al-Lawatiya district, which is walled and segregated and with clear 'Keep Out' notices. This sect keeps itself apart from visitors and does not welcome intrusion.

The souk consists of a covered intricate labyrinth of stalls, curio shops and winding alleys, more extensive and complex than anywhere else in the country. Indian merchants are predominant. Even in the 1960s you could buy a Chinese tricycle, a Mexican gold sovereign, an old bedstead or a Penguin paperback. The basis of the economy in trading here was selling dates and limes in exchange for cloth, rice and coffee. Today you can buy coffee pots, incense burners, rose-water sprinklers, henna, Arabic coffee, oregano, dried limes, dried chilli peppers, frankincense, perfumes, pashminas, *dishdashas*, antiques, gold, silver, chests, rugs, handicrafts and even the essential Teletubby. *Khanjars* are popular

EASY HILL AND WADI WALK

From the parking area beside the Riyam Park [map page 93] you will notice a brown trekking signpost which is the start of the way-marked walk C38. In the winter months or in the late evening or early morning in the hotter months, this walk along a rocky path is recommended to give you a proper feel for the setting of Muttrah and Muscat, and follows part of the ancient overland route that linked the two places before the arrival of roads and vehicles. The total distance one-way is 2.5km and it takes 90 minutes to two hours, ending behind Muttrah. From the highest points (200m above sea level) you will gain an excellent view over the coast. At one point the path also descends towards an ancient abandoned settlement with its old water cistern and *falaj* irrigation system. The path then approaches the back of Muttrah along a wadi bed.

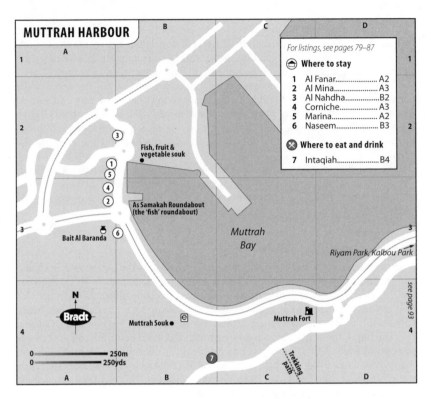

MUTTRAH HARBOUR

For listings, see pages 79–87

⌂ **Where to stay**
1 Al Fanar...................... A2
2 Al Mina...................... A3
3 Al Nahdha.................B2
4 Corniche..................... A3
5 Marina....................... A2
6 Naseem..................... B3

✕ **Where to eat and drink**
7 Intaqiah....................B4

Fish, fruit & vegetable souk

As Samakah Roundabout (the 'fish' roundabout)

Muttrah Bay

Bait Al Baranda

Riyam Park, Kalbou Park

N

Bradt

Muttrah Souk ●

Muttrah Fort

see page 93

0 ——— 250m
0 ——— 250yds

Trekking Path

souvenirs. The aromas from the spices, the incense and the perfume shops evoke an exotic sense of Arabia. In all of the souks, friendly haggling is expected. Try one of the fantastic milkshakes or fruit juices in the air-conditioned juice shops. The souk can get busy in the evenings.

Fish souk [96 B2] Close by the Marina Hotel you can watch the daily catch being sold here between 06.00 and 10.00. The variety on offer is extraordinary and fascinating. The old fish souk was replaced by a newer, more sanitised version in 2013.

Bait Al Baranda [96 A3] (*Al-Mina St, Muttrah;* ☎ *24 714262;* ⊕ *09.00–13.00 & 16.00–18.00 Sun–Thu, 09.00–13.00 Fri; adult RO1*) A new museum in a renovated 1930s house showing the history of Muscat, complete with dinosaur skeleton and many interactive displays. Fun for children.

Riyam Park [map page 93] (⊕ *15.00–midnight Sat–Thu, 08.00–midnight Fri*) This well-maintained park overlooks the sea in the Muttrah area and is clearly landmarked by the large model incense burner that sits atop a cliff. There is a children's playground. It is a grassy peaceful spot to wander around in the early evening.

Kalbou Park [map page 93] (⊕ *15.00–23.00 Sat–Thu, 08.00–midnight Fri*) This smaller park also overlooks the sea at Muttrah, but is located on the seaward edge. Take a left into the small village of Kalbou. Snacks and drinks can be bought here. Again, it is another attractive spot, with more children's playgrounds.

MUSCAT OLD TOWN

The original old town of Muscat, although only small in area, held a strategic commanding position on the entrance to the Persian Gulf, and so was chosen for its excellent harbour and natural defences. Prior to 1929, Muscat was so ringed by steep jagged rocks that it was accessible only by sea or by footpaths over the hills behind, each of which was closely guarded by watchtowers.

The first land approach by vehicle was made possible in 1929 by the hacking out of a one-lane track through the mountains by the British Royal Engineers. The name 'Muscat' means 'place of falling', thought to refer to the falling of the anchor chain (a reference to the harbour).

In the late 1830s one European said of Muscat:

> With all its barrenness and unpromising appearance, such is the advantage of position enjoyed by Muscat, commanding, as it does, the entrance to the Persian Gulf, that its harbours are filled with vessels from all ports of the East, and the busy din of commerce constantly enlivens its streets. In few parts of the world can the necessaries, nay even the luxuries, of life, be obtained in greater profusion.

With such an isolated location it is surprising that Muscat was favoured as the capital city. Muttrah, just a few bays further west, had direct access to the hinterland and was just as good a harbour as Muscat, yet was considered to be a more suitable commercial rather than political capital. Muscat also had very little fresh water within its walls, and the ring of bare hills served as a bowl which magnified the extreme heat and humidity trapped within them, preventing any cooling breezes off the sea from fanning the walled town.

The town walls that stand today were built round about the time of the Portuguese. There were only three gates: the Bab Saghir (small gate) was for pedestrians and donkeys, Bab Kabeer (big gate) was the main gate for smallish vehicles and Bab Mathaib (or Matha'eeb) was the third, used by large vehicles only permitted to drive between Muttrah and Muscat, and even then only with special dispensation granted infrequently. Curfews were imposed on the residents of Muscat; the Bab Kabeer main gate was shut three hours after sunset and could only be opened after that with special written permission from the *wali* (governor). Anyone walking within the walls at this time had to carry a *butti* (a lantern). To ensure everyone remembered, a drum was beaten from the top of Fort Merani for 20 minutes beforehand, followed by three explosions, three hours after sunset. In Muttrah there was one explosion instead of three, and even long after the gate was detached from its wall, it was still ceremonially closed each night because no-one gave the order to stop doing so. Different tribes had responsibility for different gates: the Hawasina provided ten guards each for the Bab Saghir and Bab Mathaib, while the Beni Umr guarded the Bab Kabeer gate.

The Al Bu Said dynasty, of which Sultan Qaboos is the current representative, made Muscat its seat of power in the latter half of the 18th century. The old houses were built c1820–40. Though huge from the outside, they had surprisingly small living spaces, usually just the first floor being habitable with some five rooms. The ground floor tended to be lost to a spacious hall, a small guardroom by the entrance and lots of tiny windowless storerooms. Even the inner walls were massively thick, up to 1m, to help keep the rooms cool in summer. Their design was a mix of Arab, Persian, Indian and African styles. On the flat roof there was generally a raised wooden platform, high enough to give a view over the rampart wall, offering a peaceful spot on summer evenings to catch the breeze.

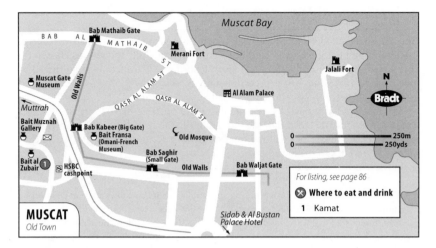

For listing, see page 86

Where to eat and drink

1 Kamat

MUSCAT
Old Town

Until the 1960s most of Muscat's houses were supplied with water by donkeys strapped with pairs of four-gallon tin drums or even by men trudging to and from Wadi Kabeer with goatskins. Only a handful of privileged houses were supplied by private pipelines. As there were no newspapers or radio stations, under Said bin Taimur's rule (Qaboos's father), his only means of communicating with his people was by noticeboard. So the gates of Muscat were utilised, announcing matters to the Omani people. Said bin Taimur's first ever public statement was made by this means in 1968 and was entitled 'the word of Sultan Said bin Taimur, Sultan of Muscat and Oman, about the history of the financial position of the sultanate in the past and the hopes for the future, after the export of oil'. Bin Taimur also had total control over all imports to the country. For example, no car could be imported without his express permission, and there were no tractors in the sultanate because he refused to give permission for them to be imported. Sometimes if he forgot or failed to reply to a request, new businesses which had already invested in buildings were left waiting over six months in limbo, unable, after all, to send reminders to the sultan himself.

GETTING THERE Take the Qurum Heights Road (which is the exit on the right of the highway just before the Qurum roundabout, where the highway splits) and then follow signs to Muscat and Al Madina Sultan Qaboos.

SHIFTING CAPITALS

Throughout its history, Oman's capital has moved locations and, although the dates are unclear, it has at various times been assigned to Qalhat, Sohar, Bahla, Nizwa and Rustaq, according to the various ruling imams and sultans. Muscat has been its capital since 1786, when the third Al Bu Said leader established residence there.

Prior to 1970, Muscat was classed as separate from Oman and the country as a whole was known as Muscat and Oman, Oman being the interior and distinctly different in character from coastal Muscat. Sultan Qaboos – the current ruler – unified the country, naming it simply Oman, and today Muscat is the hub: the site of the main international airport, the embassies, ministries, international banks and large businesses.

SINDBAD'S VOYAGE RECREATED

It was from the harbour of Muscat on 23 November 1980 that Tim Severin's ship, *The Sohar*, set sail as part of Oman's tenth National Day celebrations. It was the start of a 6,000-mile journey to China and took place amid cannon fire, music and tears from every Omani who had been involved in building the remarkable ship. It took 165 days to build, ahead of schedule.

The project had been three years in the planning, and Severin lived in the country for 12 months during the preparations and the building of the boat in Sur. He was given a mansion, rented for him by the Ministry of National Heritage and Culture, in Sur in 1980. The house was built 200 years previously by wealthy Sur merchants, had a large courtyard and was made of crushed coral. He lived in the upper rooms where the original owners would have lived, and even in the height of summer the 3ft-thick walls and wooden shutters kept the rooms cool. When he first arrived, the place was filthy, with goats browsing in the rooms and a cow penned in the yard; it took nearly two weeks for it to be cleaned up by a veritable army of 20 workers. The house was set on slightly raised ground on the foreshore, close enough to walk to the spot where the boat would be built, but too far away to sneak back to during the day.

The boat was built in traditional fashion using timbers held together with coconut rope and painted with fish oil and sugar. Severin went to the coast of Malabar in India (1,300 miles away) to get timber for the ship. All timber for Omani ships had originally come from there, since Oman had always lacked trees large enough to provide first-class boat timber. Severin and his men made excursions into the forest to hand pick the timber, called *aini*, which did not need to be seasoned for boatbuilding.

Severin's boat was named *The Sohar* (which was reputedly Sindbad's birthplace) on the express wish of the sultan, who sponsored the entire project as a tribute to Oman's seafaring heritage.

The journey took a total of seven months to sail to China. The first stretch from Muscat to Calcutta took one month. There was a crew of 28, eight of them Omani traditional sailors, all volunteers. All but one of these married young Muslim girls when they docked in Calcutta – a custom as old as the hills. They never had any intention of returning, but had to pay the girl a sum of money, which her family eagerly accepted. There was no stigma attached, even some pride in fact, and after three years the girls were free to marry again if the husband did not return. Indeed, Sindbad himself seemed to acquire a wife at every port. On the recreated journey, boxes of nuts, dried fruit, hundreds of eggs wrapped in sawdust, sacks of onions, dried peas, rice and spices were stowed aboard, along with tinned foods, sauces, Omani dates and fresh fruit. The bilges stank of rotten eggs, giving off hydrogen sulphide gas. The navigation manual which Tim Severin took on board was written by a master of 15th-century navigation: Ibn Majid, from Sur, one of the most skilled seafarers of his time. It was however difficult to follow, not least because it was written in verse. Severin managed, however, on the strength of this manual, and after some practice, to navigate from the Pole Star using nothing more than a piece of string with a knot and cardboard. Severin's book, *The Sindbad Voyage*, was published in 1983 (see book list on page 299). The *dhow* now sits on the roundabout beside the Al Bustan Palace Hotel and in front of the new National Museum in Muscat.

WHAT TO SEE The sultan's modest palace was built in the 1970s at its seafront location here in the old town. Its blue-and-gold colouring make it an unusual spectacle. If you take a boat trip (arranged through any tour operator) you will be able to observe the immaculate lawn which extends from the palace to the seafront.

A good half-day trip would be to combine an exploration of both Muscat Old Town and Muttrah corniche and souk.

Jalali and Merani forts [map page 98] The Portuguese began to build these forts in 1527, though their current versions date from 1587 and 1588 respectively. They were originally known as São João and Fort Capitan. Neither is open to the general public.

Until recently, Jalali was Oman's main jail, with many sinister tales of torture under the old sultan, Said bin Taimur. British army officers can still recall the awful conditions inside and one such officer remembers how, during interrogation of a rebel of the Jebel War, he dangled the suspect out of a high window by his *dishdasha* in an attempt to persuade him to talk. When the *dishdasha* began suddenly to rip, the British officer pulled him in quickly in a panic, but the Omani was so terrified by the experience that he told all he knew forthwith. Today Jalali can be visited only by VIPs with special permits. It is still in use as a garrison for Omani troops.

Merani (also Mirani) is still the headquarters of the Muscat garrison and in the 1960s was described as a homely military barracks with iron bedsteads and socks draped over the bed rails. Besides these forts, nothing remains of the Portuguese occupation of Muscat. Some remnants of the cathedral and the governor's residence and barracks survived as late as 1895, but were then knocked down to make way for other dignitaries' buildings.

Museums
Bait Fransa [map page 98] (Omani–French Museum) (*Qasr Al Alam St, Old Muscat;* ☏ *24 736613;* ⊕ *09.00–13.00 Sat–Thu; 500/200bzs adult/child 6–12*) This is on the right-hand side after going through the gate (under the Gate Museum). Parking is not easy in the old town, but there is a small car park here and with persistence it is usually possible to find a space.

Bait Fransa (or French House) was the original 19th-century French consulate and now is an attractive well-laid museum out chronicling Omani–French historical links from the 18th century. The lease of the house was returned to the Omani government in 1945, despite the fact the last French consul to live there left in 1920.

Bait Al Zubair [map page 98] (*Al Saidiya St, Old Muscat;* ☏ *24 736688;* e *bazubair@ omantel.net.om;* ⊕ *09.00–13.00 & 16.00–19.00 Sat–Thu; RO1/500bzs/250bzs expat/*

THE OLD BRITISH EMBASSY

In the late 1800s, Muscat was said to have a faintly zoological quality, with a tame lion and ostrich roaming the streets, together with an elephant that would regularly plod round to the British consulate where he was duly given sugar lumps. Descriptions of the magnificent consulate built around 1880 all speak of its splendid flagstoned veranda, overlooking the harbour and towered over by Fort Jalali (at that time the sultan's main prison), as one of the 'noblest' in the world. It was demolished in the mid 1990s to improve the view from Al Alam Palace – the sultan's palace – and to make way for more palace buildings.

Qaboos's father, Said bin Taimur, had no links outside his country except with Britain and India, the only two countries to have consulates in Muscat before 1970. He considered membership of such bodies as the United Nations completely unnecessary and useless, especially as its first early involvement with Oman was to condemn Britain for aggression when it responded to his request for help in the 1957 imamate revolution, stating that Oman's right to self-determination was being prevented by the United Kingdom. The old sultan's relations with his Arab neighbours and brethren were also hostile, not least because several of them had an imamate in Arab capitals like Baghdad, Damascus, Cairo, Riyadh and Kuwait. The imamates were the opposition led by Ghalib, Talib, Suleyman bin Himyar and Salih bin Isa, and they were seeking independence for the tribal-led interior of Oman (considered the Oman 'proper'). The sultan was therefore hostile to Omanis who left Oman to seek education in these conniving countries, and whom he would not then allow to return to Oman to take jobs. Ghalib was the imam-in-waiting; Talib, his brother; Suleyman, a political opportunist; and Salih an old man with little tribal influence.

Sheikh Zayed of Abu Dhabi was the only neighbour whom the sultan trusted and had time for. He once invited Zayed to Salalah and he came, after which they had a hotline installed between them. Logically, from a geographical point of view, Oman would have done well to link up in a Trucial States Federation with the Emirates – its agricultural potential and larger population (750,000 in 1968) would have complemented perfectly Abu Dhabi's colossal oil wealth, Dubai's merchant spirit and the tiny Emirates populations. Together they would have made a viable state – but personalities made such a vision impossible. Those who were true tribal Omanis of the interior remained very cut off from the commercial activity of the coast, and therefore the big Muscat or Muttrah merchants could not easily expand through branches into the interior.

Omani/child) This museum is signposted off the Muscat to Muttrah road and is located just outside the walls on Al Saidiya Street. Go through the gate and just past the bend and it is on the right-hand side, with its own car park. There are daily tours of this fine though rather over-restored traditional Omani townhouse at 11.30 and 17.30. Opened in 1998 as an Omani heritage museum and cultural centre, it is designed to give an insight into Omani lifestyles and traditions, with early photos and traditional furnishings. Inside there is a small lecture theatre, gift shop and coffee shop, as well as a reference library and a *majlis* (meeting room) with an exhibition of old maps, seafaring information and models of traditional *dhows*. The museum on the ground floor displays *khanjars*, men's dress, swords and weapons, women's dresses, jewellery, chests and household items, all well labelled and explained. Outside there are entertaining miniature reconstructions of traditional stone and *barasti* houses, with a *falaj* and running water, and even a working model of a pottery kiln.

Bait Muznah Gallery [map page 98] (*Saidiya Street, Way 8662, House 234;* e *art@baitmuznagallery.com; www.baitmuznagallery.com;* ☾ *Sat–Thu*) Just a few metres north of the Bait Al Zubair Museum, this place is a much more authentic old building, which has been tastefully restored. It displays and sells contemporary Omani art and crafts, and entry is free.

Although no French consul arrived to live in Muscat until 1894, there had been attempts to send one since a decree in 1795 (issued in Paris) announced the establishment of a Muscat consulate. Mr Beauchamp, the first appointee, spent four years in Egypt *en route* to the post and was then diverted to Constantinople by Napoleon in 1799, where he was arrested and imprisoned. The next attempt was in 1802 when Talleyrand and Napoleon appointed Cavaignac as consul. On arrival in Muscat in 1803 Cavaignac found the imam out of town (he was further up the coast fighting Wahhabi incursions) and was told he could neither disembark his baggage nor occupy the house that had been made available until the imam returned and gave his express permission. When the imam did eventually return, he did not give permission and Cavaignac was obliged to leave. Bitterly he wrote of Oman *'Ce pays et ses inhabitants sont tout à fait misérables. Le souverain n'est qu'un clef de Bédouins'* – 'This country and its people are simply wretched. The sultan is nothing but a Bedouin pawn.'

Muscat Gate Museum [map page 98] (*Al Bahri Rd;* ✎ *24 739005, 99 328754;* ⊕ *09.30–12.30 & 16.30–19.00 Sat–Thu*) This museum is operated by Royal Court Affairs and is on Al Bahri Road (which is the continuation of Muttrah corniche on towards Old Muscat, literally 'the sea road'). It is located inside the gate which spans the road. You can park in the turning on the right-hand side just before the gate, or go through it (under the museum) and follow the immediate signs into Riyam Street. You can then walk up the steps to the museum courtyard. This museum, opened in 2001, covers the history of Oman with detail of the country's ancient wells, *falaj*, forts and harbours. It also has the original pre-1970 wooden gates of the city, and good views from the top.

COAST EAST OF MUTTRAH

SIDAB سداب If you continue south out beyond Muscat Old Town you come next to the small village of Sidab, a bay area, with its fishing community. There is also a marina.

What to see and do
Marina Bandar Rowdha [103 C2] (*www.marinaoman.net*) Those interested in boating, diving, taking a *dhow* trip or simply having a meal in a beautiful, peaceful location, must visit this marina. It is open to the public and not a private members' club. It has 140 wet berths, 90 dry berths, a marine control tower, a pool, a licensed restaurant (Blue Marlin) and bar, an upstairs bar (Lighthouse Bar), and offers all the sea-based tours. The *Hatteras* is a 58ft-long luxury motor cruiser with air conditioning, television/video, stereo, microwave, fridge and radar equipment, and is chartered for fishing trips. A 32ft-long open boat is used for dolphin-watching trips. A traditional *dhow* is used for sunset trips or scenic coastal tours. The full array of tours includes diving, game fishing, snorkelling, camping, sailing, scuba, whale- and dolphin-watching, *dhow* cruising and jet skiing, or you can ask to be taken to your own private beach and arrange to be collected. You might simply like to visit this place for a meal by the pool or inside, under the protection of the air conditioning, with full marina views.

For listings, see pages 79–87

AL BUSTAN & SIDAB

SIDAB   HARAMIL   Gulf of Oman

HARAMIL ROAD

Capital Area
Yacht Club

Marina Bandar Rowdha
(Marine Science and Fisheries Centre,
and Bluzone Watersports Oman)

N

Bradt

SIDAB STREET

0 ━━━━━━ 1,000m
0 ━━━━━━ 1,000yds

The National
Museum

AL BUSTAN

Al Bustan
roundabout

Where to stay
1   Al Bustan Palace......D4

Where to eat and drink
2   Blue Marlin................C2

New Parliament
Buildings

HARAMIL حرامل   A few bays after Sidab (and before Al Bustan) is the **Capital Area Yacht Club** [103 B2] (↝ *24 737712*), which sits next to another private club marina. Beside this, set right on the water's edge, is the **Marine Science and Fisheries Centre** [103 C2] (↝ *24 736449; ⊕ 08.00–14.30 Sun–Thu, 15.00–19.00 Fri, 08.00–13.00 Sat; free*). Opened in 1986, the centre belongs to the Ministry of Agriculture and Fisheries. Inside there is an aquarium, which has recently updated its tanks and has expanded its varieties of fish. It has a particularly fine collection of turtles and its emphasis is on conservation of ecosystems.

AL BUSTAN البستان   A few bays further on you come to Al Bustan Bay, where the village of Al Bustan was long ago moved to the northern corner of the bay and modernised, to make way for **Al Bustan Palace Hotel** (see page 79), which dominates the mountain-hemmed bay. At the roundabout leading up towards Al Bustan Palace Hotel sits the *Sohar dhow*, which was used by Tim Severin in his 'Sindbad' journey (see box, page 99). The bay has rather sadly but perhaps inevitably become the site of massive government development and spending, with the new parliament building and the new Oman National Museum dominating the approach road to the Al Bustan Palace Hotel. The museum is scheduled to open in 2013. Its imposing white traditional three-storey building houses ten exhibition galleries, classrooms and a 70-seat indoor café. The 6,000-year history of the country is presented using many interactive devices.

QANTAB قنتب [map page 104] Qantab is another fishing village and local fishermen will take you fishing if you ask.

BANDER JISSAH بندر جصة [104 C3] There are five dive sites in this area (also spelt Bandar Jussa), and its shallow depths are particularly suited for beginners and night dives. Turtles, spiny lobsters and cuttlefish have all been spotted here. It is a rocky coastline with small bays, one occupied by the **Oman Dive Centre** (see pages 91–2 for more details).

BANDER KHAYRAN بندر خيران [map pages 72–3] The small secluded bays of Bander Khayran (or Bandar Khairan) make excellent camping, picnicking, diving and snorkelling spots. There are several dive sites in this area, which you can only access by boat.

FAHAL ISLAND [map pages 72–3] Otherwise known as 'Shark Island', this is reportedly excellent for diving, offering the largest variety of coral in the capital condensed into one area. There is a tugboat wreck close to North Bay. Black-tip reef sharks, rays and turtles are all to be found here.

YITI [off map, pages 72–3] With a lovely mountain backdrop 25km south of Muscat, Yiti beach is a good place to take a picnic, and close enough if you want to escape the hubbub of the city for an afternoon, though there is no public transport so you will need to take a taxi or have your own transport. The small **Al-Moosa Beach Resthouse** (24 886119; e *anosh@omantel.net.om*) here has eight furnished apartments, each sleeping five people, with a small shop for provisions. For the future there is a Yiti beach tourism project being planned www.yenkit.com (see page 23).

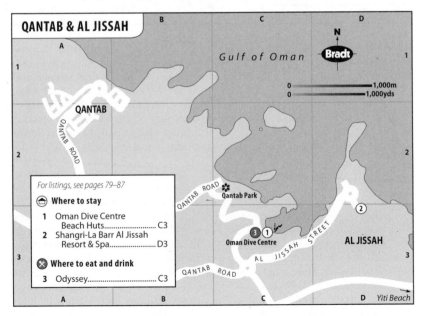

Getting there The road to Yiti is accessed by exiting at the Hamriya roundabout in Ruwi then continuing straight on, taking the small right-hand turn at the place where the road bends round at a right angle (the start of Ruwi Souk St). This small road will take you through a narrow street and upwards steeply, and you can look back over fantastic elevated views of the large town of Ruwi.

JEBEL SIFAH This new Swiss/Omani Muriya development (*www.jebelsifah.com*) lies beyond Yiti and is a 45-minute drive south from Muscat. It is an exclusive 'marina town' complex set in its own bay and beach against a mountain backdrop. As well as housing Oman's first Four Seasons Hotel, there are also the large five-star Banyan Tree Hotels & Resorts and Hotel Missoni, together with the smaller Sifawy Boutique Hotel (*www.sifawyhotel.com*) right on the waterfront, with its 25 rooms and 30 suites. The marina has a capacity of 100 berths. The road currently ends here.

QURIYAT قريات [map page 106] Historically one of the main coastal towns of Oman, Quriyat refused to submit to the invading Portuguese in the early 16th century, and had its inhabitants slaughtered as a result. Set at the start of a wide plain, its salty *khor* (or creek), which centuries ago was a major port and famous harbour, has now silted up. Fishing and agriculture remain the mainstay of the local economy and the fish souk is busy. It has been known for rows of sharks, including hammerheads, and stingrays to be sold here. The sharks used to be dried in the sun, and then cut into strips of dried flesh, which were used as flavouring for rice. The plain in which the town is set used to be breeding grounds for the horses for which Quriyat was famous for exporting.

Getting there To join the road to Quriyat, you need to exit the main highway at Wadi Aday roundabout. Shared taxis costing RO2 or microbuses costing RO1 can be picked up here for the hour's drive of 82km. The new highway to Quriyat winds and climbs, passing *en route* the Wadi Sareen Nature Reserve, created for the protection of the Arabian tahr (the half-goat) and not open to the public. After less than an hour's drive from Muscat you climb to a plateau, from which there is a steep descent for several hundred metres on to the plain of Quriyat (90km from Muscat). The distance from Quriyat to Sur is 120km.

What to see and do There are three fortifications here. Opposite the souk is **Quriyat Castle** [map page 106] (⊕ 08.30–14.30 Sat–Thu; 500bzs), restored and fully furnished to help you imagine readily what life was like for its inhabitants. The watchman takes pleasure in showing visitors around. On the coast is **Al Sahel Fort** [map page 106]. The third fort of the area is **Dagh Fort** [off map, page 106], which was built when the Portuguese occupied the country. Inland the dominant mountain is Jebel Aswad (the Black Mountain), peaking at 2,050m.

For the serious adventurer it is possible to **trek the canyon** that runs from Suwqah to Al Suwayh in the Quriyat *wilayat*. Known as the Quriyat Canyon, it is not for the faint-hearted and it would be advisable to take an accompanying guide with knowledge of the route, and be prepared and fully equipped. The 15km trip is about a six-hour trek, reportedly far more difficult than the 18km trek through Wadi Dayqah (see page 237). At Quriyat roundabout, turn right in the direction of Daghmar and about 7km further along this road there is a signpost for the highlight of Wadi Dayqah. Head along this off-road trail for roughly 8km before turning right for Wadi al Arbiyeen, where this trek begins. Suwqah is the upstream end of the canyon and can be reached only from the Dima wa'Tayeen side (also in the

QURIYAT TOWN

AL HAJIR

N

Bradt

Gulf of
Oman

AS SAHIL

AL HAJIR STREET

AS SAHIL STREET

0 ——————— 200m
0 ——————— 200yds

Quriyat Castle

AS SIRAH FORT ST

AL MUSLA STREET

Quriyat
Souk

$

Al Sahel Fort

AL MALAH

$

$

AL JINAYN STREET

AL JINAYN

Quriyat
Lake Park

AL HISN STREET

Expressway,
Dagh Fort

Sharqiya region). For this upstream end, you will need to drive from Ibra, following signposts to Wadi Na'am to reach Samaiya, an oasis village in Dima wa'Tayeen *wilayat*. Just 3km before Samaiya there is a trail that leads you to Suwqah, about a 27km off-road route. The canyon at this point is usually dry.

RUWI روي

Ruwi is now a busy business district and suburb, with the greatest concentration of high-rise buildings in the whole country. It is also the country's transport hub, with the main bus station for destinations all over Oman. The business district is sometimes referred to as the Central Business District (CBD) or the Muttrah Business District (MBD), or even 'Little India', as so many of the businesses here are run by Indians.

Until the 1960s, Ruwi was a small village serving as the market garden for Muscat and Muttrah. It had a large fish shop with an open-roofed kitchen beside the road, and donkeys would bring panniers full of fish from Muttrah Souk to be cooked here. Ruwi was also the location of the customs checkpoint, comprising only a mud hut with a red flag, where taxes were levied on goods moving between Muscat and Oman. Complex rates of tax were levied: 5% for dates and 15% for tobacco, for example, with everything having its own rate.

The Ruwi area may at first seem a little difficult to negotiate for the newcomer, as one flyover/roundabout can seem to resemble another. The dual carriageway also bends round sharply at Ruwi, which can play havoc with your sense of direction. The Sheraton Hotel is a good landmark from which to re-establish direction.

Coming from the airport end of the motorway it is useful to remember that Qurum Heights Road (the exit on the right, just before Qurum, and where the motorway splits into two) leads up and over to the Sheraton. Alternatively, keeping straight on the motorway leads you to Ruwi Souk Street (see page 109). There are various budget hotels in the Central Business District off Al Fursan Street and Al Baladiyah Street (see pages 83–4).

WHAT TO SEE

Currency Museum [108 C4] (*Inside Central Bank of Oman, CBD;* 🖕 *24 796102;* ⏱ *08.30–12.30 Sun–Thu; 500/200/100bzs adult/child/child under 6*) Opposite the HSBC Bank, this museum showcases a collection of coins and notes.

National Museum [108 A4] (*Above the Islamic Library, off A'Noor St;* 🖕 *24 701289;* ⏱ *09.30–13.30 & 16.00–18.00 Sat–Thu; 500/200/100bzs adult/child/child under 6*) Operated by the Ministry of Heritage and Culture, this museum is close to the Abdulredha Mosque (not far from Al Falaj Hotel). It houses traditional Omani costumes and household items retrieved from Bait Nadir (a traditional home that was destroyed by fire in 1988), and has a room displaying medals and regalia, photographs, portraits and jewellery from the history of the royal families of Zanzibar and Oman. It also temporarily houses archaeological artefacts (some from the Bat tombs near Ibri) from the Oman Museum (near the Ministry of Information), which is being renovated. Many of the exhibits may eventually be moved to the new Oman National Museum in Al Bustan (see pages 103–4).

Sultan's Armed Forces Museum [108 B2] (*Al Mujamma St;* 🖕 *24 312642;* ⏱ *08.00–13.00 Sat–Thu; RO1/500bzs adult/child, military personnel exempt*) Also operated by the Ministry of Defence, this museum is reached by heading past Al Falaj Hotel (coming from Al Burj flyover/roundabout). You may alternatively approach it taking the first or second exit off Bait al Falaj Street (from Bait al Falaj flyover/roundabout). Opened in 1988, it is set in the immaculately groomed gardens of the Bait al Falaj Fort whose tall white tower dominates the surrounding area. It has an impressive display of Oman's military history – the land force, air force, navy and royal guard – and an informative guide can lead you around. Downstairs has an account of Oman's wars against the Portuguese, while upstairs there is information about the Dhofar War against the communists in the south and about the armed forces in Oman today.

INDIAN MERCHANT COMMUNITY

A considerable vacuum would be left if every Indian merchant left the country. The most powerful ones are in Muttrah and Ruwi, but even in the interior most shops are run by Indians, with Omanis running only a few stalls in the older souks like Rustaq and Nizwa. Elsewhere, especially all along the Batinah, at the meat, fish and vegetable souks, you will be hard-pressed to find an Omani selling instead of buying. The Omanis who are most active in business and trade tend to be the Beluch, the Baharina and the Khojas (Hyderabadis), whose families came originally from Iran, Pakistan, India or Iraq, but who now hold Omani passports and are Omani citizens. In the past these Omanis, all of whom settled on the Batinah coastal plain, were not permitted into the interior, or only with special permission.

RUWI

A B C D

1 Lulu
Hypermarket
BAIT AL FALAJ

Bait Al Falaj
Roundabout

2 RUWI STREET

AL MUJAMMA STREET

BAIT AL FALAJ STREET

MUTTRAH STREET

Sultan's Armed
Forces Museum

Bait Al Falaj
Fort

3 ①

Al Burj Street
Roundabout

AL WASHAL ST

⑦ ⑫ ⑪
AL BURJ STREET

Star
Cinema

4 National
Museum
AL ISKAN STREET

AL FURSAN ST

⑥

⑨ Currency Museum
⑩

DHL

AN NUR STREET

AL FARAHIDI STREET

RUWI STREET

⑧
Pizza Hut

⑬

5 Qaboos
Mosque

② O.N.T.C.
bus terminal

⑤

AL JAMI STREET

BAIT AL FALAJ STREET

④

③ Ruwi
Roundabout

KFC

Ruwi
police
station

AL WADI AL KABIR

AL FURSAN STREET

Ruwi
Cinema

Bustan

6 AN NAHDAH STREET

RUWI (SOUK) STREET

STREET 41

Muscat Gold Souk

STREET 37

Al Nasr
Cinema

SUQ RUWI ST

AL BALADIYAH STREET

7 Hamriya
Roundabout

STREET 45

SUQ RUWI STREET

0   500m
0   500yds

NOTE
For key to accommodation
and eating and drinking,
see opposite

A B C ↓Yiti D

N
Bradt

Bait Al Falaj Fort [108 C2] (⊕ *08.00–13.30 Sat–Thu*)

The fort was said to have been built as Sultan Said bin Sultan's weekend country house in the early 1800s, but from 1957 until 1978 served as the Sultan's Armed Forces (SAF) headquarters. Squeezed into the space beside it was the country's only civil and military airport until the 1970s, when Muscat International Airport was built. Most visitors to Oman arrived by plane and used to watch anxiously as the hills got closer before the plane dipped in through an obscure gap to land on the small plain. The explorer Ranulph Fiennes arrived this way in 1968 and stepped out into a heat he would not have believed possible, only to be told: 'It's just beginning to get hot here, but not too bad yet. Just wait till July.'

SHOPPING

Ruwi Souk Street [108 B6]

To get here, exit the main highway at the Hamriyah roundabout and continue along the road straight ahead (the main highway bends sharply off to the left here). This road is the start of Ruwi Souk Street, which itself loops around to the left (virtually parallel to the highway). Soon after joining this road you will find metered parking on the right-hand side (you will need 50bzs coins). There are usually plenty of free spaces at this upper end of the street, so it might be best to park here and walk down, rather than get caught up in the traffic congestion that usually ensues further down.

In this street, there is a plentiful selection of shops selling gold and silver, fabric, electrical goods, souvenirs and fake designer wear, as well as the street traders that sell DVDs and clothes from mats laid out on the floor. Ruwi Souk Street can become busy in the evenings and even more so on Friday evenings, when it turns into a miniature Mumbai!

QURUM القرم

Originally just a little fishing village on the southern end of the Batinah, Qurum (which translates as 'mangrove') is now part of the modern sprawl of the Capital Area, where most of the beach hotels are situated along the wide sandy shore. The marshy estuary with mangrove swamps, designated a nature reserve, is in fact the mouth of the Wadi Adai and still floods into the sea after heavy rains. It is a good birdwatching spot, more peaceful than most places within the Capital Area. The landscape is enhanced by the rocky headland at the far eastern end of the beach, now built up with apartment blocks and home to the Crowne Plaza (formerly the Gulf Hotel), which benefits from the breezes and elevated views.

Qurum can appear rather complicated on first arrival, but once you have mastered the positioning of the two roundabouts (at the splitting of the highway), things become a little easier.

SHOPPING Qurum is home to most of the modern shopping plazas; to access these you will need to keep straight on the dual carriageway and come off at the main

Qurum roundabout (which is the next one along from the Khuwair roundabout). Taking the left turn at the roundabout (last exit) and the subsequent first right will lead you into the main group of shopping malls. They are all generally open 09.00–13.00 and 16.00–22.00, with some slight variations.

Al Harthy Complex [110 B6] ✆24 564481; information desk ✆24 560454; e ahcmpx@omantel. net.om. On the right-hand side of the highway (away from the main group); stands out for its interesting dome design. For access to this complex (& the Sultan Centre, opposite), keep straight on the highway & once you have passed the Qurum roundabout (over the flyover) get over to the right & slow down. The entrance comes up immediately after the flyover. There are plenty of ATMs outside, & as you enter there is an upmarket chocolate gift shop on the right, just inside the automatic doors. There is a Kargeen Café located upstairs. For the children, there is an extensive play & amusement area called Sindbad's Play City as well as a novel 'Happy Child' hairdresser's dedicated to distracting children while they have their hair cut (one TV per chair, playing cartoons continuously).

QURUM HEIGHTS & COMMERCIAL AREA

Gulf of Oman

PDO Golf & boating
PDO Club (private)

QURUM HEIGHTS

RAS AL HAMRA STREET
AL FAHL STREET
FUHUD STREET

Mina al Fahal (port)

MARMUL STREET

Oil and Gas Exhibition Centre & Planetarium

FUHUD STREET

For listings, see pages 79–87

❌ **Where to eat and drink**
1 China Town............A4
2 Jean's Grill..............B5
3 Pizza Muscat..........B5

Qurum Natural Park

SAYH AL MALIH STREET

Sayh al Malih Roundabout
Capital Commercial Centre, China Town

STREET 10

QURUM HEIGHTS ROAD

STREET 10

Muscat Old Town

Royal Oman Police Immigration Office
Qurum Commercial Centre
Al Araimi Complex
Sabco Commercial Centre
Al Khamis Plaza
Capital Stores

AL WALLAJ

MAYDAN AL FATH STREET

Seeb
Al Qurum Roundabout

Al Asfoor Plaza

Police Club
Police Stadium

STREET 7

AN NAHDAH STREET

N
Bradt

Sultan Centre (supermarket), Jean's Grill
Al Harthy Complex, Pizza Muscat, FedEx
Al Wattayah Roundabout
Ruwi

0   500m
0   500yds

Capital Commercial Centre [110 A5] ✆24 563672; e cccqurum@omantel.net.om; ⊕ 09.00–13.00 & 16.30–23.00 Sat–Thu, 16.30–22.00 Fri. This centre combines a supermarket & a mall. Fast-food eateries here include McDonald's, Fuddruckers, Pizza Hut, Bollywood Chaat, Subway & Baskin Robbins (ice cream). There is a small souk inside here, for handicrafts & souvenirs, & a good internet café with a drinks menu.

Capital Stores [110 A5] ✆24 797236; e csoman@ omantel.net.om. Close to Sabco Centre. There are also branches at Ruwi, Muttrah & Seeb (as well as Salalah in the south of the country).

Sabco Commercial Centre [110 A5] ✆24 563943, 562761, 566701; e sabcocen@ omantel.net.om; www.sabcogroup.com; ⊕ 09.00–13.00 & 16.00–22.00 Sat–Thu,

16.30–22.00 Fri. This is the longest-established complex (opened in 1985) & apart from the usual array of shops, it has the Body Shop, Nine West, Elle, Godiva, Wrangler, a pet shop, a beauty salon & a small-scale, modern, air-conditioned souk, which has 27 small individual units selling silver jewellery & handicrafts, incense burners, *dishdashas, kummahs, mussars,* pottery, *khanjars,* leather goods, *bakhour* (traditional scented wood), frankincense & other artefacts. If you haven't got the time to visit the real thing at Muttrah, this miniature souk is a good place for buying gifts to take back home.

Sultan Centre [110 B6] It is a large, excellent supermarket, which has a restaurant upstairs called Jean's Grill (✆24 567666), serving good buffet b/fasts.

WHAT TO SEE

Qurum Natural Park [113 F2] The park is accessed from two sides: from the gate at the base of the hill that is home to the Mumtaz Mahal Indian Restaurant, and from the road that extends from the Qurum roundabout up to the Qurum Heights peninsula. This is one of the venues for the Muscat Festival (see box on page 114), held each January/February, when a traditional village is constructed beside the lake, and Omani rural lifestyles and crafts are depicted. When the festival is on the park does not open till 16.00, and stays open till late. There is also camel racing and an equestrian show, art exhibitions, a laser show and poetry recitals, as well as concerts with popular Arab singers held in a specially constructed temporary amphitheatre. The amusement park – Marah Land – includes rides, games and a food court.

Museums

Children's Science Museum [113 F3] (*A'Saruj/Shatti al Qurum;* ✆24 605368; ⊕ 09.30–13.30 *Sat–Thu; 500/100bzs adult/child under 12*) Operated by the Ministry of Heritage and Culture, this museum is located on the right-hand side of the road that approaches the Qurum Natural Park entrance and the Mumtaz Mahal Restaurant. It is inside one of the dome-shaped buildings and focuses on interactive scientific experiments to promote interest through exploration.

Oil and Gas Exhibition Centre [110 C4] (*Seih Al Maleh St;* ✆ 24 677834; ⊕ 07.00–12.00 *&* 13.00–15.45 *Sun–Thu, 08.00–13.00 Sat; free*) The exhibition centre can be found on the right-hand side just before the Petroleum Development Oman (PDO) Gate No 2. It was donated to the people of Oman by PDO back in 1995 and guides you through the discovery and excavation of oil in the country. It is interesting for both adults and children, with interactive models and computer information all in English.

Planetarium [110 C4] (✆24 675542; e planetarium@pdo.co.om; www.pdo.co.om/ pages/planetarium; *shows at 10.00, 11.30 & 16.00 Sat only; free*) This was built in 2000 and is adjoined to the Oil and Gas Exhibition Centre. It is best to book in advance for the shows.

Qurum Beach, or Shatti Al Qurum in Arabic, is a prime beach area where three excellent five-star hotels (Grand Hyatt, InterContinental and Crowne Plaza) and two five-star hotel beach clubs (Sheraton and Radisson Blu) are located. The beach is popular with Omani families as well as hotel guests in the early evening. It is a lovely place to watch the sun go down before going for a meal in O Sole Mio or a cocktail in Trader Vic's.

SHOPPING
Jawharat A'Shatti Commercial Complex (Jewel of the Beach) [113 D3]
(*Shatti al Qurum;* ✆ *24 692113;* e *jasco@omantel.net.om*) Instead of turning right into the entrance of the InterContinental Hotel, keep straight and this will take you to this shopping complex, which has O Sole Mio (a good Italian restaurant) on its corner. There are plenty of spaces to park, but in the evening it can get busy. Inside the complex there is a Starbucks coffee shop, a café with outdoor terrace (D'Arcy's Kitchen), the Omani Heritage Gallery (shop), a card shop, Muscat Pharmacy and even a balloon shop. This area is popular with Omani families in the evening, as access to the beach is good. It is also a good place to take a stroll. You might like to pop into the Sheraton Beach Hotel (which is the beach club of the Sheraton in Ruwi), located on the beach (at the opposite end to O Sole Mio), and have a drink in Feeney's Bar (⊕ *12.00–15.00 & 18.00–midnight*). This area is within easy walking distance of both the InterContinental and Beach hotels.

Omani Heritage Gallery [113 D3] (*Jawharat A'Shatti Complex;* ✆ *24 696165, 696974*) Authentic crafts, jewellery and clothing are for sale here, close to the

---

PDO

Petroleum Development Oman (PDO) is the main oil company of the country, 60% owned by the government, with Royal Dutch Shell as its operator and main private partner. In the late 1960s, Petrol Development Oman Ltd, a subsidiary of Shell, constructed the Mina al Fahal oil terminal and refinery at this hilly outcrop at Qurum. They accompanied it with its own purpose-built village called Sahil Mahla, set on a cliff above a sandy cove known as Blackpool Beach! Many PDO officials had their wives and children with them, and a car to take them shopping in Muscat or Muttrah. Each employee had his own Portakabin with air conditioning, freezer and sea view, and fresh food coming in each week from Australia in refrigerator ships. The technicians spent 11 days upcountry at the wellheads followed by four days' rest back at the village. The pay was high, with extra hardship money for the difficult climate. Bored by the long separations, some European wives began affairs with young bachelors on the compound. Omanis employed as caterers or cleaners on the compound observed everything at first hand and went back to their villages reporting on the European lifestyle, the plush bars, the well-equipped hospital kept busy with cases of mild sunburn and stomach ulcers, the piped water, the light switches and the children's schools. The contrast of lifestyle with their own was enormous: could they be blamed for wondering when, if it was the oil that was making these foreigners so rich, they would enjoy a little of the same.

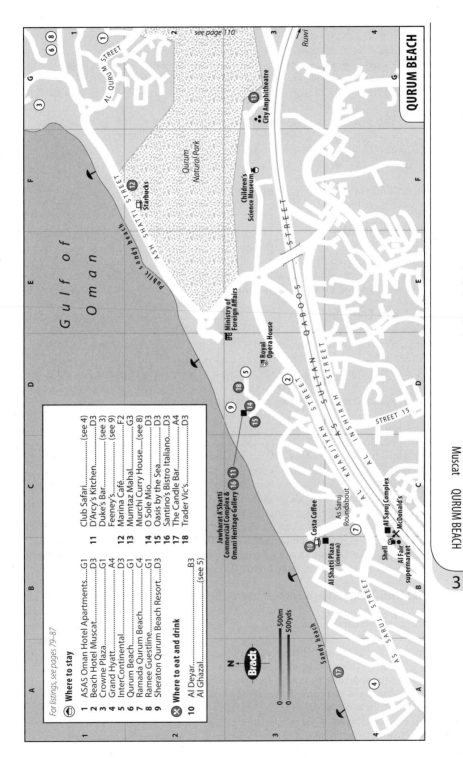

see page 110

QURUM BEACH

Gulf of Oman

Qurum Natural Park

Ruwi

Public sandy beach

ASH SHATTI STREET

AL QURUM STREET

Starbucks 12

City Amphitheatre 13

Children's Science Museum

Ministry of Foreign Affairs

Royal Opera House

STREET

SULTAN QABOOS STREET

AL KHARIJIYAH STREET

AL INSHIRAH STREET

STREET 15

18

5

9

14

15

16 11

Costa Coffee 10

Jawharat A'Shatti Commercial Complex & Omani Heritage Gallery

Al Shatti Plaza (cinema)

As Saruj Roundabout 7

Al Saruj Complex

Shell

Al Fair supermarket

McDonald's

2

4

17

AS SARUJ STREET

Sandy beach

For listings, see pages 79–87

Where to stay

1	ASAS Oman Hotel Apartments....G1	
2	Beach Hotel Muscat.................D3	
3	Crowne Plaza........................G1	
4	Grand Hyatt..........................A4	
5	InterContinental.....................D3	
6	Qurum Beach.........................G1	
7	Ramada Qurum Beach..............C4	
8	Ramee Guestline.....................G1	
9	Sheraton Qurum Beach Resort....D3	
11	Club Safari...................(see 4)	
	D'Arcy's Kitchen................D3	
	Duke's Bar...................(see 3)	
	Feeney's....................(see 9)	
12	Marina Café....................F2	
13	Mumtaz Mahal..................G3	
	Murchi Curry House.......(see 8)	
14	O Sole Mio.....................D3	
15	Oasis by the Sea...............D3	
16	Santino's Bistro Italiano......D3	
17	The Candle Bar.................A4	
18	Trader Vic's....................D3	

Where to eat and drink

10	Al Deyar........................B3
	Al Ghazal.................(see 5)

N

Brädt

0   500m
0   500yds

InterContinental Hotel. This gallery is a not-for-profit company and therefore all proceeds go direct to the artisans themselves. Good for gifts and souvenirs.

Al Madina Gallery [113 C4] (*145/6 Al Inshirah Street;* ✎ *24 691380;* e *almadga@ omantel.net.om*) Near the British Council on the way to Madinat Qaboos. Private villa whose ground floor is converted to an interesting shop selling local arts and crafts, greetings cards, paintings and photographs taken by the owner, Richard Woodhead. Good for unusual souvenirs.

Al Saruj Complex [113 C4] (✎ *24 691311;* e *taherent@omantel.net.om*) This complex is situated close to Shatti Al Qurum, but just a little farther back and adjacent to the highway. It is accessible from both the highway side and Al Kharijiyah Street on Hayy as Saruj. It has a Shell garage, a car wash, a drive-in McDonald's, an Al Fair supermarket and an HSBC cashpoint. There is also a pharmacy and coffee shop, a Baskin Robbins, a physiotherapy clinic and a small outdoor amusement area for children. It's a good area to get all things done.

MADINAT QABOOS مدينة قابوس

This area is known locally as MQ, and you will probably see it shown as Madinat Al Sultan Qaboos, Madinat Qaboos, Madinat A'Sultan Qaboos, Medinat Qaboos, etc, in various maps and publications. It is a modern residential area popular with Western expats, and occupies an elevated position on the right-hand side of the highway immediately after the Khuwair roundabout. The central shopping arcade has some good restaurants as well as an Al Fair supermarket, a Family Bookshop, a Muscat Pharmacy, an HSBC cashpoint, Pizza Hut and a Starbucks coffee shop. The Pavo Real Restaurant, the Golden Dragon Restaurant and the quaint Kargeen Caffe labyrinth are all highly recommended, and make this small MQ arcade area worth a visit.

GETTING THERE One way of getting there is to exit the highway at Al Khuwair flyover/roundabout. Once at the roundabout (and therefore off the highway), take the first roundabout exit leading up to Madinat Qaboos traffic lights (which are referred to often when asking directions, and thus a useful landmark). Go straight over at the lights, and a little further along the road at the bend you need to take a left. Follow this road round until you spot the Pizza Hut on your left. This is the start of the shopping complex (see map on page 115).

Alternatively, you can exit the highway taking the slip road immediately after Al Khuwair flyover/roundabout. This will lead you along parallel to the highway for a little way, before you need to take the right up Al Bashir Street and then the first left. The British Council is located on the left, close to the beginning of this road. Follow

Inset

British Council

AL BASHIR STREET

Starbucks

Pharmacy • • Family Bookshop

HSBC cashpoint

Al Fair supermarket

Pizza Hut

AL BASHIR ST

Madinat As Sultan Qaboos Street

B **C** **MADINAT QABOOS**

N

Bradt

Gulf of Oman

D

0 _____ 500m
0 _____ 500yds

Costa Coffee

Al Shatti Plaza (cinema)

AL MUNTAZAH ST

As Saruj Roundabout

Ruwi

AS SARUJ STREET

Shell

Al Fair supermarket

Al Saruj Complex

McDonald's

AL INSHIRAH STREET

SHATTI AL QURUM

AS SULTAN QABOOS STREET

Al Madina Gallery

AL BASHIR STREET

see inset

AN NADHAYER ST

British Council

MQ

Madinat As Sultan Qaboos Shopping Centre

AL BASHIR ST

AL BASHIR STREET

Abu Qais Decoration & Trading Co

Al Khuwair Roundabout

Seeb

MQ traffic lights

MADINAT AS SULTAN QABOOS ST

Bait Adam Museum

DAWHAT AL ADAB ST

City Plaza & Home Centre

Zakher Shopping Mall

For listings, see pages 79–87

🛏 **Where to stay**

1   Grand Hyatt Muscat.......... A2
2   Ramada Qurum Beach......D2

✖ **Where to eat and drink**

3   Al Deyar.....................................C1
4   Golden Dragon.............(see inset)
5   Grill House Company................B5
6   Kargeen Caffe................(see inset)
7   Pavo Real........................(see inset)

Muscat   MADINAT QABOOS

3

the road up the hill and you will come to the MQ complex on the right-hand side, where there is plenty of parking.

WHAT TO SEE

Bait Adam Museum [off map, 115 D5] (*Bldg 2881, Way No 2 (opposite MQ bridge turning);* \ *24 605033;* e *baitadam@omantel.net.om;* ⊕ *09.00–13.00 & 16.00–19.00; visit 2–3hrs in duration; RO3 museum only, RO15 pp museum & lunch or dinner*) This is so much more than a museum. This private collector's home in Madinat Qaboos displays art, coins, maps, books and treaties and other treasures and artefacts from Omani history, dating back to pre-Islamic times. Latif al Bulushi (whose English is excellent) and his family offer you the chance to join them in either an authentic Omani lunch or dinner in their home. Here you will experience Omani etiquette and hospitality first hand, from taking your shoes off when you enter the home, being served coffee and dates, and sitting at floor level to eat with your hands. It is a great opportunity to experience a slice of the Omani way of life. Call in advance to arrange your visit, as this is a real Omani home. Highly recommended, but difficult to find.

AL KHUWAIR الخوير

Lower Khuwair is home to all the various ministries, and lies on the left of the highway (the seaward side, when coming from the airport). This ministries' area is clearly signposted 'Wazarat' (meaning 'ministries').

Upper Khuwair is largely residential, but there is a selection of furniture shops, fast-food establishments, bakeries, a book/stationery shop, electrical goods shops, and even an ice rink on the Khuwair slip road, running parallel to the highway on the right-hand side (coming from the airport) and accessed via the Shell petrol station. The Khuwair slip road is often referred to when obtaining directions, so it will be useful for you to keep an eye out for it. Khuwair is also home to the Radisson Blu Hotel, which lies further back from the highway and elevated from it. At the farthest end of Khuwair, just before MQ traffic lights, is the large City Plaza and Home Centre furnishings and clothing shop.

SHOPPING There are several shopping malls in Al Khuwair, including:

City Plaza & Home Centre [117 G3] Near Safeer Plaza Hotel; \24 698988. Sells sportswear, clothes, makeup, toys & Western-style furniture & homeware.

Zakher Shopping Mall [117 F3] \24 730619; e zakii@omantel.net.om. In an area far less busy than both Qurum & Ruwi. There is a CD/DVD shop inside here, an internet café, clothes shops, sporting & diving equipment, a card shop, a Body Shop, a café area, a large furniture store & a good Iranian restaurant (unlicensed).

WHAT TO SEE The ministries are largely located in Al Wazarat Street in lower Khuwair.

AL KHUWAIR
For listings, see pages 79–87

🛏 **Where to stay**
1	Al Khuwair Hotel Apartments	D4
2	Bowshar International	A4
3	Holiday Inn Muscat	B3
4	Ibis Muscat	B4
5	Radisson Blu	C4
6	Safeer Plaza Hotel Apartments	C4

Off map
	Muscat Holiday	A4

❌ **Where to eat and drink**
7	Automatic	D4
8	Bait Al Turath	C2
9	Bin Ateeq	B3
	Churchills	(see 3)
10	Golden Spoon	C3
11	Grill House Company	G2
12	Happy Days	C4
13	Kamat	E3

AL KHUWAIR

3

AL KHUWAIR

SHATTI AL QURUM

NOTE
For key to accommodation
and eating and drinking,
see page 116

Desalination
plant

Grand
Hyatt

EMBASSIES AREA

UK

USA

Diplomatic
Club

AL WAZARAT AREA
(THE MINISTRIES)

Al Khuwair
Roundabout

Abu Qais Decoration
& Trading Co 11

MADINAT AS SULTAN
QABOOS STREET

City Plaza &
Home Centre

MQ

MQ traffic
lights

AL BASHIR ST

DAWHAT AL ADAB ST

Zakher
Shopping Mall

Muscat Rugby Club

AL KHUWAIR

13

DOHAT AL ADAB STREET

Al Khuwair
Shopping
Area

Philips electrical goods
showroom

Burger King
Ice rink

Zawawi
Mosque

AS SULTAN QABOOS STREET

AL WAZARAT STREET

A' SAFARAAT STREET

AS SARUJ STREET

AS SULTAN QABOOS ST

AL KHUWAIR STREET

AL KHULEIAH STREET

1

7
5
12

AL KULIYA STREET

6

Ministry of Heritage & Culture
The Natural History Museum

Shell
McDonald's
Al Fakir
Bookshop

9
10
3

City Bowling

Sports stadium

DOHAT AL ADAB STREET

18TH NOVEMBER STREET

AL IZDIHAR STREET

Lulu
Hypermarket

Al Ghubra
Roundabout

Muscat Holiday
Hotel, Seeb

2

Bowshar
Roundabout

4

N

Bradt

0   500m
0   500yds

8

Natural History Museum [117 C2] (*Al Wazarat St;* ✆ *24 604957, 641510;* ⊕ *09.30–13.30 Sat–Thu; 500/200/100bzs adult/child/child under 6*) This is a small museum, opened in 1985, next door to the Ministry of Heritage and Culture in the ministries area of lower Khuwair. The entrance is virtually opposite the large Zawawi Mosque (all the way over the other side of the highway) and close to the small roundabout. There is ample parking space.

The displays cover a small area on the ground floor, with examples of the natural environment and wildlife heritage of the country: mammals, reptiles, birdlife, insects and seashells. The Whale Hall next door has an impressive collection of skeletons.

Turtle permits used to be issued from the Ministry of Heritage and Culture here, but are now easily obtained on site in the Ras al Hadd and Ras al Jinz turtle reserves in the Sharqiya region – part of the country's drive to facilitate tourism.

BOWSHAR بوشر

Before the construction of the dual carriageway, Bowshar [117 A4] used to be a six-hour journey from Muscat Old Town. Now it takes 30 minutes. It is signposted from the Ghubra flyover/roundabout. It lies off the main dual carriageway inland towards the mountains but there is no public transport so you must take a taxi or have your own vehicle. It has really become a suburb, with extensive building of private villas. Under Sultan Qaboos's benign rule all Omanis, men and women, are entitled to 600m² of land on which they can build themselves a house. If they are from Muscat that land has to be within Muscat province, so Bowshar has become a favourite spot.

There are two separate areas of Bowshar which you can explore. One is the signposted Bait al Makham. The other is behind Bowshar in Wadi al Ghail, where a path leads for a 30-minute walk over the hills to the village of Al Ghala, with hot springs (30°C) called Bou Souman. Following the tarmac road back towards the sprawl of Muscat, watch out for the ruins on the hillside ridge above of ancient beehive-style graves, mainly collapsed.

WHAT TO SEE
Bait Al Makham (✆ *24 641300, ext 142 (call in advance);* ⊕ *08.00–14.00 Sun–Thu; 500bzs*) This fortified house was built at the turn of the 20th century for a wealthy lady. Restored in 1992, her apartment was at the top of the house with excellent views. Local boys from the village will delight in showing you round, leaping about on the walls and towers.

Bou Souman Springs The mineral-rich waters are said to cure arthritis and rheumatism.

GHUBRA الغبرة

Ghubra [map opposite] is largely a residential area, with older buildings. There is a handy HSBC cashpoint at the first mini-roundabout you reach (coming off the highway at Ghubra and going towards the sea). In the evenings this can become quite a busy area. There is a variety of small street shops here, selling fruit and vegetables, foodstuffs and building materials, plus a pharmacy, an optician's, a bakery, coffee shops/café-type local restaurants and an internet café. The **National Trading Company** (*showroom at St 44, Villa 57, near Bowshar roundabout;* ✆ *24 697014*) sells Omani carved doors or shutters converted into coffee tables, Omani chests, traditional weaving and jewellery.

AZAIBA

For listings, see pages 79–87

Where to stay

1 Al Madina Holiday Inn....... A5
2 Majan Continental.............. C5
3 The Chedi............................ D1
4 The Treasure Box................ C4

AZAIBA الأذيبة

Azaiba [map above] (also Al Udhaybah or Al Athaibah) is the newest of the residential areas in the city and you will find large, detached and quite grand homes here. There is a seemingly endless stretch of beach close by, the potential of which has been fully recognised, and is being utilised by the development projects of The Wave and the Journey of Light (see page 23). This same stretch has been enjoyed for many years, almost exclusively, by the Civil Aviation Recreational Club [off map, 119 A1], which now is housed within a smart, sizeable building (constructed c2002), and contains the longest bar in the country. It has been a bold, optimistic step away from its small, dated Portakabin-type origins, which remain next door.

Azaiba Beach is excellent for morning or early-evening walks, and local fishermen will sell their latest catch to you. The tides can be strong at times and there have been fatal accidents in the nearby waters. So if you want to swim here, do take advice (speak to any dive centre representative) and use your common sense. Note that there are no lifeguards on duty. The calm bays of the Oman Dive Centre, Al Bustan and Shangri-La hotels, for example, offer a far safer and more inviting experience.

GETTING THERE To get here, exit the highway at the Azaiba flyover/roundabout (also referred to as the Ghala flyover/roundabout). For the Grand Mosque, take the road up to the mountains (rather than down towards the sea) and you will soon reach a smaller roundabout. Take the last exit on this roundabout and you will clearly see the large entrance and road leading up to the extensive car-parking area. Local buses stop outside it plying their way from Seeb to Ruwi.

WHAT TO SEE
The Grand Mosque [119 B4] (⊕ 08.00–11.00 Sat–Thu. *Women need to cover their hair with a headscarf – don't rely on the men at the entrance to lend you one – and all visitors need to follow the conservative dress code. Even bare feet need to be covered with socks*) This mosque is awe-inspiring and is certainly worth a visit, if simply to appreciate its magnitude, craftsmanship and the architectural design-and-build achievement it represents. Even the non-religious visitor will probably be moved in some way by a tour of its interior. Construction began in 1995 and took six years to complete. Made from marble, sandstone and wood, the four corner minarets measure 148ft high, and along with the taller central minaret, represent the five pillars of Islam. There are ablution areas, a library, an administrative quarter, stained-glass windows, carved wooden doors and 35 chandeliers. The Persian carpet (in the main prayer hall) is made of fine wool and cotton in 28 colours, measures 70m by 60m, includes 1,700 million knots and weighs 21 tonnes. It was made in Khurasan in Iran and occupied 600 female weavers fully for four years. The appearance of the magnificent 50m-high central dome and the 8m-wide by 14m-high central Swarovski crystal chandelier in the main prayer hall, with its 1,122 lights, is breathtaking. The hall has a capacity of around 6,600 and the total capacity is estimated at 20,000 worshippers. The tranquillity and serenity of the *riwaqs* (open-air arcades), archways and courtyards is quite an experience in itself. The Grand Mosque in its entirety stands as an assertive symbol of Oman's confidence and spirituality.

SEEB سيب

Seeb [map page 121] is like Muscat's garden suburb, with many fine weekend villas of the wealthy set among gardens and palm groves. The **Royal Stables and Equestrian Centre** and the **Royal Guard** of Oman are both here, and just off the dual carriageway is the private road leading to the sultan's Seeb palace – **Bait al Baraka** – which is not open to the public. Between the highway and Bait al Baraka is the First Royal School of Music, which houses the **Royal Oman Symphony Orchestra**, formed in 1985. It may be that you will be in town to hear one of their regular performances (see local papers and publications such as *Oman Today* for details, or ✆ 26 894021).

Seeb is a relatively large town, with a one-way system. Follow the signposts from the highway to A'Seeb. If you approach it from the coastal road (continuing from Azaiba) you will pass many gardening and plant shops on both sides of the road. Follow the road all the way along. When you reach the town you will notice the plentiful fabric

Gulf of Oman

For listings, see pages 79–87

Where to stay
1   Al Bahjah

Off map
        Dream Resort Hotel

Dream Resort
Hotel &
Naseem Park

Local coffee shops

Seeb Souk
Area

AS SOUK STREET

STREET 42

STREET 34

Bradt

N

DAMA STREET

Royal Guard
(private club)

STREET 26

WADI AL BAHAYIS STREET

AL ADIYAT STREET

Royal Stables &
Equestrian Centre

STREET 24

AR RAWDAH STREET

Al Burj
Commercial
Centre

Seeb Palace
(Bait al Baraka)

Al Qasr roundabout,
Barka, Sohar, Dubai

First Royal
School of Music
(Royal Oman
Symphony Orchestra)

Al Adiyat
roundabout

AL ADIYAT ST

AS SEEB STREET

McDonald's

Markaz
al Bahja Plaza,
City Centre
(shopping complex),
Carrefour (hypermarket)

0 ———— 500m
0 ———— 500yds

Muscat International Airport,
Al Khoud, Muscat →

shops; Seeb is in fact well known for its tailors. If you bring along a favourite shirt, dress or skirt, choose a fabric you like in one of the fabric shops and the tailors can copy it for you within a day. Continue on this road till you come to a large impressive gold-domed mosque. The right-hand turn just before the mosque leads you to a small parking area. You might like to park your car here and wander around the fruit and vegetable souk. The fish souk is over by the sea's edge. Seeb is an interesting place, well off the usual tourist track, a typical Omani sea town going about its business. It is also a good place to walk along the 8km of sandy beach collecting shells.

SHOPPING

Markaz al Bahja [map pages 72–3] (*Al Mawaleh roundabout*; 24 540200; e *markaz@ajaygroup.com; www.albahja.com*) To get here you need to drive north from Muscat International Airport roundabout and exit the highway at Al Mawaleh roundabout (as for City Centre and Carrefour). You will see it on the right-hand side of the highway here at Al Hail. Marks & Spencer and McDonald's are also here. It is a large, new, three-level complex, with two cinemas, fast-food outlets, bowling alleys, a snooker and pool centre, and an internet café.

Muscat City Centre and Carrefour Hypermarket [map pages 72–3] (24 558888; e *mccinfodesk@mafgroup.co.ae; www.muscatcitycentre.com*) This is the first 'super-mall' in Oman (similar to those in Dubai), with 1,500 parking spaces, and can be a little difficult to access if you are a first-time visitor. Keep on the main highway north past Muscat Airport (going away from Muscat). Don't take the Nizwa exit. Although it is very close to 'the clock' roundabout (and only 3km from the airport) you need to continue straight up the highway and exit at Al Mawaleh/ Al Hail roundabout. Go all the way around this roundabout and come back on yourself on the highway. Get on to the parallel slip road as soon as you can (the bus-stopping areas can make this a little confusing). If you've missed it and find that you are driving past it again on the main highway don't worry. You can drive into the Shell petrol station (just past City Centre), and go round the back of it, and to the right, and enter City Centre via this back way.

Inside City Centre there is a Mango, Next, Mothercare, Adams, Starbucks, and the Body Shop, among others. There is a KFC, a McDonald's and more in the large food court section at the far end, and an amusement and play area for children.

WHAT TO SEE
Naseem Park [off map, map page 121] (⊕ *16.00–23.00 daily, 16.00–23.00 Tue (women and children only)*) Opened in 1984, this vast park, set between Seeb and Barka (on the very outskirts of the Muscat region – see *Batinah Coast* map on pages 128–9), is about 30km away from the airport on the coast and is signposted from the dual carriageway. It has an aquarium, lake, waterfall, flower garden, Arabic and Japanese gardens, a maze and a playground, which are all a bit run-down now. A railway transports you around, on account of the park's size. The park is popular with Omani families and gets crowded at weekends (Fridays and Saturdays).

The Amouage Perfumery [map pages 72–3] (✆ *24 540757 ext 103, 110 or 111; www.amouage.com;* ⊕ *09.00–13.00 & 14.00–16.30 Sun–Thu; free guide for a tour*) Guided tours of the perfumery are offered and an explanation of how the world-famous frankincense-based Amouage perfume is created. Perfumery has a 2,000-year history in Oman. (See box, pages 276–7.)

AL KHOUD الخوض

A little south of Muscat International Airport is 'the book' roundabout from where you can turn off in an inland direction to Al Khoud and the Sultan Qaboos University [map pages 72–3]. It took its first (557) students in 1986 and by 1995 had a total of 3,500, one-fifth of whom were female. Now there are more female than male students, a phenomenon that has spread throughout the Gulf, and total student numbers exceed 15,000.

The campus lies on the flat open plain but beyond it the road climbs through the foothills to drop again to the old town of Al Khoud, the place where the historic Treaty of Seeb was signed in 1920, a British-mediated truce between Muscat and the tribes of the interior. Here on a hill to the right rising above the palm plantations is the magnificent Al Khoud castle fort built in 1865, with a Zanzibari carved door and elegant windows showing east African influence. It was lived in continuously by the descendants of the original sheikh until 1979, when the 90-year-old resident finally moved into the modern buildings next door.

Also in Al Khoud, dinosaur and fossilised tree remains, 65 million years old, were discovered in 1997, indicating the existence of large forests in the area at the time. The dinosaurs were carnivorous therapods and giant long-necked herbivorous sauropods. The Oman Botanic Garden is being constructed here (see page 6).

EXCURSIONS BEYOND MUSCAT

Most of the trips in and around Muscat will provide you with a taster of the country. However, a short journey outside of the capital will allow you to see more of Oman's natural wonders and allows for the more adventurous of trips. You could go 'wadi bashing' (riding in a 4x4 through the dry riverbeds in the mountains) or picnic by peaceful hot springs (see pages 131 and 147).

For the seriously adventurous and energetic there is rock climbing, mountain ravine trekking and even caving (see below). The stock tours include visits to the Wahiba (usually with overnight camping in the desert), the wadis (Wadi Beni Khaled, Wadi Tiwi, Wadi Shab, Wadi Dayqah and Wadi Abyadh being the most popular), the jebels (Jebel Shams and Jebel Akhdar), the turtle reserves at Ras al Hadd and Ras al Jinz, mountain village tours, fort tours, coastal town and village tours and desert town tours.

Most tours to places beyond Muscat need to be arranged through one of the tour operators in the city (see pages 76–8). If you are travelling independently around your chosen region, yet want a sand safari (which requires a 4x4 and a driver/ guide), it is safest to pre-arrange this through a tour operator in Muscat who will collect you from your hotel, if you are already in the region.

Jebel Akhdar is a great full-day trip (see page 195). Nakhal Springs and the Rustaq Loop is another excellent day trip from Muscat (see page 145). Wadi Bani Auf and Bilad Sayt is a popular 'wadi bashing' destination for those staying in Muscat and can now be completed as a loop across the mountains to Nizwa, returning via the interior (see pages 148–9).

For further information see page 36.

LAND-BASED ACTIVITIES

Birdwatching For information on birds and birdwatching, see page 91.

Camping The desert (whether rubbly – that is to say, in the vicinity of mountains – or sandy) and the beaches of Oman are perfect for outdoor adventure. You have virtually free rein of the country for camping spots.

The small secluded bays of Bandar Khayran (or Khairan) make excellent camping and diving/snorkelling spots, accessible by boat only. Seifa too is excellent for camping. The Oman Dive Centre bay no longer permits camping, but has *barasti* huts on the beach available for rent (see page 83).

Various tour operators offer equipment rental on request, tailored to your requirements. Owing to large tour groups organising camping tours, it would certainly be best to reserve your equipment in advance with a tour operator, if you are travelling independently. They provide everything, except a sleeping bag. If you're not bringing one from home, sleeping bags can be purchased in Muscat at the hypermarkets. Try Lulu, Al Fair, Sultan Centre (up the stairs) or Carrefour. Alternatively, the sports shops may have a supply (within the plazas at Qurum and dotted around the capital as independents). Try Ruwi or Rusayl industrial area if you can't find what you're after in Qurum. Other camping equipment can be bought easily from the hypermarkets.

Caving and rock climbing The more adventurous excursions of caving and rock climbing take you outside of the Capital Area. **Jebel Ghul**, **Jebel Misfah** and **Jebel Misht** in the Dakhiliyah region offer excellent rock climbing possibilities. Jebel Misht has the biggest rock face of all. Tour operators in the capital will advise you of the various levels each site offers and it is necessary to join an organised group session with skilled guides.

For those interested in caving, the **Majlis al Jinn** ('meeting place of the spirits') is located in the Sharqiya region. The main cave chamber is said to be larger than the great pyramids of Egypt. The Majlis al Jinn is accessed by a free abseiling descent. Again it is imperative that you are accompanied by experienced cavers, on a trip arranged through a tour operator, who will also provide the necessary specialist equipment.

The **Al Hota Cave** in Dakhiliyah region, near Hamriya, is easily accessible since it has been developed for tourism (see page 211). So too is **Al Kittan Cave**, near Ibri, in the Dhahirah region (see page 178), which contains gypsum flowers and tiny fibrous hair-like crystals formed by water. The **Teyq Cave** in Salalah is one of the largest in the world.

Caves of Oman, by Dr Samir Hanna and Mohammed al Baloushi, is published by Sultan Qaboos University and is a recommended read.

Desert safari For a desert safari, or dune bashing as it is otherwise known, you will need to make arrangements through a tour operator, because of the potentially dangerous nature of the terrain. A 4x4 is a necessity; so too is the driver/guide that comes with it. See listings on pages 76–8.

Horseriding Outside of Muscat, trails are offered by Al Sawadi Beach Resort in the Batinah region.

Mountain trekking Trekking is a fantastic way to see and experience Oman's mountainscape (see box, page 189). As this needs no specialist equipment, you can do it independently but trekking trips can be organised through tour operators, who offer a choice of itineraries with different degrees of difficulty. With trekking, a certain level of fitness is necessary and it is always recommended that you join an organised trek, for safety reasons.

A global positioning system (GPS) device is a great tool if you like to stay informed of which direction you are walking in, and your position within the globe. You can track your walks, which can be quite thrilling when you take a later trek elsewhere and discover it brings you out very close to where you had travelled previously (perhaps just the other side of the mountain). Some GSMs (mobiles) also work in the mountains. Equip yourself with enough food and water for the journey. A useful guide to get hold of is *Adventure Trekking in Oman* (see *Appendix 3*, page 299).

Wadi bashing For 'wadi-bashing' trips, you will need to venture out of Muscat. See any of the regional chapters for further details of particular wadis that are worth a visit. As just one example, Wadi Bani Auf in the Batinah region is a 'must-do' wadi, and can be managed easily in a day trip from Muscat. Tour operators will arrange a trip for you, if you do not wish to explore independently. It is always sensible to go in a convoy of at least two cars for your wadi initiation.

WATER-BASED ACTIVITIES
Diving and snorkelling Oman's waters have much to offer in the way of scuba diving, with 63 registered dive sites. The Daymaniyat Islands, the waters off the eastern coastal bays of the capital, the Musandam peninsula and Dhofar region all offer excellent diving and have nearby dive centres (see the regional chapters for further details).

Special diving packages with accommodation are offered by Al Bustan Palace Hotel and Al Sawadi Beach Resort, to name but two, and there are also independent dive centres (not linked to hotels), like the Oman Dive Centre, offering their own packages. Hire of equipment is included in the dive trip or course costs, as are dive permits. The full range of courses, from beginner to advanced diver, are offered, culminating in the award of internationally recognised certificates from PADI (Professional Association of Diving Instructors) or BSAC (British Sub Aqua Club).

The spring and summer months are best for diving, with clear and settled water, but diving is possible all year round, except in Salalah (in the Dhofar region) during the June to September monsoon period.

Fahal Island, about a 30-minute boat trip from Oman Dive Centre, is one of the most popular dive sites in the capital, along with Ras Abu Daoud, the MS *Mimoona* wreck at Quriyat, Bander Khayran (about 15–20mins away by boat) and Bander Jissah. The Daymaniyat Islands are a top dive site and are about a 45-minute drive from the capital (or 1½hrs by boat). Night dives, wreck dives and dive courses are widely available. Cemetery Bay is another good location for diving, and the *Munassir* wreck has been purposefully sunk. For night dives in the winter a 5mm-thick wetsuit is recommended; night dives in the summer require a 3mm-thick wetsuit. To arrange a dive, contact or visit any of the dive centres in Muscat (see pages 91–2).

Snorkelling Snorkelling costs around RO17 per person based on a minimum of three passengers and can be arranged through most tour operators. This can be combined with dolphin watching for a cost of around RO28.

Dolphin and whale watching
Dolphin-watching tours generally last for around 1½ hours and cost about RO20 per person. Fahal Island is good for whales and spinner, common and bottlenose dolphins both in the early morning and around sunset.

Game fishing
It is possible to charter a private boat for a half-day fishing trip (4–5 hours) with a boat captain and experienced local fisherman for a cost of RO150, for up to a maximum of six people (two rods in the water). A full day's fishing costs RO220. Call Arabian Sea Safaris (✆ 24 693223), Grand Hyatt Boat House (✆ 24 602888), Muscat Game Fishing Club (✆ 99 322779), Marina Bandar al Rowdha (✆ 24 737288), Muscat Diving and Adventure Centre (✆ 24 485663) or Oman Dive Centre (✆ 99 379031). Also call any of these tour operators for **surfing** or **kayaking**. A permit is no longer required for game fishing, bottom fishing and deep-sea fishing. Spear-gun and arrow fishing are not permitted, and net fishing is permitted for traditional Omani fishermen only. This can be observed along many of the extensive beaches along the sultanate's coastline.

Sailing and boat trips
Sailing, boat trips and *dhow* trips are all available and can be tailored to suit your requirements; speak to any tour operator for full details. Generally, these cost around RO40-50 per person (for a minimum of two people) and last for about four hours. You can try your hand at fishing in the traditional Omani way with a handline, or the modern way with rods (all equipment provided). You are even invited to cook your catch.

Sunset or scenic cruises cost around RO20 per person and again can be arranged through most tour operators. The tour takes you past the two 16th-century

Portuguese forts of Muscat Old Town, and the surrounding bays of Bander Jissah and Muttrah harbour.

⊿ **Capital Area Yacht Club** ☎24 737712
⊿ **Castaways Sailing Club** ☎24 494751
⊿ **Grand Hyatt Boat House** ☎24 641234

⊿ **Marina Bander Al Rowdha** ☎24 737288
⊿ **Muscat Diving and Adventure Centre**
☎24 485663

4

The Batinah الباطنة

Telephone code: 26

When I sink I am eaten by fish, and when I float I am eaten by birds.

THE BATINAH COAST

The Batinah coast is an extensive stretch of beach beginning at Barka and continuing unbroken (except by wadis running out to sea) for some 200 miles (320km) all the way up to the Khatmat border at the entrance to Fujairah in the United Arab Emirates. After the Muscat governorate it is Oman's most populated region. To use an anatomical analogy (see page 4), the flat coastal plain, which runs for about 25km inland, is Oman's 'underbelly', and that is the literal translation of 'Batinah'; in the same vein, the western Hajar Mountains, which lie at the end of the plain, are the 'spine'.

Today, populations in the Batinah have expanded so much that the settlements virtually run into one another for the full length of the coast. A major four-lane highway has been built from Muscat to the UAE's Wadi Hatta border post, running 2–3km inland, so that the sea is never visible unless you take one of the many turn-offs down to it through the towns and plantations.

The region has a history of maritime and commercial industry and activity. Centuries ago, Sohar (located roughly halfway up the full coastal stretch) was the main trading city, renowned for its copper, and archaeological evidence of the extraction of this resource dates back 5,000 years. The whole of the Batinah coast is littered with forts and fortified enclosures (*surs*), evidence of Oman's problematic history of tribal warfare – although the warring between neighbouring tribes in this region was less than in the interior. Both Sohar and Rustaq have been the capital of Oman at various times in the past, reflecting their respective strategic positions.

Today, fishing is the mainstay, and most of the settlements along the coast are fishing towns and villages first and foremost and agricultural centres second.

GETTING THERE

From the airport Muscat International Airport is situated on the southern extremities of the Batinah in the Muscat region. You will need to rent a car or take a bus or taxi from the airport to your destination (see page 74). Taxis are around RO30 from the airport to Al Sawadi Beach Resort.

By road A good four-lane highway runs parallel with the Batinah coast, and it is an easy, pleasant drive. The road is quieter at the weekends (Fri–Sat), when the large industrial traffic lessens.

For listings, see pages 132, 133, 135, 138, 150

Where to stay
1 Al Nahda Resort & Spa
2 Al Sawadi Beach Resort
3 As Suwaiq Motel
4 Shimook Guesthouse
5 Sohar Beach

Where to eat and drink
Al Sawadi Beach Resort (see 2)
As Suwaiq Motel (see 3)

By bus All ONTC buses from Buraimi to Muscat take the Batinah coastal route, with request stops along the route. The main Sohar stop is at the Penguin Restaurant on the highway. The town bus stops are marked on the town plans.

WHERE TO STAY Any of the three international-standard hotels along the Batinah coast (Al Nahda Resort and Spa, Al Sawadi Beach Resort and Sohar Beach Hotel) make a good base from which to explore, and eliminate the extra driving time from Muscat. However, don't dismiss the mid- and lower-range hotels, if you are simply looking for a cheap room for a night or two. Listings are given under the relevant town.

WHERE TO EAT Good restaurants can be found within the upper- and mid-range hotels of the region. However, there are many cheap eating places beyond the hotels

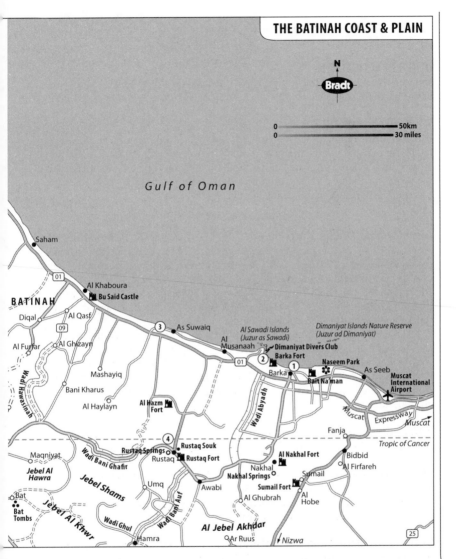

Gulf of Oman

Saham

01

BATINAH

Al Khaboura
Bu Said Castle

Diqal   Al Qasf
09
Al Furtar   Al Ghizayn

As Suwaiq
3

Al Sawadi Islands
(Juzur as Sawadi)

Dimaniyat Islands Nature Reserve
(Juzur ad Dimaniyat)

Al Musanaah

Mashayiq

01
2

Dimaniyat Divers Club
Barka Fort

Bani Kharus

Barka

Naseem Park

Bait Na'man

As Seeb

Muscat
International
Airport

Al Haylayn

Al Hazm
Fort

Wadi Abyadh

Wadi Hawasinah

Muscat
Expressway
Muscat

Maqniyat

Wadi Bani Ghafir

Rustaq Springs
Rustaq

Rustaq Souk
Rustaq Fort

Fanja

4

Tropic of Cancer

Jebel Al
Hawra

Jebel Shams

Nakhal
Nakhal Springs

Al Nakhal Fort

Bidbid
Al Firfareh

Umq

Awabi

Sumail Fort

Sumail

Bat
Bat
Tombs

Jebel Al Kawr

Wadi Ghul

Al Ghubrah

Al
Hobe

25

Hamra

Al Jebel Akhdar

Ar Ruus

Nizwa

The Batinah   THE BATINAH COAST

4

which are worth a try, largely in the form of Indian-run coffee shops, serving the local community. They can be found in any row of shops on the street and usually

OLD-STYLE TRAVEL

Until the 1970s, the easiest way to visit the Batinah coast was by boat, as the roads between the settlements were poor and intermittent. Eccentric British consuls used to wear bathing suits under their clothes, so that they could disrobe and leap ashore, then reappear in immaculate clothing to meet local dignitaries. In 1930, it took seven days by camel to reach Sohar from Muscat, and the first graded track was not built until 1930.

serve chicken, fish and rice dishes. Those looking for a simple Omani meal could try Alawi al Ghawi, just north of Sohar (see page 139).

OTHER PRACTICALITIES

Batinah Police HQ ✆26 840096

Rustaq Hospital ✆26 875055

Sohar Hospital ✆26 840299

Sohar Post Office ✆26 840003

WHAT TO SEE AND DO

Bullfighting Bullfighting (see page 29) is popular in this region and takes place on Fridays in the winter months, rotating between Seeb, Barka, Sawadi, Sohar, Suwaiq and Saham. Any hotel along the Batinah should be able to advise you of the venue for the next event. Alternatively, you can arrange for a tour operator to transport you from Muscat, taking in other sights as well.

Diving

Daymaniyat Divers Club (Ocean Extreme) (*Al Sawadi Beach Resort;* ✆ *26 795545, 895545; www.extradivers-worldwide.com*) This dive centre is the only one in the region and is a PADI five-star Gold Palm Resort. Owing to its commitment to marine environmental conservation, it is also a *National Geographic* dive centre. In addition to the usual half-day dive trips, two-day diving packages to the Daymaniyat Islands are offered. Night dives to Al Sawadi Islands can also be arranged, as well as snorkelling trips to the Daymaniyat Islands.

PADI dive courses are available: PADI Open Water diver, taking about four days to complete; Advanced Open Water course; Open and Advanced watercourse combo; Rescue Diver; Emergency First Responder, CPR and Rescue Diver combo Divemaster, and Bubblemaker for children aged 8–10 in the swimming pool. All-inclusive diving and weekend packages are available – up-to-date prices are given on the website.

Horseriding
Your best option for horseriding in this region is to enquire at Al Sawadi Beach Resort, which offers escorted riding trails along the beach.

Wadi trips
These can be arranged either through your hotel in the region, or in advance through any tour operator in Muscat. Wadi Bani Auf, Wadi Sahtan and Wadi Bani Ghafar are the three most popular wadis of the region, all of which are easily explored in day trips from Muscat.

Options for exploring the Batinah
You may like to explore the whole of the coast up to the Khatmat border, before coming back on yourself and taking the two main roads inland – one being the hinterland of Sohar, the other being the Rustaq Loop. Alternatively you might like to exit the dual carriageway at the Barka roundabout to do the Rustaq Loop first, and then further up at the Sallan roundabout (after Sohar roundabout) exit the dual carriageway again through Wadi Jizzi towards Buraimi.

It is quite possible to visit the attractions of the Batinah coast as day trips from your base in Muscat. The Rustaq Loop, for example, would make a good day trip. Or you might like to visit the Nahkal Springs as a relaxing afternoon trip. It is even possible to dive the Daymaniyat Islands as a day trip from Muscat; this can be done either as a pre-arranged boat trip from one of the dive centres in the capital, or by driving up the coast to Al Sawadi Beach Resort and arranging the trip from the dive centre there. Your choice will depend on your plans post-dive. For all of these

A wadi is a dried natural watercourse which has been formed over millennia by rains washing down from the mountains and out to sea. Wadi bashing is the popular name for taking a 4x4 through these dried mountain riverbeds. Although the name sounds quite severe, you might be relieved to hear that the 'bashing' can be done gently or exhilaratingly, depending on your personal preference. Flash floods have been known to occur, whereby rare and short-lived storms in distant mountains can result in trails of rushing water in these valleys, which sweep away everything in their path. The experienced drivers provided by the tour operators in Muscat know their stuff though and there are plenty of wider wadis that have been dry for years.

Locals, tourists and expats alike enjoy this off-road adventure, which can be done as a half-day or full-day trip, or an overnighter (if you are keen on camping) taking along a picnic or barbecue and plenty of drinking water (filling up a cool box with ice and bottled drinks is recommended). In the same way, a 4x4 can be taken through the sand deserts of the country – known as dune bashing – and these can be quite breathtaking. These trips provide an opportunity to savour the vast empty wilderness, which Oman has aplenty.

days out, aside from the diving trip (where food may be provided on the boat), taking along a picnic is highly recommended, as there are no good restaurants hidden amid the date-palm plantations to pander to the needs of the tourist. This is the Omani countryside in its raw and natural state, thankfully. However, as an alternative you might like to pick out a hotel in the region, so that you eliminate the drive from Muscat. Al Sawadi Beach Resort, although great for sheer relaxation in its isolated spot, is not the cheapest of options as a place to stay, so do consider some of the good alternatives.

Sur Rumeis (*unfenced site;* ⊕ *always*) Unusual because it is built of stone rather than mud brick, Sur Rumeis is worth a brief detour off the dual carriageway (30 minutes) if you have your own transport. It also makes a good picnic stop. Take the signposted track off to Rumeis, zigzagging between walled plantations for 1–2km until you reach a small town with shops. The road is now tarmac and you can turn left parallel to the sea for a further 1km until you see its towers on the right among the trees. Follow the track round to it and you will see that it had a moat with an old drawbridge. A crumbling mosque with a *mihrab* stands beside the moat outside the walls and inside you can still climb up on to one of the towers. The internal mud-brick rooms have largely collapsed.

BARKA البركاء

Barka was one of the prosperous historic cities along this coast, and was important as an area of export to Basra (Iraq), India and east Africa. It is about a half-hour drive north from Muscat Airport and if you do not have your own transport you can flag down one of the microbuses plying the route. The exit is clearly signposted on the dual carriageway and, once you have taken the turning, the road continues for 5km towards the sea, bringing you right up to the fort and fish souk. Vegetables and fresh herbs are sold from mats laid out on the ground or from the back of pick-up trucks surrounding the fish souk, and, to one side, animal guts and skins are laid out in a small walled-off enclosure. A few interesting old derelict buildings remain in the open space beside it, attractively shaded by dark-green mango trees. Virtually every other shop in the village is for 'Ladies' Tailoring', except, notably, the one for the 'Sale of Ice Cubes'.

🏠 WHERE TO STAY   For location of listings see map pages 128–9.

🏠 **Al Nahda Resort & Spa** (109 chalets) 📞26 883710; www.alnahdaresort.com. Located in Barka, off As Seeb St, this luxury hotel is set in 30 acres of gardens. Marketed as a 'wellness retreat', with a gym, fitness studio, spa & volleyball/tennis courts, this is a beautiful 5-star resort complete with 1- & 2- bedroom villas as well as a bar & live entertainment. **$$$$$**

🏠 **Barka Farm House** (6 rooms) 320 Barka, no direct website, but can be booked via www. booking.com. 40min drive to Muscat International Airport. Family-run farm complete with petting zoo, peacocks, cows & chickens. Rooms have en-suite facilities, TV & A/C, there is a large garden & shaded pool. 15min drive to the beach. **$$**

WHAT TO SEE

Barka Fort (⊙ 08.30–14.30 daily except when the guardian is praying or eating; 500bzs) The fort was restored in 1986 and is in fact two forts – the first Ya'arubi, the second Al Bu Said. This is the reason for the double gate, the original Ya'arubi one now being on the inside. The inner ground level is raised up to allow good drainage of rainwater or even seawater in heavy storms. There are three gun towers (look out for the bats) and two wells.

Barka Fort in its Ya'arubi form was the scene of the historical event that resulted in the ousting of the Persians from the Batinah coast and the start of the current Al Bu Said dynasty. Ahmad Al Bu Said, a merchant promoted to *wali* of Sohar, signed a trick agreement with the Persians in 1748, then invited them to a grand feast in celebration at Barka Fort. After the Persians had feasted themselves witless, the Omanis slaughtered them. Ahmad's position was therefore consolidated and he founded the dynasty the following year in 1749, before setting about the reconstruction of the Omani navy.

Ostrich Breeding Farm (📞26 884869; ⊙ Sun–Thu; 500bzs) Also in the *wilayat* of Barka there is an ostrich farm open to the public, which is an agricultural business unit too. Ostrich produce, such as leather and meat, are sold on the international market. These inquisitive, flightless, sizeable birds come to greet you, surrounding your vehicle, before casually walking away. The breeding season is April–September and there is a souvenir shop here. Exit the highway at the Barka roundabout and travel inland for about 4km in the direction of Nakhal to reach it.

Bait Na'man (📞 24 641300, ext 142; ⊙ 08.30–14.30 Sun–Thu; 500bzs) An English-speaking Omani will guide you around. Signposted off the main dual carriageway just south of Barka (roughly 30 minutes' drive from Muscat), this unusual castle (fortified country house), restored in 1990 and recently renovated, is easily the most charming of its type in Oman, and made very accessible by the furnishings that bring it to life. The scale, unlike so many of the vast forts which become rather indigestible after a while, is domestic and homely, and most visitors have no trouble imagining what it would have been like living in such a house a century or two ago. There are also excellent wall plaques explaining the function of each room.

Built by Imam Saif bin Sultan (who died in 1711) in the prosperous Ya'arubi times, the house was for his exclusive use as a country retreat (a sort of Chequers); it was originally three days' journey from Muscat. He planted 30,000 date palms and 6,000 coconut trees around it. The gardens were irrigated by a *falaj* from Nakhal, 25km away, which is now dried up. The outside courtyard was where the soldiers would have camped, several hundred of them to protect the imam, and there was a big raised-up cistern where rainwater collected. Inside, the high ceilings are attractively decorated and allow for coolness. The accommodation was suitable for a family of eight or nine members. On the ground floor were the toilet, bathroom, date store, kitchen and women's jail. New carpets have been laid as floor covering, too big to give an authentic feel – as original Omani rugs were and still are very small. Rush matting would have been the usual floor covering.

Halfway up the stairs was the guards' room, to stop people entering the private quarters, and the first floor had living areas only. The towers on the roof floor have cannon holes, though the cannons themselves have been taken off to Barka Fort or to the Ministry, as they were too heavy to get back *in situ* after the restoration. The walls are 1.5m thick, made from traditional Omani *sarouj* plaster which was typically soaked for 25 days, not just the one day as is the practice today. As a result the *sarouj* is less strong now than it used to be centuries ago.

AL SAWADI السوادي

There are beautiful stretches of beach at Al Sawadi, where there is a beach resort of the same name, and from where you can take boating and other adventure trips out to the Daymaniyat and Al Sawadi Islands.

🏠 **WHERE TO STAY** For location of listing see map, pages 128–9.

🛏 **Al Sawadi Beach Resort** (100 rooms) PO Box 747, PC 320, Barka; ☎26 795545; www. alsawadibeach.info/about-us. Situated on a beautiful expanse of sandy beach in a very peaceful & picturesque setting, this upper-range resort was built in 1996. Roughly 45mins drive from Muscat Airport (90km from Muscat), or 2hrs drive from the Wadi Hatta border, it lies approximately 15km off the main dual carriageway, & is well signposted but difficult to reach without your own transport. You can catch a microbus from Muscat or Rustaq to the Sawadi turn-off, but the final 15km requires a taxi. The disabled are catered for, & a concrete path to the sea edge facilitates easy access. Rooms are all single-storey & just big enough to squeeze in 2 extra beds

for children. Each has a good-sized private sea-facing patio area. Its food outlets are all licensed. Although the beach is not private to the hotel, they have erected *barasti* (palm leaf) sunshades for the benefit of guests. Being driven by golf cart to your room is a nice touch. This resort is for total relaxation. The hotel supports the cleanliness & marine life preservation campaign of the government & conducts a 'beach cleaning day'. There is a Bodylines health & fitness centre & a business centre. There are good health & sports facilities & the Daymaniyat Islands are on the doorstep. Boat, dive or snorkelling trips to the Daymaniyat & Sawadi Islands (see page 134) are arranged from the dive centre of the hotel, www.extradivers-worldwide.com.

WHAT TO SEE

Al Sawadi Islands These islands lie just offshore and boat trips can be arranged through the dive centre of Al Sawadi Beach Resort. Alternatively you can negotiate with the local fishermen to take you to them. One island (Al Mugabra) has a sandy beach where you can picnic under municipal shelters. On another island (Jebel Sawadi) there is a watchtower whose stairs you can climb. These islands are also good for birdwatching. Snorkellers and novice divers are taken here.

Daymaniyat Islands Nature Reserve These are a string of nine small islands situated about 16km off the Batinah coast (in both the Seeb and Barka *wilayats*). They are about a 40-minute boat trip away from the nearest resort, which is Al Sawadi Beach Resort. The waters around the islands look remarkable from the air, when coming in to land at Muscat Airport.

The islands have been proclaimed a conservation area since 1996, and are rife with bird and marine life. You can explore the waters around the islands by diving, snorkelling or swimming, but the islands themselves are protected and inaccessible. They are nesting grounds for the endangered hawksbill turtle and the green turtle, and from April to September it is the birds' breeding season, when ospreys and red-billed tropicbirds, among others, nest here. The surrounding waters also have protected zones, the purpose of which is to preserve the coral reef. Al Sawadi Beach Resort obtains permits from the Ministry of Regional Municipalities and Environment to take guests and tourists to the waters surrounding the islands, and so all the formalities are done for you these days.

Reportedly one of the best dive sites in Oman, there are more than 20 set dive locations where coral reef, clownfish, rays, honeycomb moray eels, barracuda, tuna, green turtles, fusiliers, zebra sharks and leopard sharks have all been seen. In addition there are marine and terrestrial snake species, and marine mammals such as the bottlenose dolphin, the common dolphin and the humpback whale.

The islands are broken up into western, central and eastern areas, and they are named Al Kharaabah, Al Hayoot, Al Jibaal al Kibaar Island, Al Joon, Al Jebel as Sagheer, Memlehah, Al Loomiyah, Qismah and Awlad al Joon. Camping is

PICNIC STOPS ALONG THE BATINAH

If you are travelling south from the Wadi Hatta border post there is, almost immediately, a delightful area to the right, with mountain wadis flowing all year round. There are many places where cars can get close to the wadi bottom and the only downside here is the accompanying litter, especially at weekends.

The road south passes out of the mountain scenery within 15 minutes, and after that the easiest picnicking spot is not until Sohar, 45 minutes further on. Take the same signpost off towards the coast as for the Sohar Beach Hotel from the Sallan roundabout and in less than 1km you will see an extensive landscaped park to the left of the road. You can enter it from either end, inland by turning left at the traffic lights, or at the shore end where you can turn left into a car park area. There are toilet blocks and water fountains, shaded pagodas and children's playgrounds with a central lake. You will find it near-deserted, except on Fridays. The Sohar Beach Hotel lies just beyond it.

If you want a wilder spot, another option with your own transport is to drive further on south of Al Khaboura (1½ hours from the Wadi Hatta border). Turn off towards the coast at Qasabiyat along dirt tracks through the banana and mango plantations until you reach the tarmac road parallel to the main dual carriageway. Follow this as it winds scenically past date palms till you come to the point where the tarmac crosses a picturesque wadi flowing with a wide river. Leave the car beside the main road and then walk along either side of the riverbank to find a picnic spot among the palm trees. The birdlife here is stunning.

permitted on Jibaal al Kibaar and Al Joon only, with designated areas for camp fires, and a list of strict rules and regulations.

AS SUWAIQ السويق

From the dual carriageway Suwaiq is clearly signposted off to your right taking you out towards the sea. It's quite nice to take a detour here, if simply to break the monotony of the dual carriageway. It is a quaint old village with a restored seafront fort and its share of mosques. There are four springs, the most picturesque being at Wadi Jahawar. The beach is deserted and makes a great picnic stop. The area is known for its agriculture, and bananas, citrus fruits, mangoes and herbs are grown. Bullfighting takes place here.

From Suwaiq you can follow the tarmac road close to the coast for roughly 15 minutes north to Khadra Al Bu Rashid, which winds through fishing villages, past a crumbling fort and palm plantations. Between As Suwaiq and Al Khaboura there is a cluster of three restored *surs* (walled fort enclosures) standing close to the roadside. They all have either square or round towers at their corners with gun ports. Their doors are always kept locked, but in any event they look impressive from the outside. For location of listing see map, pages 128–9.

⌂ WHERE TO STAY

⌂ **As Suwaiq Motel** (15 rooms) PO Box 455, PC 315; ☎26 862241, 862243. This simple, 1-star hotel lies about a 1hr drive (100km) from Muscat International Airport towards Sohar. Take the right-hand turn towards the sea, & the motel is about 3km down the road, about 4km from the sea. Licensed restaurant; live Arabic & Indian entertainment. No pool. **$$**

WHAT TO SEE

Bu Said Castle Just before (south of) Al Khaboura look out for signs to Qasr Bint Al Za'ad (towards the sea) and follow the dirt track as it leads between two shops and into the lush date-palm plantations. After about 1km you will hit tarmac again and turn left to follow the road at right angles to the coast. This is an extremely attractive road, almost devoid of traffic, and gives you a real feel of the fertility of the Batinah and the serenity it enjoyed before the days of the dual carriageway. It passes a very pretty wadi outlet to the sea, making a good picnic stop. Keep going and follow signs for Qasr Bint Al Bu Said until you reach the crumbling *sur* of that name, set right on the beach beside a small modern village, disappearing further into the sand year by year. The cannon, once wedged on one of the walls, has now vanished.

AL KHABOURA الخابورة

Al Khaboura itself is unremarkable except as a centre for traditional weaving, the products of which are sold in the Muscat heritage shops. Leather tanning and boatbuilding are other occupations, and sugar cane, dates, wheat and cotton are grown here. Its fort is in ruins except for one tower by the beach.

WHAT TO SEE

Wadi Hawasinah At Al Khaboura a left turn at the roundabout heads you southwest towards Ibri through the Wadi Hawasinah, a picturesque wadi day trip where you can have an energetic trek to a pool and waterfall, using the 'chains' (metal couplings with stirrups) hanging from the rock face to help navigate tricky places. The tarmac now continues all the way to Ibri, a drive of 130km, taking around two hours.

Saham صحم Between Al Khaboura and Sohar, Saham is signposted 3km off the main road. It is about 1½ hours from Muscat International Airport – or the same time from the Hatta border. Saham is an attractive old fishing town with an interesting seafront. Camel and horse racing are popular here, along with bullfighting events, which are held on alternate Fridays to Sohar's.

Keep straight on over the roundabout with the herons, following signs to As-Souk, until the road leads you on to the seafront, where it fronts the beach for 1–2km to reach the fort with its red flag flying at the far end. On the way you pass some decayed seafront houses, once the homes of rich merchants. Traces of blue and white paint remain along the decorated arches and windows that look out across the sea from the balustraded verandas. A few old *shasha* (reed) boats are usually pulled up on to the beach, still in use. The town souk is beside the fort, on the beach, and though the fort is theoretically open to the public it is in practice difficult to coincide a visit with a guard being present to open the door. Sultan Qaboos holds one of his royal camps at Seih al Taybat, which is in this *wilayat*.

SOHAR صحار

Muscat to Sohar is 230km and takes about 2½ hours. Sohar, once known as Majan (*ma-jan* means 'ship's skeleton' or 'chassis'), has great historical significance as a major trading port and for this reason stood as the capital of Oman in past centuries.

Sohar in its heyday was described by the 10th-century Arab geographer Istakhri as 'the most populous and wealthy town in Oman. It is not possible to find on the shore of the Persian Sea nor in all the land of Islam, a City more rich in fine buildings and foreign wares than Sohar.' His contemporary, the Arab historian Al Muqaddasi, described Sohar as 'the hallway to China, the storehouse of the East'. Traders disembarked from Sohar on their journeys to China, and the legend of Sindbad is said to have originated from here. The city was destroyed in the 10th century and never regained its former glory.

However, for over 1,500 years, until 1749 when the Al Bu Saids moved their headquarters to Muscat, Sohar was still Oman's most prestigious and influential town. The *khor* (creek) beside the fort, which was once its splendid harbour, is now silted and almost completely vanished. The only evident reason today for the success of the town's location is its situation at the end of the Wadi Jizzi (see page 142), one of the few east–west passes across the Oman mountain range, and from where copper was exported to Mesopotamian cities over many centuries.

When the Portuguese arrived in 1507 they found it a thriving town needing 1,000 people to defend the fort alone. An Augustine church was subsequently built

---

ARAB NAVIGATION

The Arabs had three grades of navigator: the lowest was the man who knew coastlines and could follow them safely, avoiding reefs and other dangers; second was the man who could cross open water, following a direct course until he made his landfall; third and highest was the man called a *mu'allim*, who could navigate at all times out of sight of land, from port to port, using only the stars and his knowledge. It was the medieval Arabs who developed this art of astro-navigation. Ibn Majid, a famous Omani navigator, was said to have been hired by Portuguese explorer Vasco da Gama for the Arabia to Calcutta stretch of his journey to discover a sea route to India in 1498.

there by the Portuguese, who retained it until they were driven out in 1650 by the native Ya'arubi sultans of Oman.

Sohar during the Al Bu Said dynasty was the stage for just two more moments of high drama: one in 1866 when a sultan was shot by his own son while asleep; and the other in 1952 when the present sultan's father, angered by the Saudi occupation of Buraimi, ordered his army to gather at Sohar for the march up Wadi Jizzi to Buraimi – in the event the army never set off, dissuaded from action by the British.

GETTING THERE AND AROUND Taking the right-hand turn at Sohar roundabout you pass over several smaller landscaped roundabouts. Keep straight over these until you come close to the sea and then you have the choice of turning right or left at the final mini-roundabout. The left turn takes you past a Shell garage (on your left) and if you continue onwards the Sohar Beach Hotel lies on the right-hand side of the road just before the traffic-lights crossroads. The hotel is set in a whitewashed stone wall enclosure, with large impressive wooden gates, but is frustratingly not clearly signposted. Back at the final mini-roundabout the right-hand turn takes you round to the coast road which, a little later, bends round and back on itself past the Sohar Fort (now on your left), which occupies an elevated position opposite the clearly signposted *wali's* office. For a visit to the fort you can drive up its sloped frontage to a car-parking area. The entrance door is just here, hidden behind a tree and flanked by two cannons.

ONTC **buses** run from Muscat (starting in the main Ruwi Bus Station) to Sohar about four times a day, taking three hours and costing RO5, and from Sohar to Muscat twice a day. They drop passengers off at the small hospital near the centre of town then continue north to Buraimi or Dubai. **Microbuses or taxis** can then be used for local travel. Expect to pay about RO18 for a taxi to Rustaq or Nakhal.

Today the sprawl of Sohar remains considerable. The northern edge is at the Sallan roundabout, from where the Sohar Beach Hotel is signposted. The southern edge is the Sohar roundabout, which is identified by its vast globe statue. From here, Sohar town centre is signposted off towards the sea. The old part of town is called Harat al Hajara, and the fort and *wali's* office are located here.

Simple fishing boats lie on the dark sand and after 2–3km you will see the Sohar fish souk, a series of stalls set right on the beach. This is a hive of bustle in the mornings, when the freshly caught fish are laid out. You need a fairly strong

The Batinah SOHAR

4

UAE,
Musandam

Alawi al Ghawi
Restaurant (4km)

④

AS SULTAN QABOOS RD

①

Sallan
Roundabout

KASHMIR STREET

Fish souk

ONTC Buses 🚌

Local taxis 🚗

AT TRAYE STREET

AL-BATHA STREET

②

AL WIGAYBAH ST

Friday
Market

Handicraft
Market

Sohar Fort
Museum

AL HAMBAR ST

Pizza
Hut ✕

Sohar
Roundabout

Bullfighting
Arena

ASH SHATTI STREET

Sohar
Port

AL BUSTAN ST

Dohar Hospital
(5km)

AL BAHJAH STREET

③

N

Bradt

0 ——————— 2 km
0 ——————— 1 mile

As Suwayhirah
Roundabout

Muscat

Gulf of

Oman

For listings, see pages 138–9

⌂ **Where to stay**

1 Al Wadi
2 Atlas Hotel Apartments
3 Green Oasis
4 Sohar Beach

✕ **Where to eat and drink**

Off map
   Alawi al Ghawi

stomach to stroll through it, especially as the sun gets stronger, heating the mounds of entrails.

Sohar also makes a good base from which to explore the Batinah Plain (see pages 140–54). For location of listings see map, page 138.

⌂ WHERE TO STAY

⌂ **Sohar Beach Hotel** (40 rooms) PO Box 122, PC 321, Al Tareef, Sohar; ☎26 841111; www. soharbeach.com. The hotel is about a 3hr drive from Muscat Airport – or a 45min drive from the

Wadi Hatta border post. It is roughly halfway between Muscat & Dubai airports & provides a good stopover if you want to split the approximate 4hr drive either to or from Dubai. This is a gem of a hotel, on Sallan Beach in Sohar. It sits on the road that loops through Sohar & rejoins the highway, although not at all clearly signposted from the Sohar roundabout. Instead continue on the dual carriageway past the Sohar roundabout, & exit at the Sallan roundabout (north of Sohar) in the direction of the sea. The hotel is signposted from here, & from this end it is just past the only set of traffic lights on the loop road, & sits within its high walls on the left-hand side. The hotel is like an Omani fort in appearance, with 4 round crenellated towers. The rooms, suites & chalets are arranged on 2 storeys in a semicircle round a large pool & situated within 11 acres of landscaped gardens. Facilities include Al Sallan coffee shop, Al Zafran Arabian nightclub, serving *meze*, seafood & grills, Al Jizzi lounge for residents & members & Al Taraif lounge public bar. BBQ evenings every Thu in winter, & private BBQs for 5 or more guests can be arranged. There are lots of activities for kids, like crazy golf, croquet, go-karts, beach buggies, beach volleyball, water scooters, watersports & pleasure boat rides. The room rates are cheaper than the Sawadi Beach Resort, & the décor & the welcome far superior. Accepts credit cards. **$$$$**

⌂ **Al Wadi Hotel** (80 rooms) PO Box 459, PC 311, Sohar; ✆ 26 840058, 841995; e gmalwadi@ omanhotels.com or reservationsalwadi@ omanhotels.com; www.omanhotels.com. At the Sallan roundabout (the next one up from the Sohar roundabout, 10km from Sohar), take a left. The hotel is signposted & has a small pool. Al Sallan is the licensed restaurant offering continental, Indian & Chinese cuisine (⊕ 06.00–23.00). There is Al Waqbah bar (⊕ 12.00–15.00 & 18.00–01.00) & a licensed restaurant – The Oasis (⊕ 19.00–01.00). Al Majaz is the club bar for residents only (⊕ 19.00–01.00). This hotel is one of four in the group which includes Al Falaj Hotel, Ruwi Hotel & Sur Plaza. Does not provide airport transfers. It uses Budget & Hertz for arranging hire cars. **$$$**

⌂ **Atlas Hotel Apartments** ✆ 26 858009, 26 853010; e royalint@omantel.net.om. Has large dbl rooms. **$$**

⌂ **Green Oasis Hotel** (42 rooms) ✆ 26 846442; www.greenoasishotel.com. Close to the Sohar Hospital, a peaceful mid-range place with a restaurant, pool & gym. **$$**

✗ **WHERE TO EAT** **Alawi al Ghawi** (nicknamed Cute Ali) is at the roadside 9km north from Sohar roundabout and 4km north from Sallan roundabout. On the coastal side of the road, this is a simple house made of *barasti*, serving rice with fish in spicy sauce with onions, limes and lettuce, dates and water, followed by sweet herb tea. The menu is fixed and the prices low, although it is unlicensed. You eat on the floor, in traditional style, under ceiling fans in the room to the right. The room to the left is for prayers.

WHAT TO SEE

Sohar Fort Museum (✆ *26 844758;* ⊕ *08.30–14.30 Sun–Thu; RO1/500/250bzs non-Omani/Omani/child*) To reach Sohar Fort from the Sallan roundabout take the road towards the coast, passing the Sohar Beach Hotel on your left and following the tarmac as it bends to run parallel to the coast. From the 'globe' roundabout follow the road for some 2–3km until you reach the white painted fort of Sohar, now converted to a museum, and set overlooking the black sandy beach.

Passing through the gateway into the Sohar Fort courtyard there are various outbuildings including a prison. Before you walk over to the tall square keep, which houses the museum proper, you will need to pop into a small central building to pay your entrance fee. A small booklet can also be bought for 300bzs. On the left of this central reception building are the visitors' toilets.

The four-storey keep/museum, opened in 1993, is laid out well with many old weapons, rifles and navigation equipment, including artefacts from the area's ancient copper trade. These are accompanied by a comprehensive historical summary of Sohar's navigational and overseas trading history, especially of the princes of Hormuz and the medieval fortress of Hawra Burghah (see page 142).

Sohar Fort dates to AD795, although it was renovated in the 14th and 15th centuries by the emirs (or princes) of Hormuz. There is said to be a 10km-long escape tunnel, leading from the fort to the beginning of the *wilayat* of Buraimi, which was used during sieges. The current buildings are thought to be 200–300 years old. Fully restored in 1985, it has a commanding location just in front of the beach, opposite the *wali*'s (governor's) office. The surrounding gardens have been well landscaped.

Outside, excavations in the sand are clearly visible. Conducted in 1980–82, these revealed fine quality brick-built foundations of a 14th/15th-century fort and houses of rich merchants thought to be the princes of Hormuz, who had a strong garrison here. Many fine pieces of Chinese porcelain were discovered, confirming Sohar's extensive trade links. The empire of the princes of Hormuz, with their headquarters on the island of Hormuz (in the strait of that name), fell to the Portuguese in 1507 after two centuries of rule here.

Just behind (inland from) the fort, a handicraft centre (⊕ *08.00–12.00 & 16.00–21.00 Sat–Thu*) has been built in traditional style with domes and courtyards, selling and displaying local crafts.

Sohar port There is now a modern fully operational industrial port at Sohar, a little further along the coast from Sohar town (in the direction of Muscat), which received its first vessel in 2004. It is an industrial-free zone, concentrating on cargo. Further development is planned, with a hospital and even a university. Oman's other two ports are the Raysut Port in Salalah and the Sultan Qaboos Port in Old Muscat. *Mina* is the Arabic for port.

LIWA لواء

Continuing up the main highway from Sohar, the next village you reach is Liwa, signposted 2km off the main dual carriageway. Past the village and date plantations is the castle. To reach another picturesque picnic spot or campsite, continue on, after Liwa Castle, towards the beach, turning off to the right before the houses along a track that leads to a smaller ruined fort. Beyond lies a stretch of water like a lake bounded by low dunes, rich in birdlife and pleasantly wild. In the Harmul area the Awla Ya'rab Fortress, built of white clay, is located on the beach.

WHAT TO SEE
Liwa Castle The central keep has very elaborate decoration and with care you can still climb to the upper rooms via a crumbling outer staircase to see the decorative niches and plasterwork of the top *majlis* (men's sitting room). A modern settlement just behind the fort means that young children are prone to follow you round the fort, not always in a way that is welcome.

SHINAS شناص

This town is the most northerly of the Batinah region and has a number of castles and forts, including Shinas Fort, as well as a park noted for its forest of mangrove trees (or *qurum*, in Arabic). Fruits and vegetables are grown in the vicinity. A twice-weekly ferry runs from Shinas to Khasab (see page 52).

WHAT TO SEE AND DO
Shinas Fort Restored in 1997–98 and now open to the public, the fort is signposted 2km off the main highway towards the sea. The simple classic coastal design has

four crenellated walls enclosing a rectangular courtyard with a round tower at each corner, built of mud brick and faced with traditional Omani *sarouj* plaster. There is a free-standing mosque in the courtyard. The fort was built in Shinas's heyday around 1800 when the town was allied with the Persians, and quite separate from the rest of Oman. Shinas fought with the Ras al Khaimah Qasimi tribe against British shipping in the Gulf. The British and Omani mainstream retaliated and in 1810 the fort was sacked and forced to surrender.

From Shinas to the Khatmat Malahah border post
From Shinas, the road to the north leads to the Khatmat Malahah border post with Fujairah, which would be the way to travel to reach Musandam, or Sharjah or Ras al Khaimah emirate.

From Shinas to the Wadi Hatta border post and Wadi Khabab
Instead of continuing straight up the coast road to the Khatmat border and on to Musandam, taking a well-signposted left at the roundabout leads you to Dubai and the Wadi Hatta border post. There is magnificent scenery along this route, which culminates in the Wadi Khabab.

The drive from Muscat to the Wadi Hatta border post, non-stop cruising at the 120km/h speed limit, takes three hours minimum – roughly one hour to Sawadi Beach, another hour to Sohar and the third to reach the border post – though in practice, with stops for petrol and leg-stretches, most people would allow at least four hours. Coming the other way, from the UAE into Oman, the Wadi Hatta border post is the easiest and quickest of all the crossing points, mainly because there is no UAE exit post. This means that only one set of forms needs to be filled in and only one checkpoint needs to be crossed, followed by the standard vehicle search.

Wadi Khabab Immediately before the border (on the Oman side) the scenery is magnificent with jagged mountain peaks dominating the wadi gorges, many of which have year-round running water. If you want to camp in this area of the northern Batinah, but more off the beaten track, follow the sign left to Tumait for 9km, shortly before the Wadi Hatta border post. The dirt track crosses the wadi bed and climbs a steep track out of the valley. Take the first left fork after the wadi (approximately 500m from the Tumait sign) and stay on this for some 6km until you reach date plantations set above a gorge, flowing with water. This is the Wadi Khabab, known for its blue pools, created by deposits of calcite in the rock and the reflected light. It has to be full daylight for you to appreciate the colour, with the blue sky above. There is no village here and the track continues along the right of the wadi, arriving at an open space beyond the plantations, which is ideal for camping. The track is good and can be negotiated by a saloon car, as long as the water level in the first wadi by the tarmac is low. The pools themselves are not deep and are more for splashing and wallowing than swimming.

THE BATINAH PLAIN الباطنة

The Batinah Plain is fertile from the mineral-rich soil washed down from the mountains into the wadis, namely Wadi Jizzi, Wadi Hibi and Wadi Ahin, and it is watered by many wells. These have been drilled to excess in recent years, leading to seawater seepage into the soil. However, the land still produces dates and limes together with tomatoes, carrots, onions, aubergines, cauliflowers, peppers, lemons, bananas, mangoes, guavas and even tobacco. Inland, this fertile plain gives way to gravel plain that reaches back to the mountains, broken up only by a few scrubby bushes and trees.

WADI JIZZI وادى الجزي Few people are aware how much there is to see in the hinterland of Sohar, but with your own transport an enjoyable few days can be spent based at the Sohar Beach Hotel (see page 138) exploring Wadi Jizzi with its ancient copper-mining sites, the medieval stronghold of Hawra Burghah and the ziggurat (temple) at Arja. All are likely to be deserted and all are set in landscapes of wild beauty. There is no public transport. This wadi was one of the two major inland corridors permitting access to the sea; the other was the Sumail Gap that links Muscat with Nizwa and the interior. Sohar grew up here because it was the natural port for the copper dug from the ancient mines along the Wadi Jizzi, copper that was destined eventually for Mesopotamia via Umm Al Nar (now Abu Dhabi) and Dilmun (now Bahrain).

Getting there Wadi Jizzi is reached by forking inland at Falaj Al Qubail roundabout some 20km north of Sohar, a roundabout recognisable by its landscaped artificial rocks, model goats and waterfall. It starts off very wide and becomes narrower and more mountainous as you head further inland towards Buraimi.

HAWRA BURGHAH FORTRESS This worthwhile excursion from Sohar is now easily drivable even in a saloon car since the construction of the wide graded track to the Wadi Al Jizzi Dam. The 13th-century fortress is dramatically sited on the summit of a rock outcrop that rises 200–300m above the Wadi Jizzi which it straddles.

The medieval fortress was the most important of several forts built by the Nabahina dynasty of hereditary kings in their attempts to resist the invading Hormuz princes. Its strategic location at Hawra Burghah enabled it to dominate the passageway through Wadi Jizzi to Buraimi. Beyond it to the south stands the unmistakable triangular **Sohar peak**, the highest mountain in the area at 1,600m and used by early navigators as a landmark. Its huge white limestone cone rises directly behind the town of Sohar as seen from the sea.

The name *Hawra* means 'white limestone' in Arabic and *Burghah* means 'garden' in Persian. It is the defence walls and the elaborate water system of dams, cisterns and plaster-lined *falaj* channels (see box, page 190) that make the exploration of the hilltop interesting and which give it its name. In its heyday the various terraces and levels must have been lush with crops and vegetation, enabling the inhabitants to hold out against long-term sieges, and testament to the fact that rainfall must always have been high enough to sustain life on this magnificent hilltop.

The ascent of the steep hill takes 10–15 minutes and is best made from the north side, where the track nearly touches the foot of the hill and where there is a breach in the walls through which you can enter. The upper section of the hill is quite a scramble and requires good strong footwear. Once on top it takes the best part of an hour to look around the surprisingly extensive city. Try to avoid the midday period as there is no shade on the summit.

Getting there Take the road inland towards Buraimi from the Falaj al Qubail roundabout for some 13km until you reach the blue sign marked left for Wadi al Jizzi Dam (4km). As you head inland, and once you reach the foothills, try to attune your eyes to the beehive tombs along the ridges on both sides of the road – there must be upwards of 50. Before reaching the turn-off to the Wadi al Jizzi Dam, archaeology enthusiasts who want to take a closer look at these tombs might like to turn off to a town called Willi – a sorry collection of hovels to the left of the road.

From Willi a dirt track to the left leads on through the low hills with many beehive tombs lining the ridges to either side, within easy scrambling distance of the track. Though they are mainly in a collapsed state, their sheer size and number are nevertheless impressive. Following the track out beyond these hills brings you close to an interesting group of rocks shaped like a falcon's head, an excellent perch for a picnic.

Back at the Wadi Jizzi turn-off after this detour (take the second turn after the sign to avoid the village), follow the track for 3km and continue straight at the fork that heads left towards the dam. It is a wide, dark-brown graded track that crosses the wadi stream in two places, before reaching the foot of the distinctive outcrop which it skirts right round to the left. At times of heavy rain the wadi crossings can be impassable to all but 4x4s.

THE ZIGGURAT AT ARJA This archaeological ruin is remarkable not for its scale or size, but for the fact that it exists at all. The only one of its kind in the whole Arabian Peninsula, a ziggurat is a very early kind of temple, built in terraces, similar to a step pyramid. The earliest and most famous ziggurat was at Ur of the Chaldees in southern Mesopotamia. Arja itself was the main centre for copper mining in Oman up to the 12th century. A total of 32 copper smelting sites have been identified in this area, centred on Wadi Jizzi. Estimates suggest that in medieval times Arja produced 48,000–60,000 tonnes of copper. Copper was massively exploited here for nearly 4,000 years, the result being the gradual deforestation of the entire mining area to provide fuel for smelting. Omani copper has a high nickel content and the copper deposits here were formed millions of years ago at the bottom of the ocean, in the lavas now exposed in Oman ophiolite rocks.

One side of the ziggurat has a clearly recognisable processional ramp leading to the summit, which would have been used by early priests making sacrificial offerings. The exact nature of these practices is a matter of pure speculation – as is the position of this ziggurat which appears to be oriented towards a dramatic dark pyramid-shaped peak on the far side of the valley.

Archaeologist Paolo Costa and English orientalist T G Wilkinson conducted an archaeological study in 1978 on Arja and the ancient copper-mining settlements, the results of which were published by the Omani Ministry of National Heritage and Culture. The ziggurat, as well as ancient houses and furnaces found in the area, were dated by this study to the 10th century.

Getting there The journey from Sohar in search of the ziggurat takes you through some attractive mountain scenery and gives you the chance to see some of the more remote villages. There are no buses here so you will need your own transport. From the main road inland to Buraimi, ignore the blue sign to the right signposted Arja (6km) which you reach some 23km from the Falaj al Qubail (Falaj of Tribes) roundabout (recognisable by its rocks, model goats and waterfalls), and continue to the massive modern smokestack of the copper smelting factory. Leave the main road and head towards the factory entrance, then immediately turn right and follow the tarmac road through the factory area (it's a public road!). Stay on this tarmac road for about 7km, driving straight on at all crossings. Eventually you'll see the ziggurat on the right just beneath the road with the mosque of Arja a little further off.

Continuing on the road leading away from Arja village, the route passes the old mine, now close up to your right, and comes to a dead end in a huge open-cast mine ringed with a wire fence.

LUSAIL (AL ASAYL) COPPER MINE This is the most spectacular of the copper mines, mined as recently as 20 years ago, but now abandoned. It is about a 1½-hour detour off the main coastal highway. Here stands a famous rock arch – its date and origins unknown – beside the huge open-cast mine. All around the foot of the arch are extraordinary rock colours showing the mineral wealth in reds, whites, purples and yellows.

Lusail is not marked or signposted off the main road. To reach it look out for the old tarmac road roughly 1km after the chimney stack of the modern copper smelting factory, running on the left, parallel to the main road. Get on to this road and turn right, then follow it over a wadi crossing, up and over a hill with a Pakistani mining settlement of Portakabins to the left. Then continue down over the second wadi crossing and arrive at a dead end with 'Danger: no entry' signs. This is where you park and walk on.

The deepest ancient gallery at Lusail was 88m below ground, and the length of the galleries was 20–30m with the roof supported by acacia wood and date palm. Food and water for workers was raised and lowered by winches, many parts of which have been unearthed. Tools and the mined ore were also transported this way. When functioning in the 1980s Lusail used to produce 2,500 tonnes of copper ore a day, while Bayda and Arja each produced 1,000 tonnes, and in total the factory produced 20,000 tonnes of refined copper a year. The Majis jetty, 17km north of Sohar, was specially constructed in 1983 for exporting the copper.

Crossing over the earth rampart on the way to the mining area, many samples of turquoise/green copper can be found in the rocks, as well as some fool's gold. Correctly known as copper pyrites, fool's gold is made of copper, iron and sulphur. It looks bright and yellow when freshly unearthed, but tarnishes with exposure. The rock arch lies about a ten-minute walk further on, passing a few sealed-off mine shafts on the way.

Returning to the junction at the modern copper mine and its smoking chimney stack, fork to the right on to the track opposite the chimney and climb up, leaving the bridge over the road to your left, then continue straight on over the crossroads. Follow this wide track for 2km along the ridge until you reach a small track forking to the right, then follow this for 500m to reach the edge of the ridge overlooking the Wadi Jizzi, with the remains of an ancient settlement and field systems. This makes a good picnic spot.

According to Sumerian texts there were 32 mining settlements built along the great wadis and foothills of these mountains. This copper-mining area was referred to as Magan, and there are at least 50 mentions of Magan in Mesopotamian texts of the 3rd century BC. From these texts we know that the farmers of Magan grew sorghum, wheat, barley and dates, and that they had herds of camels, cows, sheep and goats. The landscape was evidently much more heavily wooded and the climate wetter than now, but the necessity of chopping firewood for the furnaces resulted in the gradual deforestation of the region. The miners' houses were built of stone with imposing towers, inside which were wells. Their circular graves, now known as Umm Al Nar style, were 5–13m in diameter with up to 200 skeletons inside. Besides copper, the other resource of this area that interested Mesopotamia was diorite. Mesopotamia lacked such stone, suitable for carving into statues, and here it was easily gathered as the rains washed it down from the mountains into the wadi beds and thence to the coast, where it was collected and loaded on to ships.

TO BURAIMI VIA WADI JIZZI It is about an hour's drive from the Falaj al Qubail roundabout on the coastal dual carriageway to the Wadi Jizzi Omani border post, which you have to pass in order to get to Buraimi (although Buraimi is in Oman!). The good tarmac road bends and weaves through low-level jebels and past old villages with their mosques, forts and watchtowers. As this is not dual carriageway, it requires alert and aware driving, as other vehicles may overtake in risky fashion. (For further information on Buraimi, see page 181)

THE RUSTAQ LOOP

Al Sawadi Beach Resort (see page 133) makes an excellent base for the inland circuit via Nakhal, Rustaq and Al Hazm, three of Oman's finest forts. Each fort takes at least an hour to visit so set aside a day, or ideally two, for the round trip. Alternatively, if time is not an issue, the locations on the loop can easily be visited in a series of outings from Muscat. You can flag down local microbuses anywhere on this route to reach the main towns on the tarmac, but to head into the wadis you need your own transport, preferably 4x4.

The more scenic approach of the two ways into the loop is opposite Barka, taking the inland route marked Nakhal and Rustaq. This brings you to Nakhal after 15 minutes and then on to the 40km stretch to Rustaq, which leads through some spectacular mountain scenery in the approaches to Jebel Akhdar, with many water-filled wadis and picnic spots. The stretch from Rustaq onwards via Al Hazm to the coast opposite Wudam is by contrast dull and flat, with no wadis and the mountains ever more distant; there's little to see here.

MUSLIMAT مسلمات Just before Nakhal you will notice a turn-off to Muslimat. The modern town now engulfs the 300-year-old walled village, recognisable from a distance by the squat round tower rising above the date plantations. Continue round, following the walls, until you reach the point where you notice the arched gateway entrance beside an impressive two-storey mansion – built c1900, but recently restored. The old *falaj* follows the edge of the walls, fast flowing and wide, but has lost much of its charm through modern concrete reparatory and maintenance works. Immediately to the right after entering the gateway, some steps lead up to the old mosque – which is still in use – with a deep well on the raised platform beside it. Inside it has round pillars with arches and a beautifully decorated plaster *mihrab* niche.

Many of the two-storey houses can be explored in the now-deserted village, a fascinating testimony to the lifestyle lived just a few decades ago by many Omanis.

The other main feature of the town is the huge round defence tower set by itself in the centre of the village. Now locked, its rooftop was used in the past to signal to the fort at Nakhal.

AL NAKHAL FORT قلعة نخل (*Roughly 120km from Muscat;* ☏ *26 781384;* ⏱ *07.30– 18.00 Sat–Thu, 08.00–13.00 Fri; 500bzs*) Built to protect the oasis and trade routes through Nizwa to the coast, the fort's construction seems to have been a rather piecemeal operation. It is believed to be pre-Islam, although it was restored in the 3rd and 10th centuries AD, during the reign of Bani Kharous and Ya'aruba imams. It was then reportedly built upon further in 1649, by the Ya'arubi family, for whom it served as headquarters throughout the 18th century. The gate, fence and towers of the fort were built later, in 1834, during the reign of Imam Said bin Sultan. Final restoration works were completed in 1990, at which time rooms were labelled and furnished with crafts and antiquities.

From a distance it is dwarfed by the mountainous backdrop, but the closer you get (once you fork off at the signposted turn), the more impressive it becomes. The fort has six towers, with walls that ingeniously follow the natural contours of the high rocky outcrop on which it sits. Labelled rooms, such as the *majlis*, the judge's room

THE RUSTAQ LOOP

Muscat, Barka, Muslimat

Nakhal
Al Nakhal Fort
Nakhal Springs
(Ain A' Thowarah)

Al Khadra

10km
6 miles

N
Bradt

0
0

Al Abyadh

Wadi Mistal

Al Ghubrah

Wadi Abyadh

Al Mahalil

A l   J e b e l   A k h d a r

Ad Dar

For listings, see pages 150, 210

Where to stay
1 Shimook Guesthouse
2 Village Resort Motel

Off map
Sun Rise Resort

Awabi
Awabi Fort

Wadi Bani Kharous

Sital
Al Hijayr
Al Mahsanah
Al Hajar

Wadi Hijir

Al Mazahit   Al Hazm Fort

2

Wadi Bani Auf

At Tikah

Al Alamayn

Rustaq Souk
Rustaq Fort

Rustaq Springs
(Ain al Kasfah)

Wadi Bimah
(Snake Gorge)

Wadi Bani Ghafir

Sun Rise Resort,
Ibri

1

Tabaqah

Wadi Sahtan

Uinaq

Maqammak

Az Zammah

Bilad Sayt

Al Hota Cave, Hamra

J e b e l   S h a m s

and the jail, aid an understanding of past times. You can then progress upwards and inwards through a second gateway into the private family quarters. This is the most charming area furnished with cushions and ornaments, and with the guest room boasting a painted ceiling. As in all forts, the layout ensures that the men's living areas get the best position to catch the prevailing wind through their windows, while the women's quarters get the less comfortable inland side. The *wali* still conducts weekly meetings in the public *majlis* room and there is an antique gun collection.

NAKHAL SPRINGS (AIN A'THOWARAH) عين نخل These hot springs are probably the best known of all the springs in Oman and make a popular picnic spot, so popular that the plentiful rubbish bins struggle to cope, especially at weekends. The springs are situated about 3km beyond Nakhal, accessible only via the tarmac road behind the fort. This road winds on through the date plantations, past old decaying houses (some still lived in, to judge by the washing lines and satellite dishes). The road then arrives at the flowing stream of the springs beside some shops, and you park and walk on through the picnic area, laid out with tables and shades. You can walk further up to the actual source of the springs at the end of the picnic area. There are steps down to the stream, which flows all year round, and little fish swim about in shoals. Children can even frolic a bit here when the water is high.

These springs are an important water source for the residents of Nakhal, stemming from Wadi Hammam. In spring, white lilies grow among the green pastures in the shade of the palms. The waters are said to have medicinal and healing qualities. A notice beside the stream forbids cars from driving across, but local vehicles tend to take no notice and drive over to the houses and village on the other side. The village women still come down to the stream to collect water, balancing the containers on their heads. Together they wash their clothes and dishes in the running water, chatting as they work to ease their chores.

WADI MISTAL وادي مستال With a 4x4 you can take a fork to the left after Nakhal to explore the natural phenomenon of the Ghubra Bowl (6.5km off the tarmac) surrounded by the high peaks of Jebel Akhdar. Beyond is **Wekan**, a mountain village known for its terracing, especially pretty in February when the almond and apricot trees are in blossom. The total distance to the end of the drivable track is about 30km from the tarmac.

WADI ABYADH وادى أبيض Some 6km beyond the turn for Wadi Mistal, a turn on the right signposts Al Mahaleel and leads into Wadi Abyadh (White Wadi). This wadi is famous for its blue pools, caused by the white calcite covering the pool bottoms that reflect the blue sky. Fork immediately right along the tarmac, then bear left after 1–2km into the gravel plain that leads to the narrow wadi. A 4x4 is essential and your speed must be kept up to avoid getting bogged down in the loose gravel. Water always flows here and is very plentiful in the winter rainy season. The pools themselves lie about 10km into the wadi from the main road and you can walk from that point for about 1½ hours to reach the village of Abyadh. There are many delightful picnic spots among the lush vegetation.

AWABI عوابى From the Mahaleel turn-off the road towards Rustaq now enters some of Oman's most spectacular scenery in the foothills of Jebel Akhdar. Geologists call these reddish-brown jagged rocks **ophiolite**, meaning ocean crust, now pushed above ground. The wadi you are crossing time and again is the Wadi Bani Kharous, which starts high in the hills and flows out here to merge with the Wadi Abyadh.

Socially and economically, the date is the most important fruit crop in Oman. You can fertilise 500 female date palms from a single male date palm (one Omani even called his male palm King Solomon in recognition of its fecundity). A date palm lives for 50 years and in the plantations each patch has an individual owner. Every part of the tree is used: the frond for braiding into baskets, food covers, flooring, sleeping mats and fans; the fibre for ropes and scourers; and the ribs for fish traps, chicken coops and clothes fumigators. Together with timber from local acacia for the beams, palm ribs and fronds were used in roofing, fencing and the summer housing – *barasti* huts – especially on the beaches where the breezes could pass straight through the gaps to give natural air conditioning. The dates are harvested in May, June and July by climbing the trees assisted by a back support (*sibta*) made of date palm trunk fibre, which leaves the hands free for picking. Perhaps unsurprisingly, Oman has its own Date Palm Research Centre, based in Rumeis near Barka, one of six research centres that fall within the Ministry of Agriculture and Fisheries. See www.aarinena.org/rais/documents/Newsletter/Vol15No2/10-11.

The tarmac now sweeps round to Awabi, more or less at the centre of the inland loop from the coast. Having virtually passed the town, a tarmac road forks off to the left towards the old fort of Awabi, at the head of the gorge leading into the mountains. This fort has been fully restored to a high standard.

Beyond it the road leading into the gorge, the start of Wadi Bani Kharous, has now been tarmaced and after 1.5km on the left, close beside a rusting black water gauge pipe, are a series of rock drawings on the cliff face and boulders, mainly of fighting men and animals. The drawings are thought to be 1,500 years old.

Awabi has been home to Omani scholars, poets and the literati, and was known as a place of eminent learning.

WADI BANI KHAROUS وادى بنى خروص
If you have a day to spare, you can continue up this spectacular wadi, dominated by high mountains, to explore the villages. The remotest of these villages, **Al Mahsanah**, has highly decorated castellated houses of a style unique in Oman, but reminiscent of Yemeni architecture. The distances are not great and Mahsanah is only about 30km from Awabi, but the drive is slow and takes the best part of an hour. A further 20km on is the village of **Al Hajar**, which has a famous old mosque called Al Ghamama. All these villages are in the process of being linked by tarmac roads. The rocks in this upper part of the wadi are some of the oldest found in Oman, ranging from 250–600 million years old.

As the road leaves Awabi, the next settlement you reach, on the very edge of Rustaq, has an attractive tower surrounded by a group of ruined two-storey houses, with the modern village then spreading out below.

WADI BANI AWF وادى بنى عوف, BILAD SAYT بلاد سيت AND WADI BIMAH (SNAKE GORGE) وادى بيما
Beyond Awabi (by about 10km) is the signposted track to Far and the start of Wadi Bani Awf, considered by many to be the most scenically spectacular of any of Oman's mountain drives. It culminates at Bilad Sayt, probably Oman's most picturesque mountain village, with extensive fertile terracing. A 4x4 is essential and the drive is not for the faint-hearted, with steep climbs and dizzying

drops. The first 10km is along the bumpy gorge floor, green with mango, lime and oleander. After rain the pools of water here can be tricky to negotiate. The sparkling white stones scattered about on the wadi floor are natural quartz. At 14km from the tarmac the track forks, with a right turn signposted to Al Jafa, leading (after 10km or so) to the Sahtan Bowl set directly at the foot of Jebel Shams (Oman's highest mountain at 3,048m), and making an interesting circuit via which to return to the Rustaq Loop and then Barka.

For Bilad Sayt, keep left and continue along Wadi Bani Awf through splendid scenery till you come to the village of Zammah, 22km from the tarmac. A good shaded picnic spot is about 17km along the road before Zammah, where a deep ravine on the right appears to be blocked by boulders. In fact, behind the boulders are a series of pools connected by waterfalls. You can park opposite at a little side road.

Bilad Sayt lies a steep 6km beyond Zammah, requiring a 4x4 for the vertiginous winding track. Its name is said to be a corruption of 'the town I forgot' (bilad nasaytuhu), so called after a Moghul general sacked the villages of the wadi but overlooked this remote one.

The road is signposted to the right and after 26km (where the track drops into a dip) there is a parking area big enough for two or three vehicles. The narrow cleft in the dip is known as Snake Gorge because it twists and turns across pools, rocks and waterfalls. Snake Gorge can be tackled by trekkers and is a 3km-long walk, bringing you out at Zammah. The first 2km of this is very rough going with climbs and slippery rocks, unsuitable for young children. Even for grown-ups it is not to be undertaken lightly and a local guide is recommended. People have been drowned here in flash floods and it is difficult to monitor the weather when you can see only a tiny piece of sky above you. Speak to any tour operator about this, quite separate, adventure.

After Snake Gorge the graded track forks again with the left turn taking you 3km to Hat, the end of the wadi. The right fork leads you for 1km to reach Bilad Sayt, the view opening up in spectacular style as you round a bend. Another way to enter the village, less intrusively and with a bit of exercise, is to continue on the Hat track for just a few hundred metres until on the right you notice the entrance to a slim shady defile. The 30-minute walk along the well-polished rock path here leads past deep pools where villagers do their washing and children play. It helps if you can speak Arabic here so that the villagers feel less like animals in a zoo that you have come to gawp at. From Hat the track improves and is now mainly tarmac as it continues over the Jebel Akhdar to the Al Hota Cave and Hamra (see pages 211 and 209–10,).

WADI SAHTAN وادي صحتان If you wish to continue your loop round to Rustaq you should return to the fork marked Al Jafa. There are many villages in the vast natural Sahtan Bowl and some are known for their traditional beekeepers. Using date-log hives made into 1m-long hollowed-out palm-tree trunks, they stack the logs in threes and put a small piece of honeycomb inside. The ends are blocked up leaving only enough space for the bees to enter. From the time of nesting the bees take two months to produce the honey and the beekeeper repeats the process three times a year by opening the ends and smoking out the bees, and then removing the honeycomb before starting all over again. It can be a profitable business, with a single honeycomb fetching as much as RO60. One hive produces around 100 bottles of honey a year. A rapport seems to develop between bees and keeper and the beekeepers wear no protective clothing and say they never get stung – either that or they no longer notice.

The village of An Nid ('the nest') can be used as the start of an ascent of **Jebel Shams**, taking a guide and donkey from the village to carry water. Donkeys are regarded as essential on such a trip and the recommended number is one donkey per person to carry water, food and bedding for the two days. From Rustaq, An Nid is a one-hour drive.

Leaving the Sahtan Bowl to complete your loop, you enter some 8km of narrow ravine which follows the course of the Wadi Sahtan. It is a bumpy drive, with strewn boulders and running water at most times of year and the occasional piece of rock art etched on to the boulders.

Once out of the ravine another 2km along the track brings you to **Tabaqah**, a village with an impressive and photogenic fort on a cliff edge, guarding the entrance to the Wadi Sahtan. The women of the village are often found doing their laundry in the flowing stream beneath the fort. A steep descent takes you out of the wadi and on to the new tarmac road that forks left via Wadi Bani Ghafir to Ibri, or along the tarmac to Rustaq, 9km further on. For locations of listings see map, page 146.

WHERE TO STAY

⌂ Village Resort Motel Wadi Beni Awf; ☎ 99 214873/97 588818. 1km from the beginning of Wadi Bani Awf, between Awabi & Rustaq, 31km from Bilad Sayt. A brown sign announces 'Visit your second home'. A simple stopover. **$**

⌂ Shimook Guesthouse Rustaq; ☎ 26 877071. Located at the start of the road from Rustaq to Ibri. Rooms are basic. **$**

RUSTAQ الرستاق

Rustaq, which means 'market town', is about a two-hour drive from Muscat International Airport or about 1½ hours from Sawadi Beach Resort via Nakhal.

The town served as the Omani capital for some 150 years, first as the Ya'arubi imams' base from 1624, then in the early part of the Al Bu Said dynasty from 1744. In the late 18th century, Hamad bin Said established Muscat as the capital and it has never been contested since.

Today, Rustaq is still a major administrative centre. The town owes its importance to its strategic location at the exit of a wadi on the coastal side of the mountains, so it served as a commercial centre for trade between the jebel and the villages of the interior and the coastal Batinah towns. The people from the mountains and the foothills of Jebel Akhdar brought fruits such as grapes, peaches, pomegranates, plums, figs and apricots for sale here, while the coastal people brought fish, lemons and bananas. Pure Omani honey is most sought after and of high quality. Beekeeping is one of the main occupations in Rustaq.

As a result of its political and commercial influence, various industries grew up in Rustaq, notably silversmiths famous for *khanjars*, ornaments, copperwork and other traditional crafts. Normally, remnants of these crafts remain in Rustaq old souk opposite the fort (see page 152). Wooden storage chests can be found, and old weaponry on the antique stalls. Date packing has long been carried out here and today there is a proper date-processing factory. Omani *halwa* (see box, page 152) from Rustaq is also famous.

Today the town of Rustaq is a shadow of its former self, though still easily the largest of the inland towns set on this side of the Jebel Akhdar. The presence of two or three roundabouts and sets of traffic lights seems rather incongruous. The approach is entirely modern, with shops run by Indians lining the dual carriageway as you follow the signposts to Rustaq Fort and town centre.

GETTING THERE Microbuses run round the Rustaq loop and can be picked up at the Barka roundabout and on the main road a few hundred metres from Rustaq Fort. A shared taxi to/from Sohar costs RO4.

WHAT TO SEE

Rustaq Fort (⊕ *winter 08.00–17.00 daily, summer 08.00–18.00 daily, closed 11.30–13.00 Fri for prayers*) The fort is said to have been built four centuries before the arrival of Islam in Oman and is one of the country's oldest. It sits at the foot of Jebel Akhdar and it is easy to miss the left turn at the traffic lights leading directly to the fort, tucked down the side of the wadi bed. However, you can just as easily follow the main road as it loops round to the left, giving you views of the fort before you drive down along the bumpy track through the wadi to reach the main entrance.

You can park by the main entrance beside a telephone box that looks more like a summer gazebo under the shade of a tree, and this will then serve for visiting the old souk.

A tour of the fort, which is built on three levels, has four towers and is furnished with old items, can take between one and two hours, depending on your level of interest. In addition to the fort itself there is a large courtyard area that you enter on stepping through the tiny entrance door. Strolling in a circuit right round will give you glimpses of wonderful butterfly life among the wild plants and the chance to use the old *falaj* system to refresh yourself. The water still flows strongly and is hot. The castle inhabitants used to collect this water in pottery jars and hang it in a shady place to cool, after which it could be drunk.

To the right as you first enter is the large 32-pillared mosque, which used to be the Friday congregational mosque for the town before the large green-and-white one with twin minarets was built on the modern outskirts. Known as Bayadha Mosque, it was an institute with a fine reputation from which many eminent scholars graduated. To the left as you enter (after shedding your shoes) is a magnificent elaborately sculpted plaster *mihrab* marking the direction of prayer towards the holy city of Mecca. The mosque is still used sometimes on Fridays as the overspill for the new mosque.

To the right as you walk towards the main castle entrance, the building that is raised up and overlooked by the double towers (the Red Tower and the New Tower) is where the *wali* stays when he comes to town. The sultan has issued a new decree that once a month the *wali* and the judge (*qadi*) must come to the fort and hold an open *majlis* session for the townspeople and surrounding village people in the official suite of rooms within the fort, designed for this original purpose – a fine revival of the old tradition in its authentic setting.

Inside, the most splendid rooms with painted dark red-and-white ceilings are the imam's rooms, up on the second storey to catch the prevailing wind. The central beam on the ceiling carries Koranic inscriptions listing some of the 99 attributes of God, eg: the king, the wise, the holy. Note too the women's tiny mosque, barely big enough for two to enter, with its minute *mihrab* to the left.

Continuing up as far as you can you come to the left (southeast) corner of the Tower of Winds, the largest of the four towers, with its British steel cannons guarding all directions set round the huge central pillar. The date of 1821 can still be seen on them, and one has its end blasted off where it was hit by the enemy cannons before it could fire. From one of the window seats you will see the white domed tomb of Imam Saif bin Sultan, raised up on a hill. The highest tower of all, to the right (northwest) corner, is the mysterious Devil's Tower (Burj A'Shayateen) which has no entrance and appears to serve no function whatsoever. You can walk up along the parapet round

Rustaq and Nizwa were traditionally the most famous for halwa making, though in practice it is made in every town in Oman. Halwa is not made from grapes, as many foreigners fondly imagine, but of ghee, semolina and sugar mixed for several hours over the fire with a copper spoon, then flavoured with almond and cardamom. An early missionary described it as delicious to the connoisseur, 'but to the stranger smells of rancid butter and tastes like sweet wagon grease'. Another early traveller commented that one should on no account watch it being made 'for feet are usually employed to stir it, and the knowledge of this is apt to spoil the flavour'.

the courtyard to approach it, but nowhere can it be entered. The two graves in the courtyard belong to two previous imams and the big long windowless room along the back of the courtyard was a barracks for the guards.

Back down at the same height as the imam's rooms are the *wali's* offices, which are the only way through to approach the two more modern towers, the Red Tower and the New Tower. On the ground floor are prison cells, stores and an armoury.

The earliest castle on this site pre-dates Islam and was built around AD600 by the Persian governor who controlled the area at that time. A second fort was built on the ruins of the early Persian fort by a tribe called the Julandas in 1250, and then the first Ya'arubi imam moved his capital here from Bahla and rebuilt Rustaq Fort again in 1650. The Red Tower was added in 1744 by the Al Bu Saids and the New Tower in 1906. The fort also featured in the 1950s Jebel War, when it served as home to the dissident Taalib bin Ali. Its greatest heyday was in the 18th century under the Al Bu Saids, when Ahmad bin Said, head of the Al Bu Said dynasty, used it as his capital from which he co-ordinated the expulsion of the Persians and restored independence to the country.

Rustaq Souk سوق الرستاق   The old souk has been completely rebuilt, though it is still in the same location by the wadi beside the fort entrance. The best time to visit the souk is before 11.30 and Fridays are the busiest days. The old souk was far more atmospheric, one of the most interesting in the country, featuring *barasti* roofs, and with herbs and spices, walking canes, shoes, etc on offer for a pittance, and even the occasional old *khanjar* and belt. Water bottles, colourful cow-tethering bands, mousetraps and tools were among the collection of eclectic items. The Omani stallholders were getting on in years, white-bearded with lined faces, but extremely friendly to visitors. Having passed on it is unlikely the younger generation will take their place.

Ain Al Kasfah Springs عين الكسفاة   These hot springs, not far from Rustaq Fort, are less attractive than the springs at Nakhal, but nevertheless are said to have the same healing and medicinal properties for rheumatism and skin complaints (due to the sulphur content). They have been walled to create segregated bathing areas for men and women. A famous 15th-century doctor, Rashid bin Umeirah, lived nearby (the remains of his house and clinic can still be seen) and wrote his medicinal expositions on the illnesses of the day and how to cure them in the form of long descriptive poems, which could be memorised more easily.

The springs today are fetid and the attendant rest area is neglected and rubbish-strewn, with a thriving hornet population.

above	The sharp ridges of the dunes of the Wahiba Sands are constantly on the move according to the prevailing winds (OMOT) pages 230–3
right	A few women in the more remote parts of the Wahiba desert still wear full face masks (SS)
below	A typical Bedouin tent where guests are sometimes invited to drink cardamom coffee (SS) pages 231–3

above   Al Khandaq fort at Buraimi is surrounded by defensive trenches (SS) page 184

left   The traditionally furnished interior of Bait Na'man, private home of an 18th-century imam (DD) pages 132–3

below   The 16th-century, Portuguese-built Jalali fort, once Oman's main jail, still guards Muscat's harbour

(IP/S) page 100

above left   Looking down at Nizwa fort from its massive circular tower (SS) page 203–5

above right   The complex interior of Nakhal fort on the Rustaq Loop (L/S) pages 145–7

right   The interior of Jabrin Castle is more elaborate than most of Oman's other forts (CE/S) page 217

below   The newly restored fort of Bahla, Oman's oldest and largest, is a UNESCO World Heritage site (SR/S) page 216

above   **Steppe eagle**
(JDM/S) page 8

left   **African rock bunting**
(BMJ/S) page 10

below   **Domesticated goat**
(IP/S)

above left	**Isabelline shrike** (E/S) page 8
above right	**Fennec (desert) fox** (WC/S) page 7
right	**Green turtle** (K/S) page 11
below	**Domesticated camels** (SS) page 30–1

Some mountain villages are abandoned, others are still clinging to life thanks to their terrace agriculture (H/FA/A) *above*   **The distinctive comb-shape of Jebel Misht, near Ibri** (C/S) pages 123–4

right   **Wadi Shab has water all year round** (SS) pages 238–9

below   **The village of Wekan is high in the Jebel Akhdar** (OMOT) page 147 *top*   The virgin white sands of Mughsail Beach, near Salalah in the south (OMOT) page 280

above   The dramatic Yiti Beach, south of Muscat, has been earmarked for development (IP/S) pages 104–5

below   Musandam offers spectacular *dhow* trips into its fjords, with dolphin watching thrown in
              (SS) pages 161–3

Getting there To reach the springs, take the sign to the right marked Ibri off the main road into Rustaq and follow this as it loops round for 1.5km.

Al Hazm Fort (⏲ *08.00–14.00 Sat–Thu; 500bzs*) This fort is located about 15 minutes' drive further along on the loop from Rustaq Fort (the loop leads you back to the main highway). Your first sight of Al Hazm Fort, squatting in the sandy plain set well forward of the mountains, gives no inkling of the architectural complexity within. Built by the Ya'arubi imam Sultan bin Saif II in 1711, it is an example of Omani Islamic architecture, its exterior plain, even a little disappointing, though its scale once you are close up more than compensates. The Arabic Al Hazm means 'the vanquishing one' and when you have completed your tour you will understand why the fortress was itself never vanquished. An Arabic-speaking guardian greets you, in full Omani regalia complete with rifle and cartridge belt.

The roof is built on columns and the walls are at least 3m thick. In the courtyard is the first of the three wells, the other two lying within the impregnable walls, impossible for the enemy to cut off or poison. The fort also had its own running

---

FORTS

There are over 1,100 fortifications in Oman, an extensive network of forts, fortified castles and watchtowers built throughout all the regions to defend against foreign invaders like China, Persia, Europe and Africa, but also from other internal rival tribes.

Forts and fortified castles went beyond defence and also contained law courts, the *wali's* residence and office and Islamic schools. Watchtowers were used to raise alarms, collect taxes and protect the local water supply.

The design of forts was intended to delay and disorientate the enemy. The outer walls were the delaying method, where the enemy encountered the date honey poured through the slit over the entrance. If they did succeed in entering, they were confused by towers, spiral staircases and doors at all levels, ever-changing design features in each fort. It is often impossible to tell if one room is a new room or an extension of the previous one and without help it is difficult to find the way out. As the last resort there were also tunnels for the escape route, sometimes linking neighbouring forts, and sometimes so tall that soldiers on horseback could ride through them.

The sheer number of forts in Oman can lead after a time to 'fort fatigue', reminiscent of Freya Stark's 'tomb fatigue' in Lycian Turkey – 'The time came when D B and I looked at each other and said, "Do we really have to go and look at that tomb?"' The fact that so many exist is a reflection of the essentially warring nature of the Omani tribes. The fort was the centre of authority, headquarters of the main sheikh or the *wali*. Any pretender to authority had to control the fort, and anyone who had something to protect like a water source or fertile ground would build watchtowers and forts on prominent hilltops to ensure they stopped a neighbouring tribe from taking it. War was a way of life in order to survive in a country not overly blessed with natural resources. The *sur* (walled enclosure) was built as a refuge for the villagers.

Since the coming to power of Sultan Qaboos, the major forts of the country have undergone a gradual process of restoration. This is continuing and being stepped up, in line with the country's relatively recent concentration on, and investment in, tourism.

water supply throughout the ground floor, in the form of the *falaj* system (see box, page 190). The restful sound of running water can be heard in many places on the ground floor. This too could not be cut off by the enemy, as it only appears within the castle. In the washing area the water has a faster flow.

Defence and secrecy have been the dominant factors influencing the remarkable labyrinth of corridors and rooms inside. Among the more amazing features of the castle is a series of prisons which you can still climb down inside. Prisoners were left here to die with no light, food or drink. The horses were kept upstairs on the roof and the water was pulled up by bucket to a trough. You will be shown the imam's intercom system leading from his private room to downstairs, enabling him to give instructions to his servants. The imam himself slept up on a raised platform where it was both cooler and safer. A secret passageway links the east and west towers. This passageway is the coolest place in the fort, as it is set between the first and ground floors, with massively thick walls, its only connection to the outside world being some small ventilation holes. There are also secret passages leading outside.

Thursdays and Fridays are the busiest times, when there may be several hundred visitors a day, but on other days 10–20 a day is more normal. There are two Omani guides, both speaking some English. The guided tour takes one hour.

5

Musandam مسندم

Telephone code: 26

Land is better than money.

Musandam is a paradox. While it is Arabia's least-known and least-populated corner, it overlooks one of the world's busiest and most strategic waterways: the Strait of Hormuz. The strait is only 55–95km wide, but a large percentage of the world's crude oil trade passes through it.

Isolated from both Oman and the United Arab Emirates by its own rugged mountains, which fall directly into the sea, the Musandam Peninsula belongs geographically to neither. Only sparsely populated by the semi-nomadic mountain tribes, it did not much matter to whom it belonged until the late 1960s and early 1970s when the granting of oil concessions to foreign companies meant that allegiance had to be decided and borders drawn up accordingly. The Shihuh, the most populous of the three tribes of the Musandam, decided their allegiance lay with the Sultan of Oman and hence the border was drawn along the edge of Shihuh territory to separate it from the tribes whose allegiance lay with the

INACCESSIBLE THROUGHOUT HISTORY

Roads are a recent phenomenon in this peninsula; before 1980 precipitous footpaths were the only links between the mountains and the flat open plains of Fujairah and Ras al Khaimah. Even donkeys could not be used on such paths, and the Musandam towns of Khasab, Bukha, Lima and Bayah, with their small harbours, could be reached only by small boats.

Musandam has throughout history had no exploitable commodity – no copper diorite or chlorite in ancient times, no oil in modern times – so no incentive has existed to defy nature and blast routes through the barren limestone. There is no coastal plain, and the sheer cliffs plunge straight into the sea in all but a few coves and bays where the towns and fishing villages sit. These are in turn connected by steep paths to a handful of mountaintop plains and terraces where rainfall in winter is plentiful enough to allow for limited agriculture.

Thor Heyerdahl, sailing in his replica Sumerian boat *Tigris* in the 1970s down through the Gulf towards the Strait of Hormuz, could hardly believe his eyes at his first sight of Musandam:

Above the cloud banks, raised above the earth was land, like another indistinct world of its own. Solid rock was sailing up there ... with rock walls dropping almost perpendicularly into the sea.

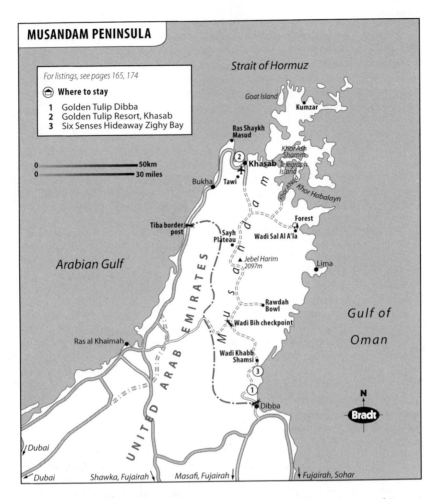

For listings, see pages 165, 174

MUSANDAM PENINSULA

Strait of Hormuz

Where to stay
1 Golden Tulip Dibba
2 Golden Tulip Resort, Khasab
3 Six Senses Hideaway Zighy Bay

Goat Island
Kumzar
Ras Shaykh Masud
Khor Ash Shamm
0 ——— 50km
0 ——— 30 miles
Khasab
Telegraph Island
Bukha Tawi
Khor Habalayn
Tiba border post
Forest
Sayh Plateau
Wadi Sal Al A'la
Arabian Gulf
Jebel Harim 2097m
Lima
Rawdah Bowl
Wadi Bih checkpoint
Gulf of Oman
Ras al Khaimah
Wadi Khabb Shamsi
3
N
1
Dibba
Bradt
Dubai
Dubai
Shawka, Fujairah
Masafi, Fujairah
Fujairah, Sohar

Sheikh of Ras al Khaimah. Musandam is therefore cut off from the rest of Omani territory by a 70km tract of UAE land. Some of the old tribesmen have been heard to mutter that they now wish they had backed the UAE horse as it may have proved more beneficial to them through possible generous handouts from the UAE federal budget.

The origins of the Shihuh themselves are unclear and, with their separate and distinctive language and culture, it is tempting to speculate that they were the original inhabitants of the region, driven up into the barren mountains by successive waves of Yemeni Arabs arriving from the south. The Shihuh live in the mountains in the winter rainy season and down in the coastal settlements in the summer, where they own gardens and run small trades.

There are thought to be some 200 villages scattered about in the mountains, half on the UAE side and half on the Omani side of the border. Of the Omani ones some 20 are still inhabited, while on the UAE side there are perhaps around five. The numbers are always declining: the Sayh Plateau, for example, was well inhabited even in the late 1980s with busy, tended fields, whereas now just a handful of villagers remain.

The scenic fissures of the mountains, locally known as Ruus al Jebel, have been likened to the fjords of Norway and, coupled with the diving of the region, are the main tourist draw.

The currents carried boats around Musandam to land on the safe shores of the Batinah, where the plentiful water and fertile coastal plain made it by far the more attractive option. In addition, the commodities needed by Sumeria (irrespective of all the copper from Wadi Jizzi), could be far more easily loaded and collected from such open coasts, in preference to the narrow beaches of Musandam with their difficult hinterland routes.

The mountain villages represent a pragmatic adaptation to the semi-nomadic way of life. In the summer months, the villages are deserted while the people migrate to the coast to fish or to tend date plantations. The possessions left behind in the village therefore need to be secured and kept safe until the autumn, giving rise to the invention of the House of the Lock (Bait Al Qufl, in Arabic). Built of local limestone, whose strata lend themselves to easy splitting into tabular blocks, the foundations go 1.5–2m below ground, giving the strength to withstand the torrential winter rains. The roof of stone and mud is supported by acacia trunks and needs frequent repair. Paolo Costa, contemporary Italian archaeologist and art historian, calls it 'the most extraordinary and unique building in the Arabian Peninsula … the result of local adaptation of the architecture to the semi-nomadic way of life'.

The Royal Geographical Society, which conducted a survey here in 1972–73, concluded that the Musandam Peninsula has tilted into the sea by up to 60m over the past 10,000 years along a fault line from Sham in Ras al Khaimah to Dibba. Wells on the coast coincide with where the main settlements are and the water table is only a few feet above sea level. There is enough water to sustain date-palm and fruit-tree oases only at Dibba, Lima, Khasab, Qida and Bukha. In Khasab they had a particularly inventive method of fertilising crops via the water system by allowing *metoot* (the local sardine) to dry and rot in the sun for a few days in the empty well reservoir. Then they started the well and the stinking fecund water was released through the irrigation system. The rains that can occur intermittently and torrentially between November and April (peaking between December and February) mean that the only way to retain both topsoil and water is by building terraces. Silt is thereby trapped behind retaining walls, creating areas of potentially intensive cultivation. To protect the precious crops (barley, wheat and lucerne) against sheep and goats, the outer retaining walls are made high and topped with thorn bushes, while the inlets of water conduits are protected by tall vertical stones. The crops in such conditions never make a surplus, but goat breeding can produce a bit of extra income as they can be sold or bartered for dates, cloth or other items.

At Khasab, a third of the date palms are owned by the Kamazirah, a secondary tribal group to the Shihuh, whose centre is at Kumzar (as their name suggests). Kumzar is a small fishing village in one of the northernmost bays of the peninsula. It is undoubtedly Oman's most remote settlement, so isolated that its only link to the outside world is by boat; its hinterland is too sheer to be crossed on foot to link with the mountain plateaux behind. As a result the Kamazirah are fishermen, boatbuilders and sailors. They even speak their own language (a kind of mix of Persian and Arabic but still distinct from either) and the women are veiled and wear black face masks. The tribal group has a limited number of goats, which they take by boat to seasonal grazing grounds on the islands, notably Jazirat Al Ghanim (Goat Island). There are ruins on Goat Island in which pottery finds have been dated to Sassanian times (3rd to 6th century AD).

The third and smallest tribal group of Musandam are the Zahuriyeen, found mainly in Khasab and Bukha. In summer they work as fishermen and as farmers in the palm gardens. Each tribe (*qabilah*) is divided into a number of clans or extended families (*ahl*). Each *ahl* breaks down into a family group (*batinah*) made up of single households (*bait*).

Administratively, Musandam is separated into four *wilayats*: Khasab, Bhuka, Dibba and Mudha.

GETTING THERE

Musandam is separated from the rest of Oman by 70km of United Arab Emirates territory and so the options are either to **fly** or catch a ferry from Muscat into Khasab, or **drive** in through one of two borders: at Thibat (from the emirates of Ras al Khaimah and Dubai) or Dibba (from the Batinah coast of Oman, after a stretch through the United Arab Emirate of Fujairah). The Thibat crossing is the main and straightforward one, but the Dibba one can be problematic as the position varies, so you should check before attempting it (see page 43). At present non-Omanis can cross the border at Dibba itself and drive up along the coast to the Golden Tulip and Zighy Bay resorts with no problem. If however you want to cross over the mountains on rough dirt roads to Khasab there is a further checkpoint inland about 50km from Dibba at which non-Omanis are currently turned back and this route requires 4x4 in any event. There is no doubt that flying in from Muscat or catching the ferry is the simplest way, as it has no visa complications since you never leave Omani territory. See page opposite and 39–40 for the flight and ferry details and for the visa position respectively.

This chapter follows the route from Dubai, entering Musandam at the Thibat border post, just beyond Sham in northern Ras al Khaimah, as most visitors in practice come this way.

CRAFTS IN MUSANDAM

A whole range of crafts centred round basketry and palm-work survives in Musandam and are still used for functional purposes like mats for drying fish and dates, conical food covers, weighing baskets, fans and date sacks. The palm ribs were used until recently, and were soaked in water then sliced into strips, for domed fish traps and chicken coops. Nowadays such things are made of wire. Chemical dyes from India are used in the decorative basket work as none of the requisite plants for natural dyes exists in the northern extremities of Musandam. The fibrous top part of the palm trunk was used by men for making rope and string, while the women used it for scouring pots and pans.

Traditional measurements are still used, based on distances from elbow to fingertip, or thumb to little finger when the hand is outstretched.

A woman can make 100 fans as well as 20 mats and food covers a month, but today as more and more artefacts for the home are bought rather than made, a woman will not make them unless there is a commission. Women have more time than in the old days, with water and electricity making household chores easier, their children out at school and men out fishing, so most would be willing to sew and braid each day if there was a demand. The crafts are no longer passed automatically from mother to daughter and father to son, as there seems little point and the children are away at school anyway.

BY AIR There is currently a daily flight on a 40-seater aircraft from Muscat International Airport to Khasab, and a return flight on the same day, operated by Oman Air (☏ *24 531 111; www.omanair.com*). Oman Air also flies to Khasab direct from Dubai.

The Muscat return ticket costs around RO55 and the flight takes 1½ hours. There is a 10kg luggage restriction.

In terms of excursions offered by the tour companies in Khasab, one or two nights is probably all you will need to get a flavour of this peninsula. As with Salalah in the south of the country, Oman Air operates package deals with the hotels that include a return economy flight, one night's accommodation with breakfast and airport transfers. For around RO75, this seems quite a good option (and you haven't got to concern yourself with arranging the short transfer from the taxi-less airport).

Seats on the right have the better view. If you are seated on the left, it appears as if the wing of the aircraft might just clip the mountains as you come in to land.

The departure lounge of this small airport is surprisingly modern and clean, complete with a flat-screen television on the wall, and all signs in English. (For details of Oman Air offices, see page 43.)

BY CAR From the Batinah coast of Oman, you can enter Musandam at Dibba (Wadi Bih) border post. If you are continuing up to Khasab there are two more border post crossings on the way up, which have to be crossed again on the way back down, travelling this route. As with entering and leaving Buraimi, there is considerable bureaucracy at the borders. Although it seems more progressive to be able to get visas and road permits on arrival at any border post between Oman and UAE (you used to have to apply in advance), visas still have to be closed down on exiting Oman and a UAE visa needs to be issued; then, on entering Omani territory at Musandam, another Omani visa needs to be purchased and the UAE visa closed. The whole process has to be reversed on the return leg. See pages 39–40, for full visa details and check with the Royal Oman Police website www.rop.gov.om to get the latest position.

The 460km drive from Muscat takes about seven hours. The drive from Muscat to Dibba takes roughly four hours on tarmac (350km), then it is about another three hours to Khasab (110km) on steep tracks for which a 4x4 is essential.

From the Dubai/Ras al Khaimah end, you enter Musandam at the border post at Thibat.

It is sometimes possible to do the whole Musandam loop, but the border post rigmarole may just dissuade you. By flying or taking the ferry, you avoid it all, but are car-less when you get there.

BY BUS To get to Musandam by bus you will need to travel from Dubai via Ras al Khaimah to Khasab. Services are very erratic and even long-distance shared taxis often only run as far as the border, with no guarantee of an onward service to Khasab. Only those with plenty of time and patience should attempt it.

BY SEA A ferry runs from Muscat to Khasab and from Shinas to Khasab, operated by the National Ferries Company (☏ *800 72000; www.nfc.om*). It runs twice a week but timings change, so check the website before doing your planning. Australian-made catamarans are used, which can carry 208 passengers and 56 cars. There are three classes of ticket: tourist, first and VIP. From the UAE it is also possible to get to Musandam by sea. For further information contact tour operators in Dubai. NFC also runs a twice-weekly car-ferry service from Shinas to Khasab (see page 52).

GETTING AROUND

BY TAXI Note there are hardly any taxis in Khasab or in Musandam and those that exist are usually already booked by local people. So it is advisable when you are making your booking with your Khasab hotel to confirm that you will be transferred from the airport. If you have booked one of Oman Air's packages then the transfer is included and should be arranged as a matter of course. If you haven't, then don't expect your hotel to prompt you to the fact that you will need to be collected from the airport – you have to do all the thinking for yourself.

BY PUBLIC TRANSPORT There are no buses in Musandam and shared taxis only operate erratically. Without your own transport hitchhiking is the only option. Always offer to pay something towards the petrol.

BY HIRE CAR You can rent a saloon car from Khasab Rent-a-Car (📞 99 447400) for around RO15 per day, but for proper exploration in Musandam you need a 4x4, which costs around RO50 per day. If you want a driver the cost for a 4x4 goes up to RO90 per day and can be arranged through Khasab Travel & Tours (📞 26 730464; e khastour@omantel.net.om). Car hire can usually also be arranged through the Golden Tulip Khasab Hotel Resort or the long-established Khasab Hotel.

Fuel stations are limited to the two in Khasab and one at Bukha. There is nothing between Khasab and Dibba.

TOUR OPERATORS

The few tour operators there are in the Musandam region are all located in Khasab. They offer the stock *dhow* cruises, mountain safaris and city tours. The most common attractions are Jebel Harim (seen on a mountain safari tour), Telegraph Island (seen on a *dhow* cruise), dolphin-watching, snorkelling, fishing, diving, fjords, birdwatching and falcon towers.

Dolphin Tourism Khasab 123; 📞 26 730813; e dolphin@omantel.om; www.dolphinkhasabtours. com. Offering an array of tours: the Khasab city tour, a mountain safari to Jebel Harim & *dhow* cruises. Full-day safaris include lunch; half-day safaris include refreshments.

Khasab Travel & Tours PO Box 464, PC 811; 📞 26 730464; Muscat office 📞 24 706463; e khastour@omantel.net.om; www.khasabtours. com. Operates from Esra Apts (opposite Khasab Airport) & also has a desk in the Golden Tulip Resort in Khasab (📞 26 831351; e omandisc@ omantel.net.om), a branch in Muscat under the name of Oman Discovery & a Dubai office (📞 +971 4 2669950; e khaztour@emirates.net. ae). Offers excursions which include half-day

dhow trips 09.00–13.00 (RO15), full-day *dhow* trips (RO30), full-day *dhow* cruise on the air-conditioned *Sindbad Dhow* (RO40), half-day 4x4 mountain safari 13.30–16.30 (RO35), full-day mountain safari (RO40) & diving trips with tank & weights (RO35). In addition it also offers an overnight stay on the *Sindbad*. Camping safaris & full equipment, kayaking, trekking, fishing expeditions & special 1-, 2- & 3-night packages, plus car hire, can all be arranged, subject to availability.

Musandam Sea Adventure Tourism 📞 26 730069, 99 346321; e sea_adventure@ msaoman.com; www.msaoman.com. Offers mountain safaris & *dhow* excursions to the fjords of Musandam.

DIVE CENTRE The region's only dive centre is in Khasab, operating from the Golden Tulip Resort:

✈ Extra Divers PO Box 498, PC 811; ✆26 730501; e info@musandam-diving.com; www. musandam-diving.com. This German-owned dive centre is located in the Golden Tulip Resort (see page 165). It offers courses, dives & live-aboard trips on a traditional *dhow* into the fjords of the Strait of Hormuz. It operates 2-tank dives by boat daily, 08.30–15.00. Guests are collected from any Khasab hotel. Extra Divers now also has its own B&B villa that sleeps 15 in a quiet location just outside Khasab centre. Diving package holidays can be booked there via UK diving specialist Regaldive (✆ *01353 659999; www.regal-diving. co.uk*) or direct using the contact details above.

🏠 WHERE TO STAY AND EAT

The only places to stay and eat in Musandam are in Khasab (see page 165) and near Dibba (see page 174).

OTHER PRACTICALITIES
USEFUL TELEPHONE NUMBERS

Police stations		Hospitals and health centres	
Bukha	✆26 828399	✚ **Bukha Hospital** ✆26 828562	
Dibba	✆26 836999	✚ **Dibba Hospital** ✆26 836443	
Khasab	✆26 730148	✚ **Khasab Hospital** ✆26 730187	
Lima	✆26 735111	✚ **Lima Health Centre** ✆26 735147	
Kumzar	✆26 733001	✚ **Kumzar Health Centre** ✆26 733047	

WHAT TO SEE AND DO

BIRDWATCHING Many tourists visit Musandam for the purpose of birdwatching alone, although there are no birdwatching tours offered by the tour operators in Khasab. The most common large birds are the Egyptian vulture, Bonelli's eagle and the Barbary and sooty falcon, which can be spotted anywhere by the vigilant as you drive the mountain roads.

CAMPING You can camp on the beach, where shades, playground and water tanks are provided, but they are not very clean and rather close to the road. The best spots in the winter months are down in the **Rawdah Bowl** and the **Sal Al A'la Forest**. In the summer, the mountains are better, preferably without a tent as the terrain is rather rocky for tent pegs. For campfires, do not use local wood and palm fronds that will damage the fragile ecology; take your own. Camping tours are offered by the three main tour operators listed opposite.

Local fishermen can drop you off at Telegraph Island for the night and collect you the next day. Their boats tend to be simpler than those used for organised boat trips, and so not as well equipped with such things as shade awnings. Ask at the boatyards on your right after passing the harbour before Khasab town as you enter from the Thibat (Ras al Khaimah) direction. This is fine if you are not too concerned about exact timings. They won't rip you off.

CANOEING The calmness of the fjords offers ideal conditions for canoeing. Speak to the tour operators at the desk in the Golden Tulip Hotel in Khasab for details (see page 165).

DHOW CRUISES/BOAT TRIPS From Khasab harbour the standard boat trips are half-day or full-day *dhow* cruises that cost around RO20 and RO25 respectively.

Children under 12 go for half price and the under fives go free. Half-day cruises include light refreshments, whereas the full-day trips include lunch. The boats are equipped with life jackets as well as snorkelling equipment, if you haven't got your own. It is best to pre-book with a tour operator on arrival at your hotel to avoid any chance of disappointment, although it is possible to arrange one on the spot at the offices opposite the harbour.

Trips take you into **Khor Ash-Sham**, a giant fjord in which Telegraph Island sits along with a few other islands, and where the water is calm and sheltered. You will spot the fishing villages of Nadifi, Qanaha, Maglab, Seebi and Sham along the route. You have a good chance of spotting dolphins in the fjord, as they like the calm water, but are also attracted by the sound and wake of the engine, swimming with the boat as if it is a giant dolphin. Once the engine is turned off, they tend to lose interest.

The *dhows* anchor at Telegraph Island (see box on page 169), and you are given the opportunity to swim and snorkel. If you wish, you can swim up to the island itself and climb the stone steps up to the top.

There are various degrees in the quality of *dhow* cruises and it may be that you prefer to go on a larger two-storey *dhow* for the extra space and elevated views it allows. These are more popular with European families and visitors. The small *dhows* can become full and cramped and are generally popular with Asian visitors. It can make or break your enjoyment, so you might like to enquire about the boat when booking your cruise.

Guests will be collected from their hotels and taken to the harbour where they join the tour.

From October to February visibility is excellent, about 20–30km. From the end of February it drops to about 5km, which detracts somewhat from the overall experience.

DIVING AND SNORKELLING Musandam is an excellent location for diving. As all divers will know, it is necessary to produce proof of your PADI Open Water qualification or equivalent, so remember to pack it.

Those wishing to gain their Open Water qualification can do so here. Extra Divers operates from the Golden Tulip Resort with fully certified tutors (see page 161). So as not to waste time in the region undergoing the theoretical side of diving (unless you have the time to spare), you can gain your qualification for this aspect of the course back in your country of residence. You will then be free to concentrate fully on the practical side of diving when in Khasab.

AROUND OMAN CHALLENGE

In 2004 and 2005, Mark Evans – a schoolteacher and geographer, who leads challenging expeditions around the world for young people – paddled a 5m kayak around the 1,700km or so of Omani coastline, a feat never attempted before. He carried a week's supply of food, tents, a GPS and a satellite phone, and was supported by a road vehicle team. He began at Khasab and spent 55 days travelling all the way to the Yemeni border, coming ashore at night to camp. The Omani government supported the event, promoting Oman as an adventure-tourist destination. Funds raised went to support local and international charities. More information can be found on www.outwardboundoman.com.

The main dive sites are Lima Rock, Oakley Island, Umm Al Farrayan, PC Rock, Red Island and Ghubbat As Shabbus. Species include reef and whale sharks, barracuda, sunfish and turtles. Those new to diving are taken to the *khors* and bays of the area for their tuition.

For snorkelling, Sibi Island is perhaps the best location in the area, as the coral and marine life is good. If you are not a diver, you can opt for snorkelling as part of a dive-boat trip, or as a *dhow* cruise. The *dhow*-cruise trips make a stop at Telegraph Island to allow for snorkelling and swimming. Trips cost around RO20.

DOLPHIN, WHALE AND SHARK WATCHING The hammerhead, nurse, reef and whale shark are found in the temperate waters of the Strait of Hormuz, especially July–September. Dolphin-watching trips are done as part of a *dhow* cruise (see page 161).

FISHING Fishing trips, which depart from Khasab harbour, can be arranged through the tour operators or the dive centre.

MOUNTAIN SAFARI If you have flown to Khasab from Muscat and are staying in a hotel here, it is likely you will arrange a mountain safari (as you won't have a car to travel this independently). The route below (from Khasab, onwards, page 165) is the one your driver will take.

BUKHA بخة

Bukha is west of Khasab and borders the UAE at Ras al Khaimah. It is potentially large and thriving, but has suffered an exodus to the oil-rich emirates next door, leaving it struggling to maintain the remaining population. New capital investment by Oman may help it to revive its considerable agricultural resources. Numerous buildings are being constructed. In among the new houses are the decaying mud-brick ones, some on two storeys with courtyards, which you can see by turning off the main coast road and following a road inland that runs parallel to the coast.

GETTING THERE There is no public transport so you need to have your own transport or hitchhike. Starting from Sham in northern Ras al Khaimah take the right fork marked Al Jer at the final roundabout by the mountains. This leads round past endless shops selling car spares and hardware to reach the border post on the coast 1km later. Queue at the first counter on the left marked 'Al Mughaadireen' ('those departing') with your passport and pink form. The second counter is marked 'Al Qaadimeen' ('those coming') and is where you will queue on your return into Ras al Khaimah at the end of your Musandam trip. Allow 30 minutes for this UAE section of the border.

The Omani border post is 1km or so further on, and you should again allow 30 minutes for the paperwork followed by the vehicle search. Go to the first counter marked 'Al Qaadimeen' with your passport and white form. The second counter is marked 'Al Mughaadireen' and is where you will go on your departure with your yellow form. After this you will be waved on to the vehicle search. Beyond the border is a Shell petrol station in case you forgot to fill up in Ras al Khaimah. The relatively new tarmac road from now on clings to the edge of the sea and had to be blasted in places where the mountain came right down to the waves. It was fully completed in 1998. Some beaches are equipped with *barasti* sunshades on iron frames (often with their *barasti* roofs missing), and sometimes have children's playgrounds and water tanks. They tend to be a bit close to the road for comfortable camping and anyway are heavily rubbish-strewn despite regular refuse collections. The first town you come to is Bukha.

WHAT TO SEE
Bukha Fort (⏰ *09.00–14.00 Sat–Thu, 08.00–11.00 Fri*) The coastal fort of Bukha, built by the Portuguese in the 16th century and renovated in 1990, sits proudly on the new road, and is open and accessible only when the watchman is there – usually workdays until 14.00. Its shallow moat, especially visible at the back, used to fill with seawater before the coastline was pushed further away by the construction of the road. A square building of stone blocks faced with mud plaster, its most unusual feature is the round tower on the southwest corner which curves inwards, giving it a pear shape which reduced the impact of cannonballs. Inside, the tower has four cannon ports. The earliest parts are thought to date back to the 16th century and the recent restoration has retained the remains of rich plasterwork wall decorations and carved doors and shutters. The main gate has the *kuwwa* or *muscat* (literally 'place of falling'), the slit found in all Omani defensive buildings, used for pouring hot date honey on the enemy or for water to quench any fire that threatened to burn down the door.

Beside the fort is a large crumbling structure built up on a raised terrace. This was the **Friday mosque**, surrounded on all sides by an extensive cemetery of headstones which have the effect of distancing the town buildings. At the back on the inland side a crumbling double set of steps leads down into the ablution area. Stairs also lead up on to the roof, in place of the minaret. Inside, the once grand mosque is in a sorry state of disrepair; most of its roof is missing and much of the delicate stucco plasterwork decorating its pillared arches is falling away, now that it is exposed to the elements. The motifs are alternate rosettes and arches. The *mihrab* niche itself is surprisingly plain and free from decoration, as are the *minbar* (pulpit) steps from where the imam would give the Friday sermon. A crude wooden *minbar* was found on these steps, but has now disappeared (probably used for firewood). The outer high walls of the mosque are pierced with elaborate decorative grilles displaying geometric and plant motifs carved in good-quality strong plaster. Despite its highly dilapidated state, this mosque is sure to be restored in the near future because old traditional congregational mosques such as these are extremely rare in Oman now; the only other remaining examples are at Rustaq (within the fort enclosure) and at Bahla (outside the fort).

Up on the hill behind Bukha stands a fine **hill fort**, a tower ringed with a defence wall. Those with the energy to climb up will be rewarded by an excellent view and a closer look at the unique domed cistern on the summit complete with pointed-arch door.

QIDA AND TAWI قضة وطوي

Just 4km before Khasab the new road winds round to the fjord-like bay of Qida, with fishing boats lining the beach. Unusually lush and green for Musandam, the oasis of Qida sits in the narrow river valley with date palms and many fruit trees. Take the signposted track to Tawi off the tarmac here, leading in a northeasterly direction into the valley, following a riverbed lined with some interesting old houses. One in particular, raised up on the left side, has attractive plasterwork in semicircular arches above the grilled windows. Follow the track beyond the village until you come to a second small village, in the centre of which, opposite a well between a group of three trees to the right, is an enormous cluster of grey boulders to the right of the road, many covered in prehistoric rock art of ships, horsemen, ibex and camels. Their date and origin are unknown. Village women, attuned to visiting foreigners, may emerge from their houses to sell you their basketry weaving. You can continue up the wadi to explore more mountain villages, some uninhabited.

KHASAB ﺧﺼﺐ

Khasab is Musandam's main town (although only a small fishing port) and is the next town you reach. Of Musandam's approximate population of 27,000, Khasab is home to 18,000 and is the northernmost *wilayat* overlooking both the Arabian Gulf to the northwest and the Gulf of Oman to the east. It acts as the seat of the *wali*, whose influence extends in practice about as far as the limits of the town. Its mainstays are fishing and agriculture, *khasab* being the Arabic for 'fertile'. Khasab has traditionally been a community of fishermen, boatbuilders, craftsmen and traders. The population swells in summer as people come from Kumzar and the mountain villages to harvest dates and to fish, thereby retaining its old way of life. The name itself is thought to be a contraction of *khawr* (Arabic for 'bay' or 'creek') and *asaba* (the ancient name for the whole peninsula coined by the Roman scholar Pliny in the 1st century AD). Its large shallow bay turns to mud flats at low tide and the type of boat built here, called the *baatil*, was quite flat bottomed but big enough for regional trading even as far as India.

The big wide bay is the mouth of the large wadi that extends inland for several kilometres, and the alluvial silt that has been deposited near the mouth by torrential seasonal flooding has enabled the extensive oases of the date gardens to build up. The old *sur* (mud and stone wall enclosure) of the Kamazirah tribe on the eastern side of town seems to have disappeared, along with the picturesque old summer houses built of *barasti* and raised up on six pillars that used to be grouped around it. Khasab town used to have many houses with traditional wind towers, a style introduced from Persia. Few now remain in the age of the air-conditioning system.

Behind the town as you drive inland – past the fort and deeper into Wadi Khasab – you will notice the wide low dam spanning the wadi floor. Such dams have been one of the priorities of the Musandam Development Committee, to minimise damage caused by violent torrential flooding. The Royal Geographic Society expedition of 1972 found a few pot shards in the alluvium of the wadi floor, which were dated to the 15th–19th centuries. Anything earlier, if it exists, is likely to be buried deep beneath the silt. Combined with that, the effect of the extreme subsidence of the past 10,000 years and the post-glacial rise in sea level would have meant any early coastal sites would now be either underwater or destroyed.

🏠 **WHERE TO STAY** For location of listings see maps on pages 156 and 166.

🛏 **Esra Apartments** (16 apts) ☎26 730562. Virtually opposite Khasab Airport & so are the furthest from the harbour. The self-catering apts (all with their own kitchen & living room) are of good clean standard &, as they are self-catering, there is no restaurant on the premises. **$$$**

🛏 **Golden Tulip Resort** (60 rooms) PO Box 434, PC 811, Khasab; ☎26 730777, 730789;

e info@goldentulipkhasab.com or packages@goldentulipkhasab.com; www.goldentulipkhasab.com. This is clearly the best hotel in Khasab, lifting accommodation in the area to a new level. Situated on its own headland with lovely sea & mountain views, it has a fully licensed restaurant (indeed the only licensed venue in town), pool bar with snacks, & a further separate bar & café. There is

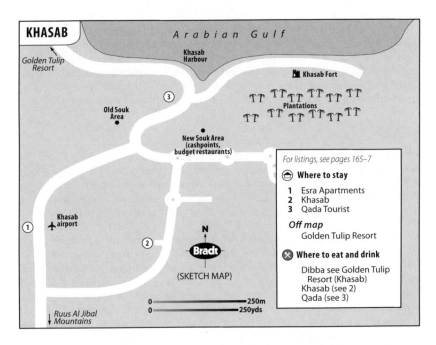

KHASAB

A r a b i a n   G u l f

Golden Tulip Resort

Khasab Harbour

Khasab Fort

Plantations

Old Souk Area

New Souk Area (cashpoints, budget restaurants)

3

Khasab airport

1

2

N

Bradt

(SKETCH MAP)

0 ─────────── 250m
0 ─────────── 250yds

Ruus Al Jibal Mountains

For listings, see pages 165–7

⬛ **Where to stay**
1　Esra Apartments
2　Khasab
3　Qada Tourist

Off map
　Golden Tulip Resort

❌ **Where to eat and drink**
　Dibba see Golden Tulip
　　Resort (Khasab)
　Khasab (see 2)
　Qada (see 3)

internet access here too (500bzs for 15mins). It has become very popular as a weekend getaway for expats working in the UAE, so needs to be booked well in advance. The hotel offers special packages that include your stay & certain excursions, which seems a pretty good option, as this will eliminate any extra hassles of arranging an independent trip. The Resort Package (RO30 + taxes) includes a welcome drink, fruit basket, overnight stay in deluxe sea-view room, b/fast & dinner by the pool or at Dibba Restaurant, guided tour to the fort of Khasab & late check-out. The *Dhow* Cruise Package (RO45 + taxes) includes the same, but with a half-day dolphin-watching cruise taking in Telegraph Island. The Fishing Package includes the same, but with a fishing trip from 17.00–20.00, which includes cooking your catch, a bottle of house wine, T-shirt, photo & a certificate for catcher of the largest fish. The Tour Package (RO120 + taxes) includes the same but with the addition of an extra night's stay, a full-day cruise & a mountain safari trip. You might like to check any updates on the tour packages offered. If you choose not to arrange one of these 'package' trips, this hotel has a Khasab Travel & Tours desk from which you can arrange *dhow* cruises, mountain safaris & trips to Kumzar independently. The tours operate all year round. This desk is helpful & informative & certainly the

most efficient place at which to organise your trips as & when you require. Accepts credit cards. Confirm your complimentary airport transfer with them. **$$$**

⌂ **Khasab Hotel** (35 rooms) PO Box 111, PC 811, Khasab; ☎26 730267; e khoman@omantel.net.om. This hotel is about 5mins' drive from Khasab Airport & sits on the left almost opposite the Shell petrol station. The rooms are laid out round a courtyard with a swimming pool. There is a simple restaurant (unlicensed) & communal lounge area with a TV. This hotel was the first to be built in Khasab & the rooms, which are a little shabby & dated, reflect this. You may find you have to work a bit harder with communication here, although the staff are pleasant & do make the effort to accommodate your requirements. A rather faceless new block has been added to expand the accommodation on offer & the new rooms are clean & bright, some with good mountain views. They will collect you from the airport, but it is safest to confirm this with them. Accepts cash only. **$$$**

⌂ **Qada Tourist Hotel** (22 rooms) PO Box 64, PC 811, Khasab; ☎26 731664, 731667; e qdahotel@omantel.net.om. This hotel is located closer to the harbour than the Khasab Hotel (its partner). The main office of Dolphin Tours is here. They will collect you from the airport, but you will probably need to remember to instruct them to do so before you leave Muscat. There is a restaurant on the premises, Dhabi al Yemen (☏ *26 731665*). Accepts cash only. **$$**

✖ **WHERE TO EAT** There are quite basic restaurants inside the Khasab Hotel and the Qada Tourist Hotel. The Dibba Restaurant, in the Golden Tulip Resort, is the only upmarket and licensed one. Outside of the hotels, there are a few local restaurants (all budget range), all located in the vicinity of the bank and souk. They serve an Indian, Arabic, Chinese and European menu, and are well worth a try.

There are also a few budget restaurants where you are likely to get a meal for two, including drinks, for under RO6:

✖ **Alshamaliya Restaurant** ☏ 26 730477. **$**
✖ **Bashair Restaurant** ☏ 26 731164. **$**

✖ **Bukha Restaurant** Old Souk. **$**
✖ **Musandam Restaurant** ☏ 26 730569. **$**

WHAT TO SEE

Khasab Fort (⊙ *08.30–14.30 Sat–Thu; free*) An impressive square enclosure with towers at each corner and an old round tower in the courtyard are all that remain of the original 17th-century Portuguese fort at Khasab. The steps up to it are shaded by an enormous *Albizia lebbeck* or rain tree (sometimes known as mother's tongue because of the large flat pods which hang on the trees for months and appear to chatter in the wind). The two separate towers to the rear house are the *wali's* private rooms for his two wives, and the front towers are the public rooms and gun-firing rooms. The fort now doubles as a museum with displays of Omani handicrafts and has been recognised with an award for being the best-presented fort in all Oman, as well as the most involved in and with the local population.

The guide leads you round from tower to tower and along the parapet walls for the tour which takes about 30 minutes. You can climb up ladders to the roof. The fort has been built from a complete hotchpotch of wadi pebbles, stones, mud bricks and careful stonework, each from a different period of construction, the oldest parts of which date back to the late 1800s.

KUMZAR كمزار

Accessible only by boat, Kumzar – a cliffside village – is the northernmost settlement of Oman, crammed into the narrow valley of Wadi Marwan and ringed with bare precipitous mountains. It takes two hours to reach it by speedboat from Khasab, nearly four by motorised *dhow*.

Back on the mainland at Khasab harbour, the road (graded track) now heads inland past the Khasab Hotel, which is on the outskirts of the town (see opposite). If you have arranged a mountain safari, this is the route your driver will take. The road continues beyond the airport and into the Wadi Khasab. Some 14km along

---

SMUGGLING TRADITION

Khasab harbour today is still busy with small boats which do a roaring trade in goats from Iran, destined for Ras al Khaimah. The Iranian smugglers then buy televisions, washing machines and cigarettes with bags of cash, returning to Iran under cover of night when the coast is radioed clear by accomplices. The authorities are not overly concerned, as it is all part of the long-standing tradition of smuggling to and from Iran that also goes on from the Emirates.

Kumzar's houses are so closely packed that there is hardly space to walk between them. There are two small mosques, each with a small graveyard, which were filled centuries ago. Recent burials have therefore been forced to take place under the floors of the houses. Kumzar *baatils* (fishing boats) were unique in the Gulf in having shell-decorated bows and zoomorphic sterns to secure the rigging. The village sheep and goats are taken regularly by boat to pastureland on Jazirat al Ghanim (Goat Island) or to other coastal bays where grazing is more plentiful. The government has now built a desalination plant, but before that everyone had to rely on a well at the back of the village. Visiting crews used to paint their ships' names on the cliffs behind the harbour, still clearly visible today.

this road (about ten minutes' drive from Khasab harbour) you come to a major junction with large signposts. The left takes you to both Khor A'Najd and Sal al A'la, potential camping spots within 30 minutes or so of Khasab. Keeping straight on leads to the military road up and over **Jebel Harim**, Musandam's highest peak, down to the checkpoint at Wadi Bih.

This checkpoint is only open to Omani passport holders or residents with a special road permit issued by the Royal Oman Police, so in practice very few people use it.

The drive over the mountain to the checkpoint takes a good two hours with no stops (approximately 60km), and relatively few make the journey right over the top and down as it tends to require another night's camping, usually in the Rawdah Bowl (see page 172).

KHOR A'NAJD خور النجد

Turning left at the signpost towards Khor A'Najd you come after 6km (a further five minutes) to the fork off left again to Khor A'Najd, the only piece of fjord coastline reachable by road in the whole of Musandam. It passes a military firing range. The track is steep and snakes up to the brow of the hill from where there is a stunning view out to sea, over the fjord and down to the *khor* (cove) itself. The total drive takes 15–20 minutes from this turn-off and is suitable for 4x4 only, because of the gradient and some bumpy sections. Only those with a high tolerance of litter and hornets would enjoy camping on the muddy beach itself, although it is geared for campers, providing sunshades and water tanks. At busy times like Eid the litter bins overflow and the water tanks become empty. The swimming is not good, as the shoreline is muddy and tacky, with rocks further out, so most people who stay here use boats – either their own or those rented out by fishermen.

SAL AL A'LA سل الأعلى

Back in the wadi floor the track continues straight on to Sal al A'la (not to be confused with Salalah, in Dhofar), a dead-end road finishing in a natural silt bowl ringed by mountains on three sides and with a few signs off to several villages on the way. The distance from here to the end of the bowl is 6km, and certainly this is the cleaner spot to camp and arguably the more beautiful. The name Sal al A'la means 'higher silt flat', reflecting its position at the head of the main valley of the largest drainage system of the Musandam mountains, flowing into the sea at Khasab.

The silt plain at Sal al A'la supports an astonishing forest of acacia trees (*simr* and *salam*), as well as *Zizyphus spina-christi* (*sidr*) and *Prosopis cineraria* (*ghaf*). The forest covers an area of 35ha and the trees reach a height of 9m. In the spring months from January to April a thick carpet of green grass grows under the trees that contrasts sharply with the barrenness of the surrounding mountains.

Sheep and goats are in paradise here, and a few donkeys are also to be found. Cows, which one could easily imagine grazing happily here, do not exist in

TELEGRAPH ISLAND

In the mid 19th century the technological revolution in Europe and the invention of telegraphy via a cable began to change the face of worldwide communications. Britain's empire and its links with colonial India had been transformed too by the introduction of steam ships in 1840 and the British India Steam Navigation Company started a postal service first to Calcutta and Rangoon, then to Ceylon and Karachi. Subsequently it extended in 1862 into the Gulf where the postal service then connected Bombay, Karachi, Muscat and Basra (Iraq). By 1858, a telegraphic landline had been laid between Baghdad and Scutari (Albania), and the proposal was subsequently made to connect this system to India via a landline to Basra, then via a submarine cable down the Gulf. After lengthy diplomatic discussions between Turkey (to which Iraq belonged at that time), Persia and Britain, the land stretch was finally completed in 1854 and the difficult submarine stretch was begun. At the Omani end there were difficulties about the placement of the telegraph terminal on the Musandam tip. This was because the local tribes, specifically the Zahuriyeen who lived on the Maqlab isthmus – the thin strip of land running between the two major fjord inlets of Elphinstone (Khor Ash-Sham) and Malcolm (Khor Habalayn) – disrupted progress for a month while they tried to establish what benefits there might be for them. It appeared that the British too had some doubts about jurisdiction over the area, but after further discussions the sultan reasserted his control over Musandam and the telegraph line was led into Elphinstone inlet and from there on to a small island to be known thereafter as Telegraph Island. The site was selected as it offered more security than the mainland against potentially hostile local tribes, and the telegraph station was built there in 1854 and maintained until 1869, the same year when the opening of the Suez Canal also brought Britain and India closer.

The terminus functioned for only five years since no-one wished to live in such an inhospitable place. Its strategic importance was felt by the British to be such, however, that in 1904 they decided to erect flags there, but could not agree what flag should fly – not the Union Jack since it was not British territory, and not the Blue Ensign of the Royal India Marine, for that would mean they might have to defend it. So the flagpoles were all taken down again, except one which was allowed to remain on Telegraph Island with no flag. None of the flagpoles were visible from the open sea anyway, but it is doubtful the decision makers in London ever realised. This tiny connection with modern technology had no effect on the lives of the Musandam tribes, needless to say, for whom life went on at subsistence level as before.

The tidal variation of two to three feet means that it is not always possible to land at Telegraph Island as the boat would be damaged on the rocks at low tide.

Musandam and are anathema to the Shihuh. Wild animals found in Musandam are leopards, wolves, foxes, hyenas and the Arabian *tahr* (a sturdy russet-haired type of mountain goat).

The spring of **Birkat al Khalidiya** ('spring of eternity') lies beyond the playground, where the track ends. The name is rather ironic as the spring is no longer maintained and has more or less dried up. As the cistern runs low, heading into April, hornets are drawn by the remnants of the water. Rubbish is still a problem, but far less so than at Khor A'Najd, and because the woodland is so large you can still find privacy even during religious holidays.

The village over in the left corner of the bowl (the opposite side to Birkat al Khalidiya) is **Limhas**, the largest settlement in the area. It has a large walled area that used to house a date plantation and fields of crops and fruit trees. The wall was specially constructed with the largest stones at the top to allow floods to pass through without resistance, keeping the strongest part at the top to prevent collapse. The settlement itself has stone Bait al Qufl houses (see box, page 173) as well as modern houses. It used to take a day for the men of the village to reach Khasab, so they would migrate there for the summer months, but now that it takes only 30 minutes they commute on a daily basis.

JEBEL HARIM جبل حريم

Jebel Harim is the tallest peak in the region at 2,097m and lies between Khasab and Dibba.

Returning to the main signposted fork at Khasab, you can now (if you have a minimum of half a day or preferably a full day) continue on the main mountain road signposted for Dibba. Again, if you have arranged a mountain safari, this is where you will head. The road runs very flat along the wadi bed, well compacted and smooth for another few kilometres until signs warn you of the impending mountainous section which requires 4x4 low ratio, especially on the descent. The road, built by the Omani military, is tricky driving, probably more difficult than the drive up to the Saiq Plateau or up the Bilad Sayt road in the Jebel Akhdar mountains, both of which are wider routes with better-compacted surfaces. You also require more of a head for heights, as some of the edges on the beginning stretch and just beyond the summit itself are extremely vertiginous.

The first section of the ascent is very steep but if you can wrench your eyes off the road for a moment, you can spot the Shihuh villages tucked into the mountainsides and perched on the edge of gorges. Old Bedouin houses (now disused) can also be spotted, at rather extraordinary heights. Look out too for the wispy bushes of the wild almond (*shu*) tree (*Amydalus arabica*) whose branches are used for the handles of the Shihuh small axe worn by Shihuh men instead of the traditional *khanjar* of Oman. This axe is unique to Musandam. It is called the *jerz* and some villagers may even offer you theirs for sale to earn themselves a bit of welcome cash. At each settlement are the white water tanks at the roadside, regularly filled by blue water tankers. If you see the water tanks with no sign of a village, rest assured that there will be a village tucked away somewhere nearby but out of sight of the road. As you get higher it becomes easier to stop and admire the views.

SAYH PLATEAU نجد صيح Towards the upper part of the ascent you will suddenly arrive at the Sayh Plateau, an extremely attractive miniature lush plateau about 2km long and 500m wide.

In the winter months the plateau is delightfully green, but starts to go brown by mid April. The settlements, most of which are on the opposite side across grassy meadows, exist to tend the small palm groves and fields of wheat and alfalfa. Donkeys, sheep and goats frolic in the pastureland.

On the opposite side of the plateau is another small settlement with Bait al Qufl houses, some of them built into the mountainside like caves. The numbers of villagers are constantly on the decline as men leave for the coastal towns.

On the summit of Jebel Harim immediately above, you can spot the grey dome (like a golf ball) that is the radar station set at 2,097m.

A climb of another ten minutes brings you right up to the summit of the pass where the Omani Air Force sits just below in its austere grey-green buildings. Half a kilometre before the final zigzags to the V-cut in the mountain pass summit is a bumpy track to the right, leading along flat ground for 2km to reach a helicopter landing pad used for delivering supplies to the air force base. There are a few small walled gardens close by that appear largely disused, and this whole area makes a fine camping spot in the summer months, the altitude providing welcome coolness – though there is virtually no shade and of course no water.

Continuing to the summit, as you pass through the V-cut to the other side of the mountain range, the most staggering view presents itself and the faint-hearted will quiver at the sight of the road they must follow for the descent. It starts by clinging to the left precipitous side of the mountain, then snakes off over a long thin ridge, before the final descent down to the wadi bed on the other side, a total of some 45 minutes' driving. The route is definitely at its most spectacular when seen from this direction – the climb back up again gives angles which are less dramatic and less vertiginous, too.

WATER PRACTICES IN THE MUSANDAM MOUNTAINS

Today the Khasab municipality runs a system of water tankers that regularly go to each village or to the closest point on a drivable track to replenish large white roadside water tanks for the remaining inhabitants of the mountain villages. This system dates back only to the early 1980s. Before that the Shihuh tribespeople devised other ways of surviving on minimal water.

The *falaj* irrigation channels so common in the rest of Oman are absent in Musandam. The nature of the terrain is such here that there would never be enough water to keep them flowing, so the high mountain villages tried instead to trap as much as possible of the heavy winter rains. To achieve this they built water-deflecting walls (*musaylah*) – following the contours of slopes where they observed the water ran best and most frequently – then caught it in cisterns built of stone and lined with mud. These can still be seen in many mountain villages, where the wall is often mistaken for a defensive structure. One of the best examples is on the raised outcrop directly above the Islamic cemetery at the junction of Wadi Bih with the track into the Rawdah Bowl.

The other practice was the use of a *khayr* (Arabic for 'good'), a large clay water jar donated by a family for public use. The benevolent donor thereby increased his social standing in the village, and it was his responsibility to keep it full. These jars were generally placed under a tree beside a main track, to facilitate travelling, or sometimes among a group of village houses. A few can still be seen in the remoter villages, and tend to have their tops stuffed with thorn bushes to keep debris out when the village is abandoned for the summer months.

5

THE RIDGE Just at the start of the ridge as the road leaves the mountain massif there is a small settlement of stone houses to the left of the track. If you fork off into this village, following the track through and beyond it for a kilometre or so, you will reach a deserted village which you can explore at leisure, to examine the exact layout of the Bait al Qufl houses and the walled garden areas. You may also notice the occasional stone plinth, apparently in the middle of nowhere, thought to have been used for the call to prayer. Another unexpected sight is the occasional use of scarecrows in the fields to protect the precious crops. The walled field systems round the tiny village settlement are remarkably complicated, the walls positioned for maximum rainwater run-off collection in harmony with the contours of the ground. Once crops were growing, the tops of the walls were rammed with thorn bushes to prevent goats jumping in and helping themselves.

After the long ridge the final descent into the wadi floor can be very bumpy, especially after rains have gouged out deep runnels in the steep track. Bulldozers and steamrollers try to repair the damage as soon as they can but occasionally it can take weeks rather than days if the rains have been very heavy.

RAWDAH BOWL At the foot of the mountain you come to a crossroads, the left of which takes you back along the gravel wadi floor to a minor settlement before reaching a dead end. The right takes you along Wadi Bih to the border checkpoint. Straight over leads you into the Rawdah Bowl – the best camping spot in the area.

From here into the Rawdah Bowl is a five-minute drive along a good track through a narrow defile which suddenly opens up into a large mountain-ringed bowl some 5km long by 2km wide. There are a few settlements in the bowl, and two interesting cemeteries. The area is large enough for you to find houses tucked away, often close to ruined stone homes, deserted in favour of newer buildings.

As you enter, your arrival will be noted by the police post on the left and if you stay the night a couple of men from the police post will almost certainly be sent out to check up on you after nightfall to make sure you are not causing trouble. A few friendly and polite words are all that is required, and even if you invite them to join you, they will respect your privacy and refuse.

The wildlife in the bowl is abundant, with owls, hedgehogs, birds of prey, numerous butterflies including tiger moths and blue pansies, and amazing cricket life, as well as the usual sheep and goats. February and March are the best for flowers and by April the grass is beginning to go brown. The bowl is heavily wooded with acacia, but is nothing like as lush as the forest at Sal al A'la.

Back out at the four-road junction at the foot of the mountain, you should fork left on to the Wadi Bih track, even if you do not intend to cross the border, for within just 1km is an extensive cemetery which deserves some attention. The **Islamic cemetery** lies to the right of the road, just round the corner from a large bluff. Its headstones are unusually tall, often over 1m, a few of them with engravings etched on to the rock, like that of the man with a spear and shield. Extremely neat and well arranged, this cemetery is one of the most impressive in the quality of masonry anywhere in Oman. Two slabs marks a male, three slabs a female grave. This is the Sunni, Hanbali style of grave, quite different from the small random stones of the typical Ibadhi graveyard. One unusual structure is circular, reminiscent in style of the foundation of an Umm al Nar tomb, with pinkish regular blocks.

The only house that remains as part of this settlement is back at the foot of the bluff on the same side of the road, a remarkable building constructed of colossal stone blocks. Again this is a mystery building, undated and unique in the country, and so perfectly crafted it almost resembles a small rural temple.

On the sloping bluff above it is a carefully constructed low double wall for deflecting water, a *musaylah*, with a few circular tower-like structures that were probably cisterns for collecting the mountain run-off.

Beyond the Islamic cemetery are a few very collapsed cairn tombs, but the better-preserved ones are on the other side of the track over towards the entrance to the Rawdah Bowl in the wadi plain. These cairn tombs, some 15 in all, are also a mystery here in Musandam, as yet undated and unexcavated. One has a long narrow chamber in the centre with roof slabs over the top. It is almost as if the loose stones have been added to cover this above-ground grave structure.

DIBBA دبا

Dibba (or Daba) is located in the southeastern edge of Musandam and has the second-largest population in Musandam after Khasab. The town is divided into three parts, although the divisions aren't clear and the signposts lacking. The southern part is Dibba Muhallah and is in the emirate of Fujairah; Dibba al Hisn is part of the emirate of Sharjah; and Dibba Bayah is the part belonging to Oman. In Dibba al Hisn there is an old simple fort, square with four towers at its corners, which has now been renovated and is open daily (⊕ *08.30–14.30; 500bzs*) except Friday. It used to be a police headquarters. Excavations have shown that this area was already inhabited c1000BC.

Most people will reach Dibba by road from the UAE, which does not require a visa. Coming from Khasab however, and with all the provisos about border crossings and visas (see page 43), Dibba can be reached following the course of Wadi Bih until it reaches the mountain pass, again built by the Omani military and announced by the same warnings of steep gradients. This road is less vertiginous and steep than the earlier section over Jebel Harim, but nevertheless impressive. As you near the top you will notice to the left of the track a large settlement set about 500m off the road, with extensive terracing. It also has two stone-built towers, one round, one square. The round one – with three levels and rather dilapidated – is

BAIT AL QUFL (HOUSE OF THE LOCK)

The Bait al Qufl style of house is unique to Musandam, and its whole construction and design is geared round security. The name 'house of the lock' reflects this and a highly complex locking device ensured that no-one could enter the house during the summer months when it was left unattended.

These houses are built from local stone. The roof is made from acacia wood, and covered with an earth and gravel mix, then edged with stone blocks. The walls never have windows. The floor level was usually 1m below ground level, and the door extended down to the sunken floor, with a deep recess, opening inwards, making it difficult to get in and out.

Inside, the inhabitants locked away all their essential items and possessions – such as storage jars, cooking utensils and tools used for crop growing. Sometimes the storage jars were so big they had to be put in the house before the roof was put on. Warmth was the secondary consideration, as the cold winter nights could reach close to freezing point. By preference, however, the Shihuh slept outdoors, only retiring to the Bait al Qufl in extreme cold. Outside there was generally a ledge or step running the length of the front of the house like a bench, where the owner would sit.

thought to have belonged to the wealthiest inhabitant. The square tower is a granary (*yanz*) in which the agricultural produce was stored. There is an opening in the side which was sealed to keep animals out, or to keep it clean when empty.

The border post is here, for crossing into the UAE and onwards to enter Oman at the northernmost tip of the Batinah coast. For location of listings see map, page 156.

⌂ WHERE TO STAY

⌂ **Six Senses Hideaway Zighy Bay** (82 pool villas) Zighy Bay, Dibba, Musandam Peninsula; ☏26 735555; e reservations-zighy@sixsenses. com; www.sixsenses.com. The ultimate getaway, super-remote, with ultra-clean sandy beaches & lavish service, the Zighy Bay is a Dubai-style resort for the super-rich. Built of local, natural materials it has a world-class spa focusing on holistic wellness & rejuvenation, with a full range of treatments conducted by international therapists. Most customers drive in from Dubai (1½hrs) via Dibba. It has 1.6km of private beach on one side & a mountain backdrop. As well as the pool villas there are 2-bed retreats & a 4-bed reserve. Restaurants

are what you might expect, including a hilltop restaurant offering international cuisine & a central restaurant with regional specialities. There is even a choice of arrival methods: a scenic drive down the mountain; a 15min speedboat ride; or as a companion passenger with the Zighy's professional paraglider! Dbls from RO245. **$$$$$**

⌂ **Golden Tulip Dibba** (54 rooms) Mina Rd, Dibba, Musandam Peninsula; ☏26 730888; www. goldentulipdibba.com. A low-rise development built in 2006, this 4-star place offers very good value for money, with plenty of deals at prices well below advertised rates on websites like www. booking.com. Good range of restaurants. **$$$**

WHAT TO SEE

Dibba Fort (*In the middle of the old town, set in a kind of central square;* ⊕ *08.30–14.30 Sat–Thu; 500bzs*) Worth popping in for a few minutes to see the layout, the fort has now been restored and its guardian has even produced a leaflet on it. There are no furnishings but the guardian will offer tea and *halwa*. You can climb up each of the four towers.

MADAH مدها

Madah (or Mudha) is the small piece of land surrounded on all sides by UAE territory and roughly 3km inland. If you are approaching from the Oman end, Madah is about 60km from Shinas. Ruins have been found here dating back to the Iron Age (1500–1000BC). There is rock art and calligraphy to be found at Jebel al Rukham (the Marble Mountain), and elsewhere in Madah, mostly dating to the 10th and 11th centuries, although some is believed to be pre-Islamic. New Madha is the new administrative part of the town with schools, health centres and government buildings.

Madah is one of Oman's least-known areas, with peaceful oasis villages, valleys, streams, springs, *falaj* and date-palm gardens; it is ideal for picnicking. The natural springs are said to have healing properties for skin disorders, as they contain sulphurous water. A local historian who is keen to preserve Oman's heritage, **Mohammed bin Salem al Mad'hani**, has filled his home with relics, handicrafts, antiques, curios, manuscripts and over 12,000 ancient weapons. We understand that it is possible to visit him, but you'll need to ask locally.

6

The Dhahirah الظاهرة

Telephone code: 25

There is a pair of scissors for every moustache.

The Dhahirah region is the vast stretch of desert plain extending from the foot of the Hajar Mountains out west into the Rub' al Khali (the Empty Quarter), which crosses the border with Saudi Arabia, and north, up to the UAE. South and eastwards, it meets Al Wusta and Al Dakhiliyah regions of Oman.

The modern significance of the region lies in its oilfields, notably Fahud which produces a third of Oman's oil. The historical interest lies in the region of Bat. Tombs have been found here dating back to c4000BC and the area is now a UNESCO World Heritage Site. Ibri is one of the main towns of the Dhahirah.

Overall, the area hasn't too much to offer the tourist, but the wadis and oases make it perfect for the camping and outdoors enthusiast.

GETTING THERE

BY ROAD You can access this region via Nizwa from the southern and eastern regions, via Buraimi from the north, or via Wadi Jizzi from the Batinah coast.

BY BUS Bus services run twice a day from Muscat to Buraimi, via Sohar, taking 1½ hours and costing around RO4.

BY TAXI A private taxi will charge around RO45 to drive you from Muscat to Buraimi, so it is cheaper to rent a car.

GETTING AROUND

There is not much public transport for moving around in this region. There are microbuses from Nizwa that take two hours to Ibri and cost around RO2, and buses

---

DURU BEDOUIN TRIBE

Oman's major oilfields of Fahud, Natih and Yibal lie in the middle of Duru territory. The three wadis of the Duru lands, Al Ain, Aswad and Amairi, disgorge into an area known as Umm As Samim ('Mother of Poison'), reputed to be an area of deadly quicksand. The Duru used to be nomadic, moving about with their livestock of camels and goats, and utilising the trees as camps, by hanging tent material around them, or by building up barasti huts around them. Since the 1970s the Duru have increasingly settled in their date groves at Tanam, near Ibri.

THE DHAHIRAH

↑ *Musandam*

Khatmat Malahah
border post

Dubai

05

**UNITED ARAB
EMIRATES**

21

Wadi Hatta
border post
(Al Wajajah)

*Jebel
Hatta*

01

Shinas Fort
Shinas
Shinas Park

Liwa
Liwa Castle
Majis

*Gulf of
Oman*

N

Awla Ya'rab
Fortress

Sohar
Sohar Fort
Museum

Bradt

• Mahadah

Huwa

07

Wadi Jizzi

Al Khandaq Fort

Wadi Jizzi
border post

Al Ain

Buraimi

1

× Saham

Jebel Hafeet

Wadi Hafeet
(Meryad border post
& customs)

• Hawra
Burghah

08

Al Filayj ○

AL BATINAH

• Al Khaboura
Bu Said Castle

Hafeet

Diqal ○

01

21

Diqal

09

○ Mashayiq

Sayya ○

Al Furfar ○

Ar Ruhbah ○

Wadi Hawasina

○ Bani Kharus

Al Haylayn ○

Tropic of Cancer

As Sunaynah •

Dank • Dut

Yanqul

**Wadi
Fidda**

Al Hayyal ○

09

Maqniyat ○

Rustaq

Jebel Shams

Al Araqi •

○ Al Dariz

*Jebel Al
Hawra*

Ibri Fort

Ibri

2

• Bat

*Jabal
Misht*

Jebel Al Khwr

*Nizwa
Fort*

DHAHIRAH

Al Sulaif ruins

Bat
Tombs

21

Bahla

Jabrin

29

For listings, see pages 178, 183–4

🏠 **Where to stay**

Abha (see 1)
Al Baraka Oasis Hotel
Apartments (see 1)
1 Al Buraimi
Al Dhahirah (see 1)
Al Masah (see 1)
Hamasa (see 1)
2 Ibri Oasis
Nafahat Al Buraimi
Hotel Flats (see 1)

❌ **Where to eat and drink**

Abha (see 1)
Al Masah (see 1)
Club Tropicana (see 1)
Ibri Oasis (see 2)
Lebanese
restaurant (see 1)

29

○ Natih

Adam

Fahud •

DAKHILIYAH

Jibal ○

0 ——————— 50km
0 ——————— 30 miles

29

that run from Muscat to Ibri taking five hours and costing about RO4. To make the most of the region having your own transport is preferable.

TOUR OPERATOR

Omani Travel and Tourism Bureau (OTTB)
Buraimi; 📞 25 655890; e otboman@omantel.net.om

⌂ WHERE TO STAY

There is not much choice in terms of places to stay in this region. There is one mid-range hotel and a few budget hotels in Buraimi, and one mid-range hotel in Ibri and that's about it.

Your only other option is to **camp**. One of the best places for camping is to head for Wadi Fidda (off the Yanqul road, see page 180), the wettest wadi in northern Oman, where you are guaranteed water pools all year round. After rains in the winter the wadi may well be too wet to be drivable, but in April and May it is perfect, with stunning gorge scenery.

From the main Buraimi–Ibri road there are two interesting diversions: one via Dank to Yanqul, the other via Ad Dariz to Bat. These can be done as a loop tour (for which you will need a 4x4), although they are described in this chapter as two separate diversions, in which case a 4x4 is not strictly necessary.

The road is signposted left to Fidda, 11km off the Yanqul road. The tarmac runs right through the wadi. This first stretch is the most scenic, so if camping, you need only allow 30 minutes from Al Dariz to find your camping spot. A 4x4 is necessary unless you camp on the very edge of the wadi.

IBRI   عبري

Ibri, located 297km from Muscat, is the main town of Al Dhahirah. It is suggested that the name Ibri may come from the Arabic root 'a-b-r', which means 'crossing' or 'traversing'. It is renowned for its oilfields in addition to its ancient tombs at Bat.

Ibri had a reputation as a fanatically Ibadhi place with a hostile attitude to Christians. After the Imamate Revolt was suppressed in 1959 its *wali* was put in prison in Jalali Fort, where he died an old man in 1968. Today it has a thriving souk and benefits from its proximity to the oilfield at Fahud. It has its own Arabic language school for foreigners wanting to learn Arabic (see page 64). You can therefore safely disregard the description of an early traveller in 1836 that 'to enter Ibri a man must go either armed to the teeth, or as a beggar with a cloth'.

Ibri is also known for its distinctive black-and-red-striped goat-hair rugs, and for its traditional dancing. There used to be about four bands that performed regularly at celebrations such as births, weddings and Eid holidays, but numbers are dwindling now. Dances were performed, as they are today throughout Oman at times of celebration, by men organised in rows and often carrying swords and sticks, who would enact a mock battle to the beat of the drums. In Ibri there was also a dance for women, and even for men and women performing together in rows facing each other.

The first road and border crossing between Oman and Saudi Arabia opened in 2012, called Ramlat Khaliya on the Omani side and Rub Al Khali (Empty Quarter) on the Saudi side, facilitating access to Mecca at times of the Hajj, and a road providing access to the Batinah coast. A good road already links this region with the United Arab Emirates, via Al Ain in Abu Dhabi.

GETTING THERE The drive from Bahla northwest towards Ibri takes approximately one hour. The summit of Jebel Kawr is 2,960m, only a little lower than Jebel Shams (the highest peak in Oman). As you begin to leave this behind to your right, the terrain flattens out and becomes rather monotonous.

As you enter the sprawling outskirts of Ibri the first signpost to the right avoids Ibri town centre completely and leads to Al Araqi, Bat (sometimes spelt 'Bath'), Yanqul and Dariz.

To see a little of Ibri itself, continue straight for another kilometre or so until Ibri is signposted off to the right. Follow the tarmac road on through the older houses, which spread up a rocky outcrop to the left with the ruins of a hilltop fort. The tarmac road then winds out through date gardens and across the wadi bed to rejoin the Al Araqi, Bat and Yanqul road that is heading east into the hills. For location of listing see map on page 176.

🏠 WHERE TO STAY

🏠 **Ibri Oasis Hotel** (27 rooms, 2 suites) PO Box 387, PC 516; ☏ 25 689955, 691626. This mid-range hotel, opened in 1999, has an international restaurant & bar. Rooms are large & well furnished. The hotel will provide you with packed picnic lunches. Works closely with Mark Tours & others. Accepts credit cards. **$$**

✗ **WHERE TO EAT** If you haven't brought a picnic with you to this region, then the best place to stop for a meal would probably be the restaurant inside the Ibri Oasis Hotel.

WHAT TO SEE

Al Sulaif ruins Your approach to Ibri is heralded by the sight on your left of the ruins of Al Sulaif across the wadi bed on a rocky outcrop. Abandoned some 20 years ago in favour of the new settlement beside it, this large walled village is well worth a detour of half an hour, to get a feel for a typical fortified Omani village. The road is signposted to the left and you can park in the new settlement close to the main gateway. A few old men are still to be found sitting near the entrance to the old souk and a small alleyway leads up to the covered main gateway, with several inscriptions carved into the rock beside it. The *falaj* still flows, if rather fetidly, and inside the walls you will find a mosque, fort, wells and many houses, some quite grand. The sloping rock up behind is ringed with watchtowers.

Forts The three main forts in Ibri are Ibri Fort, Jebel al Shahshah Fort and Al Aswad Fort. Of these, the most accessible is Ibri Fort (⏱ *08.30–14.30 Sun–Thu; 500bzs*) in the centre of the town, and over 400 years old. Within its walls is one of Oman's largest mosques to be found within a fortification, which can accommodate about 1,000 worshippers. This mosque – the Friday Mosque – has been restored and is still in use today.

WADI HAWASINA وادى الحواسنة

The road from Ibri through Wadi Hawasina to the coast at Khaboura will only ever be secondary because of its tortuous narrowness, no more than a twisting cut in the mountains carved by floodwaters and a dangerous place to be in rainstorms. The Hawasina tribe after whom the wadi is named are the most loyal and trusted tribe in Oman and for that reason the old sultan, Said bin Taimur, always had them as his palace guards in Salalah. A tarmac road to the coast at Khaboura, which was completed fairly recently, has transformed the journey time. About 3km from Al Araqi, those who have an hour or two to kill could attempt to find the **cave of Al Kittan**, said to have some of Oman's best and oldest cave decorations.

Getting there You begin by forking off to the left to follow the left edge of an outcrop. This outcrop is the only one for about 7km and comes to an end at a gravel gap in the hills. Here, maintaining your speed to avoid getting stuck in the deep gravel, keep to the left and turn round the corner of the outcrop. Almost immediately the terrain hardens as you exit the wadi bed, and you pass a ruined village on your left called Uqabiyah, with derelict field systems. Drive south from here for 3km, keeping to the right hand of the two tracks until you reach the mouth of a wadi. The cave opening is said to be a short walk on the right-hand side, but be prepared for a long and possibly futile search. If you do go looking for it, be sure to take plenty of water.

AL DARIZ الدارز

Back on the road to Al Dariz you will notice the impressive tall fort of **Al Ainayn** to your left rising from some date palms. The entrance has been blocked up, but the local sheikh has the key to the other door, if you have the time to spare.

At Al Dariz there is also an attractive sand-coloured fort beside a mosque and *falaj* in the centre of the village, still inhabited by the local sheikh.

BAT بات

The real reason for making the detour along this road to Al Dariz is to visit the necropolis of Bat with over 100 burial sites, selected by UNESCO as a World Heritage Site. The whole area was heavily settled in the earliest times here, on the intersection of several major trade routes, and pottery finds and radiocarbon tests have dated the Bat beehive tombs to c3000BC. The site is extensive. In addition to the beehive tombs there is a circular fortress and several Umm Al Nar circular tombs. It covers an area of about 2km² in total, in largely shadeless terrain – so avoid any lunchtime visits, except in the winter months.

GETTING THERE There is no public transport, so private taxi or your own vehicle are the only options. A 4x4 is not necessary as the track is good. The detour from Ibri to see Bat takes at least 2½ hours, which includes an hour to explore the site itself. The tarmac road leads as far as the modern village of Bat, and along the 14km you will frequently notice the remnants of beehive tombs along the tops of ridges beside the road. The track off to the side used to be signposted Medina Al Athar (City of Ruins) but there was no signpost at the time of writing. It forks off to the left just before the modern village of Bat and then winds round to the right. The fencing gives you a clue, erected to protect the site; but whole chunks are missing, which makes access to the necropolis straightforward.

OIL PRODUCTION

Oman had to wait a long time for its oil to be discovered and the quantities are relatively small compared with Saudi Arabia's or Abu Dhabi's reserves. The first oil concession was obtained from Sultan Said bin Taimur, Qaboos's father, in 1937, by the Iraq Petroleum Company. World War II then intervened and the poor communications in the hinterland slowed everything down enormously. Around £12 million was spent and in 1960 most of the partners gave up. Only Shell, supported by Gulbenkian interests, kept trying and in 1964 succeeded in finding commercial quantities of oil in the fields of Fahud, Natih and Yibal. They spent a further £25 million, and actual oil production and export began in 1967. A main pipeline runs from the oilfields through the Sumail Gap to reach the tanker terminal at the oil port – Mina Al Fahal – in Muscat.

Opposite the round tower you can skirt the fence to drive past the old city walls over to the Umm Al Nar tombs, seven or eight circular communal graves with a diameter of about 11m, designed for up to 200 people. Only the beautifully crafted foundations remain and the group of fenced beehive tombs beyond. Anyone who saw these tombs in the 1980s would be shocked now to see the extent of the deterioration. Not one has an intact roof and only one has an intact arched doorway. A Danish team first excavated in 1976 and found the beehive tombs to contain two to five graves each. Up on the ridge above the site there are more. The Bat Tombs are one of the most complete collections of settlements and necropolises of the 3rd millennium BC.

DANK ضنك

From the main Buraimi–Ibri road take the turning off to Dank, clearly signposted. The tarmac road goes straight through Dank and curves to the right, built up on a high flyover above the wadi and date groves from the point where the tarmac used to end but now continues through the Wadi Dank, a popular tourist attraction and a good picnic spot. There are a number of imam forts in Dank as well as the Dank Caves. Signs at this point announce Yanqul (42km) and Fidda (24km). The first 5km through the wadi is very attractive and lush. There are many pools and the water flows freely to the left of the gorge, with the occasional settlement among the date gardens.

The next section opens out into a wide gravel plain, less scenic by far.

WADI FIDDA وادى فضة

Once you arrive at Dut (or Dawt), the first village *en route* to Fidda from Dank, the gorge narrows again, and there are caves visible in the cliffs. Only when you reach Fidda, recognisable by its red flags and Red Crescent clinic, does the gorge become really scenic again, with many pools and date gardens offering shade. After 5km the wadi opens out just before the modern unsignposted settlement.

Follow the tarmac on for 4–5km to reach the T-junction from which Yanqul is signposted 11km to the left. The terrain here is unusual, with pointed mountains, some conical, some jagged, some pyramid-shaped and some in giant tabletop slabs.

YANQUL ينقل

Yanqul is considered a transit stop between the Dhahirah and Batinah regions, the most famous landmark being the mountain peak of **Jebel al Hawra**, which is

---

BAT: OMAN'S OLDEST SITE AND *FALAJ* SYSTEM

To the right of the track you will come first to a substantial circular structure, once fenced, but the fence has been washed away by flash floods from the nearby wadi. This fortification has been identified as a tower and is dated to 2750BC. It is a complex structure and seems to have a well in its centre. Archaeologists have calculated the original height was around 10m and they have found traces of five other similar towers in the vicinity. They also uncovered constructed water channels leading to the site, which would make these the earliest-known use of the *falaj* system for which Oman is so well known.

used as the emblem for the *wilayat*. Goldsmithing, carpentry and weaving are the traditional crafts carried out here. Oman's only gold mine, producing 500kg of gold a year, opened near Yanqul in 1994.

The old Yanqul Fort and settlement, now abandoned, lie just 1km further on from the point where the tarmac used to end but now continues round the corner from the flagged government building just out of sight. Park by the old main gate and take some time to poke round inside this unrestored walled village. Abandoned some 20 years ago in favour of the modern housing provided by the government, its tall building to the right of the entrance has an impressive deep *falaj* within its walls and an attractive painted ceiling in one of its upper floors with Koranic inscriptions on the beams. There are three wells within the old village, and the building at the far end also has some attractively carved doors still *in situ*. Note too the mosque with four domed chambers.

The road continues from here to loop round and rejoin the entrance of Wadi Fidda. Copper and silver have been found in the surrounding hills and gold has been produced from copper oxide deposits.

From Yanqul a tarmac road now runs through scenic gorges to Al Wuqbah (45km) on the edge of the Batinah coast, and you can now reach Sohar this way in under two hours.

BURAIMI برايمى

Buraimi and Mahadah are the northernmost *wilayats* of the region. Both are known for their farming and agriculture. In Mahadah, corn is the most common crop, along with dates and animal fodder. In Buraimi, agriculture is centred on the farming of limes, dates and alfalfa. Buraimi has a long history of conflict and its many forts are testimony to this. Its two main forts are Al Khandaq and Al Hillah.

Buraimi is significant because of its strategic situation as an oasis on trade routes between Oman, Abu Dhabi, Saudi Arabia and the rest of the Arabian Peninsula. The oasis is in fact a whole group of villages, mainly belonging to Abu Dhabi, and a handful belonging to Oman. Buraimi and Al Ain are tightly juxtaposed, and so, with British assistance, Abu Dhabi and Oman staked out a complex but agreed border, with the Omani part named Buraimi and the Abu Dhabi part named Al Ain, after the largest village in each case. Within the area itself there is no obvious indication where the border runs, and there is no border crossing within the city. Instead, the two border crossings (at Mazyad and Az-Zurub) are both well in advance of it.

In the 1960s and 1970s the differences were far more marked, with Al Ain aspiring to grow and develop, with street lights, banks and Coca-Cola stores, while Buraimi remained exactly as ever – a collection of hovels and dust. The *wali's* fort remained unmodernised, while Sheikh Zayed's new guesthouse sported air conditioning. The contrasts were extraordinary, with the Omani dirt track meeting the immaculate tarmac road of the Abu Dhabi side. Now, in the 21st century, the differences are less obvious and Buraimi, though not as affluent and buzzing as Al Ain, is nevertheless a thriving modern centre. Outside of Buraimi there is desert.

HISTORY In 1800, the Saudi Wahhabis marched into Buraimi, planted their governor there and began to dominate the surrounding territory. From its original back-to-basics beginnings, Wahhabi doctrine became single-minded and intolerant in its attempts to propagate itself over the next 70 years through a series of raids and invasions from this southeastern Arabian base. Raids were profitable and made in the name of *zakat,* the religious tax of Islam rather like a church tithe. If the British had not supported the sultan, the Wahhabis might well have conquered Oman. When the Saudis renewed their claim to Buraimi in 1952, it was because of suspected oil reserves in Abu Dhabi territory (which indeed proved to be correct), though they concocted an elaborate web of historical claims based on *zakat* payments and old documents. In 1955, the Saudis were driven out by the British and the Trucial Oman Scouts, and have never yet returned, though their claim has never been formally dropped. The Saudi presence in Buraimi between 1952 and 1955 was one of the main reasons for the Jebel War of 1957–59 in Oman, as the Saudis supported the rebelling imamate of Ghalib and his brother Talib.

GETTING THERE AND AWAY Those wishing to travel the circuit of Oman will undoubtedly be frustrated by the bureaucracy and inconvenience of the border posts. They are huge trouble to those simply wishing to do a full tour of the country, stopping overnight at the Buraimi Hotel (which is in Oman!) and continuing the following day on an Oman circuit tour down to Ibri (with no intention of visiting Abu Dhabi's city of Al Ain). Although Buraimi is Omani territory, your Omani tourist visa needs to be cancelled and a UAE one issued – which is very tedious.

As entering Buraimi causes both extra expense (in terms of visa purchases) and hassle (in terms of paperwork and security checks), it seems that skirting Buraimi would be a good option. But although the layout on the maps seems to indicate otherwise, it does not appear possible to simply go round Buraimi (and thus eliminate the border hassles), as the border post is located that much further away from Buraimi town itself; you have to go through Buraimi to access the road southwards to Ibri/Nizwa. For this reason, coupled with the fact that there is not too much for the tourist to see there, you may choose to avoid Buraimi altogether.

Entering Buraimi To enter Buraimi you can approach from two directions in Oman: one, from Ibri to the south and, two, from Sohar to the east. Either way you have to cross the border and enter UAE territory, which means you will need to have your Omani visa cancelled and a UAE visa issued. This procedure is reversed on the return leg. The route from Ibri crosses at the Mezyad (Jebel Hafeet) border post, and from Sohar at the Wadi Jizzi checkpoint. The Wadi Jizzi border is quicker, as it has no UAE checkpoint, so it only involves one stop and one set of forms to fill in.

Wadi Jizzi border post (from Omani side) This border post lies nearly 40km before Buraimi and roughly an hour's drive from the coastal dual carriageway. It consists of an Omani checkpoint with no UAE entry or exit post, taking an average of a mere 15 minutes – and where, in theory, you will be issued with an exit ticket.

Once past the signs to Mahadah you will soon reach a roundabout that is signposted right towards Buraimi. The route to Buraimi from the Omani border side takes you through mountain scenery with occasional villages and terracing. It is a good new empty road, which crosses over the wadi many times with attractive views down into the wadi floor, with rivers and pools for much of the year. At one point just after Al Wasit, a long white bridge crosses the wadi and, looking up to your right just after the bridge, you will spot a natural rock arch which can be clambered up for fine views. A plateau with a few graves lies just below the arch.

Jebel Hafeet (Meyzad) border post (from Omani side) This is a large border post stop, officially named the Mezyad Border Post and Customs, involving six stops and accessed via the long road from Nizwa through Ibri. About 20 minutes after this stop you will reach Buraimi.

Leaving Buraimi Finding your way out of Buraimi/Al Ain to continue your travels around Oman can be difficult the first time. The two border posts are at Jebel Hafeet/Meyzad (leading to Ibri/Nizwa) and Wadi Jizzi (leading to the Batinah coast). There are no signposts from the main roads in the centre of town indicating directions south to Ibri/Nizwa, or east to Sohar, no signposts indicating directions to the Jebel Hafeet or Wadi Jizzi border posts, and no signposts simply indicating the direction for Oman. You may find yourself driving blindly around the busy city of Al Ain, praying for a recognisable signpost.

Wadi Jizzi border post (from Buraimi side) Approaching from Buraimi, leave the centre of Al Ain turning right at the 'horse' roundabout in front of the *wali*'s fort and then following signs to Sa'raa. At the next roundabout with model gazelles follow the signs to Al Khadra'a Al Jadida. At the third roundabout with the model oryx, known as Buraimi Hospital roundabout, you go straight on following Sohar and Al Jizzi.

As you leave the Buraimi sprawl behind you there are fine views of the Jebel Qattar escarpment to your left and the looming mass of Jebel Hafeet to your right. You then pass through a dramatic V-cut in the rock and turn left at the roundabout following signs to Sohar. The road takes you through an open wadi with jagged mountains to each side, and there are traces of water in the wadis near the turn-off to Al Kitnah. The next turn-off right is to Al Malaqah and then within 1km you come to the Omani border post set astride the wadi.

Jebel Hafeet (Meyzad) border post (from Buraimi side) This border crossing will lead you down to Ibri and Nizwa. From Buraimi/Al Ain you need to follow signs to Mezyad to reach it, some 15km south of Buraimi. It takes about 20 minutes to drive from the Hilton Hotel (which is in Al Ain) to reach the border. Expect formalities here to take approximately an hour and incorporate around six separate police points. Your UAE tourist visa will now be cancelled and an Oman one re-issued (costing RO6). If you have the inclination, after this tedious process, you may notice the striated rock formation of Jebel Hafeet towering over the border post. Nizwa is roughly a three-hour drive from Buraimi.

WHERE TO STAY There are no upper-range hotels in Buraimi. If you are looking for something in this bracket then Al Ain (closely interweaved with Buraimi and to which you are free to travel) offers the Hilton Al Ain (*www.hilton.co.uk*); Al Ain Rotana Hotel (*www.rotana.com*); the InterContinental Hotel Al Ain (*www.ichotelsgroup.com*); and the Mercure Grand Jebel Hafeet Hotel (*www.mercure.com*), all $$$$$. For location of Buraimi see map on page 176.

Al Masah Hotel (59 rooms) PO Box 490, PC 512, Buraimi; 25 653007. This is a 3-star hotel with a restaurant & coffee shop. Travelling past the Buraimi Hotel continue straight until you meet a roundabout. Go straight over this roundabout. At the second roundabout take the left. Continue straight until you meet another roundabout where you continue straight again.

The hotel is about 500m past this on the right-hand side, behind the Toyota showroom. $$$
Al Buraimi Hotel (30 rooms, 20 chalets, 10 villas) PO Box 330, PC 512; 25 642010; e alburaimihotel@yahoo.com. On Oman's border with the UAE, this hotel is close to Al Ain (300km from Muscat). You need to 'exit' Oman & enter the UAE to stay here. The hotel is of good standard,

with a licensed restaurant called Club Tropicana & a bar. There are no internet facilities & the piped music can be loud. On the Club Tropicana menu (which is also served as room service) you have the option of grilled pigeons, stuffed pigeons & ox tongue, among the usual extensive list of pasta, 'international favourites' (steak, chicken, etc), snacks, seafood & Arabic/Indian dishes. The hotel organises camel safaris & full-moon desert BBQs. Accepts credit cards. **$$**

⌂ **Al Dhahirah Hotel** (35 rooms) PO Box 169, PC 512; ☎ 25 652992; e Al_blushi79@hotmail. com, yasser_amrea@hotmail.com. Situated 2km from Al Ain & 270km from Muscat Airport. Al Dhahirah deals with a number of car-hire companies, including Fast Rent a Car. There is a Lebanese restaurant that serves all kinds of grilled food & fish. **$$**

⌂ **Abha Hotel** (12 rooms) PO Box 577, PC 512, Buraimi; ☎ 25 654700. This hotel is located close to Buraimi Hospital. It has a restaurant offering 24hr food. **$$**

⌂ **Al Baraka Oasis Hotel Apartments** (27 apts) PO Box 17, PC 512, Buraimi; ☎ 25 650955. These self-catering apts & rooms are located about 200m further along from the Buraimi Hotel & on the opposite side. **$$**

⌂ **Nafahat Al Buraimi Hotel Flats** (8 apts) PO Box 624, PC 512, Buraimi; ☎ 25 654777. These self-catering apts are opposite the Buraimi Hospital, which is about 500m from the Buraimi Hotel. **$$**

⌂ **Hamasa Hotel** (28 rooms) PO Box 490, PC 512, Buraimi; ☎ 25 651200. This 1-star hotel is located about 2–3km from the Buraimi Hotel. With the Buraimi Hotel on the right-hand side, continue straight until you meet the 1st roundabout. Take a left here & continue straight over the 2nd roundabout. There is no restaurant here, but they will bring food to your room for you from a local restaurant. **$**

OTHER PRACTICALITIES
Hospitals
✚ **Al Buraimi Hospital** ☎ 25 652319
✚ **Ibri Hospital** ☎ 25 691990

Police stations
Buraimi ☎ 25 650199
Al Dhahira ☎ 25 650099
Dank ☎ 25 676099
Ibri ☎ 25 489099
Wadi al Jizzi ☎ 25 659309

WHAT TO SEE Most of the sights of interest to visitors lie in the Abu Dhabi section of the oasis. The only historic monuments in the Omani Buraimi side are Al Khandaq Fort and Al Hillah Castle. Because of Buraimi's strategic position on the crossroads into the rest of the Arabian Peninsula, the forts are steeped in the region's history of conflict.

Al Khandaq Fort This fort is located beside the 'horse' roundabout where the modern *wali*'s fort stands. Recently restored, it is open to the public free of charge whenever the guardian is in attendance. It provides a good example of the ancient strategy of using a defensive trench or dry moat to protect and strengthen the stronghold. From its towers you can get a good view over towards the old Buraimi oasis with its picturesque, decaying houses. You can drive over, and stroll in the winding alleyways between the date plantations, which are tended nowadays by Beluch and Pakistanis who live in huts on the edge of the oasis.

Al Hillah Castle This castle is situated in the centre of Buraimi and is notable for its plasterwork decorations and motifs. Like Al Khandaq Fort, this too has been restored.

7

The Dakhiliyah الداخلية

Telephone code: 25

The ewe that went to get horns returned without ears.

The Dakhiliyah translates as 'the interior' and is the area that begins at Fanja and incorporates the western Hajar Mountains. It consists of the eight wilayats of Nizwa, Bahla, Bidbid, Sumail, Izki, Manah, Adam and Al Hamra.

The region is an important agricultural area, both historically and currently. The unique climate of the jebels facilitates growth of a wide range of fruit trees, plants and shrubs, which are a crucial part of the country's economy.

The interior was historically considered very different from coastal Oman, largely because it looked, not to the sultan, but to the imam as leader. He was the elected head of the Ibadhi sect, an early sect of Islam which exists today only in Oman and in small pockets of north Africa, having been wiped out in all other parts of Arabia (see box, page 28).

The imamate had always tended to be inward looking and detached from the activities of the coast. By contrast the coastal population had always had contact with the outside world through maritime trade. Traditionally therefore, the interior and coastal Oman were separate, so much so that the interior was referred to as Oman, and the coast as Muscat. When local people left the coast to go to the interior they would say 'I am going to Oman.'

Problems began when the Al Bu Said dynasty in Muscat started to interfere with the traditional ways of the Omanis of the interior. These differences were not exclusively religious, for not all Omanis of the interior were Ibadhi; the problems were also tribal, and these tribal characteristics and traditions continue to exist even today.

Today, the region has eight *wilayats* and Nizwa is the administrative centre.

For an exploration of the region, Nizwa makes the perfect base, and a stay of two or possibly three nights will allow you to experience most of what the region has to offer while providing an interesting and marked contrast to the city of Muscat.

GETTING THERE

BY AIR There is no airport here for civilians.

BY CAR To reach the interior, take the Muscat–Nizwa road (Route 15) just after Muscat Airport; the excellent dual carriageway speeds you along between the mountains, through the Sumail Gap. This gap has always been the major link corridor between Oman's coast and the interior, the chief trade route of old. The drive from Muscat to Nizwa takes 1½ hours, and is dual carriageway all the way, making it an easy and quick excursion. In the past, when most of it was single carriageway, it used to be subject to flash floods.

THE DAKHILIYAH

Gulf of Oman

N

Bradt

Al Filayi
08
01
Al Khaboura
Bu Said Castle

AL BATINAH

Diqal
Al Qasf
09
Al Ghizayn
Mashayiq
Al Furfar
Bani
Sayya
Kharus
Ar Ruhbah
**Wadi
Hawasinah**
Al Haylayn
Al Mazahit

As Suwayq
Al Musanaah
Barka
Daymaniyat
Islands
Naseem Park
As Seeb
Barka Fort
01
**Muscat
International
Airport**

**Al Hazm
Fort**
11

Al Abyad
Fanja
15
**Al Nakhal
Fort**
Tropic of Cancer

Al Hayyal
09
see page 196
Maqniyat
**Rustaq
Fort**
Rustaq
Awabi
Nakhal
Sumail
Bidbid
Al Firfareh

Al Dariz
Bat
Ibri
**Bat
Tombs**

Jebel Shams
Umq
Hat
Al Jebel Akhdar
Ar Ruus
Al Ghubrah
Al Hobe

Wadi Ghul
Hamra
Jebel Al Khwr
Bilad Sayt
Tanuf
Mutti
Al Afia
**(Wadi Halfayn &
the Persian Steps)**
25

21
Al Rawdah Fort
**Akhdar
Fort**
23

DHAHIRAH
Bahla
Nizwa
Izki
Jabrin
Birkat
al Mawz
15
Samad
27
Lizq
28

33
Al Mudaybi
Sinaw
SHARQIYA

29
Natih
Adam
27
32
Fahud

31

**DAKHILIYAH
(THE INTERIOR)**

29

32

0 ――――――――― 50km
0 ――――――――― 30 miles

31

Al Ghaba
1

For listings, see page 208

⊖ **Where to stay**
1 Al Ghaba Resthouse

⊗ **Where to eat and drink**
Al Ghaba Resthouse (see 1)

AL WUSTA

186

BY BUS All buses travelling to Salalah in the south go via the interior and drop-offs/pick-ups can be made at any of the designated bus stops. Buses run twice a day from the Ruwi Bus Station to Nizwa, the main town of the Jebel Akhdar region (see page 199), taking 2½ hours and costing around RO3, and the same back again.

GETTING AROUND

CAR RENTAL This can be arranged via the Falaj Daris Hotel in Nizwa or any of the other hotels. It is possible to rent a saloon car from Muscat or the Capital Area, then switch to 4x4 just for the day to save the cost of renting a 4x4 all the time.

TOUR OPERATORS

If you are not intending to travel the area independently, it is necessary to pre-arrange any tours through operators in Muscat to avoid any disappointment. They will either collect you from your hotel in the region (which is invariably in Nizwa), or transport you from Muscat, whichever suits your needs best.

⌂ WHERE TO STAY

Accommodation in this region is mainly concentrated in and around Nizwa, listed on page 201, and there are two places high up in the Jebel on the Saiq Plateau (see page 198).

CAMPING AND PICNIC SPOTS Although the area is heavily populated compared with other regions it is still possible to find places away from villages to camp and picnic, especially if you have a 4x4 and are prepared to drive off the tracks a little.

OTHER PRACTICALITIES

HOSPITALS
✚ **Adam** ☏25 434055
✚ **Bahla** ☏25 419233, 420013
✚ **Izki** ☏25 341755
✚ **Jebel Akhdar** ☏25 429055
✚ **Nizwa** ☏25 449155
✚ **Sumail** ☏25 352236

Adam ☏25 434099
Bahla ☏25 419099
Bidbid ☏25 360099
Izki ☏25 340099
Nizwa ☏25 425099
Sumail ☏25 350099
Wadi al Jizzi ☏25 659309

POLICE STATIONS
Dhahirah Police HQ ☏25 650099

POST OFFICES
✉ **Nizwa** ☏25 410302

WHAT TO SEE AND DO

All major tourist destinations into the jebels are signposted from the Nizwa–Bahla road with large brown tourist signposts. To access these destinations you will need a 4x4. For independent travellers arriving in saloon cars, it is recommended that you pre-book any tours into Jebel Akhdar, the Hota Caves or any other jebel trips with the tour operators based in Muscat, so that you are not disappointed. Caving, rock climbing, trekking and wadi bashing are all possible in this region. For caving and climbing you will need to arrange your trip through a tour operator in Muscat.

ROCK CLIMBING Around 160 climbs have been pioneered in the region; each is rated in terms of difficulty and they range from 120–500m. Jebel Misht, Jebel Ghul and Jebel Misfah are the three rock-climbing sites and they are all in the Jebel Akhdar range in the Dakhiliyah. Climbs are arranged through most tour operators in Muscat (see pages 76–8). *Rock Climbing in Oman*, published by Apex, will certainly be of interest to you if climbing is your thing (see page 300).

CAVING Al Hota Cave near Hamra is the caving destination of the interior (see page 211), now made accessible to everyone as a major tourist attraction. For further caving opportunities in other regions of Oman, see pages 123–4.

FANJA فنجاء

If you are heading out from Muscat on your first exploration of the interior, Fanja will be your first opportunity to explore an old walled town, now deserted but with a few houses at the very edge.

GETTING THERE On the Muscat–Nizwa road, after 32km, Fanja is signposted off to the right and you follow the approach road to the new village set on the far bank of the wide wadi. If you do not have your own transport you will need to be dropped off by the bus from Ruwi Bus Station on the main road and walk the 2km into the village.

WHAT TO SEE
Fanja Tower Look carefully as you get closer to see the old town and its famous tower set up high on an escarpment above the modern village, built of the same rock as the cliff face and therefore surprisingly easy to miss. Head for the foot of the escarpment and park below near some shops now run by Indians, then walk on up the narrow tarmac road, past the running *falaj* at the roadside, to enter the old gateway into the village after a five-minute walk. Once inside you will notice one or two inhabited houses, quite smartly renovated and with television aerials, but the houses beyond are empty. Most interesting though is the walk up the sloping escarpment past the 17th-century cannon to the fortification towers, especially the unusual oval-shaped one at the very summit. There is a kind of reservoir beside it, originally used by the inhabitants before the days of piped water, and the views out over the date gardens and the majestic sweep of the wadi are very impressive, especially at sunset when the rocks glow a deep red.

On the way to rejoin the main road there are a few shops near the bridge selling pottery and earthenware made at Bahla. With a 4x4 you can also drive down into the

---

IMAM OR NO IMAM

Ibadhi are deeply conservative and traditional, and their beliefs are based on the earliest Islamic sources, the Koran and the Hadith (ways of the Prophet Muhammad). They believe the imam must be elected by the whole community and if he loses support or credibility he may be removed or deposed. If no suitable imam can be found, then the office can remain unfilled until such time as the community agrees on a suitable candidate. Thus, the status of tribes and individual leaders was constantly changing. There was no imam for 60 years from 1810–70 and at one point three elected candidates in a row refused the position.

wadi bed before reaching the bridge to drive along the Wadi Fanja back towards the coast as far as Al Khoud. This is the site of a fine fortified and decorated castle and Sultan Qaboos University. There are many pools and good picnic spots along the way.

BIDBID بدبد

Just 2km beyond the Fanja turn-off (and about 30 minutes from Seeb roundabout) you come to the Bidbid exit, where you could make a half-hour stop to visit the fort, the first one in Oman to be restored using traditional methods from the original materials of mud, gypsum and straw.

WHAT TO SEE
Bidbid Fort To reach the fort, follow the tarmac road through the village, then fork off to the left just as the main tarmac through-road starts to drop down into the wadi. The fort lies 1km along this road, rising up above the date palms on the very edge of the wide wadi bed. It is now kept locked, but there is one point at the back where you can climb in with care. The rooms are all empty, with a cannon embedded in the tower, and the whole fort has a tumbledown air with a big tree in the centre of the courtyard. Outside, flowing past the main gate, is a very attractive *falaj* still in use by the village beside the fort.

AL FIRFAREH الفرفرة

After Bidbid the dual carriageway continues and, very soon after, the road forks left to Sur and the Sharqiya (eastern province). Nearby is a small village called Al Firfareh, known for a group of four religious hermits who once lived there, all women (as are many of the Omani adherents of the Sufis, the mystical sect of Islam). They were three sisters and their aunt, and the small mosque they built for their devotions outside the village in the early 1900s still stands in a renovated form, but now incorporated into the expanded village. Today there is no continuing tradition of Sufism in the village.

THE SUMAIL GAP فجوة سمائل

The Sumail Gap – the only natural pass through the northern jebels, and separating the Hajars into the western and eastern ranges – is 60km inland from Muscat Airport and coast, and forms the main access route from Oman's coast to the interior. It starts at Sumail and ends at Izki, and today it is the main road from Muscat to Nizwa. It is not totally flat, but in fact climbs about 2,000ft above sea level at its highest point. This was the ancient, strategic route for trade and communication between coastal and interior Oman; it was the frankincense route taken by caravans as well as the road travelled by explorers such as Marco Polo and Ibn Battuta.

THE *FALAJ* SYSTEM

Thought to have been introduced by the Persians in pre-Islamic times on account of its obvious resemblance to the Persian *qanat*, the *falaj* is a channel for water that leads from its source, usually an underground spring, to the fields where irrigation is required. The concept began in Persia and dates back to 1000BC. Some 20% are open channels direct from springs, while 80% are underground channels leading water from mother wells at the foot of the mountains where the water table is higher because of rainwater run-off. Some are said to originate 40ft underground, while some never go underground at all. Some run for miles while others are very short.

Maintaining the *aflaj* (plural of *falaj*) requires much skill and money, and the state of them has therefore tended to be linked to the economic health of the community. During the prosperous Ya'arubi times (17th and 18th centuries) the *aflaj* were, not surprisingly, in excellent repair and many new ones were dug. One ingenious aspect of their construction was the way they crossed a wadi bed. They were dug down vertically on one bank to reach below the wadi floor, then continued horizontally until the wadi was crossed, then a vertical shaft was dug to a point fractionally lower than the upstream bank, thereby creating a siphon system.

The *falaj* tends to be the collective property of the village or group of landowners and a complex system evolves where each landowner pays for a certain number of minutes or hours of water a day, depending on his need (for both agriculture and domestic use), and the water is channelled to his land accordingly. An elected worthy known as the *arif* is appointed to monitor the fairness of this system, and he is also in charge of repairs, the cost of which is distributed according to the size of water share in the same way. In the recent past there were still *falaj* books with the title, sales and accounts of the *aflaj*, which would have been fascinating glimpses into the hierarchy of a rural community. In many village communities the *falaj* is still part of the essential way of life, and one of the standard exchanges for a visitor on arrival at a neighbouring village was 'And how are the *aflaj*?' 'Full, Inshallah.' It is estimated that 11,000 *aflaj* exist in Oman today, of which 4,000 are constantly flowing.

In geological terms it is also the gap between the limestone range of the Jebel Akhdar and the lower jagged volcanic hills that head off into the Sharqiya. If you are venturing out of Muscat for the first time, it is the colossal massif of the Jebel Akhdar on your right that will draw your eye. The extraordinary tilt of the layers of rock is mesmerising, even to the geological novice, with the occasional cleft snaking off into dark shadowy ravines. Its sharp lines and jagged layers make it immensely photogenic, especially in the early morning and late afternoon. Sometimes around midday the exceptional heat of the summer months can make it disappear from view altogether behind a haze, a most disconcerting experience when you know it is looming just there behind the shimmering blur.

SUMAIL سمائل Like many Omani towns, Sumail is divided into two parts, the lower (*sufelat*) and the upper (*aliyat*). Sumail Sufelat is Ghafiri and had the great fort (*husn*) where the *wali* lived until the 1960s and which also housed a Koran school, judge's office and prison. Sumail Aliyat was Hinawi and the two parts of the settlement had many fights against each other. There are around 115 forts or towers defending the area – such was its importance as a trade route – and the many small villages of Wadi Sumail, with their farms and gardens, are watered by nearly 200 *falaj* channels stretching over 16km. Some of the best dates come from Sumail.

The first Omani to embrace Islam also came from here and was responsible for building one of the first mosques – named the Mosque of Mazin – after meeting the Prophet Muhammad in Medina back in the 7th century.

Getting there If you follow the signs to Sumail from the Muscat–Nizwa road, you will **drive** through the new town and out beyond for a few kilometres where the old town is heralded by two watchtowers on a hill rising above the date gardens. Follow the tarmac road to the right and over a narrow wadi to reach the old souk on a bend in the road. Once the third-largest souk of the interior after Nizwa and Bahla, it is now all but deserted. The fort of Sumail lies further along this road, perched up on a rocky hill by the main road. Just beyond the fort is a traditional old mosque with a corner dome, crumbling, but still with a well-decorated *mihrab*.

Without your own transport you will have to get the **bus** from Muscat to drop you on the main road and walk the 2km into the town.

From mid-May the date harvest gets in full swing, and in northern Oman, Fanja souk is the centre of the date trade. Brought by the truckload from surrounding oases like Sumail, the dates are bought and sold in a traditional measure called 'manns', roughly 4kg. Between 3 and 3.5 tonnes of dates arrive every day at the souk, from where they are traded by professional date auctioneers, who take 10% commission. Prices start out high at about RO5–7 per kilo, then as the season progresses, they can drop to as low as 500bzs by peak harvest in mid-June. The yield of one tree is worth about RO20–30, making it a valuable commodity to its owner. The season ends in July and from Fanja they are traded to Dubai and further afield to other Gulf countries.

AL HOBE الحوب Still part of the Wadi Sumail fortifications but signposted separately, Al Hobe has a splendid ruined castle fort rising up on a hill above the date palms. There are five supplementary watchtowers on surrounding hills, and the castle fort itself still has a fine entrance door.

MUTTI مطي Some 8–10km before you reach Izki is the village of Mutti, built of typical jebel dry stone walls, an interesting contrast to the mud-brick villages of the wadis. From here up the twisted wadi that lies behind the village is one of the routes up the jebel, with well-cut stone steps (for other routes see box, page 195). The villagers here sheltered rebels in the Jebel War in the 1950s.

WADI HALFAYN AND THE PERSIAN STEPS About one hour's drive from Muscat (105km), you will reach this spectacular gorge. It makes a fine camping spot, as there are many large *sidr* trees for shade. A bumpy, rocky track leads for 2km to the mouth of the gorge where you can camp. A disused *falaj*, the Falaj Sahama, runs along the right-hand side of the wadi gorge. To reach it, you need your own transport. Take the turn-off to Al Afia some 30km beyond Sumail on the Nizwa road, then turn right on to the track 2.8km later, heading towards the nearby gorge. Park by the trees and continue on foot through the large boulders littering the wadi floor. One of them, on the left some 200m from the parking spot, has rock art etched into it.

The disused *falaj* on the right runs about 20ft (6m) above the wadi floor and the easiest option is to climb up to it and walk along it. Allow a full two hours for walking to the point where the *falaj* reaches the first of many deep pools. The scenery is attractive with palms and wild flowers.

Purple marks on the rocks show the trail on to the Persian Steps – 1,400 steps cut into the rock of the jebel to reach the high plateau at 6,000ft (see box, page 195). The base of the steps is marked by a box canyon with three tall waterfalls. Look for the purple marks to the right of the waterfall-stained cliff. The climb up the zigzagging steps takes a minimum of four hours and requires a moderate degree of fitness. Locals who live in the mountain villages can do it in under two hours in flip-flops, using the technique of gliding effortlessly in one flowing movement from rock to rock. This technique is especially noticeable in their descent, where they appear virtually to run down the mountain with none of the jarring movements so wearing on the knees. Allow a whole day for this trip from Muscat and see how far you get.

IZKI ازكى The Sumail Gap ends at the inland town of Izki, which lies along the course of the Wadi Halfayn, one of Oman's great wadis. The wadi is normally dry, but after heavy rain a raging torrent runs off into the desert and often blocks the main road on to Nizwa.

Izki – known as Jarnan in pre-Islamic times, and renamed Izki as a derivative of *zakah* (an Islamic alms tax) – is renowned for its tribal intrigues, as it is inhabited by both Hinawi (Yemeni from the south) and Ghafiri (Nizari from the Nejd in Saudi Arabia in the north). Intermarriage between the two was taboo until very recently, and their dialects retain separate characteristics.

Izki also has what is reputed to be Oman's oldest *falaj*, the Falaj Al Mulki, which originally, in its earliest Persian form, was known to have 370 separate channels. It is still well maintained and is a superb example of a stone-roofed tunnel, some 6ft (2m) high. Steps lead down to it where it flows about 1ft deep at 10ft below ground level.

From the main road only the modern town is apparent, but Izki does have a 150-year-old fort, now ruined, which overlooks the walled town and dominates the head of the Sumail Gap.

In the cliffs above the wadi floor is an inaccessible cave called the Jarnan Cave, where local folklore has it that Jarnan, an idol in the shape of a golden calf, was hidden after the new faith of Islam spread with its condemnation of idol worship.

At Izki the main Nizwa road bears right to follow the line of the Jebel Akhdar, while straight on there is a tarmac road to Sinaw, a market town on the edge of the Wahiba Sands (see page 230). It takes about 20 minutes by road from Izki to Nizwa.

BIRKAT AL MAWZ بركة المَوز

Roughly 70 minutes' drive from Muscat is Birkat al Mawz ('Pool of Bananas'). Like Tanuf, Birkat al Mawz was a town of the Beni Riyam whose sheikh, Suleyman bin Himyar, was the rebel leader in the Jebel War.

GETTING THERE Birkat al Mawz is signposted off the main Nizwa road and is reached via a right turn some 10km after Izki (coming from Muscat) or a left turn (coming from Nizwa). The first turning takes you past the date and banana plantations and skirts the old town, while the second turn-off has a brown signpost for Bait al Redidah, with Wadi Muaydin/Jebel Akhdar on the blue sign and which bypasses the town itself. The second turn-off bends steeply round and down. If you follow this road for three to four minutes you will see the fort on your right-hand side. By **bus** from Muscat or Nizwa you will have to ask to be dropped on the main road and walk the final part.

WHAT TO SEE
Bait al Redidah (⏰ *08.30–14.30 Sun–Thu, closed Fri & Sat; 500bzs*) The British RAF was invited by the sultan to destroy Suleyman's fine palace at Birkat al Mawz, which they did. It was restored and opened to the public in 1999 and today the serene two-storey fortified house (or castle) is known as Bait al Redidah. It guards the entrance to Wadi Muaydin, another key route up into the mountains and the point from where the military road up to the Saiq Plateau begins. Suleyman, whose base was at Tanuf, had a third private palace at Saiq, which has today completely disappeared, bombed by the RAF at the sultan's request, and then utterly demolished to serve as a lesson to the Jebel Akhdar villagers. A modern white fort was subsequently built with a detachment of the SAF (Sultan's Armed Forces) permanently garrisoned up on the Saiq Plateau ever since. Even today some people have observed a certain sullenness among the inhabitants of Saiq, who do not always welcome visitors in the normal Omani manner.

An impressive *falaj* – Falaj al Sharieh – built in the Ya'arubi era (1624–1741), in the same style as the original palace, runs out from behind Bait al Redidah, and an old mosque stands just before it, unusual in that it is built of stone and not clay.

WADI MUAYDIN   وادي مؤيدين

The road on to Wadi Muaydin (which leads up to Jebel Akhdar) runs straight ahead past Bait al Redidah, heading for the gorge beyond. About 3km past the fortified house the road splits and the right fork brings you, less than 1km later, to the military checkpoint with barrier, which is the start of the military route up to the Saiq Plateau. No permit is required but saloon cars are stopped here and not allowed to continue as there have been some unpleasant accidents with inexperienced drivers.

Taking the left fork before the military checkpoint will lead you into Wadi Muaydin, a favourite area for walking and camping. In dry weather you can drive a few kilometres into the gorge before stopping in shade and exploring further on foot. It is a demanding six-hour trek from here up to the plateau and Saiq. In wet weather you may have to stop earlier and wade through running streams. If so, keep a sharp lookout for any signs of rain higher up in the jebel, which can suddenly rush down the gorge from the higher peaks without it ever actually raining where you are.

SAIQ PLATEAU   نجد سيق

Before the construction of the military route, the ascent to the Saiq Plateau was a gruelling six-hour climb up a near-vertical path. A special kind of jebel donkey was used, tough and agile like a goat, as an unburdened, normal donkey would not cope with such an ascent, let alone when loaded. The plateau itself is at 6,000ft with temperatures to match. Even during the day you will need thick clothing here in the winter months.

Follow the military road 33km to reach Saiq. After this the ascent takes one hour of extremely steep hairpin bends, especially at the beginning, where a 4x4 with low ratio is necessary. An excellent feat of engineering, the road is well maintained and easily wide enough for two lorries to pass each other. Vehicles kick up huge quantities of dust. As you climb you often pass through wispy cloud for some way, before then rising above the clouds. Once higher the scenery and views are less dramatic and green than one might expect, certainly less dramatic than the road from Wadi Ghul up Jebel Shams on the far side of the jebel, described on page 212.

At 20km from the military checkpoint there is an unsignposted fork at which you turn left, and at 23km there is a signposted right fork to Menakhir (3.5km), at which you fork left. At 24km there is another signposted fork to Hayl Yemen (2km) where you stay on the main track. At 26km the Jebel Akhdar Hotel is signposted, and at 27km you suddenly arrive at a strip of tarmac that leads you on to the village of Saiq.

There is a seven-acre farm at Saiq, run by the Ministry of Agriculture and Fisheries, which is worth a visit for its diversity of fruit trees, including plums, peaches, pomegranates, apricots, olives, almonds, pears, apples and figs.

Just before the tarmac a rough track leads right for a further 10km past the stone-built village of Dar Hajimta. You then come to an area generally referred to as 'the meadows', a popular picnicking spot where the scenery, relatively barren up to now, becomes a little more varied with more trees, bushes and grasses growing. The area is announced by a green sign to the right addressed to 'Brother Visitor and Brother Citizens', exhorting people to look after the trees, animals and birds here. It is home to wild donkeys, lizards and birds, as well as a few ancient beehive cairn tombs found over in the far left corner of the meadow bowl.

JEBEL AKHDAR الجبل الاخضر

Jebel Akhdar, which translates as 'green mountain', refers to the mountain range whose highest peak is Jebel Shams (or 'mountain of the sun'), standing at 3,048m. The name Jebel Akhdar is misleading, as the greenery is confined to the terraces of a handful of villages on the Saiq Plateau, notably Shuraija, where grapes, peaches, pomegranates, apricots, figs, walnuts, almonds, lemons, apples, barley and desert roses grow, a large proportion of which are sold in the Nizwa souks.

Everything else is bare rock, predominantly grey with little or no vegetation. One convincing explanation of the name Akhdar is that it does not mean 'green' but 'living', in the sense that it is living limestone rock, not dead volcanic rock as is found in the foothills round Nizwa and in the Sumail Gap.

Jebel Akhdar is the home of the Arabian tahr, a unique species of wild goat. It is with the preservation of this animal in mind that the sultan has designated part of the jebel a national park.

The jebel is home to around 58 separate villages and communities, and about 300 wadis. Water from the natural springs flows through *aflaj* (ancient manmade channels) directing the water to these communities, which also receive regular deliveries of drinking water provided free by the government. The jebel has a hospital, some schools, a post office, and interconnecting roads are being slowly developed linking the larger villages.

The unique climate of the jebel allows for a diverse range of vegetation that cannot grow anywhere else in the region. Fruit trees and shrubs are a major part of the heritage of the jebel and all parts of the plants are utilised for culinary, perfumery, medicinal and beauty purposes. Pomegranate and walnut are the two most lucrative commodities here and Saiq, Bani Habib and Al Menakhar are the three main villages involved in growing them. Other Mediterranean fruit trees are being introduced to the region, the climate being ideal; pears are relatively new here. Honeybee breeding is also carried out in the jebel's plateaux.

The government is focusing on Jebel Akhdar as a major tourist destination and is slowly developing the area to accommodate visitors. A 36km road linking Birkat al

PATHS TO THE JEBEL AKHDAR

The main footpaths up the jebel are via Wadi Muaydin starting in Birkat al Mawz (see pages 193–4); via Wadi Ghul up Jebel Shams (see page 212); the track from Mutti near Izki (see page 192); from Wadi Halfayn up to Munaikhir (see page 192); and a couple of tracks from the Rustaq side, the most used of which starts from Al Awabi. Most of these ascents have stone steps cut into the rock, thought to have been the work of the Persians when they conquered the jebel in the 10th century. The amount of labour involved in such a task is so mind-boggling that one cannot help but wonder whether the summits were green and fertile at that time, to warrant the expenditure of so much effort, or whether slave labour was enlisted.

JEBEL AKHDAR & ENVIRONS

see page 146

NOTE
For key to accommodation and eating and drinking, see opposite

Bidbid, Muscat

Sumail
Al Hobe
Sumail Fort
Bawri
Sayja
Wadi Qari
Al Afia (Wadi Halfayn & the Persian Steps)
Sayma
Al Hilayw
33
15
Adam, Natih
Al Ghubrah
Al Khadra
Al Mahalif
Al Magkhir
Mutti
Zukayt
Izki
Al Ghubrah
Al Maghkir
2
Al Ayn
Wadi Al Muaydin
Birkat Al Mawz
Manah Fort
Manah
Az Zammah
Al Mahsanah
Ad Dar
Ar Ruus
8
Safa As Sabra
Saiq Plateau
Saiq
Bait al Redidah
Wadi Muaydin
7
Salalah
Awabi Fort
Sital
Al Hijayr
Al Hijar
Al Jebel Akhdar
Bani Habib
Wadi Al Abyad
Nizwa
Fara
Awabi
At Tikah
Aqbat Al Biyut
Al Far
Tanuf
Taymsa
Al Mudaybi
Rustaq, As Suwayq, Snake Gorge, Bilad Sayt
Al Hiwayjur
Fasah
Umq
Maqammak
Bilad Sayt
Al Alamayn
1
Mistah Al Abriyyin
Mibat
Al Hota cave, Sharfat al Alamayn
Oman Oil
Bahla Fort
Bahla
Jabrin
21
Salalah
Al Uqur
Damm
Barut
Al Libanah
Al Ayn
Amla
Sint
Al Ayshi
Jebel Al Khwr
Amla, Barut
Ibri
21
3
Jabrin Castle
Jebel Shams
Wadi Nakhr Gorge, The Grand Canyon, Falcon View
Jebel Shams ▲3075m
Madruj
Al Hijar
Wijman
4
5
Dar As Sawdab
Army base
Al Hajir
Ghul
Wadi Ghul
Shell
9
6
Al Hamra
Al Khitaym
Hirmt

N
Brad t

0   10km
0   10 miles

196

ABANDONED VILLAGES

As traditional communities in the interior of Oman change their lifestyles, become increasingly urbanised and move to new housing, they are leaving their ancestral homes and allowing them to fall into disuse. Some are remote mountain settlements like Bani Habib on the Saiq Plateau, others are more readily accessible like the old merchant quarters of Al Minzfah and Al Kanaatir in old Ibra (see page 228). So far the Omani government has struggled with how to handle these abandoned villages, lacking a unified policy across the various ministries involved. Sometimes, when there have been ill-thought-through attempts to develop villages as tourist destinations, such as Misfah Al Abriyeen (see page 210), the local people have resisted what they saw as an 'invasion' by curious western tourists. Respectful behaviour and proper dress is essential when visiting such conservative areas, so as not to cause offence. Often the new government-supplied housing is close to the old settlement, but residents remain deeply traditional, and retain a strong attachment to their old homes.

It is incumbent on the Omani government to address the issue of how to save these villages which form an important part of Omani heritage and culture. Local communities need to be involved in decision making so that they do not feel excluded. That way it should be possible for the villages to be restored and developed sensitively in a way that brings benefits and much-needed employment opportunities to young local Omanis, while at the same time introducing foreign visitors to this little-known aspect of Omani culture.

Mawz to the Saiq Plateau will be a fundamental aspect of this phased development and there is already more accommodation up there to encourage longer stays (see below).

From the tarmac onwards to Saiq there are various government buildings including an agricultural development centre and a host of construction sites.

JEBEL AKHDAR & ENVIRONS
For listings, see pages 198, 208, 210, 211, 214, 216

🛏 Where to stay
1 Al-Hoota Resthouse
2 Alila Jabal Akhdar
3 Jibreen
4 Jebel Shams Resort
5 Jebel Shams Travelling & Camping Centre
6 Misfah Old House
7 Noor Majan Camp
8 Sahab
9 The View

✖ Where to eat and drink
Al-Hoota Resthouse (see 1)
Alila Jabal Akhdar (see 2)
Jibreen (see 3)
Jebel Shams Resort (see 4)
Noor Majan Camp (see 7)
Sahab (see 8)
The View (see 9)

In order to see any sign of terraced agriculture, take the turn-off to Shuraija. The grapes grown here were said to have been imported by the Persians (along with many of the other exotic fruits) and were used to make wine. Suleyman's (see page 199) cellars in his Saiq palace were reputed to contain casks of wine rather than rifles and ammunition.

The village of **Al Aqr** is known for its roses, flowering mainly in April. The desert rose is unique to Jebel Akhdar. Traditionally, Omani rose water was made here from the petals picked in April before dawn and distilled in traditional mud ovens by boiling for three to four hours. It was then used not only as a perfume but also in cooking desserts and in making flavoured coffee. Today, there is a demand for the product and perfumers can be seen at work here in the new factory. Beyond the modern development you pass the firing range with its red flags and military training centre. As the road drops down into a dip beyond this on the way to Bani Habib, the village at the far edge of the plateau, you will see on the right the smashed remains of a British Venom aircraft shot down by the rebels in the Jebel War. Beside it is the grave of the pilot marked by a white marble headstone with a white cross.

You can now drive on to **Bani Habib** on the edge of the plateau and leave the car in order to walk a little and see the old village clinging to the cliff edge, its houses in terraced rows. Being such a popular spot from which to enjoy spectacular views, a sitting park has been developed, providing benches, shaded areas and even toilets. The village has now been largely deserted in favour of the new town on the top because of the lack of vehicular access. Its parlous state is a great shame, because some of the dilapidated mud houses contain colourful wall painting which is almost unique in traditional domestic architecture in Oman. So far government departments have been unable to agree on how to progress saving villages like these, let alone how to then present them as tourist attractions, where they would make a welcome addition to Oman's many forts. May they resolve their differences before there is nothing left to save, as each year the winter rains are taking their toll.

On the drive back from Bani Habib about halfway to Saiq, look out for three walled-up cave entrances in a wadi cliff side facing you, where the road does a deep bend and dips into a wadi. You can park on the road opposite the caves and scramble down into the wadi gully and up the other side to the caves, used by Suleyman (see page 199) as his final hideout. The narrow entrance requires a small adult to get down on all fours with a torch, but once inside, it opens out to be quite spacious. You can even stand up, though no light from outside can penetrate. Spending even one minute in this cave is enough to help you vividly imagine what it would have been like for Suleyman, waiting for weeks at a time while the furore of the pursuit outside died down.

The Bani Riyam, with Suleyman as their sheikh, were the leading Ghafiri tribe whose territory extended along the base of the mountains and right up into the summit area as well. The jebel itself had only once before been conquered by outside forces (in AD972), so Suleyman must have considered himself pretty safe up at Saiq in the third of his palaces. When the British SAS finally made an assault up the mountain in 1959, Suleyman was therefore not prepared for it. Although he had his caves to hide in, the SAS effectively put an end to the Jebel War, and Suleyman was exiled to Dammam, Saudi Arabia, to one of the flattest and dullest landscapes in Arabia. For location of listings see map, page 196.

⌂ WHERE TO STAY

⌂ **Alila Jabal Akhdar** (86 rooms) www.
alilahotels.com. Scheduled to open in 2014,
this Asia-based group has created a luxury
designer hideaway on the edge of a cliff, boasting
spectacular views. It has a restaurant, spa &
kidney-shaped pool with sun-bathing terrace,
& the whole complex is built to blend in with the
surroundings. **$$$$**

⌂ **Sahab Hotel** (27 rooms, from studios to
family suites) ✆ +968 25 429288; e sahab@

sahab-hotel.com; www.sahab-hotel.com. A superb
boutique hotel, located at over 2,000m on the Saiq
Plateau, beautifully designed to integrate with the
natural surroundings but with modern luxuries.
Features an infinity swimming pool, garden with
native plants, satellite TV, free Wi-Fi, minibar & AC.
The restaurant serves international & local dishes,
& there is indoor or outdoor dining with a snack-
bar overlooking the pool. The cafe serving light
meals & sandwiches displays 270-year old marine

fossils along one wall, which were found during construction. Organised options for the active include trekking, farming, goat-herding, caving & donkey rides. **$$$**

NIZWA نزوى

Nizwa is about 1¾ hours' drive from Muscat (174km). As the key settlement of the interior, Nizwa was a verdant oasis city, famous for its large, busy souk. It was the capital of Oman in the 6th and 7th centuries. When the traveller Ibn Battuta visited in the early 1300s he described it as a city at the foot of the mountains surrounded by gardens and rivers with beautiful bazaars. He observed the men's habit of bringing their own food to dine together in the mosque courtyard and said of them: 'They are a bold and brave race and the tribes are perpetually at war with each other.' Even when it was not the capital itself, Nizwa was always a centre to be captured by anyone seeking to have power in Oman.

Nizwa represents an important crossroads at the base of the western Hajars linking Buraimi, Muscat and Dhofar, and was once a centre of education and art. The Falaj Daris is the largest single *falaj* in the country. Forty different varieties of date palm grow in Nizwa; Khalas and Khunaizi are considered the top-quality and most valuable varieties.

For an exploration of the region, Nizwa is the recommended base, offering some good hotels. Any of the old villages and places of interest listed under *What to see*

JEBEL WAR – THE IMAMATE REVOLUTION

By the 1950s there was much disaffection in the country about the fact that the sultan, Said bin Taimur, who had ruled since 1932, sat mainly in Salalah and refused to delegate any decision-making, preferring instead to guard all affairs of state jealously to himself.

This led to a state of sterility which the rebel leaders – Ghalib, who had been elected imam in 1954, Taalib his brother and two tribal leaders, Suleyman bin Himyar and Salih bin Issa – aimed to overthrow. At this time too the Wahhabi Saudis, who had seized Buraimi in 1952, were at the height of their attempts to spread Wahhabism through Oman, and they lent their support to the rebels, who were able to capture Ibri and other towns north of Nizwa. To repel them, Qaboos's father, Sultan Said bin Taimur, made his only trip from Salalah with a collection of cars and trucks to Nizwa, Buraimi and Sohar, before returning to Muscat. The rebels dispersed and the country was briefly unified. This was the first and last trip he ever made to the interior of Oman.

Within a few years things had drifted back to where they started, with the rebel leaders active again, and the sultan called on the British to come and use their armed forces to crush the rebels, which they duly did. The British, however, did not wish this to become a precedent, at a time when the United Nations was vociferous on the subject of intervention, as it was only shortly after the Suez fiasco. In 1958, British Foreign Office Minister Julian Amery was sent out to negotiate an agreement as to the future security of Oman, which resulted in Britain paying £250,000 a year to the sultan, and the setting up of the SAF (Sultan's Armed Forces) and the SOAF (Sultan of Oman's Air Force) with Britain providing seconded officers to run them. The RAF was to continue to be allowed to use airbases at Salalah and Masirah.

NOTE
For key to accommodation
and eating and drinking,
see below

Bahla, Al Hamra,
Jabrin, Ibri

0 ———————— 5km
0 ———————— 3 miles

Al Khanjar
roundabout

Hashar
roundabout

Firq
roundabout

Central Nizwa

Pizza
Hut

Muscat,
Golden Tulip
Nizwa Hotel
(approx 12km)

(SKETCH MAP)

APPROACH TO NIZWA

Manah, Adam, Salalah ↓

APPROACH TO NIZWA

For listings, see pages 201, 203

Where to stay
1 Al Diyar
2 Falaj Daris
3 Majan Guest House
4 Tanuf Residency

Off map
   Golden Tulip Nizwa

Where to eat and drink
   Al Fanar Falaj (see 2)
5 Arab World
   Bahjat Al Sham (see 1)
6 Spice Village
   Tanuf Residency (see 4)

Off map
   Birkat al Mawz
      (see Golden Tulip Nizwa)
   Pool Café
      (see Golden Tulip Nizwa)

on page 203 are easily reached from here. You will need a stay of two nights or so to fit it all in, but it will certainly provide you with a different feel of the country from that which you will have experienced in Muscat. However short your visit is to the country, I would highly recommend a trip to Nizwa and its close surrounds in order to gain a fuller and more rounded impression of Oman.

GETTING THERE

By bus The Oman National Transport Company buses that link all the main cities and towns of Oman start from the Ruwi bus station and run to Nizwa twice daily at 08.00 and 14.30, and from Nizwa (souk) back to to Muscat (Ruwi) at 08.40 and 17.50. Check the online timetable on their website (*www.ontcoman.com*) for up-to-date timings as these can change. The trip by bus from Muscat to Nizwa takes two hours 20 minutes and costs around RO3. You can catch a bus from Nizwa to Salalah (10 hours, RO8) from the final roundabout where the Salalah highway forks south, 5km east of the *khanjar* roundabout.

Once at Nizwa local microbuses or shared taxis link the smaller towns, with the usual fare being around RO1–2. From the town centre the microbus fare to hotels such as the Falaj Daris and the Tanuf Residency is 100bzs. The bus stop and taxi stand are both in the middle of the wadi in front of the fort/souk area, 800m beyond (southwest of) the *khanjar* roundabout. See map on page 202.

By car Taxis from Bahla (see page 214) to Nizwa cost RO2.5. If you're driving, Nizwa is clearly signposted from Muscat Airport roundabout. This is well known as the Muscat–Nizwa highway. If you are intending to stay at the Golden Tulip Hotel in Nizwa, remember to keep a close eye out some 20km before Nizwa proper (as this hotel is closer to Birkat al Mawz than Nizwa). You will need to take a right-hand turn after emerging from the mountains (see below for further details). Built in 1996, it is the most luxurious base for exploration in the region.

At about 3km before Nizwa Old Town itself is the Falaj Daris Hotel, which sits on the left (see below). Passing the Falaj Daris Hotel, you now approach the heart of Nizwa itself, recognisable by the vast round tower of the fort beside the bright cobalt-blue dome of the Sultan Qaboos Mosque. Before you reach it, there is a wide wadi bed, usually flowing either weakly or impassable after heavy rains, as Nizwa is at the confluence of two wadis – Wadi Abyadh and Wadi Kalbouh – one of the reasons for its location. Using this water, it has an extensive network of *falaj* channels irrigating its date gardens which extend for some 8km behind the town.

It is probably best to leave your car in the extensive parking areas in front of the modern sand-coloured souk façade that faces the wadi bed. For location of listings see maps, pages 200 and 202.

WHERE TO STAY

Al Diyar Hotel (60 rooms) PO Box 1166, PC 611; 25 412402; e al_diyarhotel@hotmail. com; www.aldiyarhotel.com. Located 4km from the town centre, the spotless rooms are a little cheaper than the Falaj Daris, but it is unlicensed & so has no minibar in your room (although it does have a fridge). There is an unlicensed restaurant attached to it, called Bahjat Al Sham, offering a good cheap menu. It has a small swimming pool. Hire cars can be arranged from here (10 days' advance notice), for RO50/80 saloon/4x4 (inc driver/guide). B/fast included. **$$$**

Golden Tulip Nizwa Hotel (120 rooms) PO Box 1000, PC 611; 25 431616; e info@ goldentulipnizwa.com; www.goldentulipnizwa. com. This hotel is the plushest base for exploring the interior. It is about 1hr's drive from Muscat International Airport, in its own grounds about 20km before Nizwa town proper, which is about another 30mins' drive further on. The rooms are in a low-rise modern complex set round a large pool, business centre & 3 bars with live entertainment. There is a licensed, elegant restaurant, a poolside café, a lobby café, a large bar (Al Wasit) with a live band & a nightclub (Tanuf). **$$$**

Falaj Daris Hotel (55 rooms, 2 suites) PO Box 312, PC 611; 25 410500; e fdhnizwa@ omantel.net.om; www.falajdarishotel.com. Just the sort of mid-range small hotel Oman needs more of, this single-storey unpretentious place is situated after the Golden Tulip Hotel as you approach from Muscat & is closer to the centre of the town, about 4km before the fort. Irrespective of the end from which you approach the hotel, the signpost comes up on you at the turn into the entrance; there is no earlier indication. So don't worry if you miss the turning, as you can simply go to the next roundabout & come back. Try to get on to the slip road at the Shell garage (on the left past the Falaj Daris going towards Nizwa town centre) as the road is less hectic & you can drive more slowly. The hotel is set round 2 attractive courtyards with pleasant tropical trees & plants, & a small swimming pool in each. It has a licensed restaurant, a bar (Castle Bar) & a health club. In addition there is an Arabic bar (Sahara Lounge), the entrances for which are outside & to the left as you exit the front doors of the hotel. This has local entertainment with belly dancing from 21.00. Many Europeans stay at the Falaj Daris, which has an almost colonial feel about it. There is something special about its courtyard setting with its mountain backdrop. The rooms have showers only & no bath, but its proximity to the old town is a major plus point. **$$**

Majan Guest House (21 rooms) PO Box 1262, PC 611; 25 431910, 431912–3, 99 453884; www. majangh.com. Roughly 8km before the Falaj Daris Hotel, & just after the Firq (or Faraq) roundabout on the right-hand side coming from Muscat. Considering this is near to & pretty much half the price of Falaj Daris & has good, clean rooms & friendly staff & management, it is certainly an alternative option if you simply want to get your head down after your tours. There is no restaurant as yet. **$$**

Tanuf Residency (45 rooms) 25 411601. Right on the main Muscat–Nizwa highway, 4.5km before the *khanjar* roundabout, Nizwa's main roundabout just 800m before the fort & mosque. The rooms & beds are big with good views to the back over the mountains. A good-value place with its own adequate restaurant, though you can also try out the Arab World Restaurant next door. **$$**

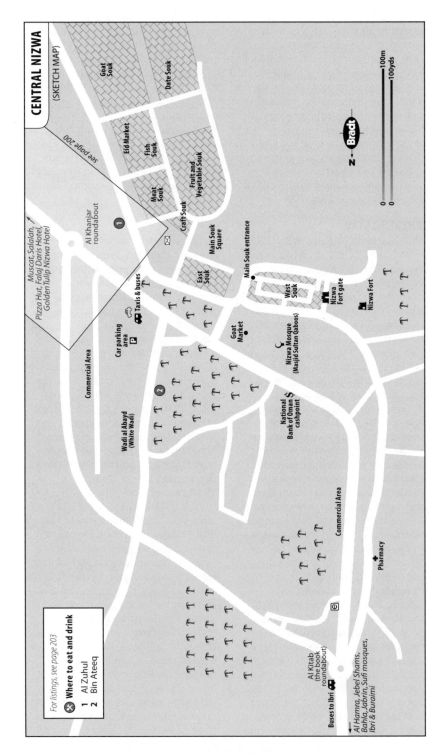

CENTRAL NIZWA
(SKETCH MAP)

For listings, see page 203

✗ Where to eat and drink
1 Al Zuhul
2 Bin Ateeq

Goat Souk

Date Souk

Eid Market

Fish Souk

Meat Souk

Fruit and Vegetable Souk

Craft Souk

Muscat, Salalah,
Pizza Hut, Falaj Daris Hotel,
Golden Tulip Nizwa Hotel

Al Khanjar roundabout ①

see page 200

Taxis & buses

Commercial Area

Car parking area

East Souk

Main Souk Square

Main Souk entrance

West Souk

Nizwa Fort gate

Nizwa Fort

Goat Market

Nizwa Mosque
(Masjid Sultan Qaboos)

② Wadi al Abayd (White Wadi)

National Bank of Oman cashpoint

Commercial Area

Pharmacy

Al Kitab (the book roundabout)

Buses to Ibri

Al Hamra, Jebel Shams,
Bahla, Jabrin, Sufi mosques,
Ibri & Buraimi

Bradt

0 ──── 100m
0 ──── 100yds

✗ WHERE TO EAT The plushest restaurants of the interior are in the Golden Tulip and the Falaj Daris hotels, both of which are fully licensed.

✗ Birkat al Mawz Golden Tulip Hotel; ☎25 431616. With an international menu. $$$

✗ Al Fanar Falaj Falaj Daris Hotel; ☎25 410500. Serves continental, Chinese & Indian dishes. $$

✗ Arab World Restaurant A good Lebanese restaurant beside the Tanuf Residency on the Muscat–Nizwa highway. It has the standard *mezze* & kebabs & is not licensed but the indoor AC eating area is a welcome retreat from the heat. $$

✗ Pool Café Golden Tulip Hotel; ☎25 431616. Serves poolside snacks & can be used by non-guests. $$

✗ Spice Village ☎25 431694. This is located a little before Nizwa. Take the road left at the Firq roundabout (if you are coming from Muscat), in the direction of Salalah. It is just a little way down on the right side, close to the Oman International Bank. Serves Thai, tandoori, Chinese, Arabic, south Indian, north Indian & Punjabi meals. $$

✗ Al Zuhul Restaurant Very simple place serving kebabs & *shawarma* where you can sit with local people on the pavement tables & chairs overlooking the fort & mosque. At night when both are illuminated it makes for a very atmospheric scene. $

✗ Bahjat Al Sham ☎25 412409. This is an unlicensed restaurant with a good cheap international menu & is located immediately next to Al Diyar Hotel (& part of it) at the first roundabout after the Falaj Daris Hotel, going towards the town centre. $

✗ Bin Ateeq ☎25 410466. A little way up the road on the right just after the vast car-parking area & clearly signposted. It is the only traditional Omani restaurant in the area, & offers a fun eating experience at floor level in the local style. It is cheap & serves good food. You are taken to your own private room behind a sliding door, where you leave your shoes. You are served dates & coffee as a matter of course & they round off the meal perfectly as dessert. A meal for one consisting of salad, fried king fish with white rice & then coffee & dates comes to a little under RO4. There have been some comments that hygiene is not that great & that the seating is uncomfortable, but it's worth a try, just to see for yourself. There are many more in the chain, in both Salalah & Muscat. $

✗ Pizza Hut ☎25 412096. If you are suffering from homesickness, this could be the place for you, situated about 200m beyond the Falaj Daris Hotel (going towards Nizwa Old Town centre). It is almost always empty & is open all day, offering a salad bar & the usual range of thin & deep-pan pizzas. It is unlicensed but has clean toilets. $

WHAT TO SEE

Nizwa Fort [map page 202] (⏱ *09.00–16.00 Sat–Thu, 08.00–11.00 Fri; 500bzs*) As the chief town of the interior and Oman's capital for many centuries, Nizwa is dominated by its vast circular tower. This colossal structure took around 12 years to build under the imam Sultan bin Saif bin Malik al Ya'arubi, who repulsed the Portuguese (who were never to return) from Muscat. He is said to have financed the construction from the spoils of sacking the emirate of Ras al Khaimah.

One of the oldest and largest forts in Oman, it was completed in 1668, to protect its strategic position at the crossroads of the caravan routes. Before the massive restoration project (completed in 1990), the *wali* (district governor) lived in the tower and had to move out whenever parts of the roof collapsed following heavy rainstorms. On the roof of the tower itself the army guards lived among scattered iron bedsteads, draped with clothes.

The massive round tower is filled in with earth and stones for half of its 30m height and 36m diameter. This solid in-fill created a strong platform for cannon to fire over the tops of the palm trees and made it impossible for rival cannon fire to breach the walls. An additional protective wall with three sets of steps to the top encircles the cannon platform, with excellent vantage points over the town. The round tower is entered via a narrow zigzag flight of steps with three sets of doors to block off the enemy at each turn.

Entering through the main gateway to the left of the round tower, you come to the courtyard in which one of the outbuildings has an interesting display of figures showing the restoration process in action, with explanations of the techniques used. It helps to see these before your tour, so that you fully appreciate the labour involved.

Once inside, the sheer extent of the main fort comes as a surprise. From the outside, the round tower appears to be the entire structure, but the other areas are extensive, with prisons, storerooms, kitchens, washing areas, sleeping quarters, a mosque, a Koranic school, *majlis* rooms, a judge's room and living quarters for the *wali*. These rooms are spread at various levels, a veritable maze in which it is easy to lose all sense of direction. Back down on the ground floor within the fort itself is a small **Omani Heritage Gallery** (e *ohgmq@omantel.net.om; www.omaniheritage. com*), which is a shop selling handicrafts. The prices are a little inflated compared with those of the souk, but you may prefer to simply pay the tag price and be gone, rather than haggle. Furthermore, it is a not-for-profit organisation which aims to

DATES OF NIZWA

Approximately 40 types of date grow in Nizwa, and entire farms now exclusively cultivate the two prized varieties of *khalas* and *khunaizi*. Below is a brief summary of the popular varieties.

HILALI OMAN Grown in various regions of Oman. It is a late-season crop, light yellow in colour, with a 60% sugar content.

KHALAS The most valuable date crop. They thrive in this region, as well as in the Sharqiya and Dhahirah regions, and Rustaq. It is 65% sugar and, arguably, the most tasty. It is bright yellow in colour and oval-shaped. It can be eaten either fresh or half-dry.

KHASAB A late-season crop, which can be dark red or yellowish in colour. Although it grows in all of the date-farming regions of Oman, quality crops stem from Rustaq, Ibri and the Sharqiya regions.

KHUNAIZI Cultivated in most areas of the sultanate. They are dark red and can cope with high humidity. They are eaten fresh in season or dry outside of season.

MEBSELLI A mid-season crop. This date is cooked, dried, then exported to markets in the Indian subcontinent (in the traditional fashion). It is also eaten fresh or naturally dried. It grows extensively here in the interior, as well as in the Sharqiya, Dhahirah and Batinah regions.

NAGHAL An early-season crop. It is sensitive to humidity and so thrives best here, in Oman's hot and dry interior. A large percentage of the *naghal* harvest goes to Oman's date-processing factories.

QASHTABAQ This date is reddish-yellow in colour and is oblong in shape. It grows in the interior, Dhahirah and the Batinah regions of the country. Sugar content is pegged at a significant 68%.

A whole range of simple traditional items are for sale as souvenirs for visitors, items which used to be part of every local household's possessions. In the renovated souk at Nizwa all sorts of souvenirs can be bought, including old silver *khanjars*, silver jewellery, antiques, pottery, metalwork, woodwork, weaving, walking sticks and fans. The flag-shaped fans were used before the days of air conditioning, and each guest was always provided with one. Various baskets and containers were braided from palm fronds, soaked in water for pliability, then dyed and graded in patterns. The basket used for storage is known as a *jrab*, while the basket for the collection of dates is known as a *qufer*. The strange latticework pyramids on sticks are clothes fumigators called *mibkhara*. Clothes were draped over them, and placed over incense burners to saturate the clothes with the fragrance. Pottery coffee pots decorated with red geometric patterns have now been replaced by Thermos flasks, and old cooking pots by aluminium from India. Pottery incense burners are the main souvenirs now, the size compatible with suitcases, their decoration appealing and their purpose exotic. The old souk at Bahla sells silver, spices and herbs. There are two pottery factories if you follow the road around the back of the town. In Jebel Shams there are rugs for sale at the roadside, which have been woven in the mountain villages by men.

support Omani artisans with a view to preserving their traditional crafts. (There is also another Omani Heritage Gallery outlet next to the InterContinental Hotel in Muscat at the Jawaharat al Shatti Complex.)

Nizwa Mosque (Masjid Sultan Qaboos) [map page 202] The mosque, with its distinctive blue and gold dome, was built by Abdulla bin Mohammed al Ibadi and lies next to the Nizwa Fort. It was modernised and developed in the 1970s. Non-Muslims are not permitted to enter, but views of the mosque and the surrounds generally are superb from Nizwa Fort.

Nizwa souk [map page 202] The renovation programme of the 1990s extended beyond the fort itself into the whole surrounding area and the modern souk façade conceals renovated areas of pristine cleanliness, sanitised for tourists. If you want to see the old Nizwa however, this façade is just that, and a few more steps will take you beyond to the medieval mud streets ripe with the usual medieval smells. Spices, seeds, berries, herbs and all sorts of intriguing produce used in traditional medicinal remedies can be bought here.

Vehicles can drive in through the main gateway in the souk façade and there is some parking within. The central area has been imaginatively recreated, with Omani craft shops selling antiques, silver jewellery, *khanjars*, swords, leather goods, copper, pottery, weaving and wooden artefacts. Artisans go about their craft in the small workshops. Prices in the souk are already low, so bargaining scope is limited.

In the area to the left, away from the round fort tower, are the refurbished fruit and vegetable souks, the fish souk and animal souk (where goat and cattle auctions take place on Thursday and Friday mornings at around 07.00–09.00 and the eve of Eid in readiness for the feasting that follows).

The Sufi mosques [off map 202] Spare an extra half-hour if you can to make this interesting short diversion to a walled graveyard on the outskirts of Nizwa, where the Sufi mystics built a series of little mosques on low hills as places where they could worship in seclusion away from the town.

Go out of Nizwa on the Bahla road and turn left by a high watchtower shortly after 'the book' roundabout. The graveyard is to both sides of the road and has some important tombs of imams and scholars. Some of the tombs have engraved stones with names and dates going back to the 7th century AD, the first century of Islam.

The road leads on through old Nizwa and its date gardens, giving an unusual contrast to the modern and renovated centre of town, until it leads back to the fort.

Falaj Daris, Mosque of the Rock and Al Shawadhna Mosque detour

Approximately 10km after Nizwa on the Nizwa–Bahla road near Marfa, look out for the small green sign indicating Falaj Daris to the right, where you can make a detour of half an hour or so. There is now a park and picnic spot here and you can climb down inside this, one of Oman's largest *aflaj*. Beside the *falaj*, there are two unusual ruined mosques tucked under the lee of the mountains. Once you have turned right off the main road from Falaj Daris keep to the left, passing the high school building, and follow the route for 2km after the tarmac runs out. To the left of the road you will see the small square **Az al Qadim** Sufi mosque (Mosque of the Rock) on the edge of a hill with a large rock beside it. There is a legend associated with the rock and the mystic who used to pray here alone away from the town, whereby the 100kg rock disappeared and reappeared inside the mosque overnight.

A further 1km along the graded road to the left are three more abandoned mosques including **Al Shawadhna**, which has a beautifully carved *mihrab* and the unusual feature of two *qiblas* (a niche marking the direction of prayer), one facing Mecca, the other facing Jerusalem. It must therefore date back to the 1st Islamic century (7th century AD) when prayer in the early mosques faced Jerusalem, before the direction of prayer was changed to face Mecca some ten years later, still during the Prophet Muhammad's lifetime.

You can stay on this track, forking right to rejoin the main road.

SEIH AL BARAKAT   سيح البركات

Before reaching Manah, some 7km from the Salalah turn-off, you will notice a high picnic spot on a hillock to your left. This is Seih al Barakat, where the sultan meets local people on his annual tour. There are a few little towers, an incense burner and some palm sunshades. The sunset views from here are very evocative. From this point also you will notice a tall sand-coloured structure standing proud of the date plantations – this is Fiqain Fort.

Without your own transport the only way to reach the following places is by hiring a taxi or hitchhiking. There is no public transport.

FIQAIN   فقين

Take the turn-off marked Fiqain and follow the tarmac as it winds round behind the tall tower. Park here where the road narrows, under a tree, and walk back the short distance through the old town gate towards this amazing building. It is a remarkable fortified **tower house** (⏱ *08.30–14.30 or whenever the guardian is* *present*), almost Scottish baronial in its narrow proportions and restored in 1988. The guardian sits below and lets you take yourself on a tour, hardly surprising given the number of stairs involved, and may offer you coffee afterwards for your exertions. The ruined town of Fiqain lies crumbling to the right of the fort, now ringed by modern houses.

The design of Fiqain Fort is quite unique, with massive stone-built walls faced with *sarouj* plaster. The tall side tower to the left as you approach is a wind tower, designed to catch the breeze and funnel it down into the top two floors of living space. This section is approached by the stairs to the left side of the entrance door, leading up to the rooftop. Each floor has a perfectly aligned circular hole for the family to shout instructions down to the servants or for raising water or food up on a tray.

It is totally separate from the second slightly larger section which is approached from the stairs at the back of the entrance hall. The rooms off the hall were for weaponry as well as cooking and storage, and the upper levels were used for the guards and soldiers defending the sheikh's family. The door through which you now enter was a secret entrance, not discovered until 1991 after an old man in the village told the authorities about it. Before that, entry was only by rope and pulley, still in place in the guard section, into the two high windows. All the restoration work was carried out through these high windows. Note also the two overhanging latrines on the top floor of the guard section.

MANAH منح

Probably Oman's most impressive ruined town, Manah is well worth the short drive (11km) south from Nizwa. Restoration work started in 2008 and although work is now largely completed, the site remains closed to visitors at the time of writing, while the government makes decisions about the future use to which it will be put. To reach the site, take the major fork south to Salalah on the eastern outskirts of Nizwa, and after 1km take the signposted turn left to Manah. The modern town of Manah has tarmac running to it, and the old town lies just behind it and can easily be approached on dirt tracks, which are fine for saloon cars. Follow the tarmac to the end of town, passing an Oman Oil petrol station on your right, until you reach a small roundabout with a restored mosque to the left, raised on a terrace. This mosque dates back to 1534 and was renovated in 1991. It cannot be visited by non-Muslims. Turn right at the roundabout on to a gravel track past a large ruined building and drive skirting the edge of the walled town until you come to the tall square tower built into the stone walls. Normally, you can park here and walk in through the gateway to see the remarkable covered street to your right. If you do gain access, go straight along the main street and then into the first building on your left, up some steps to a terrace with a well still in use. This is the forecourt of a disused mosque, inside which you can still see a very elaborately detailed green-painted *mihrab*, with a valuable blue-and-white Chinese plate as its centrepiece stuck on to the plasterwork. Wall niches still hold loose pages of the Koran.

Further down this main street are two more mosques, also with elaborately decorated *mihrabs,* one with all its Chinese plates painted over in green. The *mihrab* inscriptions show that they date to the early 16th century, and all three *mihrabs* were built by Oman's most famous mosque architect, Abdullah Al Hamaimy. The town is mainly built of mud brick and, though the houses still have many carved doors left, the walls are badly crumbled.

The overgrown *falaj* system at Manah is claimed by local folklore to have been dug by Malik bin Fahm, leader of the Yemeni Azdite tribe who settled in

Oman after the bursting of the famous Marib Dam in Yemen in the 2nd century AD. Yemeni civilisation was thereby terminated and Malik's tribe migrated east to Oman, driving out the Persians who were at that time dominant in Nizwa. Coming upon it in the late 19th century, one English traveller wrote: 'Is this Arabia ... is this the country we have looked on heretofore as a desert?' Today these words are unfitting, as the *falaj*, broken and dusty, lies off in a field smothered with dead grass. For location of listings see map, page 196.

🏠 WHERE TO STAY

🏠 **Noor Majan Camp** (13 rooms) 2km from Nizwa bypass, 5km from Manah National Park.

Wooden cabins with AC & private bathrooms, free Wi-Fi. Buffet restaurant. Surrounded by trees. **$$$**

IZZ AND ADAM عز و أدم

Neither part of the Sharqiya nor part of the true interior, the curious towns of Izz and Adam are both situated at the beginning of the road to Salalah. Izz was originally a Bedouin nomad settlement surprisingly close to the jebel. As such it had little permanent housing but had a large date grove. Adam, a large settled town a long way into the desert from the jebel, was fed by *aflaj* led in from three surrounding hilly outcrops.

Izz lies some 10km south of the Manah turn-off and Adam about 25km beyond that. Adam is roughly 295km from Muscat and is the main entrance to the interior of the country from the south. It is the last green oasis before the featureless desert stretches all the way to Salalah. It has an old quarter called Harrat al Jamii (Mosque Quarter), birthplace of the founder of the Al Bu Said dynasty. The mosque named after him, Jamii Al Bu Said, has been restored and stands outside the walls with pillars and an ornate *mihrab*. Inside the walls is an unusual small domed mosque, now disused, with two small arched doorways leading in through the mud walls. For location of listings see map, page 186.

🏠 WHERE TO STAY

🏠 **Al Ghaba Resthouse** (10 rooms) ☎ 99 358639. This budget resthouse provides basic accommodation with an international

restaurant. It is situated on the Salalah road at the southernmost point of the Dakhiliyah, 715km from Salalah. Accepts credit cards. **$$**

TANUF تنوف

About 15 minutes on from Nizwa on the Bahla road there is a brown sign marked Wadi Tanuf. There is also a turn-off to Tanuf at a point further up the main road at Al Maha petrol station (the first sign you come to if you are coming from Ibri/Buraimi). Do not take this one; it is the Wadi Tanuf sign you need to look out for.

The name of Tanuf is known today for the mineral water which is bottled from the springs at the nearby factory. A small modern settlement has grown up beside the bottling plant and is starting to encroach on the crumbling walled ruins of old Tanuf, abandoned some 50 years ago, which sit at the mouth of the spectacular gorge. Follow the tarmac road in towards the mountains, keeping to the right, for about three minutes. You will see the old ruins easily as you approach. If you follow the road around immediately behind the ruins this takes you into the wadi. After parking in the shade by the gorge you can climb the steps to explore the old town.

This ghost town is a stark reminder of the savage Jebel War, fought in the 1950s. Tanuf was singled out for destruction as a reprisal against the Beni Riyam, whose sheikhs were known as Lords of the Green Mountain. From the wadi behind the town there were escape routes up into the mountains, which is how Suleyman bin Himyar, the sheikh at the time, used to slip away up to hideouts in caves high on the Saiq Plateau (see page 198). The town was bombed by the planes of the RAF at the request of the sultan (Said bin Taimur) and what remains today is a crumbling collection of houses set on the hillock above the wadi.

The *falaj* still runs through it, offering a rare opportunity to explore a traditional Omani town without disturbing the inhabitants. The pillared mosque beside the *falaj* is still quite well preserved. If you cross the wadi, usually flowing until May, you can picnic in the playground on the other side, often accompanied by goats. There are good views of the *falaj* channel built into the sheer mountain wall. After the rains it fills to overflowing and cascades down the wall like a waterfall to join the river. The track into the gorge is drivable for 8km, passing to the right of the Wadi Tanuf recharge dam (which was completed in 1989 with the intention of increasing the supply of subterranean water feeding the *aflaj* of Daris and Tanuf). The wadi at the end, called Wadi Qashah, has good walking with pools deep enough for swimming. A whole day can easily be spent in this stunning scenery.

HAMRA الحمراء

One of Oman's most attractive and traditional towns, Hamra was founded in the Ya'arubi dynasty (1624–1741) and has Oman's most elegant collection of two- and three-storey mud-brick houses in the old part of town, many dating from the Ya'arubi era. You can reach them as you follow the tarmac road winding and twisting beside the date gardens, which are set down below street level so as to maximise rainwater collection. Unlike so many Omani towns, Hamra has no fort and no defensive walls. As a result it was never involved in tribal warfare and hence the houses are still very well preserved – indeed some are still inhabited.

GETTING THERE AND WHAT TO SEE The road off to Hamra from the Nizwa–Bahla road is signposted (Hamra 17km) and heads straight for the foot of the Jebel Akhdar where the town nestles. Taxis from Bahla (see page 214) to Hamra cost RO3. Note the sections of *falaj*, built of stone and looking like a low wall, running along the side of hills to your right, with the occasional disused building nearby. As you approach the mountain you can see two roads snaking up the jebel behind Hamra. The one on the left leads to Misfah and the one on the right is a new road to the Hota Cave. Continue straight on to the roundabout and follow the signs for Hamra East, straight on across the roundabout. This tarmac road runs through the new town, winds past the date gardens and on to the old part of town. The one-way system leads you up a ridge from where you have fine views over the old town and the greenery, and can see the watchtowers set on the surrounding ridges. What is unusual about Hamra is the large number of old houses still lived in, with air conditioning and television aerials added, especially those on the edge which are easily accessible by vehicle. The least inhabited parts are those up narrow alleys in the centre where no car can penetrate.

Dropping down from the bridge you come to a lush roundabout with a playground behind. The road to the right leads to Misfah, while straight on leads you back in a complete circuit to the original Hamra East/West signposts. Take the road to the left first, though, past the enormous stand-alone three-storey mud house with green shutters, and on into the heart of the old town. Park where the road bends and then walk in through the old gateway a little up to your left before dropping down to follow the fast-flowing *falaj* system within the walls.

The old houses here are fascinating. Some, near the edge, are still lived in with the *falaj* actually flowing through their entrance hall. Old men sit in the shaded alleyways drinking coffee and chatting about old times, and the youths hanging about may have difficulty pointing out to you which old house is **Bait al Safa**, House of Purity, where mystical Sufi women lived together like nuns. The 400-year-old house is now unoccupied and locked up, but is said to house old handicrafts. Opposite it is a small mosque built beside the *falaj*, originally for the women's use alone, now air conditioned with its porticoes glassed-in. Women in the Sufi tradition often chose to remain single and celibate, devoting their lives to prayer. Allow a minimum of 30 minutes for a stroll here, ending by the *falaj* at the *halwa* maker, his central freestanding stall piled round with wood for fires which he lights beneath the huge copper bowl. For location of listings see map, page 196.

WHERE TO STAY

⌂ **The View (Al-Hamra)** (15 luxury en-suite tents) PO Box 833, PC 112, Ruwi; ☎24 400873; m +968 98518778; reservations@theviewoman. com; www.theviewoman.com. Located 8km up a track from Al-Hamra, this is the first eco-camp of its kind in the Jebel Akhdar mountains. At 1,400m it is cool in summer & even offers conference facilities, organising annual parties, official meetings & Omani weddings. Mountain bike & hiking routes are organised to full international standards. It has its own licensed restaurant with canyon views, serving all meals & a capacity of 40 people. **$$$$**

⌂ **Sun Rise Resort** (21 rooms, mix of chalets & tents) PO Box 57, 318 Talh, Jabal Asara'h, 40km from Hamra; ☎968 97100791; e reservation@ sunriseresort-om.com; www.sunriseresort-om.com. Set high in the mountains, with a garden & children's playground. A/C & free Wi-Fi. Buffet restaurant serving traditional Omani dishes, offering breakfast, lunch & dinner for up to 50 people. Outdoor pool. Guided walking tours of 3hrs or 6hrs. **$$$**

MISFAT AL ABRIYEEN مصفاة العبريين

Misfat (also known as Misfah) is the ultimate medieval village, built into a rock face 10km up a winding road from Hamra that has now been upgraded from a dirt track to tarmac. There is even a shaded picnic area close to the village where information boards detail walking tours in the area (see page 62) as well as destinations for day trips by saloon car and 4x4 vehicles. If you want to walk through Misfah, leave your car at the car park and walk down the worn steps into the main alleyway. The lush date plantation lies directly below the village in a gully. Follow the narrow streets between the tall houses until you emerge at the other end in a green open area where the women come to wash their dishes and clothes in the *falaj* and water pools. The truly adventurous can follow the way-marked donkey trail (W9) for a six-hour trek from here over to **Bilad Sayt** in Wadi Bani Awf, a distance of 9km reaching altitudes of 2,000m with a difference of 1,050m. The return descent takes four hours. You can do this privately if you are experienced, starting from the campsite in Misfat Al Abriyeen, or hire donkeys and a guide. Speak to one of the specialist tour operators in Muscat if you would like to arrange this as an accompanied trek (see pages 76–8). For location of listings see map, page 196.

WHERE TO STAY

⌂ **Misfah Old House** (12 rooms) Can be booked via www.booking.com. Traditionally furnished house in the village centre, with mattresses, blankets & pillows. Shower & shared bathrooms. Tiled floor & large windows. Omani cuisine provided by local families. Heating, AC. No Wi-Fi. Packed lunches, hiking & horseriding can be arranged. Shuttle service by arrangement. **$$$**

AL HOTA CAVE AND SHARFAT AL ALAMAYN

كهف الهوطة وشرفة العالمين

(*www.alhootacave.com*; ☉ *09.00–13.00 & 14.00–18.00 Sat–Thu, 09.00–12.00 & 14.00–18.00 Fri, closed Mon; RO5.5*) Al Hota Cave (also Al Hoti) is one of the largest cave systems in the world, with several lakes, which provides a home to a variety of different species of fauna. There is a wealth of stalactite and stalagmite formations in the chasms below, and the cave is also home to unusual species of pink-coloured blind fish which sense their way around the lake with feelers, as well as bats and hunter spiders.

The Gulf's only show cave, this used to be accessible only to serious cavers, requiring ropes and climbing gear to descend the 30ft into the sinkhole. Now, however, it has been developed for tourism, with a visitors' centre, a Lebanese and international restaurant called Zajal, a ticket counter, a souvenir shop, a geological museum and a railway station with an Austrian-made 36-seater train that makes a four-minute journey along a tunnel for a distance of 2.7km into the cave. The train often seems to have maintenance problems, so be prepared to walk the 0.7km to the entrance to the cave, then a further 150m in a tunnel to where the guided cave tour begins and where photographic equipment has to be surrendered for safe-keeping. An illuminated walkway with stairs has been erected to view the cave, which has interesting offshoot chambers. The time needed inside the cave is not much more than 40 minutes, and the entry fee is very high, so there have been a number of disgruntled visitors complaining that there are far more impressive caves in Europe with lower entry fees. The caves have a daily capacity of 750 visitors, and when they first opened, queues of enthusiastic Omanis overflowed this limit. It is still advisable to book.

Sharfat Al Alamayn is Arabic for 'balcony of the two worlds' and, as its name suggests, is an excellent vantage point for views over Wadi Bani Awf and Bilad Sayt to one side and the Sahtain Bowl to the other. The altitude here is 2,000m and the terrain is covered in bushes and juniper trees. Even in May and early June nights can be surprisingly cool, dropping to 10°C when the temperature at Nizwa may rise as high as 45°C. Since the improvement in the roads, this route can be followed in a 4x4 to lead over the mountains, visiting Snake Gorge and Bilad Sayt on the descent (see page 148) to arrive via Wadi Bani Awf at Rustaq and return to Muscat along the coast road. Some tours even offer this as a long day's outing from Muscat.

GETTING THERE Take the right-hand turn off the Nizwa–Bahla road (following signs to Al Hamra), setting your milometer to zero. As you approach the mountain you can see two roads snaking up the jebel behind Hamra. The one on the left leads to Misfah with the one on the right to the Hota Cave and Sharfat al Alamayn. After 3.7km take the right-hand turn, signposted to Qalaat al Masalha. Then at 8.3km turn right. At 8.5km turn right again, then bear left at 9.3km and right again at 9.5km. This is where the road to the cave begins. At 14.8km you reach a fork. For the cave, take the left road and after a further 0.9km turn left. Following this road, you will reach the cave entrance at 16.7km. The drive from Nizwa to the Al Hota Cave takes 20 minutes. For Sharfat al Alamayn, take the right at the fork which leads you up a steep bumpy track. For location of listing see map, page 196.

🏠 WHERE TO STAY

🏠 **Al-Hoota Resthouse** (30 rooms) Haat St, 112 Bimah, 24km from the Hoota Cave; www. booking.com. Chalets with private bathrooms & AC set high up on Sharfat al Alamayn. International restaurant, children's playground. Packed lunches. Free Wi-Fi in public areas. **\$\$\$**

WADI GHUL وادی غول AND JEBEL SHAMS جبل شمس

The best time for an exploration of **Ghul** village, abandoned on its rocky outcrop, is late afternoon to dusk. The colour of the stone is brought to life by the red sunset, and the contrast as night approaches, between the eerily empty houses on one side of the valley and the noisily bustling modern village on the hilltop opposite, is all the more striking. The name *ghul* in Arabic (from which we get our word ghoul) means a kind of evil (*jinn*), usually female, that feeds on dead humans and appears in monstrous shapes, especially to travellers alone at night. This ties in with the reputation of nearby Bahla for witches and black magic.

Fork off the main track as you cross the wadi bed itself, heading towards the old village and the little mosque set at its foot just beside the *falaj* system. Leave the vehicle here, where a footpath leads past the mosque with steps down to a private ablution spot, and then forks to the left. After being a bit vague initially, the path soon turns into carefully made steps which zigzag up the rock to bring you within a minute or so into the main street of the village, heavily overgrown now, and full of collapsed stone walls from the adjacent houses.

Clambering about in and among the houses can take anything from 15 minutes to an hour depending on how exhaustive you wish to be. If you have the time it is well worth gradually making your way to the very top of the rocky outcrop, where the remains of an impressive fortification are to be found. At the entrance is a rock drawing showing a warrior with sword and shield. The views from the summit give a sense of strategic command.

Returning down through the main street, look out for the rock drawings of men on horseback chiselled into the flat grey rock faces. There is a particular concentration of some 12–15 drawings about halfway down the street. Close by is a smooth worn hole in the rock, like a grinding mill in the grey stone, though quite why this is in the middle of the street remains unclear.

Jebel Shams ('mountain of the sun'), the tallest mountain in Oman at 3,048m above sea level, is a popular tourist destination because of its spectacular gorges, ravines and breathtaking heights. Trekking trips can be arranged through local tour operators such as Muscat Diving and Adventure Centre (*www.holiday-in-oman.com*) (see page 77). Its popularity has led to the construction of a modern campsite facility with five independent stone cabins with en-suite toilets and five open-style units, with plans to

---

GRAND CANYON OF OMAN TREK

This dramatic three-hour round-trip trek follows the course of an ancient donkey path starting from the Jebel Shams plateau at the village of Al Khateem. The ground underfoot is stony but quite easy going, covering a total distance of only 3.5km, and with a difference of just 100m and a highest altitude of 1,900m. The at times vertiginous path skirts the western edge of the Wadi Nakhr Gorge (popularly known as Oman's Grand Canyon) and leads to the abandoned village of As Sab. It is way-marked as W6 with the yellow, white and red stripes. The village once housed some 15 families who used to grow watermelon, onion, chilli powder, tomato, wheat, pomegranate, lemon and basil. You can still see a flour grinder among the houses. It had its own water supply, still visible above the village in the form of the pool known as Bi'r Dakhiliah (Inner Pool) below a cave. Do not take anything from the houses. There is also some cave housing and a ruined tower.

add more rooms and a restaurant. Tourists are permitted to use the kitchen and cook their own meals. The water for this site comes from Wadi Ghul. Summer camping up here can be surprisingly cool, so take thick clothes and blankets for the night. The contrast when you drive down to the plain again can be as much as 30°C.

Tiny villages are signposted off the main track and occasionally visible clinging to the hillside with terracing. Children from these villages aged ten or over go by 4x4 down to Hamra to school daily. Boys and girls aged seven to nine are mixed in small village schools learning the basics of reading and writing.

En route to these villages is **Wadi Nakhr** which, with its large water pool, is a major site of interest within Jebel Shams, and another popular camping area. Al Khateem village lies on the edge of a gorge with fantastic views, and this is where the trek to reach the cliff dwellings in the canyon begins. It is also the spot from where Bahla and Al Hamra can be seen in the distance – probably one of the best spots for an appreciation of Jebel Shams. **Falcon's View** is another outstanding spot in the mountains from which to take in spectacular panoramic views.

It rather goes without saying, but good care must be taken if camping hereabouts with children on account of the precipitous location. Nights with a full moon are said to be the best. Do carry plenty of food, water and camping gear.

You may well encounter some of the children up on the plateau by the Wadi Nakhr rim, who can be over-enthusiastic in their desire for a sale of their handmade crafts. Remember not to stand too close to the edge as you back off from their zealous approach! Their skin is noticeably weathered and their eyes lined with *kohl*, which can be rather alarming. However, the cash they make from any sale of their little weaving creations, such as key-ring tassels in colourful patterns, I am sure makes a welcome contribution to their existence in this part of the desert.

Near the top Dar Sawda village is signposted 1km off to the left, while the main road continues straight on up to the restricted military zone. You must continue and turn right after 500m on to a road signposted 'Al Hail' that brings you after another 4km to the plateau. The main road itself ends at Al Khateem, the tiny village on the edge of the rim, but smaller tracks fork off left before that to reach the edge of the rim. The Grand Canyon of Oman is truly spectacular, with near-vertical drops of 1,500m to the wadi bed below.

From Al Khateem village you can, if you have a good head for heights, follow the 'rim walk', which takes at least five hours to complete. It is a very narrow steep track and starts by leading down to a deserted village. Then it carries on across large boulders and along an old *falaj* channel to the other side of the canyon. The terraces over here are irrigated by a large natural bowl, Bir Dakhiliya (Arabic for 'interior well'), and are supported by a gigantic arch of rock.

The trees at this height are wild olive and juniper, while on the lower slopes in springtime you will see the delicate pink flowers of the *Moringa peregrina* (*shu*). For the rest of the year it is virtually leafless, but its seeds are crushed to make oil with medicinal properties, said to be beneficial for fevers, skin and stomach problems. Children will sometimes offer handfuls of wild juniper berries (*boo'ot*), delicious and full of vitamin C. The rock itself is often littered with shells and marine fossils, showing that it was once the floor of a warm shallow ocean aeons ago.

GETTING THERE Shortly before Hamra, a new surfaced road runs through Wadi Ghul (10km) and Jebel Shams (37km) and is signposted to your left, by a petrol station. The road was built by desert-line projects to enable military vehicles to gain access to the defence installations on the summit of Jebel Shams. The first 10km to

Wadi Ghul itself is along a wide graded track, mainly flat and easy driving, until you reach the villages of Ghul, old and new, one each side of the wadi bed.

Once through Wadi Ghul, the road leading to Jebel Shams is surfaced for most of the way. The final winding 7km track until the turning to the villages of Al Hail and Al Khateem is not too steep and therefore no longer requires 4x4. From Ghul, allow an hour for the steep 27km drive up Jebel Shams, as well as some time to stop and examine the goat-hair rugs woven and sold by the villagers at Ghul and at several other points during the ascent. (Prices range from RO30–60, depending on size, and the striped geometric patterns can be very attractive. The predominant colours are red, black, brown, white, and occasionally grey and yellow, using both vegetable and chemical dyes. The women's job is to spin the wool, but unusually, the men do the weaving, something that is perhaps reflected in the more masculine patterns and colours.)

At 2,000m, the Jebel Shams plateau is the highest drivable point anywhere in Oman. There are campsites located at 3km from this turn, and a further 2km will get you to the small modern bungalow/camping resort. For location of listings see map, page 196.

WHERE TO STAY

🏠 **Jebel Shams Resort** (35 rooms) ☎99 382 639; e reservations@jebelshamsresort.com; www.jebelshamsresort.com. There are three levels of accommodation: detached 'luxury' chalets, stone-built rooms & Arabian black traditional tents. The chalets & rooms are simply but adequately furnished, complete with en-suite bathroom, verandah, AC & heater. The tents have shared facilities. There is a good restaurant with terrace & garden that also provides packed lunches to trekkers & BBQ facilities. Service is very friendly & the place is entirely Omani-run. **$$$**

🏠 **Jebel Shams Travelling and Camping Centre** (6 chalets & 6 tents) ☎24 635222, 99 228489. The camp is approx an 80km drive from Nizwa (so plan petrol stops accordingly), also on the Jebel Shams plateau. Modern AC & en-suite apts (but no fridges or towels in rooms). **$$**

BAHLA   بهلاء

A sense of the magnificence of Bahla can be gleaned from the extraordinarily extensive wall remnants that still surround the town for a distance of some 12km and which you cannot fail to notice as you approach from the direction of Nizwa. For the best view of Bahla Fort, rising majestically above the oasis palms, drive beyond the town and then double back to approach from the Jabrin side of town, crossing the wide, fertile wadi bed. If you have come from Buraimi, this will be the first view you get, and it is an impressive one as you approach via the winding road. The walls enclose not only the fort and the town, but also an extensive area of date gardens and irrigated fields. While Bahla was the capital of Oman for four or five centuries (mid 12th to the 17th) under the Nabahina dynasty, a special group of slaves used to guard the walls during this period, when the Ya'arubi took over. The walls are said to have been designed by a woman named Ghaitha 600 years ago, and have 15 gates and 132 watchtowers for sentries at regular intervals.

As you approach from Nizwa, the turn-off to the right immediately opposite the fort (clearly signposted) leads into the old souk area of town, which lies to your right as you advance slowly along the narrow road. Now that Bahla Fort restoration is complete, work is scheduled to begin in 2013 on the old souk area with its 163 shops. Immediately opposite to the right, just before the one-way system begins, you will see a gateway into the old enclosed souk. At the centre of this gateway once stood a famous gnarled tree, said to be inhabited by jinn. The villagers were afraid the jinn might fly off with their tree, so they tied it down with chains. According to locals, when the tree was cut down, a spontaneous fire arose. A new tree has been planted in its place, surrounded by a low concrete wall. If you have the chance, visit this souk just before an Eid holiday, when a special traditional market called a *habta* is held. There are a few places here to park your car if you'd like a little walk around.

As an alternative approach from Nizwa you may like to slow down and take the track towards the three 'flying' mosques just 500m after the Shell petrol station on your left. The track leads through a vast cemetery of plain traditional graves, reflecting Ibadhi beliefs that graves should be as simple as possible. Clearly there was no question of revisiting a grave, as it was impossible to distinguish one from the other. Saint worship was strictly against Ibadhi and Orthodox Islamic beliefs, but in this part of Oman mystical Sufis held sway, with another Sufi fraternity, or more accurately, sorority, dominant in Hamra. The three mosques are now in ruins, and have to be climbed up to from the track. You should allow 40 minutes to explore all three. They are said to have belonged to religious hermits and the highest one 'flew' here one night from Rustaq, hence the nickname.

In its colourful history Bahla was built and rebuilt many times, sometimes as a result of rainstorms, sometimes as a result of enemy attack. One such razing was in 1610, so most of the current fort was almost certainly rebuilt by the Ya'arubi, the same as in Nizwa, Jabrin, Rustaq and Al Hazm. Until the 1960s the *wali* used to live in the best-preserved part.

Bahla has long had a reputation for magic and sorcery, with witches, flying mosques, magic trees and a range of people who continue to claim extra-sensory experiences while in and around the town at night. The Bahla Motel has a domed and porthole design, appearing just like something that flew in overnight from outer space.

Bahla is famous for its pottery and the ancient craft can be watched at the Aladawi pottery factory (see page 217).

GETTING THERE Microbuses run to and from Nizwa's main pick-up point in the wadi opposite the fort to Bahla for 300bzs, taking about 45 minutes. A shared taxi

THE MAGIC OF JINN – ORIGIN OF OUR WORD 'GENIE'

The three mosques on little hills just before Bahla are also known as the Mosques of the Saints. In Orthodox Islam there are no saints, but to the Sufis, the mystical sect of Islam, saints' tombs are revered and often held to have miraculous powers such as healing the sick. The origins of Bahla's magical roots are not known, but it may simply be that three mystics or religious hermits settled here and their reputations grew.

The prophet Muhammad was himself a sincere believer in the existence of good and evil jinn, and the Koran has a sura (chapter) entitled Sura Al Jinn. In one of the Traditions of the Prophet it is said 'The jinn were created of a smokeless fire.' They were also meant to have a great fear of metal – hence the chains on the market tree – and someone who felt himself pursued by a jinn would shout 'Hadid, hadid!' ('Iron, iron'), to protect himself. The existence of jinn in Islam is completely accepted and through the use of magic they have extended into folklore. A man who died by violence, for example, was commonly thought to become a jinn spirit and haunt the place of his death, just like our ghosts.

will cost around 500bzs, or a private taxi around RO6. Buses stop on the corner of the road that leads to the souk. For location of listing see map, page 196.

🏠 WHERE TO STAY

🏠 **Jibreen Hotel** (29 rooms) PO Box 733 Bahla, Jibreen Junction, 3km from Jabrin Palace/Fort; 📞 25 363340/363371; e jibrnhtl@omantel.net.om. Very good value & location, a welcome modern addition to the sparse accommodation in this area. Restaurant with varied menu. **$$**

🍴 WHERE TO EAT

As Bahla is so close to Nizwa, you might just as well move on there to eat, as there is nothing much to be found in the village, aside from cheap eats inside the local coffee shops and the simple restaurant at the Bahla Hotel.

WHAT TO SEE

Bahla Fort (⊕ *08.00–16.00 Sat-Thu, 08.00–11.00 Fri; RO1*) Bahla Fort rates in UNESCO's World Heritage Sites list as a 'monument of global importance'. It is considered Oman's most significant monument, closely followed by the archaeological site at Bat and is the country's oldest fort, dating back to 1000BC. The UNESCO restoration project began in 1988 and over £6 million was spent by the Omani government between then and 1999. Work finally finished in summer 2012, when the Ministry of Culture and Heritage handed it over to the Ministry of Tourism, which now has the massive problem of how best to present such an important site to the public, hence the trial opening. No thought had been given by the restorers to such practicalities as electricity installation, so there was not even any lighting provided. The restoration project was conducted under the supervision of two Moroccan architects and a team of Indian and Pakistani labourers, with a handful of Omanis from the Ministry of National Heritage and Culture who were trained in management and restoration work. Their task was enormous and the state of disrepair so advanced that when they began work, the first two years were spent clearing rubble to return to the original ground level. A dearth of old photos (pre-1960) has also meant that they have been unsure of what the original looked like in some parts. The oldest known photo was taken by a British colonel called S B Miles in 1885 and showed two incredibly tall wind towers, probably the tallest towers ever constructed in Oman. Today they have all but disappeared. The bulk of the work has concentrated on strengthening what already exists.

The internal mosque was the first building to be restored and is now in use. The main entrance is built of stone – the grey stones you can see are the originals, the orange ones newly put in. All materials used are local. In some places you can see a damp-proof course of stones about 1m up the walls, the natural height of rising damp. Maintenance is the big problem with these forts. If mud only is used it lasts a maximum of four to five years; *sarouj* plaster is much stronger. One of the high walls suffered bomb damage from the Jebel War, and the place where the hole was patched can be clearly seen. A deep well inside the main castle is divided into two with a washing area and wide pipe inside the wall.

Outside the walls on a raised terrace in the far southeastern corner stands the old mosque of **Ibn al Ass**. Before restoration with its ceiling collapsed, it permitted glimpses from above down into the pillared interior with its beautiful moulded plasterwork *mihrab* and carved *minbar*.

Getting there Your best bet is to get a taxi from Nizwa if you do not have your own transport.

Aladawi Clay Pots Factory and Sale To take a look at the pottery factory, continue through the narrow one-way system and round to the right, passing the old village shops. The road then becomes two-way, but remains extremely narrow. Locals toot to warn you of their approach. Follow the tarmac road slowly all the way around behind the town (keeping to the turnings in the road furthest to your right). After 1–2km you will come to the area of potters, with the domed kilns on the edge of the date gardens. Continuing up the winding narrow road through more date plantations and sections of old and new housing, you reach the pottery factory. The pots here are far cheaper than the ones you will find in the shops and even inside Nizwa Fort.

Continuing on this small road past the factory will take you back out to the main road (you will see more of the old Bahla town wall as you drive), where a left turn will lead you back to Nizwa, passing the Shell petrol station again. Turning right on this main road will take you along to Jabrin Castle.

Jabrin Castle   جبرين   (⏰ *09.00–16.00 Sat–Thu, 08.00–11.00 Fri; 500bzs*) It is about a ten-minute drive from Bahla to the Jabrin Castle turn-off. It is clearly signposted left from the main road. Follow this turning for three minutes inland until you reach a roundabout at which you take a right. You can't miss it, as it stands by itself in a flat open plain beside some date gardens.

Jabrin (also Jibreen, Jabreen) is set apart from all other Omani forts through its elegance and elaborately decorated ceilings, which make it appear more like a palace than a fort. It was built by Bil'arub bin Sultan, an imam of the Ya'aruba dynasty, known for his interest in scholars and poets, initially as a home in 1670, and subsequently used as a sort of retreat by the Ya'aruba imams or ex-imams. It still retains a calm and peaceful feel. The restoration – which took seven years – was the first to be undertaken by the Ministry of Culture and Heritage, and was completed in 1983. The rooms were then furnished with antiques to give as close a flavour as possible of the original atmosphere.

It was not designed to have a defensive role – the two round gun towers at diagonally opposite corners were added later, as was the outer encircling wall. A small village used to nestle at its foot, but this was knocked down after the restoration, and the government built a new settlement some 1km away back towards the main road and clearly visible from the palace roof. The large shady tamarisk tree by the gate is more permanent and has given shade for over 100 years.

Imam Bil'arub bin Sultan died here in 1692 after a siege by his brother. A later imam, Mohammed bin Nasir, then made Jabrin his headquarters, but after that it remained uninhabited from his death in 1728 until restoration began in the late 1970s. The imam is buried in the fort near the *falaj* that runs through its ramparts, said to be his favourite place in the building, to the left of the main fort door.

Inside, the three-storey structure is arranged round two separate courtyards, each with different floor levels. The main reception and guest rooms, known as the Sun Room and Moon Room, are the most elegant and elaborately furnished, with exquisitely painted ceilings. Some of the ceiling arches and passageways are decorated with Koranic inscriptions and geometric red-and-black patterns. A room on the second floor was specifically for the imam's favourite horse.

On the roof there was a Koranic school, and Jabrin became an important centre for teaching Islamic law, medicine and astrology. The students were given bananas from the gardens below to keep them alert in their studies, according to an early source.

If you need to stay the night, the Jibreen Hotel (see opposite) – about 3km from the fort – should meet your needs.

JEBEL KAWR AND AL GHAFAT جبل كور والغافات

The settlement of Ghafat, signposted 6km to the right just 15km after the Jabrin turn-off, has a fine grouping of two- and three-storey mud-brick houses set in the centre of extensive date plantations. It is the capital of the Bani Hina, from where the name Hinawi originates. There is plentiful water here, and much wheat is grown on the fertile plain beside it. Al Ghafat is set below Jebel Kawr (or Jebel Koor), a spiky rock reckoned to be one of the largest in the world. It is one of a cluster of peaks west of Jebel Shams known as 'the exotics', as the geomorphology of these peaks is somewhat different from the others in Oman. Jebel Kawr is almost as high as Jebel Shams, but far less well known. The jebel is home to the third-longest cave in Oman, at 1.5km. The cave's gaping lower entrance is easily visible from the dirt tracks that enter the wadi from the signpost for Amla (53km – which is on the road that leads in a southerly direction from Ibri).

GETTING THERE A taxi from Nizwa (see pages 199–206) to Jabrin and Ghafat takes just over three hours and costs around RO9.

8

The Sharqiya الشرقية

Telephone code: 25

The corpse washer cannot guarantee paradise.

The landscape of this eastern region contains a mixture of low-level mountains that sit in the distance at the end of an extensive gravel plain. These eastern Hajar Mountains are far less concentrated than the harsh, dense massif of the Jebel Akhdar in the interior (part of the western Hajars). *Sharq* is Arabic for 'east', and so the Sharqiya translates literally as the 'eastern part' of Oman.

The region can be split into three distinct areas: the Indian Ocean coastal stretch, the desert and the city of Sur. The coast is rather different from that of the Batinah: it is barren and cliff-bound in places, with few natural harbours. From Al Ashkhara all the way to Ras Nuss in Dhofar, the coast is desolate. The Wahiba Sands constitute the Sharqiya's southern edge.

The region has been dominated for many years by the Al Harithy tribe and its sheikhs, who are strongly Ibadhi (see box, page 28). It is believed that the east African cities of Mogadishu and Barawa were founded by Omanis of Al Harithy descent in the 10th century, and so, after the Zanzibar revolution of 1963, many of the Zanzibaris who fled east Africa sought asylum in Oman and settled in the Sharqiya, considering it to be their ancestral homeland. Qabil, the Al Harithy capital of the Sharqiya, was on the route of the slave trade from the ports at Sur and Al Ashkhara. African goods used to be imported to Oman via the ports of Sur and Al Ashkhara, and dates were exported in exchange. But when Oman lost the Zanzibar connection in the late 19th century the prosperity of this region, and indeed the whole of northern Oman, suffered a tremendous setback.

The Al Harithy people are Hinawis, yet the Hinawi tribes outside the Sharqiya do not pay allegiance to them; thus the Hinawi tribes of this region are quite distinct from those outside of it (see box, page 26).

GETTING THERE

BY AIR There is no airport open to civilians.

BY ROAD There are two ways to access this eastern region from the capital: the inland route and the more recent coastal toll motorway. Whichever route you take, it would be a good idea to come back via the alternative, if you have the time, as the full circle provides an excellent tour of the Sharqiya. The towns and villages of interest have been placed in the order that you meet them travelling the inland route from Muscat first, followed by the coastal route from Muscat. A new road has also been built between Al-Ashkarah and Shannah, improving access to Masirah Island.

THE SHARQIYA

MUSCAT
Muscat International Airport
01
Al Amrat
As Sifah

MUSCAT

Al Nakhal Fort
Nakhal
Sayh Hatat
Bidbid
13
Awabi
Sumail
Sumail Fort
15
Ar Ruus
Tanuf
Quriyat
17

Gulf of Oman

Tropic of Cancer

Nizwa
Izki
Al Rawdah Fort
Akhdar Fort
Dibab
Bait al Afreet
Bimah
Fins
Shab
Tiwi
Manah
Samad (ancient copper mining settlement)
Lizq (ancient ruins)
23
Majlis al Jinn Cave
Wadi Shab
Qalhat
Ibra
10
Oman Oil
4
3
Ibra Beehive Tombs
Sur
Ras al Hadd
Al Mudaybi
33
5
9
Ras al Jinz
Sinaw
27
Bidiyah
2
14
1
23
Adam
13
8
11
Al Kamil
Al Wafi
Ar Ruways

SHARQIYA

Bilad Bani Bu Hassan Fort
Jalaan Bani Bu Ali
35
6
A'Seela
Al Ashkharah

DAKHLIYAH
32
Bilad Bani Bu Ali Fort
Al Ashkharah

Wahiba Sands

N
Bradt

ARABIAN SEA

32
Shannah Resthouse

Al Jazeera
Muhut
Mahawt Resthouse
Masirah Hilf
12
7

AL WUSTA
Mikhaybiyah
Al Khaluf
Masirah

0 —— 25km
0 —— 25 miles

Shital / Ad Duqm, Salalah

For listings, see pages 229, 231–4, 246

🏠 Where to stay

1 1000 Nights Camp
2 Al Areesh Desert Camp
3 Al Qabil Resthouse
4 Al-Raha Tourism Camp
5 Al Sharqiya Sands
6 Areen Youth Hostel
7 Danat Al-Khaleej
8 Desert Nights Camp
9 Golden Sands Camp
10 Ibra Motel
11 Lyali Al Sharqiya Resthouse
12 Masirah Island Resort
13 Nomadic Desert Camp
14 Oriental Nights Resthouse

✗ Where to eat and drink

1000 Nights Camp (see 1)
Areen Youth Hostel (see 6)
Danat Al-Khaleej (see 7)
Masirah Island Resort (see 12)
Two Dunes (see 8)

BY BUS Buses operate from Muscat to Sur along the inland route only. (There is almost no public transport along the coastal road apart from the occasional taxi being used by local people.) Request drop-offs/pick-ups can be made at any of the designated bus stops *en route*. The inland route makes a fixed stop at Ibra. Buses run about three times a day in each direction and take about 4½ hours on the inland route.

TOUR OPERATORS

The tour operators shown below are also included on pages 76–8, but are reproduced here as they operate camps and tours in the Sharqiya region.

Desert Discovery Tours PO Box 99, PC 115, Madinat Qaboos, Muscat; ☎24 493232; m 99 328858, 99 317107; f 24 490144; www.desertdiscovery.com. Manages Al Areesh Desert Camp in the Wahiba Sands, Al Naseem Tourism Camp near Ras Al Jinz turtle-nesting beach & Al Qabil Resthouse. Also arranges mobile camping units for stays in the Wahiba & elsewhere. They collect guests from Al Qabil Resthouse. Mobile camps are arranged to suit & include 4x4s, camping gear, cooking staff, food, water, drivers & guides. The units can be moved to anywhere in Oman, or can cross the Wahiba. Tourists have the option of driving themselves with a guide. For a camp booking 24hrs notice is fine, but for the mobile units, at least 4 days' advance notice is recommended. *RO30/20/10 adult/child aged 6–12/ child under 6; inc dinner, B&B.*

🏠 WHERE TO STAY

There are a few guesthouses and budget hotels along the interior route to Sur. These are located at the larger villages, such as Ibra and Qabil, which lie on this ancient trading route. On the coastal route there is at present nowhere to stay until you get to Sur, unless you are camping. Once you have reached the vicinity of Sur on the eastern coast, you have a choice of a few hotels and a few camps at various nearby locations. If you are after a desert experience, do try one (or more) of the various camps in the region, like Al Areesh Desert Camp or Golden Sands Resort (in the Wahiba Desert) and Al Naseem Tourism Camp (Ras Al Jinz). Independent camping is best along the beaches of the coast road between Muscat and Sur, especially between Bimmah and Tiwi. You can take your own equipment or hire from a tour operator. You can camp in most places, whether mountain, beach or sandy desert, but Ras Al Jinz and Ras Al Hadd are designated camping areas. You can check with any tour operator about this. Desert Discovery Tours (see above for contact details), to name just one example, provides full camping equipment. Basic resthouses are available in Sinaw and Jaalan Bani Bu Ali (see pages 226 and 234). Masirah Island has simple accommodation both on the island and the mainland opposite (see page 246).

✗ WHERE TO EAT

Your options for eating are largely limited to the restaurants within the hotels and the resthouses. **Al Qabil** serves good curries and an international menu at budget prices and is a great stop-off point about midway to Sur on the inland route. However, each village does have its share of basic coffee shop-type cafés catering to the local community. You might stumble on a gem, but otherwise keep in mind that these villages, thankfully, weren't designed to titillate the Western tourist. Having said that, there is a Pizza Hut in Sur.

OTHER PRACTICALITIES

HOSPITALS
✚ **Al Ashkhara** ☎25 566100
✚ **Bidiyah** ☎25 581167
✚ **Ibra** ☎25 587100
✚ **Masirah** ☎25 504363
✚ **Ras Al Hadd** ☎92 177549
✚ **Sinaw** ☎25 524338
✚ **Sur** ☎25 561100

POLICE STATIONS
Sur ☎25 542599
Sinaw ☎25 524999
Bidiyah ☎25 583099
Ibra ☎25 570099
Al Kamil/Al Wafi ☎25 557420
Jalaan bani Bu Hasan ☎25 550420

WHAT TO SEE AND DO

BIRDWATCHING Masirah Island in the winter is the home of greater flamingos, seagulls, terns and herons. There are no organised birding tours to this destination, so it is very much an independent affair. Ayga Island is a 30-minute boat ride from the coast of Sur and a good birdwatching spot. This can be visited independently (by enquiring at any of the boats on Sur harbour) or through a tour operator from Muscat (if you would prefer being accompanied). For example, Bahwan Travel Agencies (see page 76) offer a day trip along the coast road to Sur from where you take a boat trip out to Ayga Island. The full-day trip costs RO170, which includes a 4x4 vehicle (accommodating four passengers), a driver/guide and the return boat trip to the island. The day starts at 07.30 and finishes back at your Muscat hotel at around 19.00. Water and soft drinks are provided. You have the option of taking a picnic along with you or using one of the basic local restaurants.

CAMEL RACING Camel racing events are held at tracks at Bidiyah and Mudaybi and are announced in the local press. For more information, see pages 30–1.

CAMPING The beaches along the Sharqiya coast are ideal for camping. Tiwi is a particularly popular spot. Masirah Island is largely deserted and perfect for camping. If your trip falls in the turtle-nesting season too, it will undoubtedly be a memorable island adventure.

CANYONING Canyoning is a special kind of trekking, and doesn't require specialist equipment. It usually involves a combination of narrow canyons with sheer rock faces, natural water pools to swim in, caverns and grottos. Wadi Shab, on the coastal route to Sur (see map on page 220) is excellent for this. If you travel to Wadi Shab independently, there are usually a couple of young Omanis at the entrance who will guide you through. Their guidance is invaluable, but it is probably best to agree a small fee with them beforehand. The *pièce de résistance* is swimming in the cavernous water pool at the end, reached by swimming through a head-width opening in the rock.

CAVING The cave near Ibra called Majlis al Jinn ('meeting place of the spirits') is one of the largest in the world (for further information see pages 227–8). It is for advanced cavers only and it is essential to arrange trips through a tour operator in Muscat (see pages 76–8).

There is also the Moqal Cave in Wadi Bani Khalid, which you can visit independently. You will need flashlights and must be prepared to enter the cave on your hands and knees. For more information see page 233.

DESERT SAFARI Of the Sharqiya region's offerings, a desert safari trip into the Wahiba Sands (otherwise known as 'dune bashing') is one of the best. It provides the 'real' sandy desert experience. It is vital in terms of safety that you have an accompanying guide – someone with demonstrable desert driving experience and logistical knowledge. A minimum of two 4x4s is also recommended, again for safety. It is advisable to arrange a trip into the Wahiba a few days in advance with a tour operator, as you may be disappointed if you are unable to organise anything while in the vicinity. See page 221, for details. You can opt for a day trip or an overnighter, which includes a barbecue and sleeping in *barasti* huts. Either trip includes a visit to a genuine Bedouin camp, dune bashing and camel riding if you want it. These trips can be surprisingly expensive, so make sure you investigate the costs fully before committing yourself.

DHOW CRUISE *Dhow* cruises around Sur Bay can easily be arranged through the Muscat tour operators (see pages 76–8).

GAME FISHING Sur and Masirah are especially good sites for this, with species such as marlin and tuna living in the waters. Tours can be arranged through operators in Muscat (see pages 76–8).

HIKING AND TREKKING Like the rest of Oman, the terrain is great for those with a penchant for trekking and hiking and, as with the rest of the country, you're never far from a mountain, wadi or canyon. Wadi Dayqah is a favourite in the Sharqiya

---

A TOUGH TREK

One of the only properly way-marked routes in the eastern Hajar Mountains, this trek is also probably the most spectacular. However, it is not for the faint-hearted as it requires either 14 hours with a light pack or 18 hours with camping gear to cover the 28km from the coast at Wadi Tiwi to the green inland oasis of Wadi Bani Khalid. That said, you do not have to walk the whole thing, and certainly one option is to walk the first, easy section from Al Aqur to Sooee, then turn back or, starting from the other end at Wadi Bani Khaled, the first section which is lovely as it overlooks the pools and the canyon. If you do walk the whole way, you will need to plan ahead and think about how to get back, as there is no transport at either end. One quite fun idea, if you have two vehicles in your group, is for each party to walk from opposite ends and to meet in the middle and swap keys – make sure you have duplicate keys with someone else in the party just to be sure it all works. On the Wadi Tiwi side the starting point is the village of Al Aqur or Sooee, and you can make an early start by camping on one of the many beaches near Tiwi. On the Wadi Bani Khalid side the walk begins just after the village of Miqil by the pools, where you can camp under the palm trees. The trek follows an ancient donkey trail and is way-marked (E35) using the standard yellow, white and red stripes, and cairns. You must take your own water for the trip and be self-sufficient in food as there is no settlement on the way. The highest altitude reached is 2,100m and the difference is 1,800m, making this one of the more gruelling and challenging treks in Oman. The fabulous landscape, with stunning views over deep canyons and green wadis, will make it a memorable experience.

8

and, for the serious trekkers with experience, the 28km way-marked trekking path from Wadi Tiwi to Wadi Bani Khalid is a fine challenge.

SURFING Oman offers excellent windsurfing at all levels from beginner to advanced. Lessons are given by Al Bustan Palace Hotel (which offers a good sheltered bay for beginners) and the InterContinental Hotel (see pages 79 and 81). Once you know the basics you can progress to Ras Al Hadd, 4½ hours from Muscat, a good location for intermediate-standard surfing, with higher waves but a good sheltered bay and no dangerous currents. A slightly trickier site is Asylah on the east coast near Al Ashkhara, 3½ hours' drive from Muscat. For the real experts the ultimate windsurfing destination is Masirah Island, six to seven hours' drive from Muscat, best reached from Sinaw on the new surfaced road to Al Hij just north of Barr Al Hikman. It is at its best during the monsoon winds that blow from mid June to late August. From Al Hij a graded road runs to Shannah, from where a ferry (RO16 each way) goes to Hilf on Masirah Island. The ferry usually takes 1½ hours. The best beaches are then reachable via graded roads some 40 minutes south of Hilf.

TURTLE WATCHING The three main turtle-watching sites are Ras Al Hadd, Ras Al Jinz and Masirah. Green turtles, loggerheads, hawksbills and leatherbacks come to nest and lay their eggs in the sand on these beaches every year. Turtles can be seen at virtually any time of year at Ras Al Jinz, though the best time to see large numbers is June–November. In January, only a few females nest per night. In July and August the number is in the hundreds, anything from 100–600 per night. August is a good month as the strong monsoon winds make it reasonably cool for camping. There is hotel accommodation on the site at Ras Al Jinz (see page 245). The beach itself is about three-quarters of a mile long, with cliffs at the back and a high sandbank. The nearest village is about 1–2km away, but is not visible from the campsite.

Visits to the sites are controlled to restrict numbers, as these are endangered species. You have to join an escorted tour that goes on to the beaches at around 21.30 and book your place through the Directorate General of Nature Reserves (✆ 24 602285). Places can also be booked through a tour operator or through any of the hotels in Sur, which all offer visitation packages.

ALONG THE INLAND ROUTE FROM MUSCAT TO SUR

The inland road used to be the best option for getting to Sur, before the Muscat–Sur coastal highway was completed as a three-lane toll motorway, transforming what used to be a difficult five-hour drive with 4x4 along the coast into a two-hour easy trip.

In all, the inland journey from Muscat to the east coast (Sur) is 335km (about a four-hour journey, including a short rest stop for petrol/refreshments). A good tarmac road takes you initially towards the interior (on the main Nizwa road) passing through the Sumail Gap, the natural divide between the eastern and western Hajar mountain range. It takes about an hour from Muscat to reach this fork. At this point there are signposts to Sur, 263km away, and the road forks off just beyond Bidbid. From this point there is no more dual carriageway for the whole distance to Sur.

The initial part of this single carriageway is attractive, winding through wadis and gorges with low hills all around. After roughly 60km the road leaves the hills and wadis behind and you reach a clearly signposted major fork at which the right turn takes you to Al Mudaybi, Sinaw and Samad. This route to Sinaw is now an excellent tarmac road; it is fast driving on dead flat terrain, and is of interest for the archaeological sites of Samad and Maysar, the hill fort of Lizq and the old market town of Sinaw on the edge of the desert. There is also now a tarmac link eastwards across to Ibra from Sinaw, so it can be an interesting variation in the route to Sur. Also, there is a tarmac road from Sinaw leading south to reach the coast (after 218km) at Barr al Hikman, close to where the ferry to Masirah operates (at Ras an Najdah).

AL RAWDAH الروضة From the Sinaw turn-off, the first signpost you see marks a right turn to Al Rawdah (also spelt Al Rowdah). A short detour can be made here to drive the 2km over to the fertile date plantation, where a fine restored fort, built at the end of the Nabhani dynasty, sits on a hilltop commanding the village. The approach to the tiny oasis village is along a gravel wadi with shallow water, fine for a 4x4. Further in, and away from the main road, is another fort, this one a ruin. The whole spot is very attractive, and an hour could easily be spent here strolling about exploring the forts and other old buildings.

AKHDAR أخضر Beyond Al Rawdah, a sign turns off to Akhdar, whose brown stone-built tower can be seen from the road. The village, with its picturesque fort in ruin, is rich in history but particularly noted for its pit-weavers (all of whom are men). If you spend half an hour here strolling in the old part of town, you can still see the weavers at work, under *barasti* shades, sitting in the sunken pits where their wooden hand looms are erected. There is a range of woven items including wall hangings, bedspreads and shawls. Prices start from RO45, the high price reflecting the labour-intensiveness and skill required to produce a beautiful item. You can buy direct here if they have any spare produce. There are several fine old houses around the tower, some of which were lived in until the late 1990s.

SAMAD صمد South of Akhdar, the road continues through low rocky mountains until you see the signs for Samad and Al Meyasar (also spelt Maysar). Samad is steeped in history with several fine forts and archaeological sites. One area of archaeological interest in the town is the copper-mining settlement from the Umm al Nar period in the 3rd millennium BC. Within the settlement are ruins of copper smelting kilns 40cm wide by 50cm high, and the foundations of a hill fort. Copper implements were found in the old houses, such as chisels, axes, needles and rings. Also at Samad is a deserted old walled town and ruined fort which can be explored rather more easily. The fort at Hozam bin Falah also lies in ruins. Date-palm groves, fruit orchards, full-flowing *falaj* and tranquil gardens surround it.

LIZQ لزق Continuing through the landscape of gentle hills you come next to a blue signpost marked Al Lizq. A detour of some 45 minutes is recommended here for those interested in ancient ruins, for on a hill to the southwest of the modern village is an impressive stone staircase dated to the Iron Age. This is the only one of its kind yet found in Oman. A staircase leads on towards a fortified citadel on the summit: the final 30m or so of the ascent is tricky for all but the sure-footed and agile. Good footwear should be worn, as the rocky terrain can be loose and slippery.

A low wall lines both sides of the stone steps and at the point where the stairs end and the ground flattens out a little, there used to be a well and two small towers guarding the entry point. From here you simply have to pick whichever way across the boulders to the summit you find easiest, as there is no clear path. The total ascent takes about 15 minutes, and less if you are fit. The view from the summit is magnificent, the hilltop commanding the land in all directions. A few scant remains of stone-built rooms and fortifications are left mainly over towards the far side of the summit, where the ground starts to dip a little. The whole area of small, almost volcanic-looking hills is attractive, and the area at the foot of the hill makes a good picnic or even camping spot. The old village, of which no trace remains, used to be situated here just at the edge of the date-palm trees.

Getting there To reach the hill drive straight through the centre of the modern village, over the tiny roundabout, veering a little left; you pass over a small humped bridge, and need to keep to the right when presented with two tracks. The dirt road wriggles through the plantations between high mud walls, passing a small round watchtower raised up on a group of rocks to the left; you then need to turn right and continue straight on and out of the village. Once you are on the outskirts of the village sprawl you need to fork left and head towards the hill that stands by itself immediately to the left of the large date plantation, a total distance of about 1km from the edge of the modern village. There are many tracks, all of which can be driven in a saloon car and it does not matter which you take as long as you focus on the hill itself. Once you arrive at the obvious parking area at the foot, the stone staircase is clearly visible rising straight up the middle of the hill.

AL MUDAYBI المديبي Al Mudaybi is now a large modern town on the edge of the desert, but until the 1970s it was still a traditional walled mud-brick town. The town would be at its busiest in the summer, when the Bedouin would come in from the desert for the date harvest and live in *barasti* huts by the date plantations until August. The old town can still be explored on foot by forking left for 1km just before the Shell petrol station.

At Al Musalla, the road south to Barr Al Hikman (Route 32) on the coast begins, but if you keep to the main road, it bends round and heads north again to reach Sinaw shortly after.

SINAW سناو Sinaw is famous for its colourful souk and cattle market, but is also visited for its attractive old town. It is signposted and sits just off the main road from Al Mudaybi to the left. Drive through the new town for about 1km to the final roundabout where you fork right to reach the market and the old part of town. The market area itself lies on your right after leaving the roundabout; it consists of a rectangle of shops each facing into the centre, where there is a roofed but open pillared area for selling fruit and vegetables. There is a one-way system in and out at each end for vehicles, through large green metal gates.

The souk is at its busiest on Thursday and Friday mornings. Some of the shops sell traditional silver jewellery as well as the more modern gold jewellery which has become popular with local women. Unusually, women sell produce in this market alongside the men. A rather unusual (and rather frightening) souvenir is the *burka* mask still worn today by Bedouin women in Oman.

Leaving the souk on your right, you can walk or drive along the dirt track to reach the old crumbling parts of town, consisting of two separate walled villages. These are now deserted, but still contain remnants of an old way of life in the abandoned multi-storey houses, such as cooking pots, kettles and plates. From Sinaw the new tarmac road takes you along flat, unexciting scenery to Izki some 60km to the north and from where you can join the motorway back to Muscat or on towards Nizwa. For location of listings see map, page 220.

Where to stay

🏠 **Ain Safnan Resthouse** (16 rooms) PO Box 269420 Sinaw; ☎ 25 524560. Basic accommodation which will nevertheless be welcome if you have been camping for a few nights. **$**

🏠 **Sinaw Motel** (15 rooms) ☎ 25 524056. A simple place in the middle of town. **$**

IBRA إبرا

Ibra is about 150km (two hours' drive) from Muscat on the main Sharqiya road from Bidbid to Sur (Route 23), past the turn-off to Samad. It is a relatively large sprawling town, with several wadis. Ibra is the chief town of the inland Sharqiya, and used to have close trading links with Zanzibar and east Africa. It is known as the gateway to the eastern region, and is famous for its fine horses and horsemen, situated as it is on the ancient caravan route from the interior to the port at Sur. The houses of wealthy merchants still stand, crumbling among the palm gardens, as evidence of the town's more prosperous days. Ibra is the home of the Al Harithy tribe, Ibadhi Muslims of aristocratic descent who have featured large in the country's history.

On occasions of celebration, camel racing takes place here as well as in Barka on the Batinah coast. For location of listing see map, page 220.

Where to stay

🏠 **Ibra Motel** (25 rooms) ☎ 25 571777; e ibramtl@omantel.net.om. Located behind the Oman Oil petrol station just off the main highway, this cheap place has the advantage of being central & close to the bus stop. B/fast can be taken in the restaurant next door for RO2.5 **$**

Where to eat There are local coffee shops (budget range) dotted about on the main road here which serve Indian, Chinese and Arabic food. The Fahad Bin Saleh Al-Hooti Restaurant beside the Ibra Motel behind the Oman Oil petrol station has good cheap food including occasionally prawns with ginger.

What to see

Ibra souk A lively place with plenty of traditional outlets including weapons and rifle maintenance, the souk, though now housed in modern buildings, is still the heart of the town. Thursday mornings are particularly busy, with everyone buying their food for the weekend.

Ibra beehive tombs (🕐 24hrs) Further along the road to Wadi Naam is the difficult and tortuous route to the Ibra beehive tombs, set to the east in the mountains of Jebel Bani Jabir on a high ridge 2,000m above sea level. There are roughly 90 in all, dating to the 3rd millennium BC, and many have survived remarkably well, still standing to three-quarters of their original 5m height. They are carefully built of stone blocks, tapering in towards the top and with a double wall. In 1994, archaeologists opened one to find skeletons, beads and pottery, which enabled accurate dating to take place. The tombs are visible from below, where the tarmac road to Wadi Naam ends. Follow the sign for Al Dammah, forking left along the main graded road where a date plantation wall ends. From this point the tombs are a gruelling 67km drive into the hills through several villages, which takes roughly two hours. You would need to devote a whole day to visiting the tombs and the 4x4 vehicle is needed to reach the tombs and for the steep ascent in the final stages.

Majlis al Jinn Cave (🕐 24hrs) The other reason for enthusiasts to come this far is for access to the Majlis al Jinn Cave ('place of the genie') in Wadi Bani Jabir, one of the largest known cave chambers in the world at 310m long and 225m wide, about the size of several aircraft hangars. The cave was 'discovered' in 1983 by an American employee of the Ministry of Water Resources.

Inside the cave – correctly known as **Khosilat Maqandeli** – you can see colourful stalactites and stalagmites. Since it is a two-hour trek from the nearest village (Karan) and then a 160m rope descent through a sinkhole to the floor of the cave, it is clearly not going to be undertaken by the average visitor to the Sharqiya. Experienced climbing guides will need to accompany you and these climbing tours can be arranged through the tour operators in Muscat (see pages 76–8). Close to this cave there is another cave system with over 5km of passages to be explored, again with accompanying guides. Camping up on the high plateau here is possible, but chilly and exposed.

Old quarters of Ibra There are two old quarters of Ibra: Al Kanaatir and Al Minzfah. They are reached by forking to the right off the main inland road where the signpost says Ibra Sufelat (lower Ibra), then following the brown signs. The hills lining the wadi are topped with watchtowers. The tarmac road brings you after around 2km into the decaying remains of Al-Minzfah, where you can park and wander round the crumbling old merchant houses. A handful have been restored, but the old pillared souk and the Mosque of the Two Qiblas (prayer niches) are slowly collapsing, awaiting a decision on how to restore them. Tragically, many inhabitants have left the area, following the death of the palm trees in the oasis from damage to the local water table. Even so, an interesting hour can be spent here exploring and examining the unusual architectural elements of the once-wealthy houses, such as porthole windows, a hark back to their maritime heritage.

AL MUDAYRIB المضيرب Al Mudayrib is 20km beyond Ibra on the road to Sur. This small town is worth a detour, especially towards the end of the day when the colour of the distant Wahiba Sands reflects a gentle redness. Don't visit at midday, as it is stiflingly hot with the full glare of the desert and little shade.

The attraction here is the fine old buildings built by wealthy merchants often resident in Africa, but intended for public use as an endowment for the town. They are known as *sablas*, and only ten remain. The public reception areas are used for meetings, wedding celebrations or halls of mourning. Each prominent family would have a *sabla* for use by its extended relations, which was like a social club

WOMEN'S SOUK

On Wednesday mornings, from 07.30–11.00, modern Ibra has a souk for women only (the only one of its kind in Oman). The women do the selling as well as the buying, mainly of items like perfumes, cosmetics, clothing, lotions, powders and textiles, as well as fruit and vegetables. It was started in 1986 and its popularity is increasing year by year as women enjoy shopping away from the pressures of men's impatience. 'Men do not enjoy shopping like we do,' says Fatima, a regular visitor. 'We like to take our time and chat while buying, but they want to get it over with. This arrangement frees them from the need to do the family household shopping.' Traditionally the household shopping was the man's role, so that his wife was not seen in public. The souk is off the main road to the right by the Oman Oil petrol station, then a further 3km along the road, past the *wali*'s office.

Under the previous sultan (before 1970) it was forbidden to replace your house with anything except what it was already built from. So if your barasti hut burnt down it had to be replaced by a barasti hut unless you could obtain special dispensation, normally only available from the sultan. All controls tended to be negative in those early days and the municipality existed primarily to tell you what you could not do. This was good in the sense that it prevented the unbridled development boom which has been gripping Dubai for years, but bad in that it hindered much progress.

for that family. Unfortunately it is not possible to enter any of these *sablas,* some of which are even fortified and on two storeys. There are also 20 small mosques scattered about the town, and it is worth climbing the hill to the crumbling 18th-century fort built on flaky black rock.

The town lies 1km off the main road to the left, and you can follow the road into the centre and park under a shady tree in the old town square, encircled by the stalls of the old souk. The old *falaj* channel runs through here by a stone bridge, making it a popular place for villagers to sit and children to play.

One of the most impressive *sablas* is raised up and overlooks the souk, and by climbing up on a little path for just a few metres you will reach its magnificently carved door, imported from east Africa in the 19th century. The locked door conceals a finely decorated room with painted ceiling beams.

Al Mudayrib is at its most evocative just before the Eid holidays, when the souk comes alive and everyone, man and woman alike, is dressed in their finest clothing and jewellery. For location of listing see map, page 220.

🏠 Where to stay

🏠 **Al Qabil Resthouse** (10 rooms) PO Box 53, PC 419; ☎ 25 581243. Just a few kilometres beyond Al Mudayrib in the little village of Al Qabil is this simple resthouse of the same name. It is on the main road (Route 23) & is signposted. It is close to the Wahiba Sands & provides a good stop-off for lunch, if you have opted for the Muscat to Sur inland route. The unlicensed international restaurant sells satisfactory food, which is very cheap. The rooms are simple but comfortable with fridge, TV, AC & 24hr room service. Children's beds can be added. Alcohol is served in the bar for guests only. Accepts credit cards. **$$**

BIDIYAH بدية **AND AL MINTIRIB** المنتيرب Bidiyah and Al Mintirib are set on the banks of Wadi Batha which heads from Qabil for 97km deep into the Wahiba Sands. Heavy rains in this area can cause floodwaters from Wadi Batha to form a huge lake, dramatically set among the dunes. The tribe here is Hijriyeen, who had their moment of glory in the early 19th century when they were the only Omani tribe to successfully ward off the invading Wahhabis from central Arabia. Today they have been largely absorbed by Al Harithys.

Al Mintirib still has a surprisingly grand main street and a very solid fort. Up until the 1960s the *qadi* (judge) could regularly be seen sitting in the sand in front of it, holding his *majlis* to decide on legal matters of dispute. The senior sheikh of the Hijriyeen at that time was a deaf old man who had a delightful garden filled with shady vines and papaya facing on to the dunes. The brown signpost off the main road announces **Bidiyah Castle**. This strong and square defensive fort, with no towers, sits by itself 2km off the main road, and is generally kept locked. Nearby

ABANDONED WEALTHY MERCHANTS' HOUSES

After entering through a fine gateway into Al Minzfah, you will find some of Oman's grandest old merchants' houses, a few of them four storeys high and built of stone faced with mud plaster (*sarouj*) like that used on the old forts. They are in varying states of repair, one or two are locked and inaccessible, while others no longer have doors and can be wandered into freely. A few modern houses have also been built now, their concrete hulks scattered incongruously among these magnificent ruins.

In the 1980s many of these houses still had blue-and-white Chinese plates embedded in the walls and ceilings, but all have now mysteriously disappeared. The Ministry of Tourism has been examining how best to display these unusual examples of Omani residential architecture to the public, and various schemes are under consideration. Sadly, indecision can be a form of decision, and in a few years there may not be much left left to display.

to the right of the fort your eye will be drawn by a tall tower house which, on closer examination, has painted green crenellations. It is still lived in, with a television aerial attached and a very fine carved entrance gateway. For location of listing see map, page 220.

Where to stay

Oriental Nights Resthouse (19 rooms) PO Box 84, PC 421, Bidiyah; 99 354816, 99 006215 e onrh@onrh.net; www.onrh-oman.com. This small hotel, near the Al-Ashkarah junction, with gardens of mango & orange trees, offers tours into the Wahiba Sands & into Wadi Bani Khalid (2-day tour RO25 pp), including food & accommodation. If you have 4 or fewer people in your group then no notice is required. Starting at around 16.00, a tour guide fluent in Italian, English & Arabic will accompany you on your trip into the desert where you can watch the sunset & have dinner under a canopy. You return to the guesthouse for an overnight stay. The following morning, after b/fast, you take a trip into Wadi Bani Khalid to see the waterfalls. At 14.00 you return to the guesthouse for lunch. You can eat in the restaurant (good Indian curries) or have food delivered to your room. Many European visitors pass through this hotel. **$$**

WAHIBA SANDS رمال وهيبة The sands are about three hours' drive from Muscat. Bidiyah Castle (see page 229) is probably the best of the many entrances to the Wahiba Sands, which are Oman's mini-version of the Rub' al Khali (the Empty Quarter – the largest desert expanse in the Middle East). The Wahiba is a true rolling-sand desert measuring 180km from north to south, 80km from east to west, and with dunes 100–150m high. Bedouin camps can be found along trails and tracks in the Wahiba. The petrol station on the main road to Sur is the last place to fill up if you are intending a full crossing of the sands, which almost certainly requires an overnight camp. Any mechanic at one of the plentiful auto tyre-repair shops will take some of the air out of your tyres to a recommended level for the desert terrain.

The most spectacular of the dunes are along the northern end of the Wahiba, and they progressively flatten out as you get closer to the coast in the south. The dunes flow in corridors north to south, making orientation relatively simple as long as you continue to drive in straight lines. An east–west crossing is very tricky, and there are almost no tracks in that direction.

If you want a less gruelling sensation of the Wahiba, there are other options. One is to drive 7km further east from Bidiyah Castle to Al Huwayah, which is a large oasis on the very edge of the Wahiba with extensive date and banana plantations. The high dunes completely encircle the oasis, giving a real sense of the encroaching desert. There is a *falaj* and a narrow one-way road running through the plantation and you can picnic in the shade here, watching the awesome dunes pressing in, or camp just outside the plantation on the very edge of the desert.

In the high summer months from June to September the Wahiba Bedouin families come to the oasis, complete with livestock, and live in the *barasti* huts on the edge of the town, harvesting their dates. A gravel road leaves from here for 24km into the desert before becoming a sand track.

Along the eastern edge of the Wahiba are extensive woodlands of prosopis (*ghaf*) and acacia (which have been shown to live on dew), with many Bedouin shanty towns scattered among them. The best way to reach this part of the Wahiba, quite different in character from the high dunes, is to take the tarmac road to Al Ashkhara on the coast, where you can fill up with petrol at the Shell station. Fork right in the village; soon after, the tarmac stops and becomes a graded track. This track leads all the way to Khuwaymah, 78km away on the coast. The woodlands can be reached by turning right, almost back on yourself, after 61km by a makeshift petrol stop, thereby completing a loop as the woodland track emerges on to tarmac by Bilad Bani Bu Ali. There is a shipwreck on the beach 15km from the start of the track, but the sand all round is too soft for easy driving.

The easiest and safest option with the Wahiba is to set up an organised trip through an experienced company like Desert Discovery Tours (see page 220 for contact details). Both use knowledgeable guides, so that the navigation and logistics responsibility fall to someone else. Alternatively, you can contact a desert camp direct. For location of listings see map, page 220.

Where to stay

Å Desert Nights Camp (24 double tents, 2 family tents) m 92 818388, 99 744266; can be reserved on www.booking.com. The most luxurious of the desert camps, very stylish & exquisitely designed. The Two Dunes Restaurant offers AC indoor dining or outdoor under the

OMANI DOORS

In Islamic architecture the door or gateway to a building is often the most elaborately decorated feature. All the effort is concentrated on the façade of the door; from the inside it is often quite plain. Oman does not have the right kind of indigenous tree for carving, so the wood was usually imported teak or rosewood from India or sometimes from Zanzibar. Omani carpenters then carved their motifs, often the traditional floral patterns of roses, Oman's favourite flower. These days, alas, there are few Omani carpenters left and most wood is carved by Indians imitating local designs. Omani doors have become popular with expatriates and tourists who like to turn them into coffee tables. To tell the difference between an old door and a new one there are two things to look for: colour and texture. Old rosewood or teak (200 years old) is dark with a deep redness to it. Young wood looks more orange. Some dealers stain the doors darker to disguise their age, but this masks the grain of the wood. Newly carved doors also have a sharp feel to their carving and edges, while old doors will have gained the smoother finish that comes from wear and exposure. Today in new houses, metal doors, often brightly coloured reflecting the east African link, are increasingly replacing the old carved doors.

The sands were the subject of an expedition by the Royal Geographical Society in 1986, the results of which aroused international scientific interest. The project director wrote:

No body of sand in the world contains such a full range of study terrains, nor has so much to offer desert scientists urgently trying to piece together the complex jigsaw of arid zone areas. Its isolation and size lend itself to field research simply because it can be studied as a complete unit. It can be circumnavigated by Land Rover in three days.

The 35 scientists involved discovered 150 species of plant, 200 species of mammals, birds, reptiles and amphibians, and 16,000 invertebrate specimens.

If you are interested in learning more, there are two titles you might wish to track down. The first is *The Scientific Results of the Royal Geographical Society Oman Wahiba Sands Project 1985–1987*; the second, N Winser's *The Sea of Sands and Mists: Story of the Royal Geographical Society Oman Wahiba Sands Project* (see page 68).

stars. Oasis Bar fully licensed. Excursions can be organised to Wadi Beni Khalid, a local souk or local Bedouin house, trekking, sandboarding or camel safaris. **$$$$**

🏠 **Al Areesh Desert Camp** (43 tents) ✆24 493232, 99 317107; www.desertdiscovery. com. This is another camp run by Desert Discovery Tours & located a few kilometres south of Al Mudayrib (which is on the inland Muscat–Sur road). The tent bungalows are covered with palm fronds in the traditional Bedu style, equipped with electric lighting & bedding. Showers, hand basins & flush toilets are also available on site. Guests can also choose to sleep on raised platforms out in the open. There is a reception/ entertainment area with cushions & carpets, where you are offered Omani dates & Arabic coffee. The camp has shower & toilet facilities. You can experience dune driving (with experienced Bedu drivers), sand skiing, camel rides or a visit to local Bedu homes. There is an evening campfire & entertainment from traditional musicians, dancers & singers. Some reports have said it feels a bit over-commercialised. *RO25/20 pp, with/without en-suite toilet, inc dinner, B&B. Short camel ride RO3 pp; long ride (2–3hrs) RO12 pp. Visit to Bedouin settlement or short dune-bashing (1hr) RO7 pp if Desert Discovery vehicles used, RO2 pp in own vehicle. Long desert trip (3–4hrs) RO25 per vehicle in DD vehicle, RO15 per vehicle in own vehicle.* **$$$**

🏠 **Golden Sands Camp** (20 en-suite chalets & large furnished Bedouin tents) ✆99 445092. The Golden Sands office is at Al Wasil. This is where you park to join a vehicle to transport you to camp. It offers a great place inside the Wahiba Desert. The dining & entertainment area is called The Oasis & there is even a small shop for essential items. Quad bikes can be hired, there is a children's adventure playground & beach volleyball, soccer, archery & golf are all available. Or you can 'star gaze' in a tent away from the camp, or take a camel ride. **$$$**

🏠 **Al-Raha Tourism Camp** (77 tents, 15 of them luxury) 20km off the road; www. alrahaoman.com. Large-scale desert experience, with central dining tent holding up to 200 people. It offers the full range of desert activities including sand-boarding, dune-bashing, quad-biking, camel riding, archery & shooting. It even boasts its own in-house dune. **$$$**

🏠 **Al Sharqiya Sands Hotel** (24 rooms) PO Box 585, PC 413, Ibra; ✆99 205112, 205113; www.sharqiyasands.com. A good hotel about halfway between Muscat & Sur (at 180km) on the inland route, & a welcome find after a monotonous drive with only rubbly desert plain to look at. The rooms are of a good standard & pleasant décor, positioned around a garden courtyard area & swimming pool. It is peaceful & serene here & a major plus factor is that you can buy a cold beer (& there are not many places in the Sharqiya where you can). There is a licensed restaurant & a separate pub. Members of staff here are pleasant, professional & assisting. It advertises itself as 'an oasis by the desert' & it truly is. However, the hotel does not arrange desert tours. Tours should therefore be organised in advance through tour operators in Muscat (see pages 76–8) to avoid disappointment. It is a good place to stop off at either for refreshments or an overnight stay if you plan to tour the Sharqiya, the sands, or take a trip south to Masirah Island. Rooms are available on a B&B, HB or FB basis. **$$**

🏠 **Nomadic Desert Camp** ✆ 99 336273; e info@nomadicdesertcamp.com; www.

nomadicdesertcamp.com. A more intimate experience of the desert, run by a Bedouin family. There is a handful of *barasti* huts with shared bathrooms, but all is clean & simple. FB including a camel ride & transport is RO40 pp. **$$**

🏠 **1000 Nights Camp** ✆ 99 448158; e info@1000nightscamp.com; www.1000nightscamp.com. An impressive set-up that even runs to a conference centre, this camp offers 'sheikh' tents & 'Arabic' tents, a small swimming pool, free Wi-Fi, with a proper restaurant & terrace. An extensive range of activities are on offer, from free sandboarding to private dune dining. **$$$**

WADI BANI KHALID وادى بنى خالد Continuing from Al Mintirib on the main Sur road you see a sign pointing left (after 15km) towards the mountains for Wadi Bani Khalid. The graded track leads over the sandy plain for 24km before reaching the start of the wadi and its numerous villages. As one of the wettest wadis in Oman, the area is lush and heavily populated – a real oasis. One of its specialities, found only here, is the red-skinned banana, which you can buy in the local shops. The end village is Miqil, from where a path leads along the wadi floor for about half an hour's walk to the entrance of the **Moqal Cave**, accessible without special gear, but with a very narrow entrance only 1m high, from which several passages lead off. A strong torch is essential and the climb to the cave becomes steep after the bridge and is difficult for younger children. See box on page 223 for a trek into the mountains.

Camping in the area and swimming in the wadi pools can be difficult because of the density of the local population, so show sensitivity to local custom by being discreet. The area round the pool has now been developed with a small car park and some shaded picnic huts. The journey to Sur for the villagers today is a two-hour drive, but before 1970 it was a gruelling seven-hour trek by donkey. For location of listings see map, page 220.

🏠 **Where to stay**

🏠 **Lyali Al Sharqiya Resthouse** (12 rooms) ✆ 25 584233. A simple place located at the entrance to Wadi Bani Khalid. **$**

Just 2km beyond the turn-off to Wadi Bani Khalid look out for some tracks to the right towards an outcrop of Wahiba dunes close to the road and easy to scale for a view or picnic stop.

At Al Kamil, 60km beyond Al Mintirib, the main tarmac road bends left towards Sur, and a secondary tarmac road continues straight on towards the coast at Al Ashkhara. The final approach to Sur (see page 240) from Al Kamil takes about 20–30 minutes and leads across a series of wadis.

AS SALEEL NATIONAL PARK حديقة السليل الوطنية This sanctuary is signposted from the main road that bends round to Sur just after Kamil – a red sign in Arabic with pictures of oryx. The park was proclaimed as a national park in 1997 and its aim is to protect and conserve the variety of wildlife in its natural habitat. It is a plain covered with acacia woodland, home to Arabian gazelles, the rare Gordon's wild cat, wolves, red fox and Egyptian vultures. Animals such as the Arabian oryx and sand gazelle are being gradually reintroduced. The park used to be a site of poaching, with unlimited access. This conservation project plans to educate as well as conduct environmental studies and research.

BILAD BANI BU HASSAN بلاد بنى بو حسن
Taking the road to Al Ashkhara (Route 35), you will meet the twin towns of Bilad Bani Bu Hassan and Bilad Bani Bu Ali (7km apart along the main road). They have a certain curiosity value for their forts and splendid fortified houses.

The first town, Bani Bu Hassan, has a neat four-towered renovated **fort** (⊕ 08.00–14.00 Sun–Thu) on the edge of the sands, signposted from the main road. One of the fortified houses in the old town, called Awlad Mushed, is 25m high with five storeys and was lived in until 1986.

JALAAN BANI BU ALI بلاد بنى بو علي
The town of Bani Bu Ali has an uneasy history of war. In the first quarter of the 19th century, the Bani Bu Ali tribe accepted the new Wahhabi creed (see box opposite), becoming a fundamentalist Muslim sect. They were the only tribe in Oman to do so.

When, in 1820, the Bani Bu Ali tribe renounced the rule of the sultan, matters escalated until the sultan called on the assistance of the British to carry out an attack. They did so, destroying the town of Bilad Bani Bu Ali in 1821. Prisoners who were not killed were shipped off to Bombay, but were shipped back again only two years later with large grants to rebuild their destroyed homes and *aflaj*. The Bani Bu Ali remain nominal Wahhabis and although some say they are unreceptive to Europeans, this does not appear to be true today. The BBC World Service arm was set up in a house in Bani Bu Ali as a temporary base while constructing the site at Asylah (from approximately 2000–02), and the lone Scottish employee, who oversaw the project, used to cycle daily through the village, to waves and greetings from the locals.

At the back of the village there is a tall 11th-century fort (often closed), which encloses a simple white mini-domed mosque in its courtyard, reminiscent of that at Al Badiyah in the emirate of Fujairah (United Arab Emirates). Restored in 1990, the mosque also has an ablution *falaj* running close by in the courtyard. Close to the fort is another very unusual small mosque with 52 domes, called Al Hamuda Mosque as both the fort and mosque were maintained by the Al Hamuda sheikhs. It is thought to date to the 11th century and was also renovated in 1990. The 52 domes have hidden ventilation for the mosque, making it surprisingly cool inside. With its courtyard and simple arches its style is almost Umayyad. A *falaj* channel runs through the courtyard for ritual ablutions before prayer. Inside it is said to be reminiscent of a miniature version of the Great Mosque at Kairouan in Tunisia, though it may not be possible to see inside as a non-Muslim. To reach the mosque turn left after the fort, then turn right at the first crossing. The mosque stands on the left of the road after about 400m. For location of listing see map, page 220.

⌂ Where to stay
⌂ **Al Dhabi Resthouse** (14 rooms) ☎ 25 553307. A simple place with basic accommodation, but the only option in town. There is a small restaurant next door. **$**

AL ASHKHARA الأشخرة
Al Ashkhara is a quiet, coastal fishing town where you can see traditional *dhows* (no longer in use) preserved on the beach as a reminder of its prestigious past. In addition, many fishing boats line the beach, these days made of

fibreglass. Al Ashkhara was the landing point for merchant ships from India, Yemen and Iran from the 11th century onwards. For location of listing see map, page 220.

Where to stay

Areen Youth Hostel 25 566266. This youth hostel is a good, clean, modern hotel at which to stay in the region. Quiet place with a good restaurant. Cash only. **$**

AS SEELAH السيلة Also spelt 'Asaylah', this is another quiet coastal fishing village. Close by is the relatively new BBC World Service relay station – the replacement for the closed site on Masirah Island.

ALONG THE COASTAL ROUTE FROM MUSCAT TO SUR

The most scenic route through the Sharqiya is the coastal road to Sur, which was a difficult dirt track requiring 4x4 till recently. Now it is a three-lane highway with toll booths from Quriyat to Sur. The journey from Muscat to Sur via this route (240km) takes about 2½ hours, though of course it will vary widely depending on the amount of stops you may wish to make – and you undoubtedly will. There is fabulous coastal scenery here, with mountains and gorges extending down to the sea, rock pools and good walks into the hills. The stretch of coastline is a series of rocky inlets reaching all the way down to Sur. Whole sections between Muscat and Quriyat where the road does not follow the coast are reachable by boat only, and some of the villages are still linked only by graded tracks.

In a couple of coves hidden from land between Muscat and Sidab are 19th-century Christian graves, including that of the first missionary, Bishop French, who came to Muscat aged 65 from Lahore, rather than settle for old age in England. He would go to the coffee houses and preach on street corners to whoever would listen. 'I cannot say,' he admitted, 'that I have met with many thoughtful and encouraging hearers or people who want Bibles and Testaments.' He died three months later of ill health.

The Muscat to Sur return drive is quite tiring if taken as a day trip, and you will miss out on a lot. However, if you are pushed for time, you could, with an early start around 08.00, set off through Quriyat, Dibab and Fins to have a picnic lunch in the Tiwi/Wadi Shab area, then complete the circuit by returning to Muscat on the

The Sharqiya   ALONG THE COASTAL ROUTE FROM MUSCAT TO SUR

8

THE WAHHABI CREED

The Wahhabi Creed is a puritanical reform movement begun by the conservative jurist Muhammad ibn Abd al Wahhab (1703–92). Having travelled round the Hejaz, Iraq and Syria, he returned home to Najd impressed with the idea that Islam had deviated widely from the orthodox practice as prescribed by the Prophet Muhammad and the Koran, so he determined to purge it and restore it to its primitive strictness. He and his followers were called Wahhabis by their opponents, and they zealously set out to rid Islam of its cult of saints, destroying many tombs, claiming they were idolatrous. Wahhabism rejects any innovations that occurred after the 3rd century of Islam, so making pilgrimages to special tombs, venerating trees, caves and such like, as well as making sacrificial offerings, were all banned. Arabia's history, from around 1750 to the present day, is largely centred on the history of the Wahhabis. Osama bin Laden is a Wahhabi, and though the doctrine is widespread in the Arabian Peninsula, especially Saudi Arabia, its influence is minor in the rest of the Middle East.

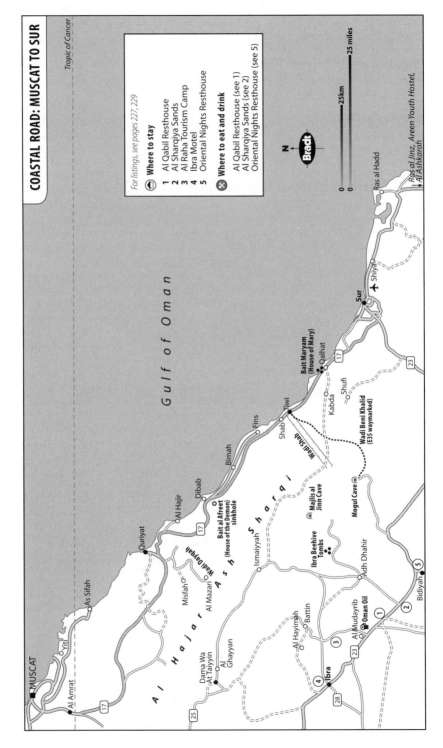

COASTAL ROAD: MUSCAT TO SUR

For listings, see pages 227, 229

Where to stay
1 Al Qabil Resthouse
2 Al Sharqiya Sands
3 Al Raha Tourism Camp
4 Ibra Motel
5 Oriental Nights Resthouse

Where to eat and drink
Al Qabil Resthouse (see 1)
Al Sharqiya Sands (see 2)
Oriental Nights Resthouse (see 5)

Tropic of Cancer

Gulf of Oman

MUSCAT
Al Amrat
Yiti
As Sifah
Quriyat
Al Hajir
Dibab
Bimah
Fins
Shab
Tiwi
Wadi Shab
Bait Maryam
(House of Mary)
Qalhat
Shufi
Kabda
Sur
Shiya
Ras al Hadd

Ras al Jinz, Areen Youth Hostel, Al Ashkarah

Bait al Afreet
(House of the Demon) sinkhole
Misfah
Al Mazari
Wadi Daygah

Al Hajar Ash Sharqi

Dama Wa
At Taiyiin
Al
Ghayyan
Battin
Al Hayimah
Ismaiyyah
Majlis al
Jinn Cave
Ibra Beehive
Tombs
Adh Dhahir
Wadi Beni Khalid
(E35 waymarked)
Mogul Cave

Ibra
Al Mudayrib
Oman Oil
Bidiyah

25km
25 miles

236

inland tarmac road (four hours' drive from Sur), arriving back in Muscat at about 20.00, having made a couple of further brief stops along the way; a good 12-hour stint. So, if you can, try to stay overnight in the area. Two or three nights here would be ideal. One night could be spent in Sur or Ras Al Hadd, the next at a turtle camp in Ras Al Jinz, and the final night in a desert camp in the Wahiba Sands. Each of these stays offers its own unique and memorable experience.

GETTING AROUND The starting point within Muscat is the Wadi Adai roundabout just before Ruwi. Follow signs to the right in the direction of Quriyat, Hatat and Watayah. This roundabout is also the place to pick up buses heading south to Quriyat and Sur.

WADI DAYQAH وادى ضيقة Wadi Dayqah is one of the most famous wadis in Oman, and links the Sharqiya with the Muscat governorate. Its name means 'narrow wadi', and is an old pack-animal route from the coast to the interior, still used as such until about 1980. It is the largest perennially flowing wadi in Oman, 14km long, with many deep pools. The head of the wadi, where it meets Wadi Tayin, is called Devil's Gap. The walls here are 1,700m high and the gap as narrow as 12m. The best scenery is this stretch to **Mazara**, which can be reached only on foot. There are spectacular cliffs and a fast-flowing river. The summit of the surrounding mountains reaches 1,885m here. Tour operators arrange trips to Devil's Gap: it is one of Oman's best canyon excursions.

Getting there Following the road to Quriyat from Muscat, and having dropped to sea level on the plain, look out for the Oman Oil station on the right (85km from Muscat, 9km before Quriyat). For the coastal road to Sur you will need to go straight on, but to reach Wadi Dayqah, this is the turn-off you must follow. It is signposted Hayl Al Ghaf, a village in Wadi Dayqah. After another 4km the tarmac road turns right to Misfah, a small mountain village with a fine *falaj* that crosses the wadi via an aqueduct. About 3km prior to reaching Misfah is a left fork – a graded road. Follow this graded road left for 5km, then left again for 1km following the sign to Al Hayl (8km). You will reach the wadi at a point where there are many lovely pools and shaded picnic spots among the rocks and trees. You can complete the loop from here by driving the remaining 7km up the wadi bed back to Hayl Al Ghaf.

Alternatively, if you have all day ahead of you and are in no rush, you could fork right at the previous junction to Mazara, to the dam from where the six-hour walk begins up the Dayqah Gorge inland through the Devil's Gap towards Wadi Tayin, with spectacular scenery and many pools.

To continue along the coast towards Sur, ignore the turn-off to Hayl Al Ghaf at the Oman Oil station and instead continue straight, taking the right-hand turn 5km later, 4km before Quriyat town. The road is tarmac and is signposted for Daghmar. At the next roundabout, 6.5km further on, take the right fork to Tiwi on the graded track. After a further 3km the track to the right enters the gorge of Wadi Dayqah and climbs up the hills for another 3km. Straight on at the mouth of the gorge would lead you to Daghmar on the coast, through which Wadi Dayqah flows; however, there is no coastal road between Daghmar and Dibab, and so you have no option but to head inland via the mouth of Wadi Dayqah. Around 8km after leaving the gorge you come to a junction at which the right takes you to the small fishing village of Dibab, 15km away. From here the road keeps to the coast for the remaining 90km to Sur.

For a scenic diversion, those with time can take the right turn at the previous junction, signposted Wadi al Arbiyeen, which leads for some 15km of steep track requiring low ratio 4x4 to Wadi Suwayh, reckoned as another of Oman's highly scenic wadis, with steep mountains, pools and lush vegetation.

DIBAB ضباب **AND THE SINKHOLE (HAWIYAT NAJM PARK)** The beaches around Dibab are particularly good for beachcombing, with unusual shells and birdlife. From the main highway the sinkhole is now labelled Hawiyat Najm Park. Follow the signs, and approximately 5km beyond the village you come to the park where trees and landscaping, with *barasti* shades, have been established to form a picnic site. Now surrounded by a 1m-high stone wall, the huge natural water sinkhole – 40m across and 20m deep – is known locally as Bait al Afreet ('House of the Demon'). The water is clear, green and slightly salty; there are tiny fish visible in the shallower part.

BIMAH AND UMQ بيما وعمق Ten kilometres beyond the sinkhole, after a drive along spectacular bays and coves rich in birdlife, you come to the village of Bimah. Bimah is unremarkable in itself, but 1km beyond the village is the start of the graded track (a dead end) that leads inland 10km to the village of Umq. This village is unusual for its mud houses built into the side of the mountain. The drive is scenically stunning and there is much wildlife in the area, including wolves, foxes and gazelles. From Umq there is a difficult six-hour climb up the 800m cliff face on to the Jebel Bani Jabir Plateau where the Ibra tombs are located (see page 227). The climb is not to be attempted without a guide.

FINS فنس **TO TIWI** طيوي From Bimah it is another 10km to Fins – the halfway point to Sur. The stretch of coastline from Fins to Tiwi has both long white-sand beaches and tiny gravel bays with rock pools. Litter can be a problem, especially on the popular sand beaches like Tiwi (known as White Beach, 6km beyond Fins). At weekends especially the beaches can become crowded.

SHAB AND TIWI شاب وطيوي These two settlements are both at the mouth of gorges which share their name. Shab comes first, and is approached by a road that has been cemented because of the steepness of the descent and ascent from/ to the cliffs.

If there is one wadi you must visit during your trip to Oman it is **Wadi Shab**. It is a place of outstanding natural beauty and peace. The wadi is not drivable, but there is a footbridge leading in at the start of the walk. A new road crossing Wadi Shab has been constructed recently. In order to get to the wadi, take the first exit signposted to Wadi Tiwi and Wadi Shab, then drive down to the hamlet at the end of the road where you can park in a kind of open plaza. Walk from here down to the river bed and across to the other side along the top of a high and wide levy. There'll be a small boat waiting here, which you will take you across the river to the other side. The 50–60-minute walk into the wadi is beautiful, leading through the steep ravine and past pools, waterfalls and lush plantations. There are several villages higher up, accessible only on foot. The *pièce de résistance* is the mountain pool at the end of the walk, deep in the mouth of the gorge. Here you can swim through a tight gap and narrow tunnel, which opens up into a cavernous mountain pool area. At Tiwi, which almost runs into Shab village, the wadi gorge is wider and drivable for 10km or so before you come to a footpath leading on to the nine villages of the wadi. At the last roundabout through Tiwi, having climbed the steep hill into the

Marco Polo wrote:

> This city has a very good port, much frequented by merchant ships from India, and they find a ready market here for their wares, since it is a centre from which spices and other goods are carried to various inland cities and towns. Many fine war horses are exported from here to India, to the great gain of the merchants.

Ibn Battuta, the Moroccan traveller, is said to have visited Qalhat in about 1330. He wrote:

> The city of Qalhat is on the coast. It has good markets, and one of the most beautiful mosques in the world. The walls of the mosque are covered with blue ceramic tiles. It stands on a hill beside the harbour. This mosque was built by an important woman named Bibi Maryam. The people here are merchants, and they bring many goods from India. When a ship arrives the people are very happy.

village and wound through the houses, you turn right on to a narrow track that leads to the wadi. The vegetation here, including banana, mango and fig, is very lush and the water flows all year round.

As you begin the drive from Tiwi towards Qalhat and Sur, you will notice black signs marking archaeological sites, which have revealed a large settlement.

QALHAT قلهات From Sur, Qalhat used to be an hour by Land Rover, then an hour on foot when the terrain became impassable, but it can now be reached quickly on the motorway from Tiwi.

It is hard to see today why Qalhat was chosen as the site of such an important port, when Sur, just 20km down the coast, seems to have such a superior natural location, with an obvious route to the interior. But until the end of the 14th century, Qalhat had a *falaj* system leading down the wadi from the hills, with many wells to supplement it. And while the *khor* (lagoon) today is just a stagnant tongue of water by the modern village, it was, centuries ago, a deep anchorage reaching right up to the north of the wadi. For the route to the interior, merchants must have used the donkey path through Wadi Hilm, which leads eventually to Wadi Bani Khalid.

Qalhat was affected by two disastrous events. First, an earthquake destroyed many of the city's fine buildings at the end of the 14th century. Then in 1507, the Portuguese arrived in Oman and ransacked Quriyat and Muscat. The following year they attacked Qalhat, killing many of the local population and burning all the ships and buildings. Qalhat was completely devastated and the survivors fled the city. The earthquake of the 14th century had put an end to the *falaj* and the harbour, and the city never recovered.

Today it is difficult to picture the great city of Qalhat. **Bait Maryam** (the House of Mary) is the only major building to survive and is in remarkably good condition, especially considering the devastation of the buildings surrounding it, most of which appear at first glance to be little more than rubble. Inside there is a brown-grey resin wax built up from the candles over the years of offerings by visitors. It was originally said to have been covered in glazed tiles. The site merits at

8

least an hour's stop. Take the trouble to explore some of the rooms, walking on little paths towards the sea. You will be rewarded by the discovery of much interesting pottery, butterflies and plantlife, to say nothing of the atmosphere of the destroyed rubble town. After a 20-minute stroll you will reach the sea, where a small harbour is still recognisable. The semicircular arched tunnels are cisterns built by the princes of Hormuz in the 13th century.

Getting there The new highway has meant that the road now bypasses the site, which lies on the sea-side a little lower down the hill. To reach it you therefore have to take the Qalhat exit and follow the road down through the village to reach the wadi bed. From here you have to leave your car and walk across the wadi into the roped-off site.

SUR صور

Sur is a quiet coastal town that played a central role in overseas trade with east Africa. It occupies a position on a large lagoon, which is still the port today.

Along with Sohar, it has been said that Sur was the home of the legendary sailor Sindbad. The town shares its name with the coastal port of Sur in Lebanon, known to Westerners as Tyre, and one attractive theory, based on Herodotus's account that the Phoenicians came from the Gulf area, is that the Phoenicians originally hailed from here, then moved on to Lebanon, reusing the same name as their home town.

Archaeological evidence to prove this theory is lacking, but certainly the rocky spit by Sur creek bears a resemblance to that of Tyre, and the origins of the Phoenicians are still disputed by experts. The reputation of the inhabitants to this day is that they are difficult and independent-minded.

The coastal town itself never had fresh water, but Bilad Sur, the large village amid the date palms a few kilometres inland, supplied all the necessary water from its wells, and water is still piped in today from the same source.

When Zanzibar and Oman split into two separate sultanates in 1861, Sur had over 100 ocean-going *dhows* in its trading fleet. Trade declined after the split, hastened by the arrival in the Gulf of the British India Steamer Navigation Company, which also took trade away from Sur. Shipbuilding gradually declined as Sur became a less prosperous port.

The modern town of Sur today has a sprawl that extends many kilometres inland and it is difficult to establish when you have reached the centre of town. The Sur Beach Hotel is signposted off to the left from one of the first roundabouts (see opposite). Sur is renowned for its horses, hence the model horse statues that flank the road. The passion for pure Arab thoroughbreds survives here in the form of a few trainers who excel in 'mastering' their horses. One, a resident of Bilad Bani Bu Hassan, trains 23 horses and has instilled his passion into his 22 children; the youngest son when aged nine could stand on a galloping horse.

If you follow the main tarmac road into the centre of town, this eventually does a big loop round the lagoon, on the edge of which are the boatyards, still in operation on a reduced scale and easily visited. You can park outside and wander in through any of the gates. The keels and hulls are made from teak imported from India, while the ribs are made from local acacia wood. No plans are ever used. The boats are built by eye, from the outside in, not the Western convention of inside out with ribs first.

Further on from the boatyards, the road loops round to pass the restored *dhow*, *Fatah al Khair*, thought to be 75 years old, and one of the last ocean-going vessels

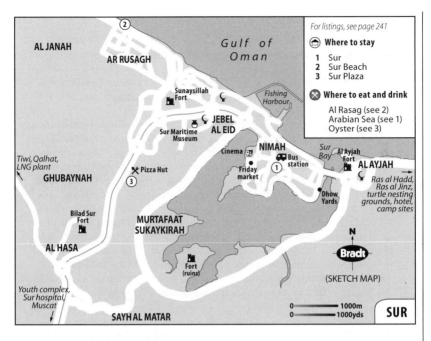

For listings, see page 241

Where to stay
1 Sur
2 Sur Beach
3 Sur Plaza

Where to eat and drink
Al Rasag (see 2)
Arabian Sea (see 1)
Oyster (see 3)

AL JANAH

AR RUSAGH

Gulf of Oman

Sunaysillah Fort

Fishing Harbour

JEBEL AL EID

Sur Maritime Museum

Tiwi, Qalhat, LNG plant

GHUBAYNAH

Cinema

NIMAH

Bus station

Sur Bay

Al Ayjah Fort

AL AYJAH

Pizza Hut

Friday market

Ras al Hadd, Ras al Jinz, turtle nesting grounds, hotel, camp sites

Dhow Yards

Bilad Sur Fort

MURTAFAAT SUKAYKIRAH

AL HASA

Fort (ruins)

N

Bradt

(SKETCH MAP)

Youth complex, Sur hospital, Muscat

SAYH AL MATAR

0 — 1000m
0 — 1000yds

SUR

built in Sur. The boat was found in Yemen and a local retired captain was delegated to buy it with money raised from Sur inhabitants to keep it here as a symbol of the town's maritime heritage. It weighs about 300 tonnes and is over 20m long. At low tide here the lagoon water disappears and the *dhows* are beached on an expanse of wet mud.

From Sur there is a tarmac road to Ras Al Hadd and Ras Al Jinz.

GETTING THERE AND AROUND The bus station in Sur is right in the centre of town close to the souk and the Sur Hotel. Buses run from here twice a day to Muscat, leaving at 06.00 and 14.30, taking the inland route and costing around RO4.5. Microbuses also run early in the morning for RO3.5. The Sur Hotel can give you the exact times, as they can change. At present all public transport uses the inland route as this is where most local people want to travel to, but this may change in future. A taxi ride anywhere in Sur should cost around 200bzs.

If you are in your own transport, follow signs for the LNG plant to get on to the new coast road to Muscat. If you follow the Muscat signs you will find yourself on the inland route instead. For location of listings see map above.

WHERE TO STAY

Sur Beach Hotel (118 rooms) PO Box 400, PC 411; ⬩25 542031; e surbhtl@omantel.net.om; www.sigoh.com.om. *En route* to the beaches of Ras Al Hadd. Al Rasag is the restaurant serving international cuisine, including excellent curries, & Al Bahar is the coffee shop. Sur Bar has live music. There is a swimming pool. Accepts credit cards. B/fast included. **$$$**

Sur Plaza Hotel (102 rooms) PO Box 908, PC 411; ⬩25 543777; e reservationsur@ omanhotels.com ; www.omanhotels.com/surplaza. Part of a chain of hotels that includes Al Falaj Hotel & Ruwi Hotel in Muscat & Al Wadi Hotel in Sohar. It is a large hotel, set inland, with a licensed restaurant (Oyster Restaurant) & 2 bars, both with live entertainment. Captain's Bar has easy-listening music played by the resident duo; & the Sambuq &

Sur has long been famous for *dhow* building and is still the centre for *dhow* and *sambuk* (fishing boat) building in Oman today. A large *dhow* (200 tonnes) will take five to six months to build, and only one or two are built in a year. In the 19th century some eight *dhows* a year were built and launched. The workers today are all Indian.

Many natives of Sur – some 3,000 in the early 1960s – had worked abroad in India, east Africa and the rest of the Arabian Gulf, reflecting a marked contrast to the inwardness of the natives of the interior. Among their particular interests abroad were the slave trade and arms trafficking – perfectly normal forms of trade at that stage and not tainted or associated with any moral wrong locally. The British attempts to eliminate these trades were always met with a certain incomprehension, and Sur was viewed with great disdain by Britain for its chosen activities. Even after the sultan in Muscat signed anti-slavery treaties with the British, implementing them in Sur was virtually impossible; the established routes inland to Saudi Arabia did not involve Muscat. The first anti-slave trade treaty was signed with the British in 1822, when it was recorded that some 4,000 slaves were imported into Sur. Later, the British began to control shipping more strictly.

Al Shabaka Bar have Arabic/Indian bands. There is a Budget Rent-a-Car desk here. **$$$**

🏠 **Sur Hotel** (25 rooms) Off Souk St; 📞 25 540090. Right in the middle of town close to the new souk area, this place is very good value with its clean rooms. It is also close to the bus station. The trade-off is the noise & urban setting. Meals including b/fast are offered by the ground floor restaurant, called the Arabian Sea, & the management can also arrange tours for turtle watching or even into some of the nearby mountain wadis such as Tiwi & Wadi Bani Khalid. **$**

✖ **WHERE TO EAT** Your best option for eating is within either of the two mid-range Sur hotels or at the Arabian Sea Restaurant on the ground floor of the cheaper Sur Hotel, a lively place popular with locals serving good kebabs and even vegetarian bean dishes. Alternatively, local coffee shops are easy to find.

OTHER PRACTICALITIES There are several cash machines in Sur Town.

WHAT TO SEE
Sur Maritime History Museum (📞 24 541466 ⏱ 09.00–16.00 Sat–Thu; free) Situated opposite Sunaysillah Fort, a white building identified by the ship's wheel on the wall. It has displays showing the shipbuilding tradition with several models of *dhows* and everything related to Oman's sea trade and maritime history.

Bilad Sur Fort (⏱ 08.30–14.30 Sun–Thu; 500bzs) Set well inland just left of Main Street, it is recognisable by its unusually shaped tower. The location was chosen to protect the town against raiding tribes from the interior and it was originally one of five forts that guarded the town along with numerous watchtowers. It is surrounded by lush groves of date palms.

Sunaysillah Fort (⏱ 08.30–1430 Sun–Thu; 500bzs) Standing on a mound much closer to the sea and harbour, this 300-year-old fort is a simple design with an archetypal square plan and round towers.

Shipbuilding yards and the Fatah Al Khair *dhow* (see page 240 and opposite). Always open.

AL AYJAH العيجة

There are very few elegant 18th-century merchants' houses in Sur today and you will get a better picture of old prosperous merchant housing in Al Ayjah, a small traditional fishing village. A new suspension bridge takes you across the bay, or else the original road still loops right round from Sur, skirting the edge of the lagoon past mangrove swamps to reach Al Ayjah – both routes make the ferry trips across the narrow *khor* unnecessary. The citizens of Al Ayjah, who belong to the Bani Bu Ali tribe, used to relish this separation, and in the early 20th century set up their own customs post and flag independent of the customs post in Sur. It then took the sultan two years to get the flag down and back over to the Sur side, even enlisting the help of the British Resident in the Gulf.

Late afternoon and early evening are the best times to see Al Ayjah, when the sun sets over the lagoon and casts a reddish-purple tinge over the water. The new lighthouse overlooks the bay where the road ends, and the town's youth play football on the sands below. The road winds into the town, passing the **old Al Hamoda Fort** (☉ *08.30–14.30 Sat–Thu; 500bzs*), and you can simply follow the tarmac road slowly through the old houses and park somewhere near the lighthouse.

Take the time to stroll about among the houses, especially those that face directly out to sea away from the sheltered lagoon. Some of these are imaginatively decorated with maritime memorabilia like old anchors and nets.

GETTING THERE You can still catch the small ferry used by local people that runs from the jetty on the Sur corniche near the *dhow* yards. It takes five minutes and costs 50bzs. Alternatively, you can drive round the lagoon or use the new suspension bridge.

RAS AL HADD رأس الحد

Ras Al Hadd is Arabic for 'headland'. Scenically unprepossessing, this is the point where the turbulent Indian Ocean meets the calmer Gulf of Oman; it is not a

---

TURTLE-WATCHING RULES

Some visitors demonstrate an extraordinary lack of sensitivity when attending this natural spectacle, determined to get good photos at any cost and even posing sitting on the turtles. The turtles are easily disturbed and if they feel intruded upon, will simply head back into the sea. To enjoy the process and to allow others to enjoy it too, just follow a few guidelines.

* Do not make any noise or disturb their peace.
* Do not use flash photography, as the lights unsettle the nesting turtles.
* Do not touch the turtles or their eggs.
* Do not stay overnight on the beach.
* Do not leave any litter.

dramatic promontory but a flat sandy spit at the end of a monotonous plain, and a lot of litter tends to get washed up here, making the beaches rather unattractive.

An RAF staging post was built here in World War II and the remains of the airstrip are still in evidence. Nearby was a collection of *barasti* huts where simple fishermen lived, with a **fort** above them. This fort, now painted white, still stands, worth visiting for the views from the towers (⊕ *08.30–14.30 Sun–Thu; 500bzs*).

The beaches of Ras Al Hadd and Ras Al Jinz provide nesting grounds for an estimated 20,000 turtles each year that migrate from as far as the Red Sea and the East African coast. Turtles can be seen virtually year round, but September to November is the best time for observing them. Tourists are only allowed access to Ras Al Jinz. For location of listings see map, adjacent.

GETTING THERE There is no public transport to either Ras Al Hadd or Ras Al Jinz. A saloon car can complete the drive from Sur in an hour, as the roads are now tarmacked.

WHERE TO STAY

Ras Al Hadd Beach Hotel (60 rooms) PO Box 400, PC 411, Sur; m 99 376989; e surbhtl@ omantel.om; www.surhotelsoman.com. This is one of 6 hotels in the Sur International Hotels Group, with welcoming staff who will greet you with dates & coffee in the tradition of Omani hospitality. The rooms are good sizes & decorated pleasantly. There is a licensed restaurant & separate bar. Turtle tours to Ras Al Jinz turtle reserve can be arranged by the hotel & they will provide you with a visitor's permit. It is always best to confirm in advance to avoid any disappointment, although you might be lucky to turn up & arrange something for the same day. The usual pattern is to leave the hotel at 21.00 for a short drive along to the camp at Ras Al Jinz for a 2hr round trip. A 4x4 is not necessary. Accepts credit cards. B/fast included. **$$$**

Turtle Beach Resort (50 beach cottages) PO Box 303, PC 411, Sur; ☎ 25 540068; reservations,

RAS AL HADD & RAS AL JINZ

(SKETCH MAP)
Scale approximate

Gulf of Oman

Ras Al Hadd

③ ①

Khawr al Hajar

ARABIAN SEA

Eastern Hajar Mountains

Sur

Eastern Hajar Mountains

②
Turtle Beach
Nature Reserve

N

Bradt

0 —— 3km
0 —— 2 miles

Asylah ↓

For listings, see pages 244–5

⊖ **Where to stay**

1 Ras Al Hadd Beach
2 Ras Al Jinz Turtle Reserve
3 Turtle Beach Resort

✖ **Where to eat and drink**

Al Ghanga (see 3)
Ras Al Hadd Beach (see 1)
Sambuk (see 2)
Turtle Beach Resort (see 3)

25 543400; e info@tbroman.com; www.tbroman. com. This resort is located 8km from Ras Al Hadd town. The simply-furnished beach huts occupy a spot on the private beach, & there is a *dhow*-shaped restaurant (resembling its 16th-century predecessor) & bar (Al Ghanga) on the beach serving Asian & continental food. *Dhow* & speedboat trips can be arranged for dolphin watching. There is a lagoon for snorkelling, fishing & swimming. Khor al Grama Island (a peaceful location) is near to the resort. The resort works closely with tour operators such as Mark Tours & Bahwan Travel Agencies. The habitat for turtles is close to the resort. Offers RO25 boat rides to see turtles in the evening. **$$$**

RAS AL JINZ رأس الجنيز

Ras Al Jinz (also spelt Junaiz or Junayz) is about 17km southeast of Ras Al Hadd. The Turtle Beach Nature Reserve has been established here, complete with a campsite that provides simple *barasti* huts, water, toilet blocks and rubbish bins. It is staffed by guides who escort you to the nesting beach at dusk to watch the large female turtles come ashore and lay their eggs. The evening tour (RO5 per person) begins about an hour after dark, and the guide drives on to the beach with no headlights to find the best places, then summons you over. Alternatively, you can go just before dawn and watch the eggs hatching and the baby turtles scurrying to the sea before the hungry gulls or crabs have a chance to eat them. Many do not make it. The wardens have to keep records of the numbers nesting each night but in the morning for the hatching process there is no need to record anything, which is why you may go unescorted. No torch or camera is allowed. This early morning experience can often be more enjoyable than the evening before, as you can avoid the crowds.

A new research centre has been built by the Ministry of Tourism and there is a museum (*www.rasaljinz-turtlereserve.com*) designed to showcase both the turtles and the unique marine ecology of the eastern coast of Sharqiya region. The modern complex houses an indoor turtle pond, a café, information desk, ticketing counter and study rooms. The exhibits provide visitors with comprehensive insights into the ecosystems that sustain turtles, charting the complete life-cycle stages of the turtle from hatchling, to nesting, to migration. In addition, antiquities uncovered during ongoing excavation work in the area are preserved in the museum.

Italian and French archaeological teams were at work at a site behind the turtle beach camp here in 1998. A brick building divided into several elongated chambers was found, together with some burial sites. Items included a necklace and seals dating back to the Egyptian civilisations, c2200BC. The seals have letters in an unknown language but the finds indicate trading links between Egypt and Oman at that time. For location of listings see map, opposite.

WHERE TO STAY

Ras Al Jinz Turtle Reserve (31 rooms) m 96 550606; www.rasaljinz-turtlereserve.com. Right on the Ras Al Jinz beach itself, this swish & pricey place has replaced the old Al Jinz Turtle Beach Camp. As well as its elegant Caraspace rooms & Sambuk restaurant there is also the scientific & visitors' centre with excellent new natural history exhibits & explanations, as well as a gift shop selling traditional local handicrafts & souvenirs. The whole character of the site has now gone very upmarket. **$$$$**

MASIRAH ISLAND جزيرة مصيرة

Masirah is Oman's largest island, about 70km long, sitting 20km off the mainland, just south of the Wahiba. It is accessed by a ferry from Shannah (Ras an Najdah) on the mainland, which transports both vehicles and foot passengers. The ferry trip takes an hour and costs RO12. There are usually four trips each day, although these are dependent on the tides.

Masirah was said to have been visited by Alexander the Great, who referred to it as 'Serepsis'. The main occupation of the locals on the island today is weaving and making fishing nets and the population is about 6,000.

The island remains largely untouched, though the first luxury hotel is now open, but with many isolated beaches it still makes a fantastic getaway destination. Camping here is excellent if you come fully equipped.

The eastern side of the island is good for surfing and windsurfing; 4–6ft waves are the norm, and surfing is particularly good in the *khareef* (June–September). Camping is good on the beaches and there are small shops from which to buy your essentials. Turtles come to nest here.

There was an RAF base here that played a central role in both the Jebel War of the late 1950s and the Dhofar War of the 1960s and 1970s. The BBC World Service had a relay station here – the British Eastern Relay Station (BERS) – which no longer exists. Its modern replacement has been constructed and is fully operational at As Seelah, close to Al Ashkhara (see page 234).

A book by Colin Richardson called *Masirah: Tales from a Desert Island* reports the history of the island, enlivening it for the visitor (see page 299, for more details).

GETTING THERE To get to the island you need to take a 1½-hour ferry trip from the ferry station at Shannah, in Ras an Najdah. It costs RO12 for a vehicle and its passengers to be ferried. There are no fixed timings, as the journey is dependent upon the tide – it cannot get off the ground in low tide. You simply need to turn up and queue at the ferry stop.

GETTING AROUND There are no taxis in Masirah and no car-hire firms. You will need to bring your own transport. For location of listings see map, page 220.

⌂ WHERE TO STAY

⌂ **Masirah Island Resort** (21 rooms, including a few chalets) PO Box 135, PC414, Masirah Island; ☏ 25 504274; e reservations@masiraislandresort. com; www.masiraislandresort.com. Run by Swiss Belhotel, this new luxury hotel is on the northeast of the island, a five-minute drive from the ferry landing point. Set on a beautiful beach it offers a pool, tennis courts & a fitness centre, as well as an international buffet restaurant & a bar. It hosts the Masirah Wildlife Museum with a vast collection of exotic shells & details about Masirah's 328 bird species & 4 sea turtle species. **$$$$**

⌂ **Danat Al-Khaleej Hotel** (25 rooms) ☏ 25 504533; e info@danat-hotel.com; www. danat-hotel.com. 2km from the ferry terminal, this is a budget option on the outskirts of Hilf, Masirah's only town, the best place to use as a base if you don't want to camp but still want to enjoy the beaches. It offers very good value, with AC, free Wi-Fi, a multi-cuisine restaurant & a beach-side coffee shop. It also gives free island tours, free turtle trips, & will organise boat trips, car hire & camping. **$$**

9

Al Wusta الوسطى

Telephone code: 23

A man without cunning is like an empty matchbox.

The Arabic name Al Wusta means the 'central area' and that accurately describes this chunk of central Oman which is neither north nor south. It is Oman's least-populated province – most people simply drive through at speed on the long, central, inland road from Muscat to Salalah, longing for a sight of something other than gravel and featureless desert. In fact, the only area of interest is the coast, undoubtedly Oman's most dramatic and unspoilt, on account of its sheer inaccessibility. The sights of the Wusta region are all natural; there are no forts or buildings of historic significance. There are no tarmac roads beyond the main through road, only graded tracks, and many of them difficult. The pace of travel here is correspondingly slow with limited petrol, often sold from oil drums in the villages. Along with the Dhahirah, this region is home to Oman's oil installations.

To do justice to this part of Oman you are probably looking at a week of self-sufficient **camping**, definitely in the cooler winter months as there is no shade to be found at all – there is no vegetation to speak of. Birdlife, however, especially gulls and flamingos, exists in abundance along the coast – to date 130 different species of bird have been recorded. The beaches are rich in shells, and dolphins and turtles are also frequently spotted. A few Arabian gazelle and oryx still roam freely in the gravel desert of the Jiddat Al Harasis, reintroduced by the sultan in 1974, having been hunted to near extinction (see box, page 250). Perfectly adapted to the desert, the oryx can go without water for 22 months as long as it has plants to graze on with high water content. The region is also home to Nubian ibex, caracal, lynx and desert rabbits.

The beaches of Ras Madrakah are dramatic, with stretches of white sand interspersed with black volcanic rocks and cliffs. Several shipwrecks still stand, rusting quietly on the beaches where they were washed up. Near Qahal (or Kahil) are the unique Pink Lagoons caused by algae, and at Shuwaymiyah is a box canyon quite unlike any other in Oman, with sheer white cliffs.

GETTING THERE

This region is accessed via the long Muscat to Salalah road.

⌂ WHERE TO STAY AND EAT

On the drive from Muscat to Salalah there are several simple resthouses, with basic restaurants which are unlicensed. In the order that you meet them on the drive from Muscat, these are Al Ghaba (Dakhiliyah, page 208), Haima (Al Wusta), Al Wusta, Al Ghaftain (Al Wusta), Qitbit (Dhofar) and Thumrayt (Dhofar, both

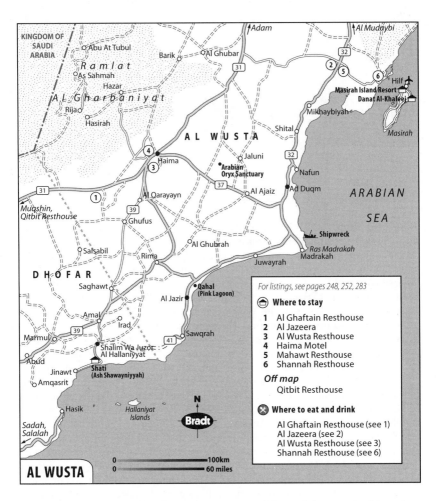

Map labels (within image):

KINGDOM OF SAUDI ARABIA

Adam
Al Mudaybi

Abu At Tubul
Barik
Al Ghubar

Ramlat
As Sahmah

Hilf
Masirah Island Resort
Danat Al-Khaleej

Hazar

Al Gharbaniyat

Rijad

Mikhaybiyah

Hasirah

Shital

Masirah

AL WUSTA

Jaluni

4
Haima
3
Arabian Oryx Sanctuary

Nafun

31

Al Qarayayn
39

37
Al Ajaiz
Ad Duqm

ARABIAN

1

Muqshin,
Qitbit Resthouse

Ghufus

SEA

Salsabil
Rima

Al Ghubrah

Shipwreck

Ras Madrakah
Madrakah

Juwayrah

DHOFAR

Saghawt

Qahal
(Pink Lagoon)

For listings, see pages 248, 252, 283

Amal

Al Jazir

Where to stay

Marmul

Irad

39

Sawqrah

41

1 Al Ghaftain Resthouse
2 Al Jazeera
3 Al Wusta Resthouse
4 Haima Motel
5 Mahawt Resthouse
6 Shannah Resthouse

Abud

Shalim Wa Juzor
Al Hallaniyyat

Jinawt
Amqasrit

Shati
(Ash Shawayniyyah)

Off map
Qitbit Resthouse

Hasik

Hallaniyat Islands

N

Where to eat and drink

Sadah,
Salalah

Bradt

Al Ghaftain Resthouse (see 1)
Al Jazeera (see 2)
Al Wusta Resthouse (see 3)
Shannah Resthouse (see 6)

0   100km
0   60 miles

AL WUSTA

---

page 283), mostly owned by the Arab Oryx group. Three of them are in this region. For location of listings see map, above.

⌂ **Al Ghaftain Resthouse** (10 rooms) m 99 485881. This is another of the basic resthouses that sit on the main Muscat–Salalah road, 408km from Salalah. Impeccably clean rooms. There is an international restaurant with good inexpensive food. Accepts credit cards. **$$**

⌂ **Al Wusta Resthouse** (16 rooms) Haima; ☎ 23 436016. Very close to the Haima Motel, on the opposite side of the road just before

reaching the town of Haima. Simple but adequate accommodation with a good basic restaurant. **$$**

⌂ **Haima Motel** (15 rooms) ☎ 23 297103. This is a small hotel offering cheap rooms if you need a break from the unending Muscat–Salalah road. Note that there is no restaurant, so if you need to eat you'll need to travel a little bit further to Al Ghaftain Resthouse. **$**

MUSCAT–SALALAH مسقط صلالة (Route 31)

The 1,000km tarmac road from Muscat to Salalah can be done in just over eight hours' solid driving if you keep your speed at 120km/h. Most people find this too strenuous and deadly dull, and therefore take typically 10–12 hours, allowing for stops at the rather uninspiring series of resthouses along the way – each of which has petrol and a small service garage. Note that this route covers three of Oman's regions, and four if we include the early part of the route (Route 15) from Muscat. It therefore could have been included in any of those other regional chapters.

Of the resthouses you meet along this seemingly endless road, **Al Ghaba Resthouse** (see page 208) is the first. It is 319km from Muscat, near which a small diversion can be made to see the **Qarat Kibrit saltdome** with its salt stalactites. For centuries the Bedouin used to mine salt and sulphur here, which they then carried by camel to Nizwa for trading. It is a 45-minute diversion from the main road and to reach it you fork right before the resthouse on a graded road signposted for the oilfield at Ghaba North. You follow the track for 22km until you reach a roundabout where the Qarat Kibrit is signposted.

Follow the road south of Ghaba Resthouse for 207km and you will reach Haima. The small settlement here has petrol, shops, a motel and even a hospital.

From Haima, one option is to head for the coast towards Duqm, subject of a massive development including an airport, hotels, residential complexes, schools, dry dock, commercial port and shipbuilding yard, then to camp at Ras Madrakah, possibly taking in a visit to the now downgraded Arabian Oryx Sanctuary *en route*, if you have pre-arranged a permit (see page 251). A second option is to take the road (a little beyond Haima) signposted Marmul, which leads to Qahal (or Kahil) of the Pink Lagoons (see page 253) and then Shuwaymiyah. Note that without a guide these places can be tricky to find as there is a dearth of landmarks or signs.

Continuing on the main Muscat–Salalah road south, 86km beyond Haima you reach the **Al Ghaftain Resthouse** (see opposite), from which point onwards you are skirting the edge of the Empty Quarter with open sand landscapes. The high dunes, reaching over 100m, are much deeper into the desert and therefore more difficult to reach.

Qitbit Resthouse (see page 283) lies 130km further on. Both the Ghaftain and Qitbit resthouses serve the oilfields of the area. A further 196km through uneventful scenery brings you to **Thumrayt**, with its small hotel and restaurant. From here the easy-graded track is signposted to Shisr (described on page 283).

From Thumrayt it is 82km to Salalah, the final 32km of which is the reward: the much longed-for and interesting descent of the Qara Mountains to Salalah on the coastal plain. This is especially beautiful during the *khareef* season when the landscape is verdant. On the descent, views over the Salalah plain are spectacular

TRIBES OF SOUTHERN OMAN

The three major Bedouin tribes of southern Oman are the Jenaba, the Wahhabi and the Harasis. Since they are all nomads, their tribal areas are never entirely clear-cut, but as a rule the Jenaba live along the coast from Bar Al Hikman (the mainland opposite Masirah Island) to the Dhofar border, the Wahhabi live in the Wahiba Sands and eastwards to the coast, while the Harasis live in the tedious expanse of desert known as the Jiddat Al Harasis, northeast of Salalah. The Harasis have always been the purest nomads in Oman, with no date groves to return to, just the inhospitable Jiddat lowland where they move about with their camels, speaking a south Arabian dialect incomprehensible to any other Arab. They are noted for their excellent sense of direction.

and hold their promise of company, activity and respite after the protracted drudgery of the long desert road from the north.

Much of the Omani desert between Nizwa and Salalah is not rolling sands at all, but flat dark gravel plain, black or occasionally purplish green. The stretch from Adam to Haima is the most tedious. Curiously in the mornings there can be dense fog around Haima, caused by just the right combination of sea breeze and desert heat. After exceptional rainfall lakes form in the desert which can linger for months and extend to several kilometres, still deep enough to swim in. Reptiles whose eggs have lain dormant for up to ten years then hatch out, newt-like, and live in the lakes. The number of flint arrowheads, axe heads and other tools found here suggests that maybe the wetter climate in earlier times meant that human settlements were possible.

The **Nejd** is the desolate area to the north of the Dhofar mountains, on the southern fringe of the Empty Quarter. Ranulph Fiennes wrote of this area: 'The Nejd looked both harmless and lifeless. In reality it was neither: every crack in the crumbling surface concealed something that crawled or slithered.' If you camp anywhere on this desolate stretch, the kind of wildlife you may encounter in the evening includes fennec foxes with their gigantic ears, jerboa, desert hares and lizards. The dhubb lizard is a great delicacy for the Bedouin, for whom it used to constitute a rare source of free meat, and they had many ingenious methods of

THE ORYX LEGEND

The white oryx, a kind of large desert antelope the size of red deer or reindeer, are held very dear in the Arabian Peninsula generally, always viewed as part of the local heritage. They are perfectly adapted to their desert environment, their white coat reflecting the sun's rays and their splayed hooves making it easy to walk in sand. They are very hardy to drought and live solely on the dew that falls every night in the desert here. Legend has it that the oryx is in fact the ancient unicorn, and certainly when seen in profile, the horns do often appear as one. The ancient Egyptians were said to bind the horns of young oryx together to make them fuse into one as they grew. Both sexes have horns and the ones of the female are longer and thinner than those of the male. A law passed in 1982 banned their hunting, and a 40-strong herd was re-introduced then, the last animal having been shot in 1972. By the late 1990s the numbers had increased to over a thousand animals. A victim of its own success, the herd has now been decimated by intermittent poaching, so easy now that rifles are freely available. Oryx were traditionally hunted for their meat and white skins, and the price that they can now fetch has been too much temptation for the poachers, who are thought to be local. Further attempts to re-introduce the species are unlikely here, as the same thing may well happen again. However the Abu Dhabi government has funded successful reintroduction of oryx into Jordan and is considering doing the same in Yemen.

Oryx are extremely hard to spot as they have a keen sense of smell and tend to disappear over the horizon, leaving their tracks and droppings as the only clues that they were there. Local tribesmen say they can be approached from upwind by lying flat on a camel's back, as oryx have no fear of camels. Gazelle are also shy and nimble-footed. It can therefore take a long time driving through the sanctuary before you spot either.

catching it. Another type of larger lizard is called Abu Ruwwal, with a scaly tail that it swings about aggressively and an intimidating snake-like hiss. The Harasis tribe treats the fennec fox as a kind of private mascot and so would never kill it; instead they leave food out for it (scraps from their own meals). The Jenaba tribe along the coast of the desert do the same thing for the turtle.

ARABIAN ORYX SANCTUARY

The Jiddat Al Harasis lies equidistant from Muscat and Salalah, in the *wilayat* of Haima (or Hayma). From Haima it takes about an hour (50km) to drive to the reserve here, signposted with a brown nature reserve sign. A sanctuary was established in 1994 and covers approximately 27,500km². Its purpose is to conserve the desert habitat and protect the oryx from extinction. It used to be a UNESCO World Heritage Site, but its status as such was withdrawn in 2007 due to heavy poaching and the awarding of oil exploration rights, so the park size has dwindled along with the size of the herd. The headquarters are at Jaaluni, which is roughly halfway between Haima and Duqm.

The sanctuary lies on bird migratory routes between Africa, Europe and central Asia, and provides good opportunities for birdwatching. The Jiddat Al Harasis attracts a fog which sustains life within the area, whose inhabitants include Arabian oryx, Nubian ibex, caracel, Arabian gazelle, sand gazelle, sand cat, houbara bustard, lizards, snakes, spiders, birds and endemic plant species.

For the people of the sanctuary, the oil companies and the Arabian Oryx Project are the two largest employers. Prior to 1974 camels were their only means of transport, but by 1980 each household had a truck. Before 1956 they relied on fog water to sustain them; now water is available at the desalination plants within the sanctuary. The first school in the area was built in 1982.

GETTING THERE To get to the sanctuary, take the Muscat to Salalah road. At Haima, turn left towards Ad Duqm. After 80km on this road take the signposted left to Matar Hab Hab or Hab Hab Airport. Continue for 15km along this stretch, which is lined by oil drums. Jaaluni (or Yaloony) is on the right-hand side (not signposted). You will need a guide to help you follow the graded track to Jaaluni. After 15km along the track, you will reach the camp at the sanctuary. A permit is required for visiting, which you will need to have set up in advance through the Office of the Advisor for Conservation of the Environment (✆ 24 693536; e *acedrc@omantel.net.om*). It costs RO22 per group. The guide himself is likely to be local and not speak English. Maps and GPS are needed to tour the reserve and at least two vehicles should travel together, for safety reasons. It is possible to camp at the reserve in a prescribed place, but you will need to be entirely self-sufficient in food and water.

COASTAL ROUTE FROM MUSCAT TO SALALAH VIA MUHUT, DUQM AND ASH SHUWAYMIYYAH

If you want lots of beach **camping** in unspoilt landscapes, have your own 4x4 and are completely self-sufficient in supplies, this route may appeal to you.

From Muscat you drive via Sinaw to reach the coast at **Filim**, where there is a desalination plant on the beach recognisable by its big green water tanks. The 410km journey to Filim takes at least six hours from Muscat and the drive on south to Duqm takes another two to three hours. For location of listings see map, page 248.

⌂ WHERE TO STAY AND EAT

⌂ **Al Jazeera Resthouse** (18 rooms) Muhut; ☏99 820882. Situated at the junction of the main road south towards Duqm with the crossroads to Muhut & Masirah Island (see pages 245–6). A simple place set beside a petrol station, but with adequate rooms & a basic restaurant. **$$**

⌂ **Mahawt Resthouse** (16 rooms) On the road towards Masirah, just north of Muhut, a handy

place to stop if you are heading to the island (see pages 245–6). Clean simple accommodation at a reasonable price. **$$**

⌂ **Shannah Resthouse** (14 rooms) Close to the ferry crossing point for Masirah Island (see pages 245–6), beside the small town of Shannah, a simple place with basic accommodation & food, where you can wait for the ferry. **$**

After Filim head to the coast at **Khaluf**, a small village with traditional houses. A nearby fish plant sells fresh fish and ice. Beyond the village is a track that leads behind a rocky headland and ends at one of the most beautiful beaches on the whole coastline. You need to be experienced at sand driving, but at low tide driving on the hard sand is no problem. Watch out for the sand above the high water mark which is much softer and easier to bog in. The beach makes excellent camping especially with children.

Returning to the main road and continuing south towards Duqm the landscape changes to low hills and cliffs, and along this stretch till just before Duqm you can see some of Oman's oldest rock formations, with black dolomites contrasting against reddish sandstones and shales. Some 108km south from the Khaluf junction a track turns off, signposted Sidarah, which runs towards the coast and more secluded

---

BEDOUIN LIFESTYLE

The Bedouin of the south in the 1960s had a lifestyle so harsh it is hard to conceive. They owned nothing save their camels, goats and a few leather bags. The children would sleep squashed among the goats. Their close dependence on nature, where they could die if a well dried out or a camel died, gave them a deep sense of the will of Allah, and the Koran was their only education. Even though they had so little, the rule of the desert was to share with guests and unexpected visitors, even if this meant their own family going without. No Bedu would eat or drink until their companions had all reached the well; no-one would take more than their share. Petty theft within a tribe was despised as dishonourable, yet it was acceptable, even manly, to raid another tribe's camels and kill the tribespeople in order to steal for your own. Freya Stark in her book *The Southern Gates of Arabia* observed: 'Crime is practically unknown in the Hadramaut; such things as robbery and murder, being done according to established rules, come rather under the heading of legitimate warfare.' Blood feuds are also a question of honour; they are not crimes.

The camel – the lifeblood of the Bedouin – does not normally sweat until its body temperature exceeds 104°F, thereby conserving its water for long periods even in excessive heat. So the Bedouin relied on her milk in the desert long after his own water ran out. A Bedouin was said to be able to tell from the footprint of a camel who its owner was, when and where it had drunk last by the amount and frequency of the droppings, and in which wadis it had last eaten, from the texture. If one Bedouin owned she-camels, he would arrange a meeting with a he-camel belonging to another man and borrow his services in exchange for milk or food.

beaches with many birds, especially Socotra cormorants, the only endemic seabirds of the Arabian region, landing and taking off in their thousands.

You next reach **Duqm**, an industrial oil town that is undergoing massive development in a bid to attract tourists and citizens to come here to enjoy the good climate. The hope is to turn it into a maritime getaway destination, and work is well under way on constructing a new airport, hotels, residential complexes, an oil refinery, free trade zone, power station, hospital, schools, shops, recreational facilities, dry dock, commercial port and a shipbuilding yard. The development is planned to open in stages, and will obviously take many years to complete. Ras Duqm is one of the most splendid bays on the coast and was where PDO (see box, page 112) first landed in 1954. The mudflats and *sabkhas* of the coast support a large population of indigenous and migratory birds.

The next section of coast from Ras Madraka to Ash Shuwaymiyyah has some of the most varied and unscarred scenery in Oman. At **Ras Madraka** the black volcanic rocks contrast with the white coral sand, and the beach itself is covered with beautiful shells, and dolphin and whale bones. The route to Ras Madraka is signposted off the main road and the scenery begins to change a few kilometres before you arrive. The rocks turn black and the landscape becomes more rugged, almost lunar. The village of Madraka sits at the foot of black hills near the beach beside a desalination plant. Two tracks lead out of the village to more beautiful beaches, and after 2km another track forks right to another three small beaches, two of them used by local fishermen, but the third utterly deserted and very beautiful. In the hills behind the beach you may even spot gazelle. Following the track 2–3km further north from Ras Madraka you will reach a shipwreck, a rusting cargo vessel, washed up on the beach below a headland. Camping anywhere round here is excellent, as is shell collecting. Rock oysters cover the black rocks and ghost crabs scurry in their hundreds along the sand, looking for dolphin and whale bones to pick clean. The male crabs build towers just above the tide line to lure females. Returning south to Ras Madraka itself you can swim across to the small island that sits just off the headland.

Back at the main road, 45km further south from the Ras Madraka junction is a small lagoon, **Khor Dhiris**, also known as Three Palm Tree Lagoon. Camels come here to drink and flamingos, spoonbills, herons and ducks are also drawn by the shallow water. It makes another fine camping spot, but make sure you have mosquito protection.

Continuing south, 96km from the Ras Madraka junction is the desalination plant of Haytam with its big green water tanks, and then another 33km to the junction at Rima. About 20km beyond Rima is the village of Qahal, near which is the largest and most scenic lagoon of the coast, **Khor Ghawi**, separated from the sea by a narrow sandbar which makes a good camping spot and excellent place to observe birds and sealife. Thousands of flamingos usually visit this 6km-long lagoon in the winter months. The 'Pink Lagoons' lie 4km further north up the coast from the northern end of Khor Ghawi. They are completely cut off from the sea so have become very saline, encouraging a particular kind of algae which blooms to give the water a deep pinkish colour, with thick red and white salt crusts round the edge used by fishermen to dry their catch.

Returning to the main road at Qahal, continue south. There is a fork off to **Sharbithat** on the coast, near where there are more good **camping** spots. On the main road, some 22km beyond Shalim, the road arrives at a major escarpment where the road plunges down 300m to the coast, an incredible engineering achievement. The village of **Ash Shuwayymiyah** is well known as a centre for basket

9

weaving and the local people are very keen to sell their wares to all comers. On the coast here there is a resthouse (Shatti Ash Shuwaymiyyah Resthouse) offering 16 simple rooms and decent inexpensive food, a welcome break maybe, after several nights' camping. Offshore the Kuria Muria Islands, now the Halaniyat Islands (see page 280), can be seen.

Just after the village take a right turn on a graded track into Wadi Shuwaymiyyah. This will bring you to a canyon unlike any other, with vertical bluffs of white limestone, making it like a box canyon. A few deep pools can be found up against the cliffs in some palm groves. Where the track ends is a good flat place for camping. Children will love exploring the wadi higher up, with more pools and vegetation, where hyena, ibex, gazelle and the small rabbit-like rock hyrax can sometimes be glimpsed.

To continue to Salalah you now have to head inland to rejoin the main road, passing Marmul, where the major oilfield is indicated by its nodding donkeys, flaring gas and the PDO camp beside it in a large depression below. The drive from Ash Shuwaymiyyah to Salalah takes about half a day.

10

Dhofar ظفار

Telephone code: 23

Every non-fighter recommends war.

Dhofar is Oman's southernmost province and covers roughly a third of the country. It is famed for its frankincense, and was the trading centre of this aromatic gum resin with Rome, Greece, Egypt, India and China. Its presence here kept southern Arabia wealthy into the 6th century AD.

Dhofar itself has its own dramatic regional variances of weather and terrain; it contains one of the largest expanses of sandy desert in the world – the Empty Quarter or Rub' al Khali – extensive gravel desert plains, lush green coastal plains and the Qara Mountains, with their gushing waterfalls and streams.

Salalah, on the southern coast, is Dhofar's administrative capital, and has quite a different feel to it from the rest of Oman, extending from Dhofar's mountain plateaux northwards. This is largely due to its monsoon, which can last from June through to September, and results in the narrow band of land from the Qara Mountains to the flat coastal plain becoming green and lush, giving rise to the name 'the green city'. The greenness of the September hills contrasts dramatically with the camel-coloured aridness of the rest of the country, yet by late October all traces of greenery from the monsoon have disappeared.

Unlike the rest of Oman, the temperature of this narrow band rarely exceeds 30°C. From October to February the temperature is guaranteed warm (28°C), sunny and dry, and therefore attracts European and North American visitors seeking to escape their cold winters. January and December are the coolest months, with temperatures averaging 25°C. From March onwards until the monsoon begins in mid June the climate becomes muggy and unpleasantly humid, and there are fewer visitors. The waves can reach a dramatic 8m during the monsoon season and the sea is then too dangerous for swimming. The average wave height outside the monsoon season is just 1m, but swimming can still be tricky because of undertows. Notices at the few beach hotels warn of the danger and absolve themselves of any responsibility in the event of an accident.

Agriculture and fishing are the key industries of Dhofar, followed by traditional crafts and tourism. In addition to its plentiful fruits, sweet potatoes, corn and wheat are grown in the region. Sardines, prawns, abalone and lobster are common catches in the waters off the Salalah coast.

Dhofar is now being promoted as a stand-alone holiday destination. For today's visitors it offers the three archaeological sites of Al Balid (Old Salalah), Sumharam (east of Salalah) and Ubar which, collectively, are UNESCO-listed (together with the little-known ruins of Andhur, another frankincense-gathering city) as the 'Land of Frankincense'. Apart from the souks of Salalah, the other sites of the region are mainly natural and scenic, like the Mughsail blowholes, the dramatic road to Yemen

Dhofar

10

255

DHOFAR

For listings, see pages 248, 252, 283

Where to stay
1   Thumrayt Resthouse

Off map
     Qitbit Resthouse

Where to eat and drink
2   Al Marnif
3   Al Mughsail Beach Tourist
4   Al Shara Tourism
     Thumrayt Resthouse (see 1)

Off map
     Qitbit Resthouse (see Qitbit Resthouse)

Rub al Khali ◄
(The Empty Quarter)

Pools of Ayun,
Shisr (Ubar) ◄

Wadi Dayqah,
Qitbit Resthouse ◄

Al Mazyunah

Tawsinat

Qafah

Al Mathafah

Tudhu

Aybut

Mudayy

Harwib

Sarfayt

Difa

Dalkut

Raykhut

Hilal

Jebel Qamr
The Mountains
of the Moon

Wanat

Ar Raydah

Al Mughsail

Mughsail blowholes &
Al Marnif cave

Mushaylah

Job's Tomb
(Nabi Ayoub)

Al Mathafah

Salalah

Raysut port

Ain Razat
(springs)

Ain Garziz
(springs)

Ambishaq
Atin Gardens

Ain Hamran
(springs)

Taqa

Taqa Castle

Babah Forest

Sumharam,
Queen of Mirbat,
Sheba's Palace/
Khor Rori

Tawi Attair
(Well of Birds)

Ayn Hut

Wadi Darbat

Teyq (cave
& sinkhole)

Jufa

Mirbat Castle

Bin Ali's Tomb

Arabian
Leopard
Sanctuary

Jebel Samhan
Nature Reserve

Sadah
Sadah Fort

Hadbin

Dhahbun

Rabkut

Dhanajit

Thumrayt

Jazal

Sayyad

Barazum

Harzan

Qatbit

Andhur

Amal

Amal

Qafah

ARABIAN SEA

ARABIAN SEA

Dhofar Mountains

Jebel al Qara

Jebel Samhan

256

and the lush Wadi Dirbat with its cave paintings. Of Salalah's 12 coastal creeks, nine are designated nature reserves.

HISTORY

Dhofar is in many respects a separate country to Oman – different in climate, people, customs and currency. Its only link to Oman was that the sultan, Said bin Taimur (Sultan Qaboos's father), chose to live here on and off for 35 years.

The sultan's presence in Dhofar meant that a contingent of the Sultan's Armed Forces (SAF) was based there to protect him. Said bin Taimur regarded Dhofar as a sort of personal property – a favourite retreat – taking responsibility for it from 1879. He spent the last ten years of his reign continuously at Salalah, together with the young Qaboos whom he restricted to the palace under a form of arrest. This was to ensure that Qaboos was not corrupted by outside influences after he returned from his Sandhurst military training in England. The ageing sultan's army consisted of about 1,000 fighting men, of whom half were Beluchi mercenaries led by a handful of British volunteers.

Sultan Qaboos has always had a special affection for Dhofar: he was born there and his mother was a Dhofari from Wadi Dirbat. His mother and sister lived in the Mamura Palace just east of Salalah until his mother's death, and his sister lives there

THE KHAREEF AND ITS FESTIVAL

Through a quirk of nature, the mountains of Dhofar and the Salalah Plain are exposed to a monsoon climate, with daily rains from mid June to mid September blowing in from Africa. As the rain-filled winds brush past the island of Socotra off the southern coast of Yemen, the vacuum created by the vast searing deserts beyond sucks the winds against the Qara Mountains. Known as the *khareef* (meaning 'winds of plenty'), the clouds shed 15 inches of rain over those three months, causing the wadi beds to flow with deep rivers and spectacular waterfalls that plunge over sheer cliffs. The area becomes filled with mist and fog. Camels are forced to leave the mountains, which become slippery and dangerous, and are kept in the plains until the rains abate. When they return to the mountains in September after the rains the pasture is rich and plentiful. This is the season in which the region is most popular with Omanis from the northern provinces as well as other Arabs of the Gulf, who seek to escape their own hot dry summers, and enjoy the lush green landscape here.

Each year, at this time, there is a six-week-long carnival, much like that of the Muscat Festival but organised by the Dhofar municipality. The festival, like its Muscat counterpart, is a showpiece for Omani customs and traditions, and hotels and flights can get booked to capacity. The Baladiya Entertainment Centre is one of the principal centres where festivities take place. It was purpose built, with a heritage village, two theatres (one open-air) and a fairground. Al Marooj Amphitheatre, which can hold 7,000 people, was opened in 2005 and is located in the east of Salalah, in the Ateen Plain. The festivities include folk bands, song and dance, art exhibitions, handicraft demonstrations, information on conservation projects of the region, as well as other exhibits displaying and promoting the culture and heritage of the region and country.

still. His mother is now buried in the cemetery at nearby Taqa. He spent much of his childhood there, as well as the period of near house-arrest as a young man after his return from Sandhurst. Now he comes every *khareef* season, staying in Al Husn Palace – the original stone-built residence of his father, now hidden from view by a huge wall. The newer Robat Palace is a smaller building, though its grounds are extensive; it tends to be used by his senior staff.

Although nominally under the rule of the Muscat sultans since the late 1800s, the sultans' authority only extended over the Salalah Plain itself, a fertile stretch 15km wide by 48km long. The Qara Mountains tended to be a law unto themselves, with the tribes frequently at war.

The sultan had an arrangement with the British that any British army officer could volunteer for a two-year attachment to the sultan's army and continue to be paid by Her Majesty's government. The British explorer and writer Ranulph Fiennes first came to Oman this way. In return the British were allowed to use the island of Masirah as an RAF base and a listening/transmitting post. One of the conditions set by the sultan was that the RAF had to maintain the airstrip and base at Salalah. The British did not require this base while they had Masirah, but the sultan insisted on its maintenance for his own personal safety.

From 1969, child recruits from among Dhofari villages were sought, first with parental consent, then without, after the first method yielded limited results. When one mother protested to the soldiers and tried to help her boy escape, she was stripped and flogged, then picked up by her ankles and swung round and round, faster and faster, moving ever closer to a cluster of rocks, until on the final swing her head was cracked open like a watermelon. After that there were no more rebellious parents.

The young teenagers who were sent off to be trained in Russia or China returned with beards shaven and preaching against God, strangers to their own families. The

THE COUP

On the afternoon of 23 July 1970, when the old sultan was resting, a group of ten Omani soldiers led by the *wali's* son, Bareik, entered the palace in Salalah unopposed. Winding through a labyrinth of dark passages they came in the end to the sultan's private quarters. The startled royal bodyguard opened fire, and a ricocheting bullet hit Bareik in the stomach. Next, Captain Tom Greening, Qaboos's young intelligence officer, appeared with more Omani soldiers and all but two of the slave bodyguards surrendered. The old sultan was wounded and refused to leave without the local British colonel. The colonel came and comforted the sultan while his wounds were dressed, and he then agreed to sign the letter of abdication in favour of Qaboos, his son. An RAF plane then flew him to London with three of his palace staff where he lived in a private suite in the Dorchester Hotel until he died in 1972. Bareik later became Wali of Dhofar.

The younger Qaboos's first act was to withdraw all troops from the Qara Mountains and to declare an amnesty for all the guerrillas. This led to a steady stream of deserters from the Dhofar Liberation Front (reaching 1,000 within the next three years) and included many who had received their training in Russia or China.

Over half the oil revenues had been spent on the war (£50 million a year) but Qaboos joined the Arab League and the United Nations and soon became creditworthy. World oil prices rocketed and in 1975 Oman's oil revenue was £300 million.

methods of the Russian and Chinese revolutionaries were also barbaric. The village elders often tried to preach against this assault on Islam, but all such insurrection ceased after two respected sheikhs had their eyes put out. The revolutionary who performed the blinding, remembered by the villagers as an idle boy who shirked his duties with the cattle, was nephew to one of the men, and used a pocket knife heated in the fire. The men died only a few days later.

A British army officer and explorer, Ranulph Fiennes wrote of the grimness of war, after killing his first enemy soldier:

> I found sleep elusive. I had often shot at people hundreds of yards away; vague shapes behind rocks who were firing back; but never before had I seen a man's soul in his eyes, sensed his vitality as a fellow human, and then watched his body ripped apart at the pressure of my finger. I tried to force away the image of his destruction but his scarred face stayed watching me from my subconscious and a part of me that was still young and uncynical died with him and his comrade the commissar, spread-eagled on a thornbush with his red badge glinting in the hot Qara sun.

THE DHOFARIS

Dhofar's people are closer to the Hadramaut tribes (Yemen) than to the northern Omanis, linked by centuries of shared interest in the frankincense trade routes. They are said to descend from a mountain tribe that arrived with the Queen of Sheba when she colonised the frankincense orchards before her legendary journey to King Solomon. Numbering around 10,000–15,000, the Dhofaris speak four different languages – Mahra, Shahra, Kharous Harusi and Botahari – all linguistically different from Arabic.

The Qara Mountains were inhabited until very recently by hostile tribesmen. The Qara people, like the Dinka tribes of the Upper Nile, lived for their cattle. They often named their eldest son after their favourite cow, and no healthy cow would be killed even when the owner's children were dying of malnutrition. After the death of a Qara tribesman, up to half his herd was slaughtered as a kind of death duty to save his soul. If a cow slowed down its milk production, they believed the cure was to blow as hard as possible up the cow's vagina, an act only permitted to Qara males.

An illuminating comparison between the society of northern and southern Omani provinces was made by Ranulph Fiennes who revisited Dhofar in 1985, his first visit since leaving in 1970, Fiennes commented: 'If the northern Omanis had leapt in a single generation from the Middle Ages into the 1980s, then the Dhofaris had bounded from the Old Testament into the 1950s and were straining at the leash to close the remaining gap.'

GETTING THERE AND AWAY

BY AIR Oman Air operates three daily flights from Muscat International Airport to Salalah Airport in Dhofar. Check its website (*www.omanair.com*) for exact timings, which vary seasonally. The flight takes 1½ hours and the price for a return ticket is around RO80. Oman Air usually offers good package deals, and so it may be worth enquiring at the time of your visit as to what is available. A package deal, which includes accommodation, costs around RO105 (five-star) and RO85 (three-star), based on a return economy flight, two nights' stay with breakfast and airport transfers. Travelling independently, a transfer to any hotel in Salalah town will cost roughly RO4 by taxi, although some hotels offer a free transfer.

DHOFAR LIBERATION FRONT

In 1963, the Dhofar Liberation Front consisted mainly of dissatisfied Dhofaris who were Arab nationalists intent on seizing Dhofar back from Oman. They were supported by what was then the People's Democratic Republic of Yemen (PDRY). The Front began as a simple movement of non-Marxist tribesmen who wanted Dhofar for the Dhofaris, but once Russian and Chinese involvement began it turned into a political war, where the ultimate goal for the Russians and Chinese was control of the oil markets through control of the Strait of Hormuz.

Dhofaris were trained as Marxist rebels for spells of up to 18 months in Russia or China, and in 1968 the Marxists took over leadership.

By the mid 1970s, approximately 2,000 Dhofaris broke with the movement, and later agreed to support Sultan Qaboos bin Said and fight against the insurgency. They retrained and were incorporated into the Sultan's Armed Forces (SAF). Jeapes and Drury's book *SAS Secret War: Operation Storm in the Middle East* (see *Appendix 3, Further information*, page 298) tells the story of the SAS involvement in the Dhofar War of the 1970s and the defeat of the communist rebels.

The departure lounge of Salalah Airport is small but comfortable, and you can get yourself a cup of tea, coffee or a cold drink, plus light snacks at the counter at the back. There are only a couple of small shops inside the lounge, selling postcards, papers, cigarettes and phonecards, but nothing much else. The toilets are clean, and payphones are situated next to them at the back of the lounge. The seating area has a family corner with comfortable padded chairs.

Announcements are made in Arabic and English (although the English is indecipherable). The staff on the coffee counter at the back speak good English and will be able to clarify the message.

BY CAR Route 31 runs from Nizwa all the way south to Salalah. The distance from Muscat is approximately 1,000km. The single-carriageway tarmac road runs virtually parallel to the Empty Quarter (or Rub'al Khali) and is a long 10-hour journey (including stops). Travelling by bus is your cheapest option, but if you have others in your party who could perhaps share the driving, then a hire car would be a good alternative. That said, the drive itself is rather tedious, with long stretches of featureless bleak landscapes, often a flat and gravelly desert.

BY BUS Buses operated by the Oman National Transport Company (ONTC) (check www.ontcoman.com for exact timings) run about four times a day between Muscat and Salalah, from the Ruwi Bus Station in the Capital Area to Salalah Bus Station in the new souk, close to the Salalah Tourist Hotel and some 200m north of 23 July St, the main street which runs east–west through the town. The journey takes 12 hours and costs around RO8.5/12 single/return. ONTC also runs services to Nizwa and Buraimi from Salalah. There are also two private bus companies, Malatan Trading and Bin Qasim Transport, which have offices in Salalah (see map, pages 264–5), and operate a once-daily bus service to Muscat at 16.00 and at 16.30 respectively. The journey time and fare are the same as with ONTC. For buses to Yemen the Gulf Transport Company (✆ 23 293303) runs three buses a week to Mukhalla in Yemen, setting off at 09.30 from the main Salalah bus station on Mondays, Wednesdays and

Fridays. It takes six hours and costs around RO14. All buses are usually on time and tickets can be bought either from the bus company office in advance or from the driver on boarding. For weekend, holiday and peak-time travel it would be wise to book a day or two in advance.

GETTING AROUND

CAR HIRE If you intend to drive yourself around and explore, you can hire a car from the airport or pre-book one from the Muscat car rental offices (see page 55). Europcar, Thrifty, Avis and Budget all have offices here, as do many other local car hire companies. In Salalah itself, Sumharam Watersports and Diving also provides a car-rental service (RO18/45 saloon/4x4, per day). Do note that if you plan on taking excursions with tour operators, it is not really necessary to hire a car, as tour companies collect you from your hotel and return you afterwards. If you plan to go off-road but think you can save money by renting a 2x2 instead of the pricier 4x4, remember that your insurance will be void if you sustain any damage to a saloon car while driving off-tarmac – the risk is therefore yours not theirs. Car hire is recommended in Salalah because of the dearth of public transport running to the tourist sites.

TAXIS Taxis are the easiest way of getting from your hotel to the city centre souks and budget restaurants, but bear in mind that prices add up as most taxi drivers

ARAB MINDSET VERSUS COMMUNISM

If the Russian and Chinese revolutionaries controlling the 2,000-strong PFLOAG (People's Front for the Liberation of the Occupied Arabian Gulf) had succeeded in overthrowing the British-led SAF in Dhofar and imposing their law, they would have soon encountered another problem – for the Arab mentality is totally at odds with the communist ideal. A regime that evens out all differences between rich and poor was irrelevant in this part of Arabia, where these differences were small anyway. Animals, land and even water were already owned collectively by whole families. Sheikhs had power only for as long as the tribe collectively permitted them. And as Ranulph Fiennes observed after several months in Oman: 'Arabs are highly individualist people, with keenly developed ideas about religion, morals, and the inferiority of other beings in general and women in particular.' In 1968, Fiennes was on the point of resigning and returning to Britain because he felt Britain was supporting the corrupt and stifling regime of the old sultan. But his Omani staff sergeant persuaded him to stay, by talking of the importance of fighting communism:

I myself have met the communists from abroad, here in Oman. They are more often than not sly men with silken tongues but their souls are empty and all their talk of revolution is without sound base. You see they try to turn us from our God and that must never be. Communism must not come here, Sahb. You must not think the British do wrong here, Sahb. They do not meddle with our way of life or our religion. If you British leave before the sultan's son Qaboos can rule, then the communists will take over without a doubt. They will force us to leave Islam or kill us. With the oil money that now pours into Oman, thanks be to God, he (Qaboos) will give us all those things which the communists promise, without changing our religion.

charge a minimum of RO3 per journey, especially from the big hotels out of town. Some visitors have reported that they regretted not renting a car as it would even have been cheaper in the long run, especially on the longer journeys, where a taxi would easily charge RO15 to Taqa, for example.

BUSES There are no buses or any form of public transport from Salalah Airport. The microbuses and taxis all tend to gather in front of the HSBC building on As-Salam Street and run to the various towns in the vicinity, not to the tourist sites. Be prepared therefore to have some long walks or to hitchhike if you rely on public transport. Microbus fares to places like Taqa and Mirbat range between 400 and 600bzs.

TOUR OPERATORS

Tour operators, which can be found inside the Salalah hotels as well as in the streets of the city centre (in Salalah), offer the stock tours of the area, albeit to varying degrees of quality and price. They may vary slightly in the sites they include in each tour. Tours can easily be arranged through your hotel, if you prefer someone else to do the organising. Alternatively you may prefer to hire a car and travel independently.

Arabian Tours Salalah; ✆23 290088. Offering a full range of tours including *dhow* cruises, scuba diving & 4x4 safaris. Also offers car hire.
Bahwan Travel Agencies Salalah; ✆23 294665, 290908; e topclass@omantel.net.om or lakshmy@bahwantravels.com; www.bahwantravels.com. This is one of the biggest tour operators in the country, established for 25 years & offering the full range of tours. It's best to arrange Salalah tours through the Muscat office (see page 76).
United Tours Salalah; ✆23 297948; e utours@omantel.net.om or utours@unitedoman.com.

Large firm with 40 4x4 vehicles & a fleet of buses offering the full range of tours, including comprehensive 8–12-day tours of Oman covering camping, safari & culture.
Zahara Tours ✆23 202581, 23 202582; e miscoman@omantel.net.om or harsh@zaharatours.com; www.zaharatours.com. Offers tours throughout the whole country. In the Dhofar region it runs 3 tours called 'frankincense', 'fabled castles' & 'serene Salalah', which incorporate most of what the region has to offer. See website for details.

🏠 WHERE TO STAY

Apart from a few exceptions like the Beach Resort Salalah in Mirbat, the hotels are mainly in the Salalah area, with the more expensive beach hotels like the Hilton located by themselves well outside the town, meaning you are dependent on taxis or your own transport (car-rental firms too are stretched to meet demand during the *khareef*). The cheaper hotels are in Salalah town. Using websites like www.booking.com you can book rooms at four- and five-star hotels (with no pre-payment) often at well below advertised rates, and can also cancel within 48 hours without penalty – this is an option well worth exploring. During the monsoon season they can get full, so advance booking will definitely be necessary.

✖ WHERE TO EAT

The plushest restaurants are in the five-star hotels in Salalah – and these are licensed. All other eating places are simple and unlicensed, though there are one or two places, like Al-Fareed (see page 267), which offer excellent food in atmospheric surroundings. Outside of Salalah city centre, places to eat are few, so packing a picnic is always a good idea (unless you're visiting the blowholes at Mughsail, west of Salalah, where there are two good beach restaurants for tourists).

OTHER PRACTICALITIES

Dhofar Police HQ ✆23 234599
Salalah Police ✆23 290099
Salalah Post Office ✆23 292933

Sultan Qaboos Hospital Salalah; ✆23 211555
Taqa Police ✆23 258199
Thumrayt Police ✆23 277099

CURRENCY EXCHANGE Money exchangers are located in Salalah along Al Nahda Street (⊕ 08.30–13.00 & 16.00–20.00 Sat–Thu, 08.30–11.00 Fri). Their rates are better than at the big hotels. There are ATMs throughout the town.

SALALAH صلالة

Salalah, the capital of the Dhofar region, is considered Oman's second city, despite having a population of only 175,000. In reality, it is just a small town of concrete buildings – hardly any Dhofar houses remain. However, where northern Oman has its dates, southern Oman has its coconuts. The route from the airport (2km north of Salalah city centre) to the Crowne Plaza Hotel winds through lush plantations of coconut, papaya, banana and mango, and the fruit stalls that line the streets give the place an African feel (eg: only 150bzs for a fresh cold coconut prepared for you to drink!). There are no high-rise buildings here. The name *salalah* means 'shining one' in the Jebali language. Sometimes known as the 'perfume capital of Arabia' thanks to the local cultivation of frankincense trees, a visit to the Frankincense Land Museum (see page 270) at nearby Al Balid will help to visualise the importance of this product to the region. Salalah became part of the Sultanate of Oman in the 19th century, becoming its capital and preferred residence of the Sultan in 1932, till 1970 when Sultan Qaboos chose to move both capital and main residence to Muscat. For location of listings see map, pages 264–5.

🏠 WHERE TO STAY
Note that all the hotels in the budget range provide comfortable, affordable accommodation. Even the cheapest have good clean rooms, and after your tours and all that fresh air, you can get your head down for a very reasonable price. The prices in summer, which for most hotels is from 1 July to 31 August, are higher, but only marginally so. Some prices include taxes and breakfast, some don't, so you might like to get this confirmed before you go. These budget hotels seem genuinely happy to accommodate you, so if there is anything you need, or would like to change, just ask. Also check whether there is a free airport transfer service provided for guests.

Luxury

🏠 **Hilton Salalah Resort** (150 rooms) PO Box 699, PC 211; ✆23 211234; e salalah@hilton.com; www.salalah.hilton.com. On the beach 12km from Salalah town centre on the way out to Raysut, not far from the 'fish' roundabout, it is well placed to catch the business trade from Raysut Port. There is a complimentary airport shuttle service to the hotel. There are 2 restaurants: Al Maha, offering international, Italian & Arabic cuisine, & Palm Grove, an outdoor restaurant situated by the beach, which offers fresh fish in the evening & light snacks during the day. The hotel has an English pub called The Mayfair. There is the Whispers Night Club & an Indian bar called Chequers. Internet access is not cheap in the hotel (RO4 for 15mins), but there are internet cafés in the street shops at approx 500bzs for an hour's usage. **$$$$$**

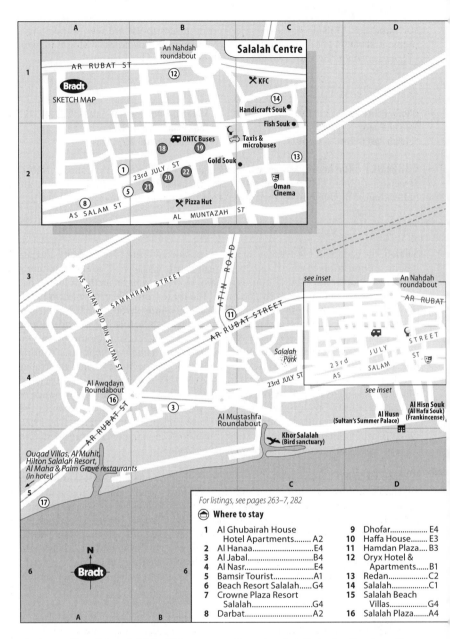

Salalah Centre

Bradt
SKETCH MAP

An Nahdah roundabout

AR RUBAT ST

⑫

✕ KFC

⑭

Handicraft Souk ●

Fish Souk ●

🚐 ONTC Buses

⑱ ⑲

Taxis & microbuses

Gold Souk ●

⑬

23rd JULY ST

①

⑳ ㉒

⑤ ㉑

Oman Cinema

⑧

AS SALAM ST

✕ Pizza Hut

AL MUNTAZAH ST

AS SULTAN SAID BIN SULTAN ST

SAMAHRAM STREET

ATIN ROAD

⑪

AR RUBAT STREET

see inset

An Nahdah roundabout

AR RUBAT

Salalah Park

STREET

JULY ST

23rd

AS SALAM

23rd JULY ST

see inset

Al Awqdayn Roundabout

⑯

③

Al Mustashfa Roundabout

AR RUBAT ST

Al Hisn Souk (Al Hafa Souk)

Al Husn (Sultan's Summer Palace)

(Frankincense)

✈ Khor Salalah (Bird sanctuary)

Ouqad Villas, Al Muhit, Hilton Salalah Resort, Al Maha & Palm Grove restaurants (in hotel)

⑰

N

Bradt

For listings, see pages 263–7, 282

🛏 **Crowne Plaza Resort Salalah** (153 rooms, 7 suites, 19 family villas) PO Box 870, PC 211; ☎ 23 235333; e cpsll@omantel.net.om; www.crowneplaza.com/salalah. From Salalah Airport turn left at the 1st roundabout, right at the 2nd & then left at the 3rd, then follow signs to the Crowne Plaza Resort. It is about 3km out of town, less than 10mins from the airport. The sandy beach is public but the hotel has put out its own sunshades. There is a large pool, tennis, minigolf & health club with sauna, jacuzzi & gym. There are 3 fully licensed restaurants: Darbat Restaurant on Dolphin Beach, Al Luban Restaurant & an Al Khareef (an English/Irish

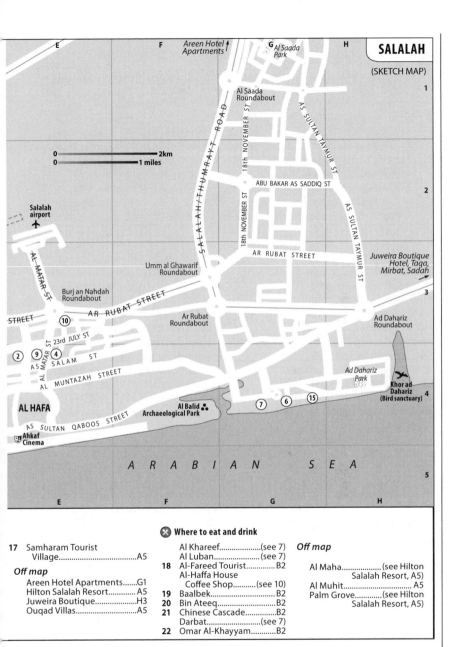

SALALAH

(SKETCH MAP)

Areen Hotel Apartments

Al Saada Park

Al Saada Roundabout

18th NOVEMBER ST

AS SULTAN TAYMUR ST

ABU BAKAR AS SADDIQ ST

SALALAH/THUMRAYT ROAD

18th NOVEMBER ST

AR RUBAT STREET

AS SULTAN TAYMUR ST

Juweira Boutique Hotel, Taqa, Mirbat, Sadah

Salalah airport

Umm al Ghawarif Roundabout

Burj an Nahdah Roundabout

AL MATAR ST

AR RUBAT STREET

STREET

(10)

Ar Rubat Roundabout

Ad Dahariz Roundabout

(2) (9) (4)

23rd JULY ST

AS MATAR ST

SALAM ST

AL MUNTAZAH STREET

Ad Dahariz Park

Khor ad Dahariz (Bird sanctuary)

AL HAFA

AS SULTAN QABOOS STREET

Al Balid Archaeological Park

(7) (6) (15)

Ahkaf Cinema

A R A B I A N   S E A

0 ————— 2km
0 ————— 1 miles

pub). There is also a 3-bar complex located just outside the hotel, a tea lobby lounge (Bird's Lounge), 9-hole green golf course (the first green course in Oman) & driving range, squash & children's playground. **$$$$**

🏠 **Juweira Boutique Hotel** (64 rooms)
📞 23 239600; www.juwairahotel.com. Unusual blend of oriental & European design, with luxury spacious rooms each with a balcony overlooking the ocean. Private beach, two outdoor pools, gym & spa. Al Fanar international restaurant, As Sammak seafood restaurant. 18km from city centre, 20km from Salalah airport, free shuttle. **$$$$**

Zanzibar, a series of islands off the coast of East Africa once famed as the main centre of the slave market, was absorbed into the Omani empire in the 1690s when the imam of Oman, Saif bin Sultan, took it from the Portuguese. Over the next centuries its importance to Oman grew, till in 1837 the greatest Omani sultan of the 19th century, Sa'id bin Sultan, decided to make it his main place of residence, building fine palaces and gardens there. On his death in 1856 his sons had a dispute over inheritance of the empire, eventually resolved with the help of British diplomacy, where one son inherited Zanzibar and its East African possessions, while the other son inherited Muscat and Oman. Sultan Qaboos still traces his ancestry to this side of the Al Bu Sa'id family. Today, Zanzibar is a semi-autonomous part of Tanzania.

Mid-range

Beach Resort Salalah (60 rooms) Ad-Dahariz Street, near Crowne Plaza Hotel; 23 236170; e reservation@beachresortsalalah.com; www.beachresortsalalah.com. New in 2013, modern hotel with spacious rooms & suites with balconies overlooking the beach, 24hr reception, complimentary b/fast. See advert page 254. **$$$**

Haffa House Hotel (63 rooms/apts) PO Box 427, PC 211, Salalah; 23 295444, 294755; e house@omantel.net.om. At the airport roundabout, so almost within walking distance (1km), this has a choice of 1–3-bed apts & has a health club, pool & tennis courts. It is popular with local families & long-stay guests. The on-site Al Haffa Restaurant serves Indian, Chinese, Continental & Arabic food, & there is an English tearoom. **$$$**

Hamdan Plaza Hotel (180 rooms) PO Box 2494; 93 201048, 93 201054 ; www.hamdanplazahotel.com. Set along Al Wadi St in the city centre, about 5mins' drive from the airport, this 4-star hotel has a host of amenities, including large outdoor pool with sun terrace, health club, tennis & squash courts, gym, hot-tub & dry sauna, billiards & table tennis. Al Lou-Lou'a Restaurant (Arabic, Indian, Far Eastern & continental food), a coffee lounge, internet café & supermarket. **$$$**

Ouqad Villas (6 apts) Ouqad, 211 Salalah; m 96 420664; www.booking.com. 5mins' drive to Al-Awaqdiya Beach, 20mins' drive to airport. Bike & car rental can be arranged, as can fishing boat excursions. **$$**

Salalah Beach Villas (8 villas, 10 apts, 25 rooms) PO Box 20, Dahariz, PC 214; 23 235999; www.beach-villas-salalah.com. In southern Dahariz, close to the Crowne Plaza Hotel, this small resort offers sea views from most of its beach villas. There is a pool & candle-lit dinners can be arranged. Also offers tours: a 4x4 for the day with driver/guide & picnic costs RO100. **$$$**

Salalah Plaza Hotel (104 rooms) Auqad, 217 Salalah; 23 210794; e salalaph@salalaph.com; www.salalahplazahotel.com. Opened in 2012 with modern décor, free Wi-Fi & restaurant. 10mins' drive from airport, 5mins' drive from beach. **$$$**

Samharam Tourist Village (46 villas, 16 chalets) PO Box 427, PC 211; 23 295444, 211420. This 4-star hotel is on the same side as the Hilton & close to it (about 10km from Salalah Airport). To access it, & indeed the Hilton, you need to continue driving past until you meet the next roundabout where you can turn around & come back. Affiliated to the Shanfari Group, this is a peaceful beachfront resort with chalets that can be let from 1 night to a medium- or long-term stay. Restaurant, coffee shop, large pool & health facilities. **$$$**

Areen Hotel Apartments (48 rooms) Saadah St; 23 234810; e admin@salalah-youthhostel.com; www.flamingo-hotels.com. In Salalah town, reasonably priced apt rooms with kitchenette, fridge & satellite TV. The hotel has an outdoor pool, restaurant but no internet access. There are facilities for the disabled. **$$**

Budget

Al Jabal Hotel (90 rooms) PO Box 1284, PC 211, Salalah; 23 210611, 23 214020; e jabalhot@omantel.net.om. On Sultan Qaboos Road, in the centre of Salalah, close to Sultan Qaboos Hospital. In the Shahrzad lounge, there is live music & entertainment, including Arabian belly dancers. There is a 24hr restaurant. **$$**

☐ **Bamsir Tourist Hotel** (35 rooms) PO Box 2851, PC 211, Salalah; ✆ 23 202556, 23 202091. There is no restaurant here. **$$**

☐ **Darbat Hotel** (53 rooms) PO Box 18532, PC 211, Salalah; ✆ 23 295877, 23 295878; e darbathotel@hotmail.com. This 6-storey hotel has rooms of various sizes. **$$**

☐ **Dhofar Hotel** (86 rooms) PO Box 2539, PC 211, Salalah; ✆ 23 292300, 23 282300; e dhfhotel@ omantel.net.om. In Salalah city centre, with a restaurant serving international, Arabic, Indian & Chinese cuisine. Does not accept credit cards. **$$**

☐ **Al Ghubairah House Hotel Apartments** (21 apts) Al Ghubairah St, PO Box 321, 211 Salalah; www.booking.com. Simple clean flats with kitchen, satellite TV & balcony, car rental & free parking on offer. **$$**

☐ **Al Nasr Hotel** (15 rooms) Airport St, 211 Salalah; ✆ 23 294815; www.booking.com.

Simple place in the city centre with free Wi-Fi. 10min drive from the airport. **$**

☐ **Oryx Hotel & Apartments** (56 rooms) PO Box 408, PC 211, Salalah; ✆ 23 296262; e oryxsll@omantel.net.om. Salalah city centre, close to Al Nahdah roundabout. **$$**

☐ **Redan Hotel** (27 rooms) PO Box 957, PC 211, Salalah; ✆ 23 292266, 23 288032; e redan@omantel.net.om. On Al Salam Street; also has 2- & 3-bedroom flats available. **$$**

☐ **Salalah Hotel** (24 rooms) PO Box 823, PC 211, Salalah; ✆ 23 295332, 23 295626. This 2-star hotel is situated on A'Suq Street close to the central market, & opposite the Oman National Transport Company (ONTC) bus station. **$$**

☐ **Al Hanaa Hotel** (25 rooms) 23rd July St; PO Box 194, PC 211, Salalah; ✆ 23 298305, 23 298306; e msarawas@omantel.net.om. Clean large rooms. B/fast not offered during Ramadan. **$**

✗ WHERE TO EAT

✗ **Al-Fareed Tourist Restaurant** 23 July St; ✆ 23 292383. Arabic, Chinese, continental & Indian food & very popular with local people. Excellent food & service. Good lobster. **$$$$**

✗ **Al Luban** ✆ 23 235333. One of the Crowne Plaza's offerings, this restaurant is also a nightclub with live entertainment. **$$$$**

✗ **Al Maha** ✆ 23 211234. Inside the Hilton Hotel, this restaurant serves international & Arabian cuisine. **$$$$**

✗ **Palm Grove** ✆ 23 211234. On the seafront at the Hilton Hotel, 12km southwest of Salalah; international cuisine & fresh fish. **$$$$**

✗ **Darbat** ✆ 23 235333. Inside the Crowne Plaza Hotel, serving b/fast, lunch & dinner, buffet or à la carte, with the option of eating on the terrace overlooking the sea. **$$$$**

✗ **Al Khareef** ✆ 23 235333. This is the pub of the Crowne Plaza Hotel, which serves hot & cold bar food & snacks. **$$$**

✗ **Al-Haffa House Coffee Shop** ✆ 23 295444. On the ground floor of the Haffa House Hotel this is a handy place for a coffee & snack. **$$**

✗ **Baalbek Restaurant** 23rd July St; ✆ 23 298834. Good & very pleasant Arabic restaurant run by Syrians. **$$**

SHARK FISHING

Shark fishing is a lucrative business in Dhofar, and the season between October and April brings hundreds of fishermen in their *dhows* from Sur and Masirah to fish the waters along the Dhofar coast. The sharks, hunted primarily for their fins and tail, are snapped up by agents on the jetties along the coast. Shark fin soup is an exotic dish with a strong consumer market, especially in Far Eastern countries. Sharks here are often 5–6ft in length and fetch around RO55–60 each. A single overnight shark fish hunt would probably yield around 12–18 sharks, so it is big business for local fishermen.

Although the warm tropical waters of the Dhofar coast offer rich pickings, and draw the fishermen in from Masirah, Sur and Al Ashkhara for a two-month season, it is in the Sharqiya where the biggest ones are caught. Eighty different species of shark are known to exist in Oman's waters.

Dhofar SALALAH

10

267

✗ Bin Ateeq 23rd July St; ☎23 292384; e binateeq@omantel.net.om. Traditional Omani food served at floor level in private rooms. Worth a visit for its excellent food & the cultural experience. Take your shoes off at the entrance to your private room. There are now 3 Bin Ateeq restaurants in Salalah. $$

✗ Omar Al-Khayyam ☎23 293004. Opposite the more expensive Al-Fareed Restaurant, it also serves a good range of Indian & Chinese fare. $$ **✗ Chinese Cascade** 23rd July St (next to the National Bank of Oman); ☎23 289844. The food here is good & very well priced. Main dishes are around RO1. $

Fast food KFC, Penguin, Chick Hut and Pizza Hut can easily be found dotted around Salalah.

WHAT TO SEE AND DO: SALALAH AND THE SOUTHERN COAST
Places of interest in the Dhofar region are largely based around the southern coastal areas. The stock tours offered by the tour operators include the 'city tour', 'East Salalah', 'West Salalah' and 'Ubar and the Empty Quarter'. These may vary a little from one operator to another, but they all take in the standard tourist sites. For example, one tour to the east of Salalah is called 'Fabled Castles', but incorporates all the usual sites, including Taqa, the ruined city of Sumharam, Mirbat and Ain Rezat. Another tour to the west is called 'Frankincense Trail' and includes Job's Tomb, a visit to see frankincense trees, and Mughsail Beach. Each set tour lasts for roughly half a day (irrespective of operator), with the option for a full-day tour to Ubar (recommended).

So, if you want to tour the area, three nights will generally be enough time; however, if you are planning to include a visit to Ubar (which is a little further out), four nights is recommended, and will give you a little time to relax and spend at leisure. There are plenty of deserted picnic spots in spectacular surroundings both east and west of Salalah.

Birdwatching The birds of southern Oman are more African in character than in the north. They include the African silverbill, Verreaux's eagle, Ruppell's weaver, African scops owl, Bruce's green pigeon, Didric cuckoo, grey-headed kingfisher, African rock bunting, singing bush lark, African paradise flycatcher, shining sunbird and Palestine sunbird. Broadly, the three best sites for birdwatching in the south are the Mughsail Lagoon (west of Salalah), Dirbat (including Khor Rori Lagoon) and A'Dahariz (about 1km east of Salalah). Ain Rezat and Ain Hamran offer good spots, too. Mirbat, Raysut and Mughsail are good for observing seabirds in the autumn. It is easy to travel to these sites independently, but if you would like an accompanied tour, speak to Sumharam Tours in the Crowne Plaza or Hilton hotels. For further information on birdlife, see pages 9 and 299).

Boat trips Diving centres (see opposite) can offer full- and half-day boat trips along the southern coast, where it is likely you will spot dolphins and whales. An afternoon trip means you have the additional pleasure of watching the sunset from the boat. Tours leave from both Salalah port (west of Salalah) and Mirbat harbour (east of Salalah). You will be collected from your hotel. A half-day trip costs RO220 for the boat, which takes ten people, and includes refreshments. The cost doubles for a full-day trip, which includes lunch and refreshments.

Canoeing/kayaking Canoeing can also be experienced outside of the *khareef* season off the Salalah coast. It costs RO24 for a full day and RO18 for half a day, from Saturday through to Thursday. On Fridays there is a special full-day canoeing trip around the lagoon of Khor Rori for RO50 including lunch. Guests will be collected from their hotels. All levels are welcome.

Caving Teyq Cave is situated between Taqa and Mirbat and is one of the largest in the world (see page 278 for further details on how to visit).

Desert tours and camping Overnight trips to the desert camp in Shisr (Ubar) are offered by local hotels, costing RO270 for the 4x4 vehicle, the driver/guide, lunch, dinner and breakfast. A day trip costs RO150 per car, which includes the driver/guide and lunch, and allows for a maximum of four people in the vehicle.

Diving Diving is permitted in the waters of the southern coast of Oman at any time outside of the *khareef* season. Avoid the *khareef* if you want to dive. The two main dive companies are **Aquadivers** (✆ 23 211234; *www.subaqua-divecenter.com*) and **Extradivers** (m 095 410213; *www.extradivers.info*, *www.divesalalah.com*).

There are several dive sites off the Dhofar coast. The best are at Mirbat and Hasik (east of Mirbat), along with the Halaniyat Islands. The Aquarium, which is located 8km east of Mirbat, is a good, easy shore dive, for divers of all levels, and makes a great site for training new divers and snorkellers. Lion fish, sting rays, clown fish, scorpion fish, puffer fish, lobsters, rays and turtles are often spotted. The Eagles Retreat dive site is 10km east of Mirbat. A shore dive is offered from Mirbat to Habeen Hasik (an ancient small village whose shores offer some of the best diving in Dhofar), and the Salalah Marriott Resort also has its own dive centre (see page 279). Close to the Halaniyat Islands there is a British wreck, which sank in 1914 on the return leg of its journey to Calcutta, carrying a cargo of tea. The *City of Winchester* lies at 30m depth. By way of example a two-night camping trip to the Halaniyat Islands, which incorporates ten dives, costs RO475 per person inclusive of everything (transport from your hotel, gear, food, camping kits), with a minimum of five people required. This has been very popular to date with British tourists. For one to two dives, including tanks and weights, it costs RO40 per person. Snorkelling costs around RO25 per person.

Fishing Fishing trips can be easily arranged through one of the diving centres (see above). The boat takes a maximum of six people and departs from either Salalah port (west of Salalah) or Mirbat harbour (east of Salalah). Hiring the boat for half a day costs RO400, while the full day costs RO650.

The delicacies of lobster and abalone are plentiful in the waters off Oman, especially in the Dhofar region and around Masirah Island in the Sharqiya. Their high commercial value has been steadily exploited, which has led to conservation regulations being established which now restrict the fishing of these species to the months of December and January.

Al Hafa souk [264 D4] (⊕ 08.00–11.00 & 16.00–19.00 Sat–Thu) Salalah's oldest souk, named after the Al Hafa district of town, is close to Al Husn, the sultan's fort, between Qaboos Street and the corniche. It is a sprawling maze of little alleys where some of Salalah's few remaining old houses can still be seen, now lived in by Pakistanis and Bangladeshis; the Omanis have moved out to more modern suburbs. Here you can bargain for frankincense of three qualities – the most expensive white variety, followed by the mixed white and brown, and then brown, the least expensive. Perfumed oils, *bokhur* (see box, pages 276–7) and incense burners are also for sale here.

There are a few shops in the souk selling old silver jewellery such as Omani *khanjars*, women's anklets, bracelets and headdresses, though these are diminishing year by year. Among the new items for sale in the souk are traditional Dhofari women's robes, now usually made of velvet or polyester and decorated with sequins or glass beads. The typical design is slightly shorter in the front, with a small train at the back. Colourfully dressed Dhofari women are often themselves the sellers, rings through their noses, bartering without inhibition. From the souk it is a short stroll to the corniche, its coconut palms leaning at amazing angles in line with the prevailing wind.

The other town souks are more modern – the new souk selling fish (mornings only), fruit and vegetables, and the old souk packed with tiny shops selling the gold trinkets that are favoured today. The gold in Salalah is very yellow, but is 24 carat. The traditional old silver Dhofari jewellery is increasingly rare, most of it having been melted down to make new items before the value of the old pieces was fully appreciated.

Al Balid Archaeological Park [265 F4] (⊕ *08.00–20.00 Sat–Thu; RO1*) Now designated as part of the Dhofar UNESCO World Heritage Site, Al Balid is the site of ancient Salalah, known as Zufar, from which the province of Dhofar gets its name. Descriptions by early visitors like Ibn Battuta (the Arab geographer) and Marco Polo referred to this ancient Salalah as 'a great and noble and fine city'. Today it is an extensive site on the Khor Salalah (Salalah Creek), a short walk west of the Crowne Plaza. It is 2km long and 600m wide.

A five-year project led by a German team from Aachen University began an archaeological dig here in 1996, discovering that many of the blocks of this ancient Salalah were pilfered to build the modern city, adding to the puzzle.

The extant ruins are from the 10th to 15th centuries, when the city was settled as a port for exporting frankincense and Arab horses, although archaeological finds date the origins of this ancient city to the early Islamic period, and even earlier. The city began to decline in the 16th century as the Portuguese took over the export trade to India.

The remains of the ruler's palace are still visible today, as are the remains of the Great Mosque, the Koran school, the cemetery and a large enclosing wall with towers. The site has an exhibition centre, called the Frankincense Land Museum, which includes two main halls (one historical, the other natural). The original Dhofar Museum (⊕ *08.00–14.00 & 16.00–20.00 Sun–Thu, Fri & Sat 16.00–20.00; free*) has been moved and incorporated into this park. The historical and archaeological exhibits from Sumharam and Al Balid and other areas in the region include rock art, pre-Islamic pottery, coins dating back to the 11th century, manuscripts and photographs, plus a natural history section on frankincense and other plants and animals of the region.

There is a gift shop, restaurant and snack bar. There is also a botanical garden with indigenous plant species, which can be visited as part of the Salalah 'city tour'.

TOURS IN AND AROUND SALALAH
Salalah city tour [map pages 264–5] The half-day Salalah city tour is likely to include Al Balid archaeological site, the frankincense souk, the gold souk, the Arabian fish market (there's a handicraft market near here too), Dhofar Museum and Al Husn, the sultan's summer palace. If you prefer to be independent, take a taxi to the gold or frankincense souk, where you can stroll about at leisure. Distances are a little far for walking if you are based at one of the beach hotels. On the coast at the

edge of town is the Al Balid Archaeological Park (see above), easy walking distance from the Crowne Plaza, but a taxi ride from the Hilton.

East Salalah tour
The East Salalah tour lasts half a day and includes sites such as Taqa, Wadi Darbat, Sumharam and the Queen of Sheba's Palace, Khor Rori, Tawi Attair, the Anti-Gravity Spot and Mirbat.

At each old village there is a small collection of grocers, Automatic Bakery stores and pharmacies, so you will always be able to grab a drink, snack or painkiller if needed. There was even a candyfloss stall (*sharr banat*, meaning 'girl's hair') at an Al Maha petrol station along the route. Tour operators usually provide soft drinks for half-day tours, and snacks and soft drinks for full-day tours, so you might like to check this when you book.

In a full day, driving about 250km, you can complete a tour of most sites to the east of Salalah. The forts at Taqa and Mirbat, and the ruins of Sumharam have brief opening hours (⊕ *08.00–14.00 Sat–Wed*), so it is best to time your visit accordingly, leaving bin Ali's tomb (⊕ *24hrs*) and the natural wonders of the baobab forest, Wadi Dirbat and Tawi Attair to the afternoon. To reach the baobab forest and the upper reaches of Wadi Dirbat you will need a 4x4, but for all else a saloon car is fine.

Leaving Salalah by the Taqa road it soon changes to a fine wide dual carriageway, the reason for which becomes clear when you realise it doubles as the approach to the Mamura Palace, residence of Qaboos's elder sister. Flanking this stretch of landscaped dual carriageway are large fodder farms and the Royal Farm, which grows grass, cereals and exotic fruits, and houses large stud farms of pedigree Arab horses, as well as dairy herds of local cattle. Next door to the Royal Farm is the extensive Southern Oman Regiment, which has been stationed here on the Salalah plain since the Dhofar War and is now positioned to guard the palace.

West Salalah tour
The West Salalah tour offered by the operators is likely to include Job's Tomb (also known as Nabi Ayoub), frankincense trees and the Mughsail blowholes, and will take roughly half a day, allowing for a picnic and refreshment stops. At the point furthest west, as far as you are permitted to go towards the Yemeni border, you meet a military checkpoint and barrier. It is not permitted to cross over into Yemen. There are no sites of historical importance on this west side of Salalah, but the natural sites and landscape make up for it. The total circuit is approximately 240km.

As you head out west from Al Husn Palace along Qaboos Street you pass the bird sanctuary to your left among the marshes of Khor Salalah. It is not possible to visit the sanctuary, which is private to the grounds of the palace.

If you still have a couple of hours of daylight left (it gets dark at 18.00 all year around) on return from your trip west of Salalah, you can continue straight on up to Job's Tomb to enjoy the sunset over the mountains, looking down towards the sea. Otherwise a full-day trip can be done to the north of Salalah by heading direct to legendary Ubar (modern Shisr), T E Lawrence's Atlantis of the Sands. The site lies northwest of Thumrayt, 180km from Salalah, so after exploring it you can have a picnic lunch in the desert, and return via the Pools of Ayun and Job's Tomb. By reaching the tomb in time for sunset, you can enjoy a drink on the terrace of the adjacent restaurant overlooking the Salalah plain from on high.

Ubar tour
North of Salalah, the tour offered by all the operators is the 'Ubar and the Empty Quarter' tour. It lasts a full day. You will be taken to the archaeological

site and small museum (for details see *Shisr*, pages 284–7), after which you will be taken for a drive over the dunes of the Empty Quarter.

An early start is usually made, and although a 4x4 is not strictly necessary to reach it, the journey over the gravel track takes rather a long time, and is not advisable by saloon car. Most organised trips to Ubar include a short spell in the desert beyond, to give the visitor a taste of the Empty Quarter and to experience the sensation, however briefly, of being surrounded by silence and sand. Sumharam Watersports and Diving Centre (in the Hilton and Crowne Plaza hotels) has a camp here, if you want an overnighter. You may find that camels lurk at a particular point beyond Ubar, the young owner ever hopeful that a party of tourists will want to experience a ride.

AIN REZAT عين رزة

The turn-off to Ain Rezat, the spring from which the Royal Farm is irrigated, is at the Mamura roundabout, where the dual carriageway ends. A private road leads to the Mamura Palace itself. This is just five minutes from Salalah and a further few minutes leads you the 7km on tarmac road to the spring, where the gardens are opened at the weekend to picnicking families. A notice warns of bilharzia snails and forbids swimming or washing in the water. Set within ten minutes' drive of Salalah, the spot is inevitably popular but the crowds can be escaped to some extent if you park and walk through the gorge, following the *falaj* systems which extend for 17km with some interesting remnants of old *aflaj* in places. The spot was the scene of heavy fighting during the 1963–75 Dhofar War. Birdwatching is good here.

AIN HAMRAN عين حمران

Just 12km outside Salalah a sign points inland to another spring, Ain Hamran, 7km away. The straight road takes you to the bottom of the cliffs, where there is no settlement as such, though during the *khareef* season a large tented encampment pitches here. The road leads round to a public area with parking, pretty and lush with trees, ending in a circular pool with steps down. Women and children can be found sitting by the pool at weekends, their washing hanging out to dry on the railings, the children splashing and swimming in the pool. Further tracks lead off among the trees with the *falaj* running through. As you leave, look out for the pre-Islamic citadel on top of a hillock that guards access to the spring, just where the vegetation stops. A little path leads up to the top – a five- or ten-minute scramble depending on age and agility. This is also an excellent birdwatching spot.

TAQA طاقة

Taqa is the first town you come to east of Salalah, an easy 20-minute drive (30km), and was once a prosperous port. There are three tarmac roads turning off to Taqa and it is best to take the first one, signposted Taqa Castle (1.5km). This leads past the picturesque Khor Edge, through the town to the little fort set in the centre (© *08.00–14.00 Sun–Fri*), with a handful of older Dhofari houses facing it. The stone used in these houses is quarried locally and starts off as white, but then goes black when exposed to the sun and air over a period of years.

On the small hill behind Taqa are four small forts guarding the town, one of which can be reached via a gravel track. Sultan Qaboos's mother is buried in the

TAQA
(SKETCH MAP)

N

Bradt

NORTH TAQA

↑ Madinat al Haqq

→ Wadi Dirbat, Khor Rori,
Sumharam, Teyq cave & sinkhole

MIDDLE
TAQA

Salalah (28km) ←

TAQA STREET

WEST TAQA

🏰 Taqa Castle

SUMHARAM ST

Khor Rori
archaeological site

🏰 Castle

ARABIAN SEA

graveyard of Taqa. The road from the fort in the centre of town loops on round in a semicircle to exit the town and rejoin the main road at the crossroads with Madinat Al Haqq, a town up in Jebel Qara.

WADI DIRBAT   وادی دربات

A five-minute drive beyond Taqa sees you crossing a bridge over the Wadi Dirbat, one of Dhofar's lushest wadis and a beautiful place for a picnic. During and immediately after the monsoon rain, the wadi is a riot of water, with lakes, pools, waterfalls and lush pasture. Even for the rest of the year it is well worth a visit for its caves and their paintings, as well as the dramatic gorge scenery.

To get to the upper reaches of the wadi you need a 4x4 to cope with the steep gradient and rough surface. With a saloon car, the most you can do is take one of the easy graded tracks after the bridge that leads up towards the vertical cliff face. During the monsoon season, the water comes crashing over here from the upper wadi in a dramatic waterfall, much photographed for Dhofar publicity material. In practice it looks like this only for about two weeks of the year, in late August/early September.

The approach to the upper wadi is from the Wadi Attair tarmac road, signposted up the hill just to the east of the wadi. Halfway up the climb to the plateau a graded track forks left, signposted Dirbat, easy at first, but soon with gradients too steep for the average saloon car. In a 4x4 you can continue 2–3km from the start of the graded track until you reach a group of huts. Above them to the right you can climb 30m to a natural rock arch, which has cave chambers with stalagmites and stalactites as well as stunning views over the lower wadi as it runs to the sea.

A short distance beyond this on the track (1.5km) is a second cave on the right of the road just above wadi level. Though small, the cave has drawings of animals, coloured with pigments from iron, coal and ochre.

From here the track is rough and steep and ends at a limestone wall 4.7km later, to the left of which is Oman's largest natural cave. The area is full of trees and especially lush in the monsoon, when the track becomes very muddy. These caves are the most accessible in Oman.

In the Arab world picnicking has a long tradition and on Fridays families like nothing better than to go en masse, with all generations from grannies to babies, and sit somewhere together out in the countryside. Shade is the primary concern when choosing the spot, rather than beauty. Carpets are spread out, and the women busy themselves with the pots and pans and food preparation. The men see to the fires and barbecues, while the children run around amusing themselves in the freedom of the environment, creating toys from twigs and whatever comes to hand. In Dhofar this ritual continues even during the rains of the *khareef*, in fact it is almost enjoyed more because of the novelty of the rain.

Whereas our Western tradition when picnicking is to head as far away as possible from habitation and other people, the Arab tradition is much more sociable, and picnicking groups often mingle freely. These occasions often go on well into the night.

TAWI ATTAIR طوي الطير

The tarmac road ends after a delightful 20-minute drive through the village of Tawi Attair, at the start of which is a track to the left signposted Khisais Adeen. Less than half a kilometre along this track is a group of small huts to the left. Turn right here along a faint track that follows the line of the water pipes heading for the village. Stop after roughly 200m when you get close to some corrugated huts, park and continue on foot for 200–300m towards the village looking out for a metal tripod sticking up in the boulder-strewn scrubby ground. This marks the edge of the gigantic and very impressive sinkhole, said to be one of the largest in the world. It is roughly 150m in diameter and 211m deep. There is water at the bottom, the same water that is pumped up through pipelines to supply the village. Pakistani labourers in the fields may help you if you cannot locate it yourself.

Also tricky to locate is the small path leading down to a platform overlooking an 80m drop to the bottom. Finding this and climbing down to it will double the time needed for your visit from half an hour to one hour. The purpose of this descent is to hear the birdsong which gives this sinkhole its name Tawi Attair, or 'well of the birds'. It is a wonderful experience in the total silence of the surroundings. The sinkhole is the start of an extensive cave system that can be entered only by experienced divers.

Beans, cucumbers, corn and mangoes are the main agricultural crops of the region of Tawi Attair. Honey production, livestock breeding and the craft of making *majmars*, which are the Dhofari-style incense burners, are all popular in this area. Diving for oysters is also practised here. The region has many natural springs and caves.

BAOBAB FOREST غابة البواباب

From Tawi Attair, if you return to the tarmac and follow the line of the graded track, this will lead you for some 16km along the plateau through sprawling meadows. You gradually climb to 1,450m, the summit of Jebel Samhan (see page 278), with stunning views to the coast. The descent of the range is extremely steep in parts, suitable for 4x4 only. To reach the baobab forest (70km from Salalah) it is preferable, if you only have one day, to approach from the tarmac coast road near Mirbat, where it is only 3km up the graded track, signposted Tawi Attair. This too requires a 4x4 because of the steepness. After 3km from the tarmac take the small track to the right that stops after 50m. Park here on the ledge overlooking the valley and you will find two paths, one leading up, one leading down. The one leading down takes you to a small wadi with a *falaj* deep in the forest. The other leads up through some rocks and reaches a small forest of huge baobab trees, some 30–40 in all. The largest, near the centre, has a diameter of 30ft and is thought to be over 2,000 years old. There is also a stream and the area is a splendid picnic spot with boulders and shade. The remaining ascent reaches Wadi Attair after 14km.

KHOR RORI AND SUMHARAM خور روري و سمهرم

Back on the main road, almost immediately after the Wadi Attair signpost at Wadi Dirbat is a sign to the right to Khor Rori. A good graded track leads you down towards the sea. At a fork after some 3km, turn right to reach the hillock on which the fenced-in ruins of the ancient city of Sumharam stand, the fine limestone walls overlooking the silted-up harbour of Khor Rori (about 35km from Salalah). To the left the track continues for another 4km or so to reach the headland right on the sea. Rockfalls and silt blocked its harbour mouth, but before that it was a safe harbour for ships from the Red Sea, Mesopotamia and the Far East. The whole area is totally deserted, with no settlement or habitation, making an excellent spot to camp in magnificent surroundings. The creek is now fresh water, having been separated from the sea by a sandy bank, and is favoured by many migratory seabirds including flamingos, waders, herons, gulls and terns.

THE QUEEN OF SHEBA'S PALACE Sumharam, the archaeological site at Khor Rori, is also known as the Queen of Sheba's Palace. There is a small hut manned by a guardian (⏲ *07.30–14.30 Sun–Thu*) but there are holes in the fence, so even when the gates are closed there is access for the curious. Unsupervised entry has led to problems, however, and wanton damage has been caused by smashing the glass cases that have been erected over the inscriptions to protect them from the elements. The site was first excavated in 1952 by the American Wendell Phillips, the first person to carry out archaeological work in Dhofar.

The only site in Dhofar that dates to before Christ, Sumharam was in 1000BC the greatest city of southeast Arabia. It was also a powerful port, which controlled the frankincense trade route inland through Arabia to Jerusalem, Alexandria and even Rome. The temple of the moon god 'Sin' here guarded the frankincense stores. The routes themselves, zigzagging across Arabia from watering place to watering place, were agreed on by the Queen of Sheba in consultation with King Solomon, her neighbour in the north. Wendell Phillips found evidence of an impregnable fortress city dedicated to a pagan god. The Romans sent an expedition in 24BC to Arabia to find the lands where the frankincense trees were grown, but they died in their thousands before reaching southern Arabia in the deserts north of Yemen.

Sumharam was the easternmost of the cities on the frankincense route, ruled by the kings and queens of Sheba and Yemen who controlled the myrrh of Yemen and the frankincense of Dhofar. From Sumharam, thought to be the greatest spice centre on earth, the bags full of frankincense would go to India and even China, or over the deserts by camel to Damascus and Alexandria. Archaeologists have now dated the site to 100BC from finds of bronze coins, amphorae and sculptures. The whole city is built from well-crafted limestone blocks. Known in ancient times as Moscha, the city was the major port for the incense trade, gateway to the inland

10

FRANKINCENSE

In ancient geography the southern area of Arabia was named Arabia Felix. Compared with the dry interior and the barren mountainous north of the region, the south was richly fertile, and home to the frankincense tree, the valuable gum from which allowed the region to flourish, giving rise to the name 'felix', meaning 'happy' or 'flourishing'.

Frankincense was used in religious rites and for medicinal purposes in most civilisations throughout the ancient world. Used in temples and at funerals, and as tribute to be paid by the Arabs to Darius the Persian king, it was a much sought-after substance and, as with myrrh, more valuable than gold at the time of Christ. In the famous words of the Song of Solomon: 'I will get me to the mountain of myrrh, and to the hill of frankincense.'

Ancient Greek and Roman writers such as Herodotus, Ptolemy, Pliny, Strabo and Diodorus relate that frankincense from Dhofar was taken by sea to all parts of the world. It was suggested that frankincense was the first commodity to lead to the whole idea of international trade routes and that the Queen of Sheba, for whom Dhofar was a colony, visited King Solomon in Jerusalem purely in order to agree a safe caravan route for the frankincense. Roman armies under Augustus went south in 24BC to try to conquer the frankincense-bearing countries, but either died or were forced back by thirst when attempting to cross the Empty Quarter. In the 1st century AD, the countries of southeast Arabia were the richest in the world as a result of the frankincense of Dhofar. At the height of the trade in the 2nd century AD, roughly 3,000 tonnes was being shipped from southern Arabia to Rome, Greece, Egypt, China, India and the Mediterranean world. Khor Rori was the centre.

Two thousand years later, frankincense is still at the centre of Dhofar's heritage. It is produced only in southern Oman, in Wadi Hadramaut in Yemen and in Somalia, but the Arabian type is acknowledged to be the best. The best of the best comes from Sawdah, Hadhbarm and Mirbat, the worst from Qushm. The Arabs divide the trees into four types, of which Hoja'i produces the highest quality. The medium-quality frankincense comes from the slopes and hill summits, while the inferior type is collected near the coast.

route to Petra and Gaza, then to Mesopotamia, and the sea route to Qana in the Hadramaut, Yemen. The inscriptions in the glass cases are the only two remaining of the eight original ones on the main gate of the city. They are written in the old southern Arabian language Himyaritic, and explain the construction of the city, built under the orders of a Sabean king for the express purpose of controlling the frankincense trade and collecting it for export. The Sabean capital was at Shabwa in the Hadramaut (from where the Queen of Sheba is thought to have got her name).

The central temple area, approached by a ramp of steps, contains a well 30m deep, now covered with protective bars, with walls 2.5m thick in places. There are also many incense storage rooms which were unearthed with incense still in them. Further on towards the seaward of the site is an excavated sunken area with three sacrificial altars. On one of the altars is a relief carving of a bull, one of the forms in which the Sabeans worshipped their lunar god. Sacrificial remains of chicken, fish and bird bones were found round the altars, together with incense residue. The other significant find was a small statue in bronze of an Indian girl playing the flute (*nai*). Dated to the 2nd century AD, the statue proves a trade link between Arabia and India at that point.

Between March and August small incisions are cut into the Boswellia tree bark to allow the milky sap to seep out, taking three to five days to dry into semi-opaque lumps. In ancient times, according to Pliny the historian, only a small number of privileged families were permitted to carry out the harvesting and tending of the trees. He explained:

> These persons are called sacred, and are not allowed, while pruning the trees or gathering the harvest, to receive any pollution, either by intercourse with women or contact with the dead; by these religious observances it is that the price of the commodity is so enhanced.

Frankincense burns well on account of its natural oil content and is used throughout Oman today largely in this capacity, burnt on coals to fragrance a room as a gesture of hospitality and in fumigators to fragrance clothing. Travelling round Oman, you will soon become accustomed to the aroma of frankincense in souks, in the shopping malls, in hotel lobbies and on the clothes of Omanis. It is also a component of a fragrance called Amouage (*www.amouage.com*), one of the most valuable perfumes in the world (see pages 122–3). The burning of frankincense is an essential part of wedding and Eid festivities and at births. An exotic version of frankincense which is mixed with other aromatic materials is *bakhoor* (or *bukhour, bokhur*). The ingredients vary and can include *oudh* (scented wood from India and the Far East), rose water, sandalwood, attar, myrrh, other perfume oils, aromatic resins and extracts. These are blended in their varying quantities, cooked, then ground down into a powder for burning on coals.

Salalah's frankincense souk is dedicated to the sale of incense and a variety of perfume, and is run by Omanis. The traditional hand-painted pottery frankincense burner (*mejmarr*) has had a revival after being used as packaging for Amouage's new perfume Salalah. Dhofari women make the pottery and then hand-paint it, thereby helping to supplement their family incomes. Frankincense and a frankincense burner make the ideal souvenir of your travels here.

From now the road heads east a little inland until, just after the graded track left to Tawi Attair that you take to reach the baobab forest after 3km, the main road does a sudden drop down to a long sandy beach. On the far headland of this beach lies the little fishing town of Mirbat. A recently built tourist complex with restaurant and playground stands right at the beginning of the beach, and sunshades are spaced at regular intervals along the sand all the way to the Mirbat end.

BIN ALI'S TOMB At the end of the beach, as the road bears round to the right, is a little unsignposted tarmac street called Bin Ali Street that leads some 300m to the tomb of Muhammad bin Ali, a local 14th-century prophet and scholar.

A mosque, which is still used for burial preparations, has been built beside the large car park and a path leads beyond it to the medieval twin onion-domed shrine or tomb of the saint. The tomb has a perennial water source in front under its own baby onion dome. Non-Muslims are permitted to enter the simple incense-filled room; all must remove shoes before entry. Surrounding the tomb is an extensive cemetery, some of the graves really very elaborate. Those with three headstones are for women and those with two are for men.

SADAH ‏سدح‎

Just after the turn-off to bin Ali's Tomb is a graded track to the left along the coast, signposted for Sadah (Suduh). This little fishing village, about 135km from Salalah, was another trading port for the export of frankincense. It has a small fort (🕐 *08.00–14.00 Tue–Fri*), and is a 1½-hour drive along a rough track through monotonous landscape far from the sea. Beyond Sadah the track is closer to the sea and the sandy bays have sheer cliffs, making them good protected camping spots for those with a 4x4. The ancient city of Hasek is here and, coupled with the scenery of Jebel Nous, it makes this place worth a trip. Livestock breeding, honey production and diving for oysters are all popular here.

The particular speciality of the sea here is abalone, a kind of sea snail (known locally as *sufailah),* whose firm white flesh the locals call 'the food of the gods'. It is also thought to be an aphrodisiac. Most of the catch is dried and shipped to the Far East where it fetches high prices. Since 1991, abalone fishing has been limited to two months a year. Excessive fishing had driven it to the verge of extinction, decreasing from a typical daily catch of over 400 in the early 1980s to barely 30 a day, prior to the law of 1991 being enforced.

BETWEEN TAQA AND MIRBAT ‏بين طاقة ومرباط‎

TEYQ CAVE ‏كهف طيق‎ The Teyq sinkhole, located between Taqa and Mirbat to the east of Salalah and about 15km north of the coast, is one of the largest sinkholes in the world. It is 250m deep and 75 times as big as Oman's Majlis al Jinn chamber (in the Sharqiya region). There is currently no conducted tour to the cave, but tourists can visit the outside of it independently. Alternatively, any tour operator in Salalah will drive you there on request.

JEBEL SAMHAN NATURE RESERVE ‏جبل سمهان‎ Proclaimed a nature reserve in 1997 and covering an area of 4,500km² the reserve extends down to the coastal plain between Marbat and Sadah, called Thalawt. The aim is to protect the wildlife in its natural habitat. The Arabian wolf, Arabian leopard, Nubian ibex, stripped hyena, Arabian gazelle, Blanford's fox and wild cats can be found here. Both green and loggerhead turtles nest here on the sandy beaches between Hadbin and Shuwaymiyah.

In a saloon car you can drive easily up the interesting climb to the plateau around Jebel Samhan, the highest point in Dhofar at 1,450m. On top, the scenery is lush and rolling and still quite green, even in late October and early November. Herds of cattle are everywhere, all over the fields and the road, interspersed with camels. Jebali villages dot the area, their simple dwellings showing the simplicity of their lifestyle. Many of their stone circular huts are still in evidence, but thatched roofs have now been superseded by plastic sheeting weighted down with old tyres. In the fields you can also see their stone-walled enclosures used for pasturing the herds.

MIRBAT ‏مرباط‎

The tarmac road continues out on the headland to Mirbat (about 70km from Salalah) and at the approach a sign points you off right to reach Mirbat Castle (🕐 *08.30–14.30 Sun–Fri; 500bzs*). The castle overlooks the harbour with fine views from the towers, and its trio of cannons, intact on a raised platform, remain as evidence of its defence against invaders from the sea.

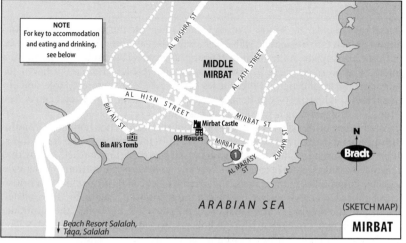

NOTE
For key to accommodation
and eating and drinking,
see below

MIDDLE
MIRBAT

AL BUSHRA ST

AL FATH STREET

AL HISN STREET

BIN ALI ST

Mirbat Castle

MIRBAT ST

Bin Ali's Tomb

Old Houses

MIRBAT ST

1

AL MARASY ST

ZUHAYR ST

N

Bradt

ARABIAN SEA

(SKETCH MAP)

Beach Resort Salalah,
Taqa, Salalah

MIRBAT

Today, the fishing village is not large but still has some fine old merchants' houses with carved doors and windows. In earlier times it too was a port for the export of frankincense, as well as a breeding centre for Arabian horses which were also exported – the name Mirbat is said to have come from *marabat al khail* which means 'place of tethering' in Arabic. There is a statue of horses at the

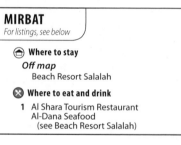

MIRBAT
For listings, see below

◉ **Where to stay**
Off map
  Beach Resort Salalah

⊗ **Where to eat and drink**
1 Al Shara Tourism Restaurant
   Al-Dana Seafood
   (see Beach Resort Salalah)

beginning of the village which indicates that this is what the area was known for. The waters at Mirbat, and to the east of Mirbat to Hasik, offer excellent diving (see page 269 for further details) and are the best places for spotting dolphins. Sports fishing tours begin here at the harbour. For location of town see map above.

WHERE TO STAY

⌂ Salalah Marriott Resort & Spa
PO Box 225, Mirbat; ☎ 23 268245; www.
marriottsalalahresort.com. The first Marriott hotel in Oman has chosen Mirbat Cove as its location, well away from any competition & in an excellent spot for diving, watersports & dolphin-watching. The white sandy beach & black rocky sections contribute to the highly scenic spot. Initial teething problems when it opened in 2010 have been resolved & it can now serve alcohol. There are several dining options, from the plush Al-Dana Seafood restaurant to poolside snacks, an Arabic café & even an English pub. Very much a place for getting away from it all. Diving centre & full health spa, huge freeform pool (the largest in Oman) & tennis courts. Good promotional rates. **$$$**

✕ WHERE TO EAT
If you want to stop off quickly for some food, take the first right after Mirbat Castle, then second right where there is a sign for Shaba Restaurant. This is actually Al Shara Tourism Restaurant, and although basic in appearance, offers an extensive international menu for a very low price, with a friendly staff and views out to sea. If you want to linger, there are of course the restaurants of the Salalah Marriott, where as well as the top-class Al-Dana Seafood restaurant, there is also an all-day (06.30–23.00) restaurant serving international fare daily.

HALANIYAT ISLANDS جزائر حلانيات

These five islands lie 200km east of Salalah, just off the coast of Shalim and Shuwaymiyah (see map, page 248). They used to be called the Kuria Maria Islands, but now are known as the Juzor al Halaaniyaal or the Halaniyat Islands, and the intention is to make them a protected zone and reserve. They are a haven for migratory birds and marine life: turtles breed here and there are large dolphin populations. Diving trips can be arranged through one of the diving centres (see page 269), and camping is possible on the islands.

The history of the islands is rather curious. They were once home to a handful of fishermen, and in 1854 the sultan gave them to the British Crown for nothing, after Lord Clarendon, the foreign secretary of the time, approached him with a scheme to extract guano (excrement of sea fowl used as manure) from the islands, a valuable commodity in those days. The scheme had been the brainchild of a British merchant called Ord, who, having spotted the guano while sailing by, duly enlisted the help of the Foreign Office, the India Office, the Colonial Office, the Admiralty and the Bombay government and a whole assortment of solicitors and MPs. The sultan refused to take any money for the islands, so Lord Clarendon felt obliged to send a snuffbox as a thank you.

The guano project, run by Ord and Company, did extract many tonnes of guano but then had its licence terminated in 1861 for failing to make royalty payments. Britain still owned the islands, however, and they were officially administered from Aden. When Aden became independent in 1967, Britain was in the embarrassing position of feeling obliged to hand over the Halaniyat Islands to Aden. The sultan of course would have been furious if Britain were to give to a third party a piece of sultanate territory which had been a generous gift to Queen Victoria. The only way out of the embarrassment was for Britain to return the islands to the sultan, which it duly did in 1967.

WEST OF SALALAH غرب صلالة

PORT OF SALALAH Located at Raysut in the industrial zone, 15km west of Salalah (out past the Hilton Hotel), this used to be referred to as Port Raysut. It began its

THE MUSLIM VIEW OF DEATH AND BURIAL

Burial in the Islamic world is a quick affair, always within 24 hours of death, and in a fairly simple grave, often with no coffin, but with the corpse just wrapped in a white shroud. The Prophet Muhammad said that if the deceased were a good man, the sooner he is buried the sooner he will reach heaven; and if a bad man, he should also be speedily buried so that his unhappy lot might not fall on the others in the house. The actual funeral service is not recited at the grave, this being thought too polluted a place for such a sacred ceremony, so it is usually held in a mosque or in an open space near the house of the deceased, either by the family imam or the *qadi* (judge). The corpse is buried with its head to the north and feet to the south, and as it is lowered all present speak the sentence: 'We commit thee to earth in the name of God and in the religion of the Prophet.' Cremation of the dead is strictly forbidden under Islam, for a dead body was considered as fully conscious of pain as a living body, and Muhammad said: 'It is not fit for anyone to punish with fire but God.'

operations in 1998 and is now one of the world's busiest harbours. Before it was built, ships could come in to berth for only six months of the year, prevented for the rest of the year by the high monsoon tides. The facility today is a world-class transhipment and container terminal, competing with the container ports of Jebel Ali and Port Rashid in Dubai, Khor Fakan on the UAE east coast, and Aden.

MUGHSAIL مغسيل Once beyond the Raysut turn-off the road narrows and is very light in traffic. Scattered frankincense trees can be seen in the wadis at the roadsides. Take the right signposted to Al Mughsail, which is the road that leads to Yemen (although the border cannot be crossed). The next landmark is Mughsail Beach, a comfortable half-hour drive from Salalah (roughly 45km). It is a magnificent 4km stretch of white sand with high cliffs at either end. The first area you can drive on to has substantial shaded shelters built of breeze block, though the quantity of rubbish littering the area is depressing, especially in view of the numerous green government notices in Arabic exhorting brother citizens to look after the environment and avoid pollution. Picnic shades stretch the length of the beach, at the far end of which is the attractively green and large Khor Mughsail, usually covered in grazing camels and cattle, with many seabirds, including flamingos, pelicans and storks.

Directly opposite the khor is the sign to Kahf Al Marnaf (Al Marnif Cave), complete with the seafront Al Mughsail Beach Tourist Restaurant, car park and Al Marnif Restaurant. The food at these restaurants (both international food, fish, steaks, omelettes, soups, salads) is good and cheap (budget range), but you might prefer to simply stop off for an ice cream or a soft drink. At Al Marnif Restaurant there are disabled toilet facilities. It is from this car park that you need to walk to reach the Mughsail blowholes.

Not visible from the road, the blowholes are clustered a short walk past the imposing rocky outcrop and cave and down some steps. They are at their most impressive during the monsoon season when the sea is at its most forceful, and water can shoot up to 30m high through the limestone rock. At other times of year the blowholes are still active at high tide, but at low tide you will mainly just hear the sea slopping about under the rocks, with the occasional soft roar and gentle spray forcing its way up through the metal grids which have been put over the holes to prevent accidents. Even a gentle spray can completely soak you so be careful what you wear, as watches, leather or cameras could be damaged. It is fun to watch people posing for photos beside the blowholes, tentatively awaiting the arrival of the huge forceful spray of sea water so that it can be captured on camera, before they hurriedly dart away to avoid getting soaked.

JEBEL QAMR جبل قمر After Mughsail, the road westwards begins its impressive one-hour climb up to the plateau of the Jebel Qamr, 'the Mountains of the Moon'. The hairpin bends wind their way up and down the first chain of mountains, the hillsides covered in frankincense trees, before the ascent proper begins leading up to the plateau. There are occasional stopping places from which to admire the views, but the best one is near the summit where a series of little tracks lead off the road towards the coast with tremendous views down over the sea. Camels, cows and donkeys are in abundance, and the ground is teeming with wild flowers and butterflies. The countryside here is not as empty as it seems at first, and you can find a spot, sit down for lunch quite alone, then be startled by a Jebali herdsman striding past as if from nowhere.

The landscape of the plateau is very different again, with extensive rolling plains covered in grass (browning by late October), trees and the occasional settlement of cow farmers. There is one checkpoint which you can pass through with no documentation, but the second checkpoint 125km from Salalah, where there is a barrier, requires a permit to continue beyond to Sarfait 40km away on the Yemeni border. A signpost points to a place beyond called Furious.

RAYKHUT ريخوت The tarmac road up on the plateau and the ascent itself are virtually traffic free with whole stretches where you do not pass another vehicle. If you take the new tarmac road to Rakhyut, a small fishing settlement and old sea port, 23km away on the coast, you come very soon to a whole succession of settlements of green corrugated-iron huts, and the amount of traffic on the road quadruples, making it feel positively crowded.

On the return drive as you approach the other checkpoint with the flags, look out for the fortification on the top of the hill to your left. It is built of well-crafted stone blocks and is very extensive. Cows are often to be found grazing in it.

✗ Where to eat
✗ **Al Muhit Restaurant** [off map, 264 A5]
This is located 5km west of Salalah on the way to

Raysut, with beach-side patios. It offers Arabian, Chinese & Indian cuisine.

NORTH OF SALALAH شمال صلالة

Travelling northwards up and out of Salalah, by the good main Muscat road, the flat coastal plain is soon crossed (within about ten minutes) and the road starts to ascend and bend as it climbs up through the clouds into the Qara mountains, with fantastic views back down to the sea. In the *khareef* (monsoon season), this plain becomes a large camping area for locals, and home to the Khareef festival for three months (see box, page 257). This is the busiest stretch of road in the Salalah region, carrying all the Muscat traffic. It is becoming busier all the time as the overland traffic transporting goods from Raysut Port begins to increase. Once past Ghadr, you can take the left to Job's Tomb or keep straight on the road to Shisr.

Cows and camels on the road are a normal feature of the climb up the mountains. They appear to wander freely with no sign of their owners, camels unhobbled, taking themselves in search of pasture. At dusk they are something of a hazard, and cows especially, being a darker colour and less easy to spot at night, can occasionally be found knocked over at the roadside, guts heaving in a mass of flies. During the *khareef* the roads become very wet and slippery and camels tend to be kept penned up as there are otherwise too many accidents.

Having climbed the mountains and reached the summit of the Jebel Qamr plateau, the landscape changes very quickly into featureless gravel desert. Signs to a tourist information centre may excite you, but the building looks as if it has been unoccupied for months. There is a police stop on the left that may or may not flag you down. Continuing straight, you reach Thumrayt (about 50 minutes' drive from Salalah), and a major crossroads from which roads head east into the oilfields around Marmul.

THUMRAYT ثمريت Thumrayt links Dhofar to the rest of Oman and therefore, throughout history, has acted as an important juncture on the ancient caravan routes. Much of Dhofar's frankincense was grown here. The town has a camel racecourse, and races are held here just twice a year, in November and January. A camel used for milk sells for RO500 but a camel used for racing can sell for a great deal more, even over RO1,000. With changing lifestyles fewer people wish to own camels as they are not really profitable and the status that used to go with owning a large herd is fast evaporating.

Indeed, many lifestyle elements have changed in recent years. Until 1991 it was a favourite pastime for men to go into the mountains for several days at a stretch and hunt oryx, enjoying the camaraderie of the camping lifestyle and the thrill of the hunt. Now that hunting oryx is banned, there is nothing to substitute for this type of hunting. The crafts of palm-frond weaving, spinning and weaving wool, and tent making are still carried out here, however. A few leopards still survive in the hills.

The graded track to Shisr is clearly signposted 72km to the left, which takes 45–55 minutes from here, depending on your preferred speed over the gravel. For location of listings see map, page 256.

🏠 Where to stay

🏠 **Qitbit Resthouse** (10 rooms) m 99 085686. North of Thumrayt, continuing on the main Muscat–Salalah road, this is the next hotel stop you will reach. This is another basic resthouse with an international restaurant, situated 275km from Salalah, but provides a welcome stop if you need it. Accepts credit cards. **$$**

🏠 **Thumrayt Resthouse** 📞 23 279371. The Thumrayt Hotel & restaurant stands over to the right on the road to Shisr & Ubar, & is the first in the series of 3 resthouses on the long Salalah–Muscat road (for details of the others see pages 208 & 248). Run entirely by Indians, it is a simple set-up despite its lavish marble entrance. The restaurant is not licensed & serves Indian or international cuisine. The resthouse at Thumrayt is a welcome stop if you are visiting the Empty Quarter & Ubar. **$$**

✘ Where to eat
By the petrol station (close to the resthouse) there are a few coffee shop/restaurants and fruit juice stalls. If you haven't brought a picnic, you might like to eat here or inside the Thumrayt Resthouse.

THE JEBALI

As their name implies, the Jebali are a mountain people of southern Oman (*jebel* is Arabic for mountain). They lived, until recently, largely on the milk and meat of cattle, goats and camels, and were dependent on these livestock for their survival and livelihood.

Omani Jebali is a different language from Arabic, and the Jebali from the Qara, the Mahra and the Shahara tribes each have a language distinct from each other (as well as distinct from the Dhofaris themselves), originating from the ancient languages of southern Arabia. Their traditional clothing is an indigo-dyed piece of material, wrapped up and over the shoulder and around the waist, forming a skirt, and the older Jebalis can be seen today dressed in this way. The younger ones have tended towards both the diet and attire of the people of Salalah town. Generally, the Jebali have been able to take advantage of the improved situation of their surrounds, in terms of education, medical care, employment, access to a wider range of foods, etc, since Sultan Qaboos took control.

The Jebali formerly lived in traditional round-stone windowless houses, which had earth and grass roofs, built slightly sunken into the ground; relatively few of these remain today. Instead they occupy concrete and corrugated-iron structures.

10

When travelling about for days in the interior, where there are no supermarkets or shops, the accepted method of feeding yourself was to take a goat along. On one occasion, Ranulph Fiennes travelled with a goat tethered between him and his driver for two days. The Omani then prepared the fire, carried it lovingly over, stroking it gently, then slit its throat with a razor blade while he held it between his knees. Sentimentality towards animals has no place in Arab culture. Travellers today, touring outside of Salalah and inland, where eating places are limited, might like to think on this and pack a picnic.

SHISR (SITE OF UBAR, ATLANTIS OF THE SANDS) الشصر و أرم القديم It takes about two hours to drive from Salalah to Shisr and a 4x4 is needed. Your arrival at Shisr is heralded by a sudden appearance of trees and buildings in the midst of the bleak landscape. You will need to drive between the two model watchtowers at either side of the entrance road to Shisr itself.

The settlement here is on slightly raised ground. The permanent water source enables year-round irrigation so there are crops growing round the spring in a fenced area. A guardian keeps the key to the fenced site, beside which stands the housing estate built in 1970 by the sultan, with a school and mosque to encourage surrounding nomads to settle. Ranulph Fiennes rented two of these houses for the archaeological team that at the time was using Shisr as a base for digs in the area, never suspecting the site of Ubar was right beside them.

A small shop selling refreshments and occasional simple lunches of omelettes, rice and chicken has been set up by the guardian and his wife at the entrance to the site. There is also a wooden hut, which is the Ubar Museum. An official comes over from a government building opposite to unlock the museum for you. If no-one is around, then enquire at the small shop. The same official gives a brief talk on the history of the site.

Inside is a collection of photographic material, including the American satellite photos which claimed to pinpoint Ubar as the genuine site alluded to in the Koran, together with photos of pretty girls shipped in to ensure volunteers from the Thumrayt army bases would come forward to boost manpower at the excavation site. Photocopies of the sensationalised international press articles are also pinned up on the walls. The articles at the time (in 1992) caused Oman much grief as the world press made many unscientifically proven claims, the most embarrassing of which was that Ubar was identified with 'Irem of the lofty pillars', as mentioned in the Koran. Outraged Muslim countries chastised Oman and the sultan for making such blasphemous claims. How could foreign infidels dare to say that they had found the holy city of the Koran?

In 1991, Ranulph Fiennes published a book entitled *Ubar: Atlantis of the Sands*, the culmination of a search that began 24 years earlier, while on secondment to the Sultan's Armed Forces during the war in Dhofar against the communist-inspired insurrection. Having read T E Lawrence's account of previous attempts to locate Ubar (sometimes called Wabar) and knowing that Lawrence suffered his fatal motorcycle accident before he had the chance to seek it for himself, Fiennes became obsessed with the idea of the legendary frankincense city. He used to take his platoon out on exploratory forays, using any opportunity to question Bedu tribesmen, often by his own admission in effect deserting for periods of a day or two to further his quest, before returning to base at Thumrayt.

Before him, others to search for Ubar included Bertram Thomas, author of *Arabia Felix*, who worked for the Sultan of Muscat as personal financial adviser in 1925, having been an administrator in Palestine. In 1930, he became the first non-Arab to make the 1,450km crossing of the Empty Quarter by camel. Next came H St J B Philby, father of Kim Philby the spy, at that time adviser to King Abdul Aziz of Saudi Arabia. He made the crossing a year later from east to west by a more difficult route. Each one claimed to have found evidence of Ubar. They were followed 14 years later by Wilfred Thesiger, born in Ethiopia in 1910, who joined the Middle East Anti-Locust Unit as an excuse to be in the Empty Quarter, having been inspired while a student at Oxford by the accounts of Bertram Thomas and T E Lawrence. In spite of many journeys across the Empty Quarter, more than any other non-Arab, Thesiger never found the city, but saw many clearly defined camel trails, especially visible in rocky areas, from many directions, all of which, according to the Bedouin guides, converged on the one same site – a city buried in the sand.

When Fiennes had first begun his search for Ubar while still a soldier, he took a big risk – he knew that the sultan would be angry if he discovered the unauthorised expeditions while on the sultan's payroll. The sultan had previously ordered the American archaeologist Wendell Phillips, originally authorised to go in search of Ubar, never to return to Oman.

Fiennes enlisted the help of NASA to provide satellite images that show up swellings of only a few feet in a flat desert setting, which, to an experienced archaeologist, can show manmade foundations. With the help of these, Fiennes eventually persuaded the sultan to fund the expedition and personally took on the logistic organisation of the project. The other key players in the expedition were Nicolas Clapp, a Los Angeles freelance documentary film-maker who had worked with Fiennes before on a polar expedition and who had long shared his obsession with the quest for Ubar. It was he who had the idea to persuade NASA to take satellite images from the space shuttle *Challenger*, which he had heard would enable a trained eye to spot buried ruins under the dunes. The expert eye, the archaeologist on the expedition, was Dr Juris Zarins, an American from South West Missouri State University who had been involved in digs in Arabia over the previous 20 years.

At the start, when the expedition was about to begin in mid July 1990, Fiennes wryly remarked:

My polar expeditions normally start in dark, freezing shacks with a handful
of comrades who know each other well and understand the minutiae of the
straightforward aim to get to the Pole. The Ubar reconnaissance expedition began
in Muscat's plush Al Bustan Palace Hotel and involved a group who were mostly
strangers to each other, none of whom knew how best to set about searching for their
goal, and each of whom had a different motive for being there.

The satellite photos were highly appealing to the sponsors of the expedition and Nicholas Clapp was entirely responsible for the film, which the Omanis had agreed was to be shot in Dhofar with the central theme being the archaeological search for Ubar. The desire to involve these satellite photos led to some frictions after the expedition was complete, when the American media began to claim that these satellite images had led to the discovery of Ubar by revealing ancient tracks of caravan routes that ran for hundreds of kilometres, disappearing under the dunes and then emerging again. The media claimed that these caravan trails converged on Shisr, which is why the expedition dug there. Fiennes and Juris knew this to be untrue, but Juris did not object, saying it was good publicity anyhow. He admitted to Fiennes, 'I never thought Ubar was Shisr even when we started digging.' In fact the discovery was achieved, in Fiennes's words, through 'a large slice of luck, a lot of hard work and the experience-honed instincts of Juris together with the support of good vehicles and generous sponsors'.

Saudi reaction to the discovery of Ubar was to belittle it, annoyed at any suggestion that Ubar or Irem was not within Saudi territory. They claimed that the Omani Ubar was nothing special and that in Saudi Arabia similar sites had been found over the past 15 years, notably Jabreen. Juris, having been involved in these excavations, was adamant however: 'Shisr is unique. There is nowhere like it in the desert for 900 kilometres.' He felt that Jabreen represented the northern end of the incense road connecting Mesopotamia with Dhofar, since it was already marked on the Ptolemy map as Labrus and was 900km away (or seven weeks' journey by camel) from the incense-gathering area. In between the two are well-spaced waterholes, but only at Jabreen and Shisr were large quantities of Roman pottery found, proving that when Ptolemy drew his map in AD150 (the height of the incense trade with Rome), trade was being carried on between Rome and Dhofar.

While speculation on the name will continue as long as no inscription is found on the site, the fact remains that the archaeological finds there were highly significant for southern Arabia. As one British professor wrote on behalf of UNESCO after visiting the site: 'The archaeological integrity of the site should not be allowed to be affected by possible disputes regarding its name.'

You approach the site today from above. Your first view is of the tallest tower, still standing some 8ft high, built of well-crafted blocks, with the first steps of the internal staircase still intact. The original height is estimated at 30ft. Around the tower are storage rooms and hearths, one blackened by wood smoke. From this tower is the spectacular plunge into the collapsed sinkhole, which is probably the most interesting feature of the site. The Arabic name for the site, *shisr*, means 'rock cleft', named after this collapsed section in the very heart of the city. Juris thought it was caused by a decline in the water-table level, leading to a collapse of the immediate surroundings into the 12m-deep limestone cavern, or even by an earthquake, and estimated the timing as somewhere between AD100–300. This natural disaster tied in well with the Koranic description of Ubar, city of the 'Ad people as described in the Sura of the Star:

ISLAM'S SODOM, THE ELUSIVE CITY

Historical references to a city in the sands, of great wealth, wickedness and idolatry, begin around AD200 with Pliny and Arab geographers, who referred to Oman as an emporium, a market set on the crossroads of the lucrative frankincense trade at the southern edge of the Empty Quarter. Pliny called its inhabitants the Ubarites. The city of 'Irem of the lofty pillars' mentioned in the Koran is known from many other historical references to have been an ancient capital of the 'Ad people of southern Arabia. It was said to have been built by King Shaddad bin 'Ad in the image of paradise. It grew to become rich and then corrupt, so that Allah saw fit to punish it and its people by total destruction – Islam's Sodom. The story of the destruction of a mythical city is recounted in the *Arabian Nights* and it is thought to allude to Ubar and to have occurred towards the end of the Roman period.

It is He who makes men laugh and weep, it is He who kills and makes alive. He is the Lord of the Dark Star, He who destroyed 'Ad of yore, and Thamud, and left none of them, and the people of Noah before them. Their cities, He threw them down, and there covered them what did cover them.

As you descend the path round the rim of the crater, you pass some of the other eight watchtowers which encircled the waterhole and which archaeologists hypothesise are the 'lofty pillars' of Irem which, rising high on this raised land, would have been visible for up to 30km in all directions. Water pipes today run into the cavern itself. The source is fresh water, unlike the usual brackish springs of the desert. Scanners detected the outline of a 4m² wellhead buried 28ft under the sand. Fiennes had a Dhofari guide who, on testing the water at Ubar, recognised it as the water from the Pools of Ayun, and another local story runs that a woman dropped her comb into the Pools of Ayun and it was later found in the well at Ubar.

At the time that excavation began here, the crater was filled in with blown sand and the bulk of the early work was in clearing the hole to reveal the original collapsed stonework around the water source. The ruins at Shisr had been written off by all previous seekers for Ubar as being only about 300 years old. Even local Omanis thought of the site as a relatively recent one, not realising what was buried underneath.

Where to stay and eat There are no obvious places to stay or eat in Shisr.

WADI ANDHUR وادي أنذر In eastern Dhofar, rarely marked on any map, lies an oasis of great beauty called Andhur, the site of a further frankincense-collecting centre. It is a difficult four-hour drive from Thumrayt requiring 4x4 and guide, and because of the distance and the terrain you would have to camp for a night. The ruins here, set in a remote valley on a hillock above the date palms, were superficially excavated by the American Wendell Phillips in 1952. They consist of a small fort with just a few rooms and a temple with a cut-stone storage tank lined with mortar. The basin and slabs in the temple are associated with Dhofari sun and moon worship that involved primitive sacrifice, possibly even human. There are rumours of girls buried alive, forcible circumcisions, trial by ordeal before the gods, and incestuous marriage.

The location overlooked water and the frankincense trails north of Mirbat. Andhur is in the region of the Mahra tribesmen and they believe the area is holy and do not take kindly to people camping or lighting fires near it.

POOLS OF AYUN On the return journey from Ubar or Andhur you can vary the route by turning right towards Ayun at the crest of the ridge of the Qara mountains to find the Pools of Ayun, which are said to be the source of the spring at Ubar. The small tarmac road runs along the top of the ridge just on the edge of the area reached by the monsoon, so the scenery is a strange mix of desert bleakness to one side, and suggestions of fertility and greenness to the other. The frankincense trees shown here on old maps have mainly died in recent years, through incorrect harvesting of the incense. After about 20 minutes you reach the signposted right turn to Ayun (6km), but almost immediately you fork left on to a graded track, bearing right when there is a choice. This leads across barren hillsides for some 3–4km and ends at a parking area on the edge of a gorge, with no settlement in sight. Though it's a little bumpy in places, a saloon car can cope.

The pools themselves lie at the foot of the gorge and can only be seen by getting out of your vehicle, walking to the edge of the gorge and looking down. The perennial pools are a lovely sight, cool and green in the barren landscape, and the only sound is reeds blowing gently in the breeze. On Fridays there may be some youths from the village, which perches out of sight on an escarpment above, but on other days you should find the spot beautifully peaceful and deserted. The climb down to the pools is more of a clamber than a walk and takes 10–15 minutes depending on your level of agility in boulder hopping. Up by the parking area are several clusters of frankincense trees, often to be found with their gum oozing from inept cuts. These days, sadly, very few Omanis know how to harvest frankincense correctly. Instead Somalis are imported to do the work, disappearing into the hillsides for weeks at a time. They are used to the work from their own country's incense trade.

THE EUREKA MOMENT

Before digging at Ubar, the expedition which began in December 1991 dug at many other sites, but always to no avail. The local Bedouin had a habit of referring to ruins as 'rubbish piles', which is what many of them had become. In one ancient well shaft, described by Ptolemy in his early map as the Oracle of Diana, the foul smell of modern garbage and animal bones defeated their attempts to find earlier debris below it.

Once digging at Ubar began, they found within weeks 60% of the remains of the citadel walls and nine towers. Some 13,000 artefacts were found, including a 1,000-year-old soapstone chess set, the only one ever found in southern Arabia. The king was called 'Shah', for modern chess is based on a Persian war game, and when the king was cornered the opponent would shout 'Shah maat', meaning 'The king is dead', a sound remarkably similar to 'checkmate'. Pottery was also found from Mesopotamia, Rome, Greece and Syria, as well as celadon and Ming plates from China, and glass bracelets from Aden. Many of the artefacts date from Shisr's trading heyday from 500–300BC, the Roman, Greek and south Arabian period. There was a decline in materials between 300BC and AD300, and the name Ubar is thought to have declined in use then also. The artefacts showed a renewal of trade during the early Islamic period from 650–1200, a period when Ubar was known also to be active.

Though the site today is small, the archaeologists speculated that this was the walled and towered caravanserai built round the strategically sited waterhole. They also hypothesised that vast tented encampments covered the hillsides around, to cope with caravans of camels carrying the incense on its route north to Alexandria and Rome, and to the ancient Sumerian civilisation in southern Iraq. Speculation is that at its zenith around 3000BC maybe 100,000 people would have been camped around its walls. Juris identified some 30 campsites on the outskirts of Ubar where caravans would have grouped and waited to enter the city. Until an inscription is found bearing the name Ubar, controversy will always surround the identification of the site, and sceptics doubt that camels were domesticated as early as 2800BC. But the evidence is compelling. Juris said defiantly:

Historians and archaeologists the world over have always had the opinion that there's nothing of value in Arabia, that nothing will ever come out of Arabia ... Only in the last 20 years have we begun to discover that Arabia is an integral part of the human experience of Mesopotamia, Palestine and Egypt.

JOB'S TOMB Continuing on the same road you begin the descent of the mountains and some 20 minutes further on from Ayun you will come to the fork right to Job's Tomb (or Nabi Ayoub, as it is known locally). The little dead-end tarmac road leads 1km and forks left up to the walled enclosure for the tomb, now with several other outbuildings grouped together in a garden of trees. Admission is free and the path leads round past the toilets and mosque to the tomb at the far end. Before you enter, the guardian may show you a footprint, reportedly that of the Prophet Ayoub. Both the footprint and the tomb are considerably large and giant-like. The guardian issues women with a green diaphanous scarf to cover their heads, and shoes must be removed by all before entering the heavily incensed single room where the large tomb lies covered in drapes. The Muslim prophet buried here is identified with Job of the Old Testament, well known for his boils.

Beyond the tomb complex, the tarmac road runs on to end at a restaurant and café with a parking area. This restaurant is well sited on the ridge with stunning views from its terrace down towards the Salalah plain and the sea in the distance.

There is also a small collection of shops. In one of the food stores you can buy anything from Red Bull to cigarettes, light bulbs to blenders, crisps to batteries, biscuits to ice cream. Even footballs are for sale here.

RETURN TO SALALAH

Back on the main road, the descent begins, winding through the extraordinary landscape of ravines and plateaux, with some excellent spots for photography. Just before reaching the outskirts of Salalah a sign points left to Ain Garziz – *ain* is Arabic for 'springs' – and a little restaurant complex sits on the edge of a garden called Ittine Natural Park. This restaurant, named Ateen Tourist Restaurant, serves full meals and has a separate family eating area ('family division'), men's eating area ('gents' division') and other attractive eating areas in tranquil flower-filled gardens. Do take time to stop here, if just for a drink. Bees are kept here and fresh honey is available. There is a *shisha* counter for those that fancy a smoke in the traditional style.

The tarmac road continues to the Ain Garziz spring at the base of the mountains, an area of lush fertility with a running *falaj* through the trees. Again, it is a beautiful, peaceful area, with not many other people about, although it is a popular picnic area at weekends (Thursday and Friday). Continuing along this road, keep an eye open for the fascinating stalls cooking and selling fresh meat on stone mounds on the ground. From here you rejoin the Ateen Road, which signposts you back to Salalah.

Bradt Travel Guides

Claim 20% discount on your next Bradt book when you order from www.bradtguides.com quoting the code BRADT20

Africa

Africa Overland	£16.99
Algeria	£15.99
Angola	£18.99
Botswana	£16.99
Burkina Faso	£17.99
Cameroon	£15.99
Cape Verde	£15.99
Congo	£16.99
Eritrea	£15.99
Ethiopia	£17.99
Ethiopia Highlights	£15.99
Ghana	£15.99
Kenya Highlights	£15.99
Madagascar	£16.99
Madagascar Highlights	£15.99
Malawi	£15.99
Mali	£14.99
Mauritius, Rodrigues & Réunion	£16.99
Mozambique	£15.99
Namibia	£15.99
Nigeria	£17.99
North Africa: Roman Coast	£15.99
Rwanda	£16.99
São Tomé & Príncipe	£14.99
Seychelles	£16.99
Sierra Leone	£16.99
Somaliland	£15.99
South Africa Highlights	£15.99
Sudan	£16.99
Swaziland	£15.99
Tanzania Safari Guide	£17.99
Tanzania, Northern	£14.99
Uganda	£16.99
Zambia	£18.99
Zanzibar	£15.99
Zimbabwe	£15.99

The Americas and the Caribbean

Alaska	£15.99
Amazon Highlights	£15.99
Argentina	£16.99
Bahia	£14.99
Cayman Islands	£14.99
Chile Highlights	£15.99
Colombia	£17.99
Dominica	£15.99
Grenada, Carriacou & Petite Martinique	£15.99
Guyana	£15.99
Haiti	£16.99
Nova Scotia	£15.99
Panama	£14.99
Paraguay	£15.99
Peru Highlights	£15.99
Turks & Caicos Islands	£14.99
Uruguay	£15.99
USA by Rail	£15.99
Venezuela	£16.99
Yukon	£14.99

British Isles

Britain from the Rails	£14.99
Bus-Pass Britain	£15.99
Eccentric Britain	£16.99
Eccentric Cambridge	£9.99
Eccentric London	£14.99
Eccentric Oxford	£9.99
Sacred Britain	£16.99
Slow: Cornwall	£14.99
Slow: Cotswolds	£14.99
Slow: Devon & Exmoor	£14.99
Slow: Dorset	£14.99
Slow: New Forest	£9.99
Slow: Norfolk & Suffolk	£14.99
Slow: North Yorkshire	£14.99
Slow: Northumberland	£14.99
Slow: Sussex & South Downs National Park	£14.99

Europe

Abruzzo	£16.99
Albania	£16.99
Armenia	£15.99
Azores	£14.99
Belarus	£15.99
Bosnia & Herzegovina	£15.99
Bratislava	£9.99
Budapest	£9.99
Croatia	£15.99
Cross-Channel France: Nord-Pas de Calais	£13.99
Cyprus see North Cyprus	
Estonia	£14.99
Faroe Islands	£16.99
Flanders	£15.99
Georgia	£15.99
Greece: The Peloponnese	£14.99
Hungary	£15.99
Iceland	£15.99
Istria	£13.99
Kosovo	£15.99
Lapland	£15.99
Liguria	£15.99
Lille	£9.99
Lithuania	£14.99
Luxembourg	£14.99
Macedonia	£16.99
Malta & Gozo	£14.99
Montenegro	£14.99
North Cyprus	£13.99
Serbia	£15.99
Slovakia	£14.99
Slovenia	£13.99
Svalbard: Spitsbergen, Jan Mayen, Franz Jozef Land	£17.99
Switzerland Without a Car	£15.99
Transylvania	£15.99
Ukraine	£16.99

Middle East, Asia and Australasia

Bangladesh	£17.99
Borneo	£17.99
Eastern Turkey	£16.99
Iran	£15.99
Israel	£15.99
Jordan	£16.99
Kazakhstan	£16.99
Kyrgyzstan	£16.99
Lake Baikal	£15.99
Lebanon	£15.99
Maldives	£15.99
Mongolia	£16.99
North Korea	£14.99
Oman	£15.99
Palestine	£15.99
Shangri-La: A Travel Guide to the Himalayan Dream	£14.99
Sri Lanka	£15.99
Syria	£15.99
Taiwan	£16.99
Tajikistan	£15.99
Tibet	£17.99
Yemen	£14.99

Wildlife

Antarctica: A Guide to the Wildlife	£15.99
Arctic: A Guide to Coastal Wildlife	£16.99
Australian Wildlife	£14.99
East African Wildlife	£19.99
Galápagos Wildlife	£16.99
Madagascar Wildlife	£16.99
Pantanal Wildlife	£16.99
Southern African Wildlife	£19.99
Sri Lankan Wildlife	£15.99

Pictorials and other guides

100 Alien Invaders	£16.99
100 Animals to See Before They Die	£16.99
100 Bizarre Animals	£16.99
Eccentric Australia	£12.99
Northern Lights	£6.99
Swimming with Dolphins, Tracking Gorillas	£15.99
The Northwest Passage	£14.99
Tips on Tipping	£6.99
Total Solar Eclipse 2012 & 2013	£6.99
Wildlife & Conservation Volunteering: The Complete Guide	£13.99

Travel literature

A Glimpse of Eternal Snows	£11.99
A Tourist in the Arab Spring	£9.99
Connemara Mollie	£9.99
Fakirs, Feluccas and Femmes Fatales	£9.99
Madagascar: The Eighth Continent	£11.99
The Marsh Lions	£9.99
The Two-Year Mountain	£9.99
The Urban Circus	£9.99
Up the Creek	£9.99

Appendix 1

LANGUAGE

Like Hebrew, Arabic is a Semitic language with a root system. The root of an idea or concept is represented by a simple verb, usually consisting of three consonants. These verbs are the very basis of the Arabic language, and all variations of meaning around the root idea are expressed by imposing different patterns on the basic root. Hence, in the simplest of examples, from the root K T B (*kataba* when vowelled) which means 'he wrote', you can make *maktab* meaning 'office', *maktaba* meaning 'library' and *kitaab* meaning 'book'. The vowels are fully conjugated, so *katabnaa* is 'we wrote' and *yatabuuna* is 'they are writing'. Arabic dictionaries list words under their root, so if you cannot identify the root, you cannot look up the word. Hunting for words in the dictionary is something the beginner spends a long time doing.

Arabic script is arguably the easiest thing about the language. Many are daunted by the script and the right-to-left flow of text, yet the alphabet contains only 29 characters and there are strict rules to determine which characters join on to which. The characters change their shape according to their position within the word but always following the same strict rules. The process of learning the characters and their shapes is therefore purely a memory exercise which can be done easily in three days and thereafter just requires practice. As for the right-to-left flow of text, it just takes a little time to adjust, rather like driving on the right instead of the left of the road.

Having mastered the script the task begins in earnest. The first conceptually difficult thing you now encounter is that only the consonants are written – you have to supply the vowels yourself. In that case, how do you know which vowels to put where? The answer is that you do not, or at least not until you have a thorough grasp of the intricacies of Arabic grammar and word structure, which takes a good three or four months' study. For this reason all beginners' texts and children's school books are fully annotated with vowel signs added in the form of dashes and dots above and below the line. Getting students to read an unvowelled text aloud is always an excellent way of assessing their level, as it instantly reveals the depth of their understanding of Arabic grammar.

Pronunciation is another area that is not as daunting as it may seem. Of the 29 consonants, 18 have direct phonetic equivalents in English such as b, d, t, l, s. The rest have no direct equivalent and range from emphatic versions of d, s, and t, usually transliterated as D, S and T, to a small handful of sounds that are genuinely difficult for Westerners to pronounce. The guttural stop or '*ayn*' as it is called in Arabic, usually represented in transliteration as a reversed comma, is probably the one that gives most trouble, sounding like a vibrating constriction of the larynx.

Arabic is, by the very nature of its structure, an extremely rich language, capable of expressing fine shades of meaning, and this is reflected in the wealth of Arabic literature, especially poetry. The average English tabloid reader is said to have a working vocabulary of 3,000 words, while the Arab equivalent is said to have about 10,000. Scholars believe that because Arabic evolved in the deserts of Arabia where life was nomadic and the daily struggle to stay alive extremely tough, the people developed a rich vocabulary to describe every conceivable nuance of material life, natural phenomena and individual activity of their lives, almost as if to counterbalance the uniformity of their environment. So there are more than a hundred words to describe a camel, for example, depending on its gender, age and qualities.

There are also many interesting features of the language which hint at the nature and attitudes of the Arab mind, notably the existence of only two tenses, perfect and imperfect. There is no future tense. In the Arabic concept of time there is only one distinction that matters: has something been finished or is it still going on? Another curiosity is that the plural of inanimate objects is treated grammatically as feminine singular.

THE ARABIC ALPHABET

Final	Medial	Initial	Alone	Transliteration	Pronunciation
ـا			ا	aa	as in 'after'
ـب	ـبـ	بـ	ب	b	as in 'but'
ـت	ـتـ	تـ	ت	t	as in 'tin'
ـث	ـثـ	ثـ	ث	th	as in 'think'
ـج	ـجـ	جـ	ج	j	as in 'jam'
ـح	ـحـ	حـ	ح	H	emphatic, breathy 'h'
ـخ	ـخـ	خـ	خ	kh	as in the Scottish 'loch'
ـد			د	d	as in 'den'
ـذ			ذ	dh	as in 'that'
ـر			ر	r	as in 'red'
ـز			ز	z	as in 'zero'
ـس	ـسـ	سـ	س	s	as in 'sit', hard 's'
ـش	ـشـ	شـ	ش	sh	as in 'shut'
ـص	ـصـ	صـ	ص	S	emphatic, strong 's'
ـض	ـضـ	ضـ	ض	D	emphatic, strong 'd'
ـط	ـطـ	طـ	ط	T	emphatic, strong 't'
ـظ	ـظـ	ظـ	ظ	Z	emphatic, strong 'z'
ـع	ـعـ	عـ	ع	'	gutteral stop, hardest sound for non-Arabs to make, called 'ayn.
ـغ	ـغـ	غـ	غ	gh	like a gargling sound
ـف	ـفـ	فـ	ف	f	as in 'fire'
ـق	ـقـ	قـ	ق	q	like a guttural 'k'
ـك	ـكـ	كـ	ك	k	as in 'king'
ـل	ـلـ	لـ	ل	l	as in 'lady'
ـم	ـمـ	مـ	م	m	as in 'mat'
ـن	ـنـ	نـ	ن	n	as in 'not'
ـه	ـهـ	هـ	ه	h	as in 'hat'
ـو			و	w	as in 'will', or 'oo' as in 'food'
ـي	ـيـ	يـ	ي	y	as in 'yet', or 'ee' as in 'clean'

GREETINGS On first meeting when travelling generally outside the cities the respectful greeting to older people is: *As-salaamu 'alaykum*, meaning literally 'May peace be upon you.' The standard reply is: *Wa 'alaykum as-salaam*, meaning 'And on you the peace.'

There are three common phrases you will hear incessantly. *In sha Allah*, meaning 'If God wills it', is used all the time in the sense of 'hopefully', because nothing is certain to happen unless God wills it. So if you say to an Arab 'See you tomorrow', he will reply '*In sha Allah*', meaning, 'Yes, if God permits it and nothing happens in the meantime to prevent it.' It can also be a polite way of avoiding commitment, conveying 'Let us hope so ...' The second phrase is *Al Hamdou lillah*, meaning 'Thanks be to God'. This is said every time something works out the way it should have done. It also expresses relief, along the lines of 'Thank God for that!' The third phrase is *TafaDDal*, meaning 'Please go ahead' or 'Come in' or 'After you'. It is always said by your host when you arrive and on entering the house or room and before eating. Literally it means 'Please be so good as to …'

Other greetings

Hello, welcome	*marHaba, ahlan*
Goodbye	*ma'a as-salaama* (literally, 'with the peace')

USEFUL ARABIC WORDS AND PHRASES

Yes	*aiwa, na'am*	More, again, also	*kamaan*
No	*laa*	Is it possible? May I?	*mumkin?*
Please	*min faDlak*	My name is …	*Ana ismee …*
Thank you	*shukran*	What is your name?	*Shu ismak?*
Thank you very		I don't understand	*Ana maa bafham*
much	*shukran jazeelan*	Where are you from?	*Min wayn anta?*
You're welcome	*afwan*	There is …	*Fii …*
Sorry, excuse me	*'afwan, muta'assif*	There is not …	*Maa fii …*
Hurry up, let's go	*yallah*	What?	*shu?*

Getting around

airport	*maTaar*	left	*yasaar*
bus	*baas*	right	*yameen*
car	*sayyaara*	near, close by	*qareeb*
suitcase, bag	*shanTa*	straight on	*dhughri, 'alaa aT-Toul*
taxi	*taksee*	where?	*wayn?*
ticket	*tadhkira*	Where is the	*Wayn Al matHaf min*
petrol	*benzeen*	museum, please?	*faDlak?*
diesel	*maazout*	How far is it to …?	*Kam kiiloometre*
far	*ba'eed*		*ila … ?*

Hotels and restaurants

hotel	*funduq, ootel*	restaurant	*maT'am*
room	*ghurfa*	breakfast	*fuTour*
soap	*Saaboun*	lunch	*ghadaa*
toilet, bathroom	*Hammam, bait mai*	dinner	*'ashaa*
towel	*manshafa*	glass	*finjaan*
the bill	*Al faaToura, Al Hisaab*	I don't eat meat	*ana ma baakul laHm*

Food and drink

bread	*khubz*	vegetables	*khuDar*
butter	*zibdeh*	yoghurt	*laban*
cheese	*jibneh*	half kilo	*nuSS kiiloo*
eggs	*bayD*	beer	*beera*
fish	*samak*	coffee	*qahwa*
fruit	*fawaakeh*	mineral water	*mai ma'daniya*
honey	*'asl*	red	*aHmar*
jam	*murabbeh*	tea	*shay*
meat	*laHm*	white	*abyaD*
sugar	*sukkar*	wine	*nabeedh*

A1

Shopping

cheap	*rakhees*	shop	*dukkaan*
expensive	*ghaalee*	market	*souk*
money	*fuluus*	How much	*bikaam? Addaysh?*
a lot, much, very	*kateer*	(does it cost?)	
no problem	*mish mishkila*		
never mind	*ma'a laysh*		

Health

chemist	*Saydaliyeh*	diarrhoea	*ishaal*
dentist	*Tabeeb asnaan*	ill, sick	*mareeD*
doctor	*doktoor, Tabeeb*		

Days and time

Monday	*Yawn Al Ithnayn*	Saturday	*Yawm as-Sabt*
Tuesday	*Yawm ath-Thalaatha*	Sunday	*Yawm Al AHad*
Wednesday	*Yawn Al Arba'a*	today	*Al yawm*
Thursday	*Yawm Al Khamees*	tomorrow	*bukra*
Friday	*Yawm Al Jum'a*		

Numbers

1	*waaHad*	١
2	*ithnayn*	٢
3	*thalaatha*	٣
4	*arba'a*	٤
5	*khamsa*	٥
6	*sitta*	٦
7	*sab'a*	٧
8	*thamaaniya*	٨
9	*tis'a*	٩
10	*'ashara*	١٠
20	*'ishreen*	٢٠
30	*thalaatheen*	٣٠
40	*arba'een*	٤٠
50	*khamseen*	٥٠
60	*sitteen*	٦٠
70	*sab'een*	٧٠
80	*thamaaneen*	٨٠
90	*tis'een*	٩٠
100	*mi'a*	١٠٠
150	*mi'a wa khamseen*	١٥٠
200	*mi'atayn*	٢٠٠
500	*khams-mi'a*	٥٠٠
1,000	*alf*	١٠٠٠
2,000	*alfayn*	٢٠٠٠

Other vocabulary

bank	*bank, maSraf*	bad	*mish kwayyis, zift*
museum	*matHaf*	hot	*Haar*
post office	*maktab bareed*	cold	*baarid*
good	*kwayyis, Tayyib*		

ARABIC SIGNS

Open	maftouH	مفـتـوح
Shut	mughlag	مغـلـق
Forbidden	mamnou	ممـنـوع
Police	shurTa, boulees	شـرطة
Gents	rijaal	سـيـدات
Ladies	sayyidaat	رجـال
Hospital	mustashfaa	مسـتـشـفـى

Appendix 2

GLOSSARY

ablution	ritual washing before prayer laid down by the Koran
ain	springs
bab	gate
bahri	sea
bait	house
bander	anchorage
bani	tribal prefix meaning 'son of ...' in Arabic
barasti	made from the branches of palm trees
bedouin	desert nomads (see box on page 252)
bustan	garden
dhow	traditional Arab wooden sailing boat
Eid	religious holiday
falaj	irrigation channel running from a spring or water source to water crops or date gardens
Ghafiri	one of the main tribes of Oman, usually in conflict with the Hinawi tribe
hadith	collection of anecdotes from the Prophet Muhammad's lifetime
halwa	Omani sticky brown sweet often served to guests with coffee, eaten with the fingers
Hinawi	one of the main tribes of Oman, usually in conflict with the Ghafiri tribe
Ibadhi	one of Islam's earliest sects, followed in Oman, very traditional and orthodox (see box on page 28)
Imam	spiritual and secular leader who is chosen by consensus among the sheikhs (see box on page 188)
jebel	mountain
jerz	simple axe with wooden handle carried only by men in Musandam, instead of the *khanjar* dagger.
jinn	spirit which can be good or evil like our 'genie'
juzor/jazirah	island
kabir	big
kahwa	Arabic coffee
khanjar	Omani silver dagger worn on the belt, with a distinctive curved blade. The more elaborate the *khanjar*, the higher the status of the owner.
khareef	monsoon season in Dhofar from mid June to mid September with heavy rain-laden winds

khor	creek or inlet from the sea; also *khwar*
madinat	town
majlis	literally 'place of sitting', meaning a meeting of an important person with others who have come to ask for something; the room where guests are received
mihrab	prayer niche in a mosque indicating the direction of Mecca for prayer
mina	port
minbar	pulpit in a mosque from where the imam addresses the congregation
oryx	creature (related to antelope) with two straight long horns, well adapted to desert life (see box on page 250)
PDO	Petroleum Development Oman, the main oil company in Oman, a subsidiary of Shell
qadi	Islamic judge
Ramadan	Muslim month of fasting (see pages 27–8)
ramlat	sandy area
ras	headland
resthouse	simple hotel generally used in transit and found on a main road
sable	fortified house used for communal activities like weddings and funerals, belonging to one family group
saghir	small
sambuk	small fishing boat
sarouj	mud plaster
shatti	shore/beach
Sheikh	tribal leader
Shari'a	Islamic law, according to the Koran and the Hadith
Shi'a	offshoot of Islam from the Orthodox Sunni Muslims, following a hereditary principle of succession after Muhammad rather than an elected or consensus method. Mainly found today in Iran.
Sunni	Orthodox Islam, following the principle of consensus selection of the next caliph or imam
souk	Arab market
sur	fortified walled enclosure
sura	chapter of the Koran
wadi	valley, natural watercourse
Wahhabi	an ultra-conservative branch of Sunni Islam aspiring to return to what it sees as the fundamentals of Islam (particularly dominant in Saudi Arabia)
Wali	local governor
Wilayat	district/area

Appendix 3

FURTHER INFORMATION
BOOKS
History

Aguis, D A *In the Wake of the Dhow: The Arabian Gulf and Oman* Ithaca Press, 2002. Documents the history of the Arabian *dhow*.

Allen, C H, Rigsbee, W L, and Rigsbee II, W L *Oman Under Qaboos: From Coup to Constitution 1970–1996* Frank Cass Publishers, 2002. Examines the political, economic and social development of Oman since Qaboos.

Clements, F A *Oman: The Reborn Land* Longman ELT, 1980. An appreciation of Oman's past glories and traditions.

Dinteman, W *Forts of Oman* Motivate Publishing, 1993. Oman's history of battles and inter-tribal conflicts.

Eickelman, C *Women and Community in Oman* New York University Press, 1989. Christine Eickelman lived in Hamra on the western edge of Jebel Akhdar in 1979 and writes of her explorations into the culture of Omani women through the life she shared with them. She sheds light on their concepts of family, privacy, propriety, status and sociability.

Frifelt, K *The Island of Umm-an-Nar: Third Millennium Settlement* Aarhus University Press, 1995. Presents the results and the material found at the settlement of Umm-an-Nar. The Umm-an-Nar culture was the most conspicuous culture in the Oman peninsula in the Bronze Age.

Gwynne-James, D *Letters from Oman: A Snapshot of Feudal Times as Oil Signals Change* Gwynne-James, 2001.

Hawley, Sir D *Oman and its Renaissance* Stacey International, 2005. An immense work on the history, geography and culture of Oman, and a beautiful book to boot.

Jeapes, T *SAS Secret War: Operation Storm in the Middle East* Flamingo, 1996. The ten-year Dhofar War lasted until 1976, taking place under conditions of secrecy. This is a first-hand account of the SAS's secret campaign in Oman.

Joyce, M *The Sultanate of Oman: A Twentieth Century History* Greenwood Press, 2005.

Laing, Stuart and Alston, Robert *Unshook till the End of Time* Gilgamesh, 2012. A detailed history of relations between Britain and Oman from 1650 till the end of the Dhofar War in 1975, by two former British ambassadors to Oman.

Peyton, W D *Old Oman* Stacey International, 1983. A fascinating and valuable album of photographs of a bygone age, with accompanying description, taken from c1900 up to 1970.

Philby, Harry St J *The Queen of Sheba* Quartet Books, 1981. Harry St John Philby was a great Arabian traveller, scholar and writer. He examines the mixture of fable, history, magic and mystery surrounding the visit of the Queen of Sheba to King Solomon, from its origins in the Old Testament and the Koran.

Phillips, W *Qataban and Sheba* Harcourt, Brace and Company, 1955. Wendell Phillips is an explorer, adventurer and archaeologist who explored the ancient treasures of the exotic civilisations of southern Arabia. In this book he unveils the history of Sheba territory in Oman.

Raban, J *Arabia through the Looking Glass* Harvill Press, 1979. An entertaining journey to explore the complex relationship between the Arabs and the West.

Al-Rawas, I *Oman in Early Islamic History* Ithaca Press, 2000. An in-depth study of the history of Oman from the advent of Islam until the fall of the second Ibadi imamate in AD893.

Richardson, C *Masirah: Tales from a Desert Island* Pentland Press, 2001. A well-researched book which recounts a wealth of first–hand stories of RAF history by those who have known Masirah since the 1930s. Illustrated with photographs.

Salil Ibn Razik, *History of the Imams & Seyyids of Oman* Kessinger Publishing Company, 2004.

Severin, T *The Sindbad Voyage* Putnam Publishing Group, 1983. The reconstruction of an ancient trade route mentioned in the legend of Sindbad; an experiment to see if a sewn wooden boat could reach China using only primitive navigational instruments.

Ward, P *Travels in Oman* Oleander Press, 1986. On the track of early explorers, an edited collection.

Wikan, U *Behind the Veil in Arabia: Women in Oman* University of Chicago Press, 1982. Unni Wikan explores the segregation of women, the wearing of the *burka* mask, nuptial rituals and place of women in Omani society.

Natural history A good selection of natural history books is available in the UK from NHBS Environment Bookstore (*2–3 Wills Rd, Totnes, Devon TQ9 5XN;* ✆ *01803 865913; www.nhbs.com*).

Baldwin, R *Whales and Dolphins of Arabia* R Baldwin, Bowlish, Somerset, 2003.
Batty, P D *Bluewater Fishing in Oman* Muscat Game Fishing Association, Oman 2002.
Bosch, D and Bosch, E *Sea Shells of Oman* Longman, 1982.
Eriksen, H and Eriksen, J *Birdlife in Oman* Al Roya Publishing, Muscat, Oman 1999.
Eriksen, H and Eriksen, J *Common Birds in Oman* Al Roya Publishing, Muscat, Oman 2005.
Hanna, S and al-Belushi, M *Caves of Oman* Sultan Qaboos University, 1996.
Larson, T B and Larson, K *Butterflies of Oman* Bartholomew, 1980.
Macgregor, M *Wilderness Oman* Ptarmigan, 2002.
Mandaville Jr, J *Wild Flowers of Northern Oman* Bartholomew, 1978.
Miller, A G and Morris, M *Plants of Dhofar, the Southern Region of Oman: Traditional Economic & Medicinal Uses* Office of the Adviser for Conservation of the Environment, Diwan of Royal Court, Sultanate of Oman, 1988.
Randall, J E *Coastal Fishes of Oman* University of Hawaii Press, 1996.
Salm, R and Salm, S *Sea Turtles in the Sultanate of Oman* Historical Association of Oman, 2001.
Woodward, T *Beachcombers' Guide to Oman,* Motivate Publishing, 1996.
Al Zubair M, *Landscapes of Dhofar* Bait al Zubair, Oman 2003.

Adventure tourism

Dale, A and Hadwind, J *Adventure Trekking in Oman* Cordee, 2001.
Explorer, *Oman Off-Road*, Explorer Publishing, 2013. Twenty-six routes complete with GPS co-ordinates and maps.
Klein, H and Brickson, R *Off-Road in Oman*, Motivate Publishing, 1996.
Mackenzie, A *Oman Trekking Guide* Explorer Publishing, 2005.

Mcdonald, R A *Rock Climbing in Oman* Verulam Publishing, 1994.

Salm, R and Baldwin, R *Snorkelling and Diving in Oman* Motivate Publishing, 1992.

Culture and tradition

Al-Azri, Khalid *Social and Gender Inequality in Oman: The Power of Religious and Political Tradition* Routledge, 2012. Rigorous investigation into the post-1970 barriers to reform in Oman and wider Islamic society, chiefly in the areas where Islamic law still places restrictions on women in marriage, divorce and inheritance.

Kendrick, I *The Bands and Orchestras of Oman* Diwan of the Royal Court, Oman, 1995.

Newcombe, O *The Heritage of Oman: A Celebration in Photographs* Garnet Publishing, 1996.

Richardson, N and Dorr, M *The Craft Heritage of Oman* Motivate Publishing, 2004.

Vine, P *The Heritage of Oman* Immel Publishing, 1995.

Biography and autobiography

Beasant, J and Ling, C *Sultan in Arabia: A Private Life* Mainstream Publishing, 2004. A biography providing insight into the character of Qaboos bin Said.

Brown, M *Lawrence of Arabia: The Selected Letters* Little Books, 2005. This is Malcolm Brown's selection of the letters of T E Lawrence – a traveller, scholar, soldier, writer, critic, politician, and a fascinating and enigmatic figure of the 20th century who played a part in the Arab Revolt.

Burrowes, J *Sultan: The Remarkable Story of a Man and a Nation* Mainstream Publishing, 2005. Biography of Sultan Qaboos.

Monroe, E *Philby of Arabia* Ithaca Press, 1998 edition. Explores the life of Harry St John Philby – one of the great Arabian desert travellers.

Taylor, A *God's Fugitive: The Life of C M Doughty* HarperCollins, 1999. Charles Montagu Doughty, an explorer, scholar, scientist, travel writer and poet, was the foremost Arabian explorer, who started a tradition of British exploration and discovery in that region. He spent two years wandering with the Bedu through oases and deserts, and returned to England to write one of the greatest and most original travel books: *Arabia Deserta*. Andrew Taylor brings Doughty to life in this biography.

Thesiger, W *My Life and Travels* Flamingo, 2003. A chronicle, spanning the 20th century, of Wilfred Thesiger's life and travel writing.

Travel writing

Allfree, Philip, *Warlords of Oman* Robert Hale, 2008. Reprint of an original classic from 1967. The author (recently deceased) describes many fascinating and colourful episodes from an Oman now long disappeared, based on his unique first-hand experiences.

Barnett, D *Dust and Fury: A Novel Set in Oman* Woodfield Publishing, 2003.

Clapp, N *The Road to Ubar* First Mariner Books, 1999. Nicholas Clapp, a noted documentary film–maker, arranged two expeditions to Oman with a team of archaeologists and NASA space scientists to search for Ubar, the city that had become known as the Atlantis of the Sands. This book is part travel journal, part archaeological history.

Doughty, C M *Arabia Deserta* Peter Smith Publishing, 1960. A classic account of two years spent with Arabian nomads in the late 19th century.

Fiennes, R *Atlantis of the Sands* Bloomsbury, 1992. Ranulph Fiennes – a leader of major travel expeditions around the globe – relates his search for the legendary Ubar in Oman.

Holden, W M *Dhow of the Monsoon: From Zanzibar to Oman in the Wake of Sindbad* PublishAmerica, 2005. William Holden follows Sindbad's journey by *dhow* relying on the monsoon winds.

Morris, J *Sultan in Oman*, Sickle Moon Books, 2003. A fascinating read from one of the world's great travel writers, who experienced Muscat prior to its development.

Owen, T *Beyond the Empty Quarter* Serendipity, 2003. Tim Owen's light-hearted memoir of his experiences in 1960s Oman.

Rollins, J *Sandstorm* HarperCollins, 2004. James Rollins's fiction based around the lost city of Ubar, in the desert of Oman.

Stark, F *The Southern Gates of Arabia* John Murray, 1936. Freya Stark – a travelling Englishwoman – relates her journey to explore the Frankincense Road, catching the spirit of people and place in this travel classic.

Thesiger, W *Arabian Sands* Penguin Classics, 1959.

Thesiger, W *Desert, Marsh and Mountain* Flamingo, 1995. Thesiger's writings are an absolute must for those interested in the accounts of previous explorers and travellers to Oman. Beautifully written. Thesiger recreates his five-year journey with the Bedu at the time before oil and the West transformed them.

Health

Wilson-Howarth, Dr Jane, and Ellis, Dr Matthew *Your Child Abroad: A Travel Health Guide* Bradt Travel Guides, 2005.

Wilson-Howarth, Dr Jane, *Bugs, Bites & Bowels* Cadogan, 2006.

WEBSITES

www.apexstuff.com Includes *Oman Today* magazine's website: the essential leisure guide.

www.askexplorer.com Essential information on living in Oman from Explorer Publishing.

www.booking.com A handy site for instant online hotel booking with no money paid up front and no fees if you cancel up to 48 hours beforehand.

www.businessdirectoryoman.com Business directory for Oman.

www.businesstoday.co.om Oman's best business magazine.

www.destinationoman.com All about Oman and getting there.

www.diveworldwide.com/oman A list of diving holiday options in Oman.

www.embassyworld.com Details of Omani embassies abroad and foreign missions in Oman.

www.nizwa.net A useful site for information about Oman generally but especially the city of Nizwa and its heritage.

www.octm-folk.gov.om Omani Centre for traditional music lovers.

www.off-roadexplorer.com/oman Directory of off-road drives.

www.oman.org/gov90.htm Details of embassies in Oman.

www.oman.org/tourism.htm General travel information, health advice, guidance for off-road routes, plus listings for hotels, tour operators and agencies.

www.omanaccess.com Listings, tourist information and community forums.

www.omanair.com Oman Air, the national carrier, with timetable information for flights to Khasab and Salalah.

www.omanet.om The Ministry of Information's website covering all aspects of the country.

www.omanholidayarchitects.net

www.omanhotels.com

www.omaninfo.com Classifieds, news and tourism features.

www.omantourism.gov.om The Ministry of Tourism's website.

www.oman-radio.gov.om All listings for Omani radio programmes.

www.oman-tv.gov.om All listings for Omani television programmes.

www.ontcoman.com Oman National Transport Company detailing bus timetables all over the country.

www.rop.gov.om Royal Oman Police – for visa information and traffic fines.

www.tripadvisor.com Useful for checking out hotel reviews.

Index

Entries in **bold** indicate main entries; those in *italics* indicate maps

BOXED TEXT

INDEX OF ADVERTISERS